The Boundaries of Data

The Boundaries of Data

Edited by
Bart van der Sloot &
Sascha van Schendel

Routledge
Taylor & Francis Group
LONDON AND NEW YORK

This book was made possible by the Dutch Scientific Organisation (NWO)'s Veni Grant (VI.Veni.201R.082) and the Digital Legal Studies research initiative, which is funded through the Law Sector Plan of the Dutch Ministry of Education, Culture and Science (OCW).

First published in 2024 by Amsterdam University Press Ltd.

Published 2025 by Routledge
4 Park Square, Milton Park, Abingdon, Oxon OX14 4RN
605 Third Avenue, New York, NY 10158

Routledge is an imprint of the Taylor & Francis Group, an informa business

ISBN: 9789463729192 (hbk)
ISBN: 9781041187356 (pbk)
ISBN: 9781003705420 (ebk)
NUR 740

Cover image: Nico Vincentini/generative AI
Cover design: Gijs Mathijs Ontwerpers

DOI: 10.5117/9789463729192

Table of Contents

1. Introduction

Bart van der Sloot & Sascha van Schendel

Abstract
This chapter sets the stage for this book, describes its background and gives an overview of its contents.

Keywords: personal data; non-personal data; anonymised data; pseudonymised data; aggregated data

1. Setting the Stage

The General Data Protection Regulation (GDPR) is one of the most well-known and perhaps the most important framework for the digital domain in Europe and beyond (Hoofnagle et al., 2019). It sets rules and standards for the processing of data, lays down obligations for persons and organisations processing data (data controllers) and grants rights to individuals whose data are processed (data subjects). Although adopted in 2016, its origins trace back to the 1970s. The decisive element for the application of the data protection framework was and remains whether the data being processed concern information about an individual (natural person).[1]

Although this determination was relatively easy to make in the 1970s, it has become increasingly difficult, especially in light of technological developments, the democratisation of technology and the push towards open data. These phenomena have meant that it is increasingly possible to derive or infer personal data from datasets that, prima facie, seem to contain no data of this kind (Finck & Pallas, 2020). In turn, this has meant that the legal status of data is increasingly volatile: since data are shared between parties and the operations performed on datasets differ substantially, the same dataset may be considered to contain personal data for one operation

1 See, for example, Article 4(1) GDPR.

Van der Sloot & van Schendel. *The Boundaries of Data.* Taylor & Francis Group, 2024
DOI: 10.5117/9789463729192_CH01

and none for another, containing personal data in the hands of party A but none in the hands of party B at the same moment.

In response, the legal regime has expanded the notion of personal data over time (van der Sloot, 2017; Purtova, 2018) In particular, in 1995 the predecessor of the General Data Protection Regulation, the Data Protection Directive, extended the scope of this notion considerably and, therewith, the number of datasets that fell under its reach. Personal data concern direct and indirect information, which refers to data through which the identity of a person can be inferred, such as descriptions. Personal data not only concern identifying data – data that can lead to a specific individual at present – but also identifiable data or, in other words, data that currently do not lead to a specific individual but that may in the future. In order to determine whether a dataset contains identifiable data, all means reasonably likely to link the data to an individual should be considered. Finally, it is not necessary to know the identity of a person; if data are used to make a decision about a specific individual whose identity is unknown, the data protection regime still applies.

These legislative changes have meant a substantial expansion of the reach of the data protection regime. At the same time, however, the framework still upholds the notion of personal data as the determining factor when deciding whether the rules contained therein apply. In contrast to the restrictive regime laid down for the processing of personal data, the European Union is also in the process of adopting other instruments that regulate data, beyond the scope of personal data, where the emphasis is on expanding the flow of such data (von Grafenstein, 2022). The Regulation on the free flow of non-personal data essentially holds that no restrictions should be set, either by the public sector or the private sector, with respect to the free flow of non-personal data. In addition, the Data Act and Data Governance Act, once in force, also aim to enhance the sharing and reuse of data. Thus, the legal qualification of whether a dataset does or does not contain personal data means that a regulatory regime of almost 180 degrees of difference applies, and the different regulatory regimes together introduce a complicated field of regulation (Graef & Gellert, 2021). It is only until the new European data strategy is fully in place that it will be possible to see how the various legal regimes relate to each other. For example, the proposed ePrivacy Regulation includes rules on the processing of metadata in addition to content data.

Now, once again, there have been further important technological and societal developments. Big Data, artificial intelligence, quantum computing and other techniques make it even easier to infer personal data from aggregated, anonymised or encrypted datasets; the democratisation of technologies means that it is even more difficult to determine the future status of a dataset; the continued push for open data and the reuse of public sector information means that the legal status of data will become even more volatile. In light of these new challenges, questions arise about how the legal regime should respond. Should the concept of personal data be stretched even further? If so, would that not mean that all data would be considered personal data in practice? Should the current distinction between personal and non-personal data be kept but a more restrictive regime be developed for non-personal data? What do these developments mean for other data categories in the General Data Protection Regulation, such as pseudonymous data and sensitive personal data?

The regulatory response has so far been two-sided.

On the one hand, the European Union is set on maintaining a strict separation between personal and non-personal data, as well as other categories of data. While personal data are protected under the General Data Protection Regulation, non-personal data are almost free from regulation, or to put it in more precise terms, the EU has adopted a regulation on non-personal data in which it dissuades public and private sector organisations from adopting any restrictions on or barriers to the free flow of non-personal data. This choice stands in a broader tradition within the EU for opting for separate, demarcated types of data, which each have their own level of protection. In addition to the distinction between non-personal and personal, the GDPR differentiates between anonymous and directly identifying data and pseudonyms, and between 'ordinary' personal data and 'sensitive' personal data. Numerous adjoining legal instruments have their own data concepts, each of which has been assigned its own scope and level of protection. Examples are the proposed ePrivacy Regulation, which makes a distinction between, among others, 'electronic communications data', 'electronic communications content', 'electronic communications metadata' and 'location data', and the proposed AI Act, which differentiates between 'training data', 'testing data', 'input data' and 'biometric data'. The presumption that guides EU regulation is that data can be distinguished and demarcated reasonably well and that separate regimes of protection can be attached to them.

On the other hand, the concept of 'personal data' has been extended in the various data protection instruments adopted over the decades. In case law, courts have also given a broad interpretation to the definition. Thus, scientific opinions, open access data, dynamic IP addresses, minutes with draft decisions about persons, registration of working hours by employees and metadata may all fall under its scope (e.g. CJEU, 2016). Various advisory bodies, such as the Article 29 Working Party (WP29), have propagated a broad approach to the material scope of data protection regimes, too (WP29, 2007, p. 136). The reason is that over time, more and more data can be used to identify a person or make decisions that affect a person. It is also relatively easy to combine various non-sensitive data points and, through predictive analysis, infer sensitive personal data – for example, saying something about a person's prospective health. What counts as non-personal, personal or sensitive personal data has become increasingly difficult to establish, and the concept has become increasingly fluid over time and will continue to do so. To provide for a high level of protection, the various concepts and scopes have been widened over the years.

The legal domain distinguishes between different types of data and attaches a different level of legal protection to each of them. As a consequence, non-personal data are left largely unregulated, while privacy and data protection rules apply to personal data. There are stricter legal rules for the processing of sensitive personal data than for the processing of 'ordinary' personal data. Metadata and communications data are regulated differently than content communications data. Technological developments challenge these legal categorisations of data on at least three fronts. First, the lines between the categories are increasingly difficult to draw and increasingly fluid: consider the increased availability of data and the democratisation of technologies that allow for combining data and inferring information from data in ways previously not possible, which makes it difficult to categorise data. Second, working with various categories of data works well when the category a datum or dataset falls into is relatively stable. However, data that is not considered personal or sensitive personal data can become so in the future, although this is less and less the case. Third, scholars are increasingly questioning the rationale behind the various legal categorisations (Quinn & Malgieri, 2021). These developments raise the question of where the regulatory framework for data is meant to go from here. The regulatory response to this reality so far has been either to maintain these strict legal categories regardless or to expand the scope of the concepts, such as including more and more data under the category of 'personal data' or of 'sensitive personal data'.

This book explores the extent to which these two strategies are feasible and the extent to which alternative approaches can be developed. It does so by combining insights from three perspectives: technology, practice and law.

2. Background of This Book

This book stems from a project conducted by the Tilburg Institute for Law, Technology, and Society (TILT) of Tilburg University for the Dutch Scientific and Documentation Centre (WODC) on behalf of the Dutch Ministry of Security and Justice. The project focused on the regulation of data within Europe in light of technical developments. More specifically, the guiding question for the project was: *What effect do current and future technical developments have on the data protection framework and the protection afforded to the different types of data with respect to the anonymisation, pseudonymisation, aggregation and identification of data?*

The sub-questions that helped answer this research question were:

Identifiability of data
1. What means are available to link (anonymous) data back to individuals, and to what extent does the availability of other (e.g. open source) data play a role?
2. What (technical) developments are expected in the coming years regarding the means to (intentionally or unintentionally) link data back to persons?

Anonymisation and pseudonymisation of data
3. What current and foreseeable technical developments can be used for the anonymisation or pseudonymisation of personal data, and what factors are decisive in this respect?
4. What technical developments in the area of anonymisation and pseudonymisation of personal data can be expected in the coming years?

Identifiability in relation to anonymisation and pseudonymisation and vice versa
5. From a legal and technical perspective, what can be said about the interpretation of the concept of 'means reasonably likely to be used'? What means can be considered reasonably likely to be used, and what factors play a role in this?
6. How do the answers to question 5 relate to developments in current and expected techniques towards achieving anonymisation and pseudonymisation?
7. When is it reasonable to say that data can no longer be linked back to an individual and that the dataset they are part of can be considered anonymous?
8. To what extent is the test for indirect identifiability objectifiable?

Consequences of identifiability and anonymisation and pseudonymisation
9. To what extent and in which cases can there be under-regulation when data are no longer linked to individuals through anonymisation and therefore do not fall within the scope of the GDPR?
10. To what extent and in which cases can there be overregulation when increasing amounts of data can be easily linked to individuals through new techniques, undoing measures of anonymisation and pseudonymisation?

Overarching analysis
11. How will current and future technical developments affect the GDPR and legal protection in a broad sense in the coming period?

In answering these questions, this edited volume was created to offer different perspectives on the GDPR and its regulation of data, as well as on alternative approaches to regulate and handle data.

The report can be found on the WODC website.[2] For this study, interviews were conducted, workshops were held and a literature study of the technical, societal and legal landscape was performed. In addition, a number of authors were invited to write a chapter for an edited volume; the result is this book. The problem with mapping the state of the art in the legal and technical fields is that expertise is spread across people with completely different backgrounds and areas of work. It is, therefore, not only necessary to have various expertise in-house and to conduct a thorough literature study and an empirical study, but it is also beneficial to have an edited volume with chapters by different authors on different topics of the study. The three domains from which the report draws (law, technology and practice) also guide the design of the book. Per domain, several authors were asked to discuss the state of the art on specific themes and consider potential future developments and normative questions that may arise.

It is impossible to provide a full overview of all relevant aspects pertaining to the discussion of EU Member States' and non-EU Member States' legal regimes and the techniques central to this study in the three domains of this book. That is why, per domain, the most relevant aspects were selected for further discussion. These were chosen on the basis of a workshop held for this study.

2 https://www.wodc.nl/

3. Contents of This Book

This book is divided into three parts: each part approaches data from a different perspective.

3.1. Technology

The first part offers a technical perspective on data through three important technological developments to explore which technologies are currently being used and will be used in the near future to process data in different categories, such as anonymisation or identification techniques.

Chapter 2, 'Object Re-identification: Problems, Algorithms and Responsible Research Practice', by Zhedong Zheng and Liang Zheng, explores techniques of object re-identification. In their chapter, Zheng and Zheng describe the importance of object re-identification techniques and algorithms for daily life. At the same time, they signal challenges for these systems in learning object features and handling environmental changes in the learning environment, especially in unsupervised settings. Unsupervised learning for object identification comes with more problems in labelling (as there are fewer labels) and data privacy issues. To mitigate challenges, Zheng and Zheng propose exploring developing algorithms with synthetic data, using data anonymisation techniques and designing economical learning schemes, which are less data reliant.

Chapter 3, 'The Quantum Threat to Cybersecurity and Privacy', by Nina Bindel, Michele Mosca and Bill Munson, explores the impact of quantum techniques for cybersecurity and privacy. In their chapter, the authors describe the quantum threat that they foresee and assess the relation between quantum technologies and various forms of encryption. The authors anticipate that quantum computing will have technical implications for confidentiality, authentication, technologies used for audio and video, and back-tracking attacks. In terms of the privacy impacts of quantum computing, they foresee the release of private information combined with a loss of agency and control over personal actions as being issues. According to the authors, the best defence against the various quantum threats is to migrate our systems and networks from current quantum-vulnerable cryptography to cryptography that is deemed to be quantum-safe, for which they describe various cryptography techniques. In addition, they propose the introduction of government policies, legislation and regulations to accelerate the building of a necessary large pool of experts who understand the quantum threat and how to mitigate it; leverage procurement, approval and funding mechanisms to demand action by the private sector; and regulation as necessary to enforce compliance with national and international standards for quantum-secure algorithms.

Chapter 4, 'Realistic Face Anonymisation', by Håkon Hukkelås and Frank Lindseth, describes how collecting and storing images has become a necessity for many applications, but it also creates data protection and privacy challenges, especially in terms of anonymising data. While traditional image anonymisation (e.g. blurring) degrades the original data, making the images unusable for many applications, developments in deep generative models have enabled a new type of anonymisation: realistic anonymisation. Realistic anonymisation replaces privacy-sensitive information with artificially synthesised realistic content. These methods preserve the privacy of individuals and generate images that are indistinguishable from the original data. In this way, realistic anonymisation techniques contribute to anonymous processing by attempting to mitigate data protection and privacy challenges.

3.2. Practice

The second part offers a perspective on the use of data in practice to assess what types of data are distinguished in various societal sectors and how data are viewed in practice outside the regulatory framework of the GDPR.

Chapter 5, 'Use of Bulk Data by Intelligence and Security Services: Caught Between a Rock and a Hard Place?', by Willemijn Aerdts and Ludo Block, describes the use of data by intelligence and security services. Aerdts and Block focus on the workings of these services: why and how do they gather their data? A specific challenge for the intelligence and security sector is the gathering of bulk data and metadata in light of individuals' privacy concerns and the supervision of these services. The gathering of data is described in different scenarios, each of which requires different data and different regulation. The authors identify three particular dilemmas for intelligence and security services concerning data, namely, data overload, sharing of raw data and special protection for persons with (legal) professional privilege. They argue that these three dilemmas are features of a democratic society in which the powers of intelligence and security services are balanced by law and various forms of oversight.

Chapter 6, 'Farm Data Sharing: Current Practices and Principles', by Sjaak Wolfert, Else Giesbers, Houkje Adema and Marc-Jeroen Bogaardt, describes how the agricultural sector is one of the most data-driven sectors in our society, and the authors present a global overview of various types of data focusing on agriculture, classified for particular groups of stakeholders and purposes. The chapter describes how raw data must be transformed into actionable management information first by using AI (for example, by service providers who invest time and effort) and how this leads to issues and risks in practice. The authors further explain these issues in terms of reasons for sharing data and obstacles to sharing data, culminating in types of potential harm or damage for farmers on sharing data. It becomes clear that data sharing in agriculture is becoming an opportunity, but there are still many issues that need to be solved to guarantee sufficient protection of data where it is necessary without compromising the innovation potential.

Chapter 7, 'Microdata Access at Statistics Netherlands', written by contributors from Statistics Netherlands (CBS), describes microdata access at their agency. The chapter shows that microdata access is a highly valued and appreciated service. The Dutch Statistical Act has explicitly enabled the granting of microdata access to researchers. In addition to the more traditional means of public use files and scientific use files, remote access to secure use files has become the most popular way of accessing microdata at CBS. However, the Dutch Statistical Act also forces CBS to maintain the highest possible standards in the protection of the privacy of the respondents. For personal data specifically, this is enforced by the GDPR as well. To reach these high standards, CBS has adopted the 'five safes' framework. This framework aims to create different aspects of protection: safe people, safe settings, safe projects, safe data and safe output. This enables the balancing of the necessary overall level of protection by assigning different levels of protection to each of the five individual 'safes'.

Chapter 8, 'Atmospheric Profiling and Surveillance in the Stratumseind Living Lab: Pushing the Limits of Identifiability', by Maša Galič, discusses whether data being processed in a typical living lab could be considered personal data. The chapter focuses on the concept of identifiability, considered through the broader socio-technical lens of profiling. The particular type of profiling taking place in living labs leads to a twofold issue. On the one hand, it adds to and further complicates the discussions around the question of whether profiling constitutes a form of personal data processing simply because of its capacity to affect individuals. This issue, which has its proponents and opponents, has not yet been settled. On the other hand, it also implies a novel type of profiling – atmospheric profiling – which tries to indirectly affect persons by affecting the general atmosphere on the street rather than singling out individuals. As such, this type of profiling does not seem to constitute a type of personal data processing. The current reach of data protection law is thus very limited when it comes to living labs and smart city projects functioning according to the surveillant logic of security, based on increasing amounts of environmental data and atmospheric profiling.

Chapter 9, 'Data Used in Governmental Automated Decision-Making and Profiling: Towards More Practical Protection', by Sascha van Schendel, explores data used in profiling and automated decision-making tools employed by governmental actors. The author illustrates how data are used in practice in that sector through two Dutch examples: System Risk Indication (SyRI) and the OxRec. An overarching problem is that the legal framework does not seem to take into account that data are often gathered in a different context than that for which they will be used during profiling and automated decision-making, or that this context comes with its own complexities. When data are collected, they are collected in a specific context, characterised at least by a specific purpose for which they are collected and a specific perspective on the subject of the data, and there is a specific actor gathering the data. Comparatively, in automated decision-making and profiling applications, this context tends to get lost or be let go of. Other problems are the bias in data bound to specific contexts, the group-oriented nature of profiles and how automated decision-making and data labelled as 'non-personal data' by the regulatory framework (such as aggregated data and statistical data) play a key role in the creation of profiles. To maintain a perspective on data used in automated decision-making and profiling that is in tune with reality, the regulatory framework needs to be able to be contextual enough to take all these factors into account and, more specifically, pay attention to the importance of groups in data and the importance of non-personal data.

3.3. Regulation

The third and final part offers a legal perspective on different aspects and ways of regulating data or categories of data.

Chapter 10, 'Data: A Very Short Introduction to the EU Galaxy and to Five Potential Paths Forward', by Bart van der Sloot, gives a broad overview of the approach in the EU to data regulation. It indicates the underlying choices of its data regulation, how these are challenged by societal and technological developments and sketches several potential solutions. The author does so by first exploring the 'where', 'who', 'what', 'why', 'when' and 'how' of the General Data Protection Regulation (GDPR). Van der Sloot explains how, with each of the approaches taken in the GDPR, questions arise, especially considering the evolving technological paradigm. The EU hopes to lay down a detailed and comprehensive legislative package for the 21st century for data. While each of these instruments contains valuable provisions, prohibitions and rights, the EU has invested little in the consistency between these and other legal instruments and the consistency between the laws applicable to the data-driven environment. To that end, alternative approaches to regulation are proposed and analysed.

Chapter 11, 'The Regulation of Access to Personal and Non-Personal Data in the EU: From Bits and Pieces to a System?', by Thomas Tombal and Inge Graef, introduces the legal implications surrounding access to data, both personal and non-personal, in the EU. In so doing, the chapter attempts to analyse the convergences and divergences of the various legislative instruments pertaining to access rights with a particular focus on the right to data portability. It problematises the heterogeneity of regulatory scopes in the construction of a coherent legal system. They note that 'the EU is becoming an inconsistent patchwork of different provisions and approaches', which market players need to deal with. In examining the elements responsible for the construction of such a framework, without prejudice to the substantive position of black letter law, the authors attach special prominence to the role that the addressees of the norm and the law enforcement mechanisms established by the regulators will play in the future.

Chapter 12, 'Regulating "Non-Personal Data": Developments in India', by Rishab Bailey and Renuka Sane, discusses the regulation of non-personal data in India. This is driven primarily by competition concerns, especially vis-à-vis foreign multinationals, as well as issues of 'fairness' and equity in distribution of the benefits of the data economy, which derive from a view that links regulation of data to India's sovereignty. It is innovative in that it recognises the community as a distinct stakeholder in the data governance debate. However, the framework seeks to regulate a vast field covering a multiplicity of sectors, businesses and relationships in a fast-changing ecosystem, which may prove to be impractical.

Chapter 13, 'Data Protection Without Data: Informationless Chilling Effects and Data Protection Law', by Dara Hallinan, discusses the concept of 'informationless chilling effects' and their relevance to information processing. Informationless chilling effects constitute a form of harm to rights, which falls within the purview of EU data protection law. Scoping concepts in data protection law offer the potential to encompass systems and contexts engendering these effects. Informationless chilling effects are a form of 'parasitic' harm stemming from information processing, without which no recognition of cues sparking subsequent chilling effect behaviours could be eventuated. Following this line, Hallinan establishes that 'whilst informationless chilling effects constitute a form of harm to rights, which has not hitherto been recognised as corresponding to purpose of data protection law, the broad, flexible and open-ended nature of this purpose' would be sufficient to incorporate the effects within the scope of data protection law. Further, the author conceives data protection law as the most suitable area of law to deal with these problems, given that there are no other areas of law that might obviously be looked to as offering a general, accessible and elaborate scheme of protection relevant in relation to systems and contexts engendering informationless chilling effects.

Chapter 14, 'Identity, Profiles and Pseudonyms in the Digital Environment', by Miranda Mourby and Elaine Mackey, shows that although the GDPR does not explicitly link the definition of profiling with that of personal data, the decisions we have reviewed have placed interference with individual rights at the heart of the concept of identification. As such, profiling provides an important illustration as to when information is sufficiently intrusive into fundamental rights so that it can justifiably be called an identification. This is contrasted with pseudonymisation, in which case the question of identification is less certain. The chapter highlights that longitudinal data showing individual behaviour over time (e.g. from a cookie) will be much more difficult to anonymise than a logfile of website visitors that only provides a single snapshot in time. Ultimately, however, our central contribution is showing that it may now be helpful to determine the scope of identity in data protection law with reference to fundamental rights and not – as is often suggested – the other way around. For all that, the category of 'identity' continues to shift as technology evolves: the underlying benchmarks of privacy and non-discrimination rights are sufficiently stable to provide a reliable sense of who we are as we navigate the digital environment.

Chapter 15, 'Biometric Data, Within and Beyond Data Protection', by Catherine Jasserand, argues that, from a technical perspective, biometric data are formats resulting from the processing and transformation of biometric characteristics used for biometric recognition purposes (one individual) or categorisation purposes (shared characteristics of a group of individuals). These formats vary from the sample captured by a biometric system to the biometric template resulting from a reduction into a numerical representation of biometric attributes used for recognition or classification purposes. A step-by-step assessment is necessary to determine whether personal data and biometric (personal) data are processed at each technical stage. Depending on the purpose or context of processing, biometric data will be classified as personal, biometric and/or sensitive data. However, it could be the case that data generated during the image acquisition and face detection stages do not reach the threshold of identifiability and remain excluded from the field of personal data. Thus, it cannot be claimed that biometric data generated during the technical processing are necessarily personal data.

References

Article 29 Working Party (WP29). (2007). *Opinion 4/2007 on the concept of personal data* ('WP 136'), 20 June 2007.

CJEU. (2016). *Breyer v Germany*, 19 October 2016, C-582/14, ECLI:EU:C:2016:779.

Finck M., & Pallas F. (2020). They who must not be identified – Distinguishing personal from non-personal data under the GDPR. *International Data Privacy Law, 10*(1), 11–36.

Graef, I., & Gellert, R. (2021). The European Commission's proposed Data Governance Act: Some initial reflections on the increasingly complex EU regulatory puzzle of stimulating data sharing. TILEC Discussion Paper no. DP2021-006. Available at SSRN: https://ssrn.com/abstract=3814721

Hoofnagle, C. J., van der Sloot, B., & Zuiderveen Borgesius F. (2019). 'The European Union general data protection regulation: What it is and what it means. *Information & Communications Technology Law 28*(1), 65–98.

Purtova, N. (2018). The law of everything. Broad concept of personal data and future of EU data protection law. *Law, Innovation and Technology 10*(1), 40–81.

Quinn, P., & Malgieri, G. (2021). The difficulty of defining sensitive data –The concept of sensitive data in the EU data protection framework. *German Law Journal* 22(8), 1583–1612.

van der Sloot, B. (2017). *Privacy as virtue: Moving beyond the individual in the age of Big Data*. Intersentia.

von Grafenstein, M. (2022). Reconciling conflicting interests in data through data governance: An analytical framework (and a brief discussion of the Data Governance Act draft, the AI Regulation draft, as well as the GDPR). *HIIG Discussion Paper Series* 2022-2. https://doi.org/10.5281/zenodo.6457735

2. Object Re-identification: Problems, Algorithms and Responsible Research Practice

Zhedong Zheng & Liang Zheng

Abstract

In this chapter, we discuss the object re-identification problem in the computer vision context of vehicles, people, etc. This task allows us to match objects under different views, which benefits many real-world applications such as public safety and traffic control. Existing works in this area focus on the development of discriminative features, ranging from backbone to loss function design. We also highlight the necessity of data-centric research, where improving and analysing data is the primary objective. Apart from these technical perspectives, we discuss responsible practices, such as the use of synthetic data instead of real data, data anonymisation and economical learning schemes. These practices would support ethical use and deployment of object re-identification systems.

Keywords: object re-identification; privacy protection; data anonymisation; synthetic data

1. Problem Introduction

What is object re-identification (re-ID)? In our daily life, objects (e.g. vehicles, people, fashion items) are encountered in certain scenarios, and re-identifying objects means recognising them in different contexts of time, in different locations or from other viewpoints. Here we usually refer to object instances instead of object categories. In the computer vision community, commonly studied objects include people, animals, vehicles and landmarks, which are captured by cameras. Specifically, given an image of an object instance or query captured by a certain camera, we aim

Van der Sloot & van Schendel. *The Boundaries of Data.* Taylor & Francis Group, 2024
DOI: 10.5117/9789463729192_CH02

to match it against a database of previously captured object images to find those containing the same instance.

In object re-identification, queries can be of different modalities, such as an image (Zheng et al., 2015), a video (Zheng et al., 2016a) or a natural language (Li et al., 2017), which contain or describe the object of interest. The query is input into the system and matched against a gallery composed of candidate object instances, and then a shortlist of highly ranked candidates is returned. Before this matching process, the object instances are vectorised using hand-crafted descriptors or deep learning features to create a shared semantic space. These features should ideally reflect the most discriminative characteristics of an instance while preserving viewpoint, illumination and resolution invariance properties. The Euclidean distance[1] is usually used when matching deep learning features; otherwise, metric learning is conducted for similarity measurements.

The study of object re-ID takes place in various settings with diverse input modalities, annotations and data distributions. The most widely considered one is image-based, fully supervised and in-distribution, where effective backbones and loss functions are designed (Sun et al., 2018). This setting can be extended in many aspects. For example, some works study the use of video clips and natural language descriptions of objects instead of image modality (Zheng et al., 2016a; Li et al., 2017). Another interesting extension is to alleviate the need for supervision, assuming the source (pre-training) dataset is partially labelled or fully unlabelled (Li et al., 2018a; Yin et al., 2021). When considering that target domains are of different distributions than the source, we could define the unsupervised domain adaptation (Li et al., 2018b) or domain generalisation settings (Zhao et al., 2021). Because of its diverse and interesting range of research problems, object re-identification has been a research hot spot in the community.

Application scenarios. Object re-identification has many real-world applications, including recognition of persons and vehicles for public safety, tracking of multiple objects in a camera network, smart husbandry by re-identifying animals and product re-identification for cargo management (see Fig. 2.1).

Main challenges. One challenge is the intra-class discrepancy when associating the same object from different cameras. Two input images may contain limited, overlapping areas of the same object instance. To address this challenge, the system should be able to spot the salient characteristics of the object while being robust to changes in viewpoint. This representation capacity becomes more critical when combined with the domain shift

1 The distance between two vectors in the Euclidean space.

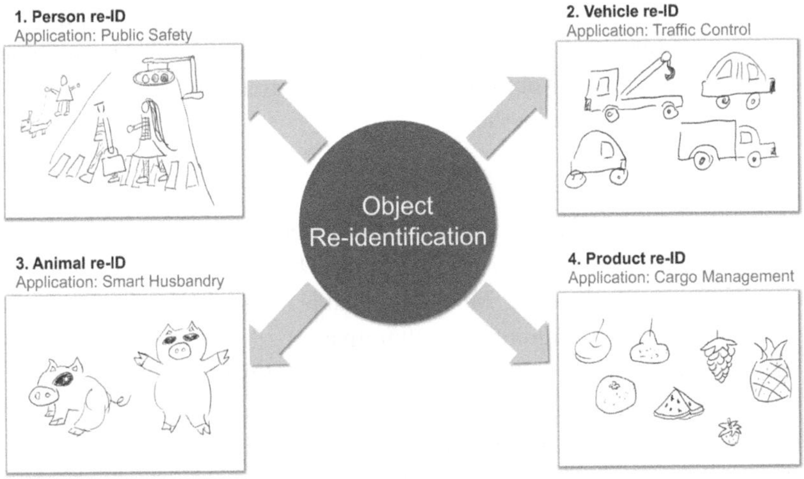

Figure 2.1. Example use cases of object re-identification regarding the subjects to be re-identified.

problem, commonly seen in the unsupervised domain adaptation setting. Another challenge is data scarcity. Due to annotation costs and privacy concerns, there is a shortage of data, the fuel of object re-ID systems. This motivates the researchers to explore data engineering, including training data optimisation (Zheng et al., 2017b) and test data analysis (Deng & Zheng, 2021). In conclusion, challenges create opportunities. These challenges, including intra-class discrepancy and data scarcity, spur researchers to develop re-ID algorithms from various angles.

2. Algorithms

Generally, recent research advances in object re-identification have been driven by large-scale datasets and deep learning techniques. On the one hand, compared with previous datasets that are small in scale, large-scale datasets (Zheng et al., 2015; Wei et al., 2018) provide more real-world data variables – such as illumination, background and occlusion – to facilitate the training of mapping functions. These datasets provide more comprehensive test sets for performance evaluation. On the other hand, data-driven re-ID algorithms benefit significantly from deep learning (LeCun et al., 2015), which allows models to be trained in an end-to-end manner. As such, it is the architecture design and optimisation objectives that matter most. In the object re-identification community, prevailing methods can generally be divided into three families. These are: data engineering, architecture design and optimisation (or objective function design). The three families are normally orthogonal to each other. In practice, it is possible to combine multiple techniques to obtain competitive accuracy. In the next section, we review some recent methods.

Data engineering

Data are the fuel of data-driven machine learning algorithms, so it is important to understand the role of data and how to improve data quality to facilitate model training. More data enable models to 'see' more object variables – such as background and illumination – during training, and thus the taught model has a stronger generalisation ability to new environments. In object re-ID, generative models (Goodfellow et al., 2014) and 3D graphical simulations are often used. Specifically, Zheng et al. (2017b) use generative adversarial networks (GANs) (Goodfellow et al., 2014) to generate more training images, which are likely aligned with the real-world training distribution. In a similar vein, Huang et al. (2018) apply an improved GAN scheme for better generation quality and a rank-based pseudo label for representation learning. The GAN methods used in these two methods are unconditional, which is not ideal for object attribute manipulation. Considering that objects have geometric structure, a few works explore pose-guided image generation. For example, Qian et al. (2018) and Ma et al. (2017) both use skeleton keypoints during pedestrian image generation, so humans are generated with arbitrary poses. Similarly, Ge et al. (2018) harness pose guidance for image generation to disentangle pose embedding and identity embedding. These works usually encode an image into a vector, the downside of which is the loss of spatial information; consequently, the reconstructed background is relatively blurred and unrealistic. In response, Zheng et al. (2019) leverage one content encoder to preserve low-level background feature maps instead of vectorisation. Comparatively, Wei et al. (2018) directly copy the background from the original inputs to the new object. Some approaches do not generate images from scratch but directly modify other real-world data. For instance, Zhong et al. (2018) transfer the camera style of images collected by different camera for data augmentation via Cycle-Consistent Adversarial Networks (CycleGANs) (Zhu et al., 2017). Deng et al. (2018) convert the style of the data collected in summer to a winter style for fast adaptation to winter test scenarios. Except for GANs, Yang et al. (2023) recently deploy Stable Diffusion models (Rombach et al., 2022) to craft a large-scale image-text benchmark, which also facilitates multi-modality representation learning.

A recent trend in the community is to explore data simulated by game engines. The simulated training data become increasingly strong and can even be comparable with real-world training sets (Zhang et al., 2021; Barbosa et al., 2018). This is particularly valuable considering potential ethical problems, such as biometric data leakage. We suspect that when cheaper and more realistic simulation is possible, this strategy will gain further popularity. In addition, it has been shown that more effective training data and validation data can be composed through simulation (Yao et al., 2020) or by searching (Sun et al., 2021). This indicates that it is not always necessary to prepare a comprehensive and large-scale dataset for training or validation purposes. Instead, datasets can be optimally generated based on test scenarios.

Despite this progress, there are still many interesting data-centric questions to study. For example, if the test data are unlabelled, will it be possible to estimate model accuracy or equivalently test set difficulty (Deng & Zheng 2021)? It would also be interesting to study what aspects are important in composing an effective training set, such as class imbalance rate, diversity and domain gap (Yao et al., 2020; Devaranjan et al., 2020). Deeper understanding of data will almost certainly facilitate the re-ID research.

Architecture design

State-of-the-art object re-ID systems require discriminative visual representations extracted by deep learning models, where a few effective backbones have been proposed. For example, Sun et al. (2018) have proposed a part-based convolutional baseline (PCB) that splits feature maps and adds class-wise supervision to different parts, yielding complementary part features. Following the spirit of PCB, Wang et al. (2018) have explored more partition strategies and difference loss functions, further improving accuracy. A few others have modified or redesigned the convolutional neural network (CNN) backbone. Specifically, Zheng et al. (2018) added a spatial attention branch to deal with image misalignment. Zhou et al. (2019) redesigned the block structure with small depth-wise kernels and achieve competitive retrieval accuracy with limited parameters. Furthermore, Wang et al. (2021) have accelerated model inference by pruning 91.9% redundant kernels while maintaining reasonable accuracy. Furthermore, some works (Quan et al., 2019; Zhou et al., 2021) directly explore network automatic search to find effective and efficient model structures during training. Recently, transformer-based approaches (Liu et al., 2021; He et al., 2021) have shown interesting potential for improving representation quality, but these potentially suffer from relatively slow training and testing (Dosovitskiy et al., 2020) and difficulties in capturing spatial patterns, like conventional CNNs and recurrent neural networks (RNNs) (Ding et al., 2022). In this regard, combining the strengths of transformers and CNNs seems to be a balanced solution.

It is also beneficial to consider using external knowledge, such as key points (Sarfraz et al., 2018; Su et al., 2017; Suh et al., 2018), semantic segmentation (Kalayeh et al., 2018; Zhang et al., 2019) and 3D reconstruction (Zheng et al., 2020). These works usually analyse the data first, then combine them with prior knowledge to better understand the geometric nature of the target objects. As a drawback, these methods may require extra annotations or off-the-shelf models, which are not always be accessible.

Objective functions

Object re-ID is an important testbed for loss design, which should reflect the underlying data relationship. According to Sun et al. (2020), this line of works can be coarsely categorised based on the used label type, i.e. pair-wise labels or class-level labels. Using the pair-wise label, it is possible to compare the distance among paired inputs, such as in contrastive learning (Yi et al., 2014). Under this loss function, models are trained to enlarge the distance between negative pairs, while pulling positive pairs closer. Taking this one step further, some works feature triplets to simultaneously compare the anchor data, positive data and negative data. The triplicate loss (Hermans et al., 2017) generally surpasses the contrastive loss in modelling the semantic space during optimisation, because it considers intra-class distance and inter-class distance at the same time. These ideas have now been widely studied in self-supervised model pretraining (Kalantidis et al., 2020).

In contrast to the pair-wise label, class-wise labels capture comprehensive relationships in the whole dataset. Typically, classification loss – including identification loss (Zheng et al., 2016b), Online Instance Matching (OIM) loss (Xiao et al., 2017), centre loss (Wen et al., 2016) and sphere loss (Liu et al., 2017) – is proposed to differentiate between different classes according to the category label. In this way, the inter-class distance is again enlarged while the intra-class distance is minimised. That said, identification loss is suboptimal in capturing the fine-grained local differences, especially for similar targets. For example, the distance between cats and dogs should be smaller than that between cats and aeroplanes. To further learn such category relationships, Lin et al. (2019) introduce object attributes – such as colour and shape – to help learning feature space align with semantic distance. Some works further explore the potential of combining both pair-wise and class-wise labels (Zheng et al., 2017a; Sun et al., 2020) and achieve very impressive results.

We have summarised some mainstream research efforts. We emphasise that there are other, important problems being studied in the object re-identification community, but due to space limitations, these are not fully covered here.

3. Responsible Research Practice

While object re-identification research has become one of the fundamental research problems in the community, there are concerns about multiple aspects of it, including privacy and ethics. Obtaining ethical approval and clearance is necessary in many institutes before starting a research project; in this section, we briefly discuss possible ways to mitigate these concerns, thus enabling responsible re-ID research.

Developing algorithms with synthetic data
While the medical research community typically uses animal models (e.g. E. coli) in research, and advanced manufacturing uses simulation, the computer vision community mainly uses real-world data, which may cause privacy concerns. Can we learn from other scientific fields by using synthetic data that are free of ethical concerns in research and only use real-world data when developing models to be used in practice? On the one hand, some recent works show that many observations made on synthetic data are consistent with those obtained through real data (Sun & Zheng, 2019; Sakaridis et al., 2018). This would encourage the community to use synthetic data to understand how systems work. On the other hand, there are strong cases of systems trained on synthetic data have comparable, if not better, performance than those trained with real data (Wood et al., 2021; Zhang et al., 2021). This can be achieved by some lightweight human design, such as increasing data diversity and applying style transfer methods. There are also automatic ways to generate training data given some unlabelled data from the target domain, such as training data search (Yan et al., 2020) and simulation (Yao et al., 2020; Kar et al., 2019). It would be interesting to study how far synthetic data can go and how to reduce the synthetic-real domain gap. Fabbri et al. (2021) put particular focus on the progress made in computer graphics. Given the above two aspects for consideration, it would be interesting to explore whether it is feasible for the community to rely on synthetic data for research purposes, only using real-world data to teach models to be deployed.

Data anonymisation
When the re-ID data have ID concerns, it would be good practice to anonymise the data before usage. One way is to edit the images, such as by blurring faces and licence plates, which can be done through a combination of detection and blurring operations. This effect is yet to be studied, but according to Yang et al. (2021), blurring faces in the ImageNet dataset does not

have noticeable influence on model generalisation ability. Another possible way to implement anonymisation is to add constraints to image features so that the original images cannot be reconstructed from their features, while the latter still maintains discriminative ability (Dusmanu et al., 2020). This active research area is yet to fully assess the anonymisation effect, since the differences between images reconstructed by various methods are usually hard to quantify and compared.

Designing economical learning schemes

By default, deep learning algorithms are data hungry, which requires a lot of labelled samples. There is currently a lot of work being put into decreasing reliance on large-scale data, which would reduce data concerns. For example, on the problem of data leaking, which may occur if a user uploads data or a server is hacked, federated learning has been proposed. Data can be stored at terminal devices without being exchanged, and a model can be trained across the terminals (Zhuang et al., 2020). On the other hand, semi-supervised learning (Li et al., 2018a), few-shot learning (Wu et al., 2018) and unsupervised learning (Yin et al., 2021) have been widely studied. There is also increasing interest in self-supervised pretraining techniques (Khorramshahi et al., 2020; Fu et al., 2021) and foundation networks (Chen et al., 2023; Zuo et al., 2023), where better pretraining models can be beneficial for existing economical learning schemes.

In conclusion, the re-ID field would benefit from model-centric, data-centric research, as well as responsible research practices. The former two aspects allow us to develop strong and robust visual matching systems, while the latter gives us confidence in stepping forward to a more sustainable future.

References

Barbosa, I. B., Cristani, M., Caputo, B., Rognhaugen, A., & Theoharis, T. (2018). Looking beyond appearances: Synthetic training data for deep CNNs in re-identification. *Computer Vision and Image Understanding, 167*, 50–62.

Chen, W., Xu, X., Jia, J., Luo, H., Wang, Y., Wang, F., Jin, R., & Sun, X. (2023). Beyond appearance: A semantic controllable self-supervised learning framework for human-centric visual tasks. In *Proceedings of the IEEE/CVF Conference on Computer Vision and Pattern Recognition* (pp. 15050–15061). IEEE.

Deng, W., & Zheng, L. (2021). Are labels always necessary for classifier accuracy evaluation? In *Proceedings of the IEEE/CVF Conference on Computer Vision and Pattern Recognition* (pp. 15069–15078). IEEE.

Deng, W., Zheng, L., Ye, Q., Kang, G., Yang, Y., & Jiao, J. (2018). Image-image domain adaptation with preserved self-similarity and domain-dissimilarity for person re-identification. In *Proceedings of the IEEE Conference on Computer Vision and Pattern Recognition* (pp. 994–1003). IEEE.

Devaranjan, J., Kar, A., & Fidler, S. (2020). Meta-sim2: Unsupervised learning of scene structure for synthetic data generation. In *European Conference on Computer Vision* (pp. 715–733). Springer.

Ding, X., Zhang, X., Zhou, Y., Han, J., Ding, G., & Sun, J. (2022). Scaling up your kernels to 31x31: Revisiting large kernel design in CNNs. In *Proceedings of the IEEE/CVF International Conference on Computer Vision* (pp. 11963–11975). IEEE.

Dosovitskiy, A., Beyer, L., Kolesnikov, A., Weissenborn, D., Zhai, X., Unterthiner, T., Dehghani, M., Minderer, M., Heigold, G., Gelly, S., et al. (2020). *An image is worth 16x16 words: Transformers for image recognition at scale.* arXiv preprint arXiv:2010.11929.

Dusmanu, M., Schonberger, J. L., Sinha, S. N., & Pollefeys, M. (2020). *Privacy-preserving image features via adversarial affine subspace embeddings.* arXiv preprint arXiv:2006.06634.

Fabbri, M., Brasó, G., Maugeri, G., Cetintas, O., Gasparini, R., Ošep, A., Calderara, S., Leal-Taixé, L., & Cucchiara, R. (2021). 'MOTSynth: How can synthetic data help pedestrian detection and tracking? In *Proceedings of the IEEE/CVF International Conference on Computer Vision* (pp. 10849–10859). IEEE.

Fu, D., Chen, D., Bao, J., Yang, H., Yuan, L., Zhang, L., Li, H., & Chen, D. (2021). Unsupervised pre-training for person re-identification. In *Proceedings of the IEEE/CVF Conference on Computer Vision and Pattern Recognition* (pp. 14750–14759). IEEE.

Ge, Y., Li, Z., Zhao, H., Yin, G., Yi, S., Wang, X., & Li, H. (2018). FD-GAN: Pose-guided feature distilling GAN for robust person re-identification. In NIPS'18: Proceedings of the 32nd International Conference on Neural Information Processing Systems (pp. 1230–1241). NIPS.

Goodfellow, I., Pouget-Abadie, J., Mirza, M., Xu, B., Warde-Farley, D., Ozair, S., Courville, A., & Bengio, Y. (2014). Generative adversarial nets. *Advances in Neural Information Processing Systems, 27,* 2672–2680.

He, S., Luo, H., Wang, P., Wang, F., Li, H., & Jiang, W. (2021). 'Transreid: Transformer-based object re-identification. In *Proceedings of the IEEE/CVF International Conference on Computer Vision* (pp. 15013–15022). IEEE.

Hermans, A., Beyer, L., & Leibe, B. (2017). *In defense of the triplet loss for person re-identification.* arXiv preprint arXiv:1703.07737.

Huang, Y., Xu, J., Wu, Q., Zheng, Z., Zhang, Z., & Zhang, J. (2018). Multi-pseudo regularized label for generated data in person re-identification. *IEEE Transactions on Image Processing, 28*(3),1391–1403.

Kalantidis, Y., Sariyildiz, M. B., Pion, N., Weinzaepfel, P., & Larlus, D. (2020). Hard negative mixing for contrastive learning. *Advances in Neural Information Processing Systems, 33*, 21798–21809.

Kalayeh, M. M., Basaran, E., Gökmen, M., Kamasak, M. E., & Shah, M. (2018). Human semantic parsing for person re-identification. In *Proceedings of the IEEE Conference on Computer Vision and Pattern Recognition* (pp. 1062–1071). IEEE.

Kar, A., Prakash, A., Liu, M.-Y., Cameracci, E., Yuan, J., Rusiniak, M., Acuna, D., Torralba, A., & Fidler, S. (2019). 'Meta-Sim: Learning to generate synthetic datasets. In *Proceedings of the IEEE/CVF International Conference on Computer Vision* (pp. 4551–4560). IEEE.

Khorramshahi, P., Peri, N., Chen, J.-c., & Chellappa, R. (2020). The devil is in the details: Self-supervised attention for vehicle re-identification. In *European Conference on Computer Vision* (pp. 369–386). Springer.

LeCun, Y., Bengio, Y., & Hinton, G. (2015). Deep learning. *Nature, 521*(7553), 436–444.

Li, J., Ma, A. J., & Yuen, P. C. (2018a). Semi-supervised region metric learning for person re-identification. *International Journal of Computer Vision, 126*(8), 855–874.

Li, S., Xiao, T., Li, H., Zhou, B., Yue, D., & Wang, X. (2017). Person search with natural language Description. In *Proceedings of the IEEE Conference on Computer Vision and Pattern Recognition* (pp. 1970–1979). IEEE.

Li, Y.-J., Yang, F.-E., Liu, Y.-C., Yeh, Y.-Y., Du, X., & Frank Wang, Y.-C. (2018b). Adaptation and re-identification network: An unsupervised deep transfer learning approach to person re-identification. In *Proceedings of the IEEE Conference on Computer Vision and Pattern Recognition Workshops* (pp. 172–178). IEEE.

Lin, Y., Zheng, L., Zheng, Z., Wu, Y., Hu, Z., Yan, C., & Yang, Y. (2019). Improving person re-identification by attribute and identity learning. *Pattern Recognition, 95*, 151–161.

Liu, W., Wen, Y., Yu, Z., Li, M., Raj, B., & Song, L. (2017). Sphereface: Deep hypersphere embedding for face recognition. In *Proceedings of the IEEE Conference on Computer Vision and Pattern Recognition* (pp. 212–220). IEEE.

Liu, Z., Lin, Y., Cao, Y., Hu, H., Wei, Y., Zhang, Z., Lin, S., & Guo, B. (2021). Swin transformer: Hierarchical vision transformer using shifted windows. In *Proceedings of the IEEE/CVF International Conference on Computer Vision* (pp. 10012–10022). IEEE.

Ma, L., Jia, X., Sun, Q., Schiele, B., Tuytelaars, T., & Van Gool, L. (2017). Pose guided person image generation. *Advances in Neural Information Processing Systems, 31*, 406–416.

Qian, X., Fu, Y., Xiang, T., Wang, W., Qiu, J., Wu, Y., Jiang, Y.-G., & Xue, X. (2018). Pose-normalized image generation for person re-identification. In *Proceedings of the European Conference on Computer Vision (ECCV)* (pp. 650–667). Springer.

Quan, R., Dong, X., Wu, Y., Zhu, L., & Yang, Y. (2019). Auto-reID: Searching for a part-aware ConvNet for person re-identification. In *Proceedings of the IEEE/CVF International Conference on Computer Vision* (pp. 3750–3759). IEEE.

Rombach, R., Blattmann, A., Lorenz, D., Esser, P., & Ommer, B. (2022). High-resolution image synthesis with latent diffusion models. In *Proceedings of the IEEE/CVF Conference on Computer Vision and Pattern Recognition* (pp. 10684–10695). IEEE.

Sakaridis, C., Dai, D., & Van Gool, L. (2018). Semantic foggy scene understanding with synthetic data. *International Journal of Computer Vision, 126*(9), 973–992.

Sarfraz, M. S., Schumann, A., Eberle, A., & Stiefelhagen, R. (2018). A pose-sensitive embedding for person re-identification with expanded cross neighborhood re-ranking. In *Proceedings of the IEEE Conference on Computer Vision and Pattern Recognition* (pp. 420–429). IEEE.

Su, C., Li, J., Zhang, S., Xing, J., Gao, W., & Tian, Q. (2017). Pose-driven deep convolutional model for person re-identification. In *Proceedings of the IEEE International Conference on Computer Vision* (pp. 3960–3969). IEEE.

Suh, Y., Wang, J., Tang, S., Mei, T., & Lee, K. M. (2018). Part-aligned bilinear representations for person re-identification. In *Proceedings of the European Conference on Computer Vision (ECCV)* (pp. 402–419). Springer.

Sun, X., Hou, Y., Deng, W., Li, H., & Zheng, L. (2021). Ranking models in unlabeled new environments. In *Proceedings of the IEEE/CVF International Conference on Computer Vision* (pp. 11761–11771). IEEE.

Sun, X., & Zheng, L. (2019). Dissecting person re-identification from the viewpoint of viewpoint. In *Proceedings of the IEEE/CVF Conference on Computer Vision and Pattern Recognition* (pp. 608–617). IEEE.

Sun, Y., Cheng, C., Zhang, Y., Zhang, C., Zheng, L., Wang, Z., & Wei, Y. (2020). Circle loss: A unified perspective of pair similarity optimization. In *Proceedings of the IEEE/CVF Conference on Computer Vision and Pattern Recognition* (pp. 6398–6407). IEEE.

Sun, Y., Zheng, L., Yang, Y., Tian, Q., & Wang, S. (2018). Beyond part models: Person retrieval with refined part pooling (and a strong convolutional baseline). In *Proceedings of the European Conference on Computer Vision (ECCV)* (pp. 480–496). Springer.

Wang, G., Yuan, Y., Chen, X., Li, J., & Zhou, X. (2018). Learning discriminative features with multiple granularities for person re-identification. In *Proceedings of the 26th ACM International Conference on Multimedia* (pp. 274–282). Association for Computing Machinery.

Wang, X., Zheng, Z., He, Y., Yan, F., Zeng, Z., & Yang, Y. (2021). Soft person reidentification pruning via blockwise adjacent filter decaying. In *IEEE Transactions on Cybernetics* (pp. 13293–13307). IEEE.

Wei, L., Zhang, S., Gao, W., & Tian, Q. (2018). Person transfer GAN to bridge domain gap for person re-identification. In *Proceedings of the IEEE Conference on Computer Vision and Pattern Recognition* (pp. 79–88). IEEE.

Wen, Y., Zhang, K., Li, Z., & Qiao, Y. (2016). A discriminative feature learning approach for deep face recognition. In *European Conference on Computer Vision* (pp. 499–515). Springer.

Wood, E., Baltrušaitis, T., Hewitt, C., Dziadzio, S., Cashman, T. J., & Shotton, J. (2021). Fake it till you make it: Face analysis in the wild using synthetic data alone. In *Proceedings of the IEEE/CVF International Conference on Computer Vision* (pp. 3681–3691). IEEE.

Wu, Y., Lin, Y., Dong, X., Yan, Y., Ouyang, W., & Yang, Y. (2018). Exploit the unknown gradually: One-shot video-based person re-identification by stepwise learning. In *Proceedings of the IEEE Conference on Computer Vision and Pattern Recognition* (pp. 5177–5186). IEEE.

Xiao, T., Li, S., Wang, B., Lin, L., & Wang, X. (2017). Joint detection and identification feature learning for person search. In *Proceedings of The IEEE Conference on Computer Vision and Pattern Recognition* (pp. 3415–3424). IEEE.

Yan, X., Acuna, D., & Fidler, S. (2020). Neural data server: A large-scale search engine for transfer learning data. In *Proceedings of the IEEE/CVF Conference on Computer Vision and Pattern Recognition* (pp. 3893–3902). IEEE.

Yang, K., Yau, J., Fei-Fei, L., Deng, J., & Russakovsky, O. (2021). *A study of face obfuscation in imagenet*. arXiv preprint arXiv:2103.06191.

Yang, S., Zhou, Y., Wang, Y., Wu, Y., Zhu, L., & Zheng, Z. (2023). *Towards unified text-based person retrieval: A large-scale multi-attribute and language search benchmark*. arXiv preprint arXiv:2306.02898.

Yao, Y., Zheng, L., Yang, X., Naphade, M., & Gedeon, T. (2020). Simulating content consistent vehicle datasets with attribute descent. In *European Conference on Computer Vision* (pp. 775–791). Springer.

Yi, D., Lei, Z., Liao, S., & Li, S. Z. (2014). Deep metric learning for person re-identification. In *2014 22nd International Conference on Pattern Recognition* (pp. 34–39). IEEE.

Yin, Q., Ding, G., Gong, S., Tang, Z., et al. (2021). Multi-view label prediction for unsupervised learning person re-identification. *IEEE Signal Processing Letters*, *28*, 1390–1394.

Zhang, T., Xie, L., Wei, L., Zhuang, Z., Zhang, Y., Li, B., & Tian, Q. (2021). Unrealperson: An adaptive pipeline towards costless person re-identification.

In *Proceedings of the IEEE/CVF Conference on Computer Vision and Pattern Recognition* (pp. 11506–11515). IEEE.

Zhang, Z., Lan, C., Zeng, W., & Chen, Z. (2019). Densely semantically aligned person re-identification. In *Proceedings of the IEEE/CVF Conference on Computer Vision and Pattern Recognition* (pp. 667–676). IEEE.

Zhao, Y., Zhong, Z., Yang, F., Luo, Z., Lin, Y., Li, S., & Sebe, N. (2021). Learning to generalize unseen domains via memory-based multi-source meta-learning for person re-identification. In *Proceedings of the IEEE/CVF Conference on Computer Vision and Pattern Recognition* (pp. 6277–6286). IEEE.

Zheng, L., Bie, Z., Sun, Y., Wang, J., Su, C., Wang, S., & Tian, Q. (2016a). Mars: A video benchmark for large-scale person re-identification. In *European Conference on Computer Vision* (pp. 868–884). Springer.

Zheng, L., Shen, L., Tian, L., Wang, S., Wang, J., & Tian, Q. (2015). Scalable person re-identification: A benchmark. In *Proceedings of The IEEE International Conference on Computer Vision* (pp. 1116–1124). IEEE.

Zheng, L., Yang, Y., & Hauptmann, A. G. (2016b). *Person re-identification: Past, present and future*. arXiv preprint arXiv:1610.02984.

Zheng, Z., Wang, X., Zheng, N., & Yang, Y. (2022). Parameter-efficient person re-identification in the 3D space. *IEEE Transactions on Neural Networks and Learning Systems*. https://doi.org/10.1109/TNNLS.2022.3214834

Zheng, Z., Yang, X., Yu, Z., Zheng, L., Yang, Y., & Kautz, J. (2019). Joint discriminative and generative learning for person re-identification. In *Proceedings of the IEEE/CVF Conference on Computer Vision and Pattern Recognition* (pp. 2138–2147). IEEE.

Zheng, Z., Zheng, L., & Yang, Y. (2017a). A discriminatively learned CNN embedding for person reidentification. *ACM Transactions on Multimedia Computing, Communications, and Applications* (TOMM), *14*(1),1–20.

Zheng, Z., Zheng, L., & Yang, Y. (2017b). Unlabeled samples generated by GAN improve the person re-identification baseline in vitro. In *Proceedings of the IEEE International Conference on Computer Vision* (pp. 3754–3762). IEEE.

Zheng, Z., Zheng, L., & Yang, Y. (2018). Pedestrian alignment network for large-scale person re-identification. *IEEE Transactions on Circuits and Systems for Video Technology*, *29*(10), 3037–3045.

Zhong, Z., Zheng, L., Zheng, Z., Li, S., & Yang, Y. (2018). Camera style adaptation for person re-identification. In *Proceedings of the IEEE Conference on Computer Vision and Pattern Recognition* (pp. 5157–5166). IEEE.

Zhou, K., Yang, Y., Cavallaro, A., & Xiang, T. (2019). Omni-scale feature learning for person re-identification. In *Proceedings of the IEEE/CVF International Conference on Computer Vision* (pp. 3702–3712). IEEE.

Zhou, Q., Zhong, B., Liu, X., & Ji, R. (2021). Attention-based neural architecture search for person re-identification. *IEEE Transactions on Neural Networks and Learning Systems, 33*(11), 6627–6639.

Zhu, J.-Y., Park, T., Isola, P., & Efros, A. A. (2017). Unpaired image-to-image translation using cycle-consistent adversarial networks. *In Proceedings of the IEEE International Conference on Computer Vision* (pp. 2223–2232). IEEE.

Zhuang, W., Wen, Y., Zhang, X., Gan, X., Yin, D., Zhou, D., Zhang, S., & Yi, S. (2020). Performance optimization of federated person re-identification via benchmark analysis. In *Proceedings of the 28th ACM International Conference on Multimedia* (pp. 955–963).

Zuo, J., Yu, C., Sang, N., & Gao, C. (2023). *PLIP: Language-image pre-training for person representation learning.* arXiv preprint arXiv:2305.08386.

3. The Quantum Threat to Cybersecurity and Privacy

Nina Bindel, Michele Mosca & Bill Munson

Abstract

Quantum computers promise to speed up and improve computations that are otherwise unfeasible on today's computers. However, they will also pose a threat to our current cryptography, which underpins cybersecurity and thus privacy. Preparing for this quantum threat by migrating to post-quantum cryptography needs to be seen as a joint responsibility of government, industry, research bodies and society at large. Unfortunately, it is likely that future technological advances will result in an ongoing need for deployment of successive generations of increasingly effective quantum-safe cryptography to maintain cybersecurity and protection of privacy.

Keywords: quantum threat; cybersecurity and privacy; confidentiality; authentication; quantum-safe cryptography

The emerging technology of quantum computing and quantum computers is a double-edged sword. Quantum computers are a new generation of computers that are more powerful than today's transistor-based computers because they use the principles of quantum physics to operate. On the one hand, they promise to speed up and improve computations that are otherwise unfeasible or take too long on our current computers. On the other hand, powerful quantum computers pose a threat to our current cryptography, which underpins cybersecurity and thus privacy.

The purpose of this chapter is to set out the privacy risks that quantum computers can be expected to introduce by way of the quantum threat. Although much of this chapter may seem overly focused on cybersecurity, this reflects the truism that there can be no privacy without security – online, at least. Even our starting point, cryptography, was initially developed to protect privacy, even if it now seems centred on security technology.

Van der Sloot & van Schendel. *The Boundaries of Data.* Taylor & Francis Group, 2024
DOI: 10.5117/9789463729192_CH03

1. A Brief Introduction to Cryptography

It seems reasonable to think that the use of secret messages to protect confidentiality and personal privacy closely followed the advent of writing. Two parties wishing to exchange secret messages by means of an intermediary while they are briefly apart would agree on one or more relatively simple steps to use to encrypt and decrypt their messages so that only they could read them. For instance, they might agree to encrypt a worded message by shifting each letter three alphabetic places to the right, and then replace it with the number corresponding to its new place in the alphabet. For example, A would become D, which would become 4. Upon receipt, the encrypted message would be decrypted by first turning the numbers back into letters, then shifting letters back to the left (i.e. 4 to D to A). In this very basic example, the steps involved in encrypting the message ensures nobody except the two parties involved can readily decrypt the message. The specific set of steps – or encryption key – must be kept secret, as decryption here involves nothing more than running the encryption key backwards. In modern cryptography, however, the algorithms used for encryption and decryption are usually known, and only a small part – the 'secret key' – needs to be kept hidden to ensure security. Depending on what kind of secret key is used, modern cryptography can be classified as either 'symmetric' or 'asymmetric' cryptography. In practice (e.g. in the Transport Layer Security (TLS) protocol, which secures most connections on the internet), a combination of symmetric and asymmetric cryptography is generally used.

1.1. Symmetric Cryptography

The core feature of symmetric cryptography is that both parties – who are often called 'Alice' and 'Bob' – know and rely on a single 'shared' set of encryption/decryption steps (i.e. a shared 'key'). This practice, which is commonly used to this day, is practical when it is possible for parties to agree privately on the key, or when the key is to be used to encrypt stored data. However, symmetric cryptography has its limits in many circumstances. For example, if Alice and Bob are remote from each other, or do not know each other, they need a way to communicate privately without meeting in order to agree on the key for encrypting subsequent communications. The same is true if personal meetings to exchange the shared key are impractical, such as for online shopping or online banking, where every customer would need to exchange separate keys prior to every interaction. This difficulty led to the invention and rapid adoption of asymmetric or public-key cryptography.

1.2. Asymmetric Cryptography

While only one shared secret key is needed for symmetric cryptography, two keys are generally necessary for asymmetric cryptography: a secret key and a public key. To explain this using the cryptographic algorithm of public-key encryption (PKE), we assume that Alice and Bob want to send encrypted messages – so-called 'ciphertexts' – using PKE. To be able to do this, each party generates a key pair consisting of an encryption key (which is made public by, for example, uploading it to a public database) and a decryption key (which needs to be kept secret at all times and should only be available to the owner). If Alice wants to send an encrypted message to Bob, she first needs to download Bob's encryption/public key from the database and then uses it to encrypt her message. She sends the resulting ciphertext to Bob, who then uses his decryption/secret key to decrypt Alice's ciphertext. It is important to mention that such encryption schemes require that the secret and public keys be mathematically related. The public key should be computed from the secret key, but it must not be possible to compute the secret key from the public key or from sent ciphertexts. This limits the set of possible mathematical relationships (also called mathematically 'hard problems' or 'security assumptions') from which cryptographic algorithms can be built. One of the best known mathematically hard problems is the Integer Factorisation Problem: factoring a very large integer that resulted from multiplying two large prime integers. While multiplying two large prime integers can be done very quickly on today's transistor-based computers, it is very difficult, and perhaps not even feasible, for today's computers to compute the prime factors of a very large integer. The integer factorisation problem is, in fact, the underlying mathematical problem in the widely used RSA scheme invented by Rivest, Shamir and Adleman in 1977. In a nutshell, the secret key consists of the two prime integers, and the public key is their product. Most of the asymmetric cryptography used on the internet today is based on either the integer factorisation problem or the similarly hard Discrete Logarithm Problem.

2. Two Sides of the Quantum Coin

Quantum computing is a way of processing, storing and communicating data in the form of physical quantum states, also called 'qubits'. These are 'bits' that are designed to be manipulated according to quantum rules, unlike the bits in our current transistor-based computing. To the general public, quantum computing and quantum computers have become almost synonymous with unimaginable increases in computer speeds, with these enormous speed-ups enabling calculations that are infeasible or very costly on today's transistor-based machines.

In general terms, quantum computers can be either 'universal' or task-specific. Universal quantum computers are capable of performing diverse operations, whereas task-specific quantum computers are tailored to solve a particular task, such as the problem of scheduling. Both kinds already exist, and some are even accessible for use by the public, even if they are still in their infancy.

Companies such as Google, IBM, Microsoft, Alibaba and many others see the enormous economic potential of quantum technology and are investing heavily in its advance. Universities and governments around the world are also showing increasing interest in developing, supporting and using quantum computing and its applications. Together, these efforts can be expected to accelerate progress toward the appearance of large quantum computers on a commercial scale. Unfortunately, the advantages of quantum computing are just one side of the coin. The other side is that the same quantum speed-ups will enable 'cryptographically relevant' quantum computers to pose a threat to our current cryptography. This is the quantum threat: that security, and thus privacy, will become vulnerable to hostile actions by actors that have access to powerful quantum computers because our cryptography is no longer strong enough to protect us. Since the quantum threat cannot manifest until a full, cryptographically relevant quantum computer is available, nobody can say with any degree of certainty when that will be[1]. However, to maintain our cybersecurity and privacy, the risk of the quantum threat must be analysed.

2.1. The Quantum Threat to Asymmetric Cryptography

Unfortunately, asymmetric cryptography, the most common form of cryptography in our daily lives, is the most vulnerable to quantum-based attacks. As noted above, most of the asymmetric cryptography used on the internet today is based on either the integer factorisation or the discrete logarithm problem. Therefore, attackers able to solve these two problems

1 In a recent study (Mosca & Piani, 2021), 46 quantum computing experts provided their opinions regarding the quantum threat to current asymmetric cryptographic algorithms. More than half were of the view that it is 'about 50% likely or more likely' that these algorithms will be threatened within the next 15 years; all but one believed this will be the case within the next 30 years.

efficiently can break the security of essentially all currently deployed public-key cryptography.

While there is no publicly known algorithm that could solve these algorithms efficiently (i.e. in polynomial time) on a transistor-based computer, Shor's algorithm can do exactly that on a quantum computer (Shor, 1999). Therefore, as soon as quantum computers large enough to run Shor's quantum algorithm have been built and are available 'outside the lab', the security guarantees of cryptography based on the two traditional hard problems no longer hold. Therefore, such 'cryptographically relevant' quantum computers will provide malevolent actors with the ability to break much of today's asymmetric cryptography in hours or even minutes. As things stand, the cryptographic algorithms that underpin the security of society's critical infrastructure – along with personal and data privacy – are at serious risk of being undermined by quantum computers in the foreseeable future (Mosca & Munson, 2019). This vulnerability is a source of great concern, as security guarantees have universal importance, such as ensuring that each party to a transaction knows that the other parties are who they say they are and that messages are legitimate. Without the assurance provided by these cryptographic mechanisms, there will be very little trust and likely fewer online transactions, whether they involve humans or the devices that make up the Internet of Things (IoT) (Mosca & Munson, 2019). For instance, security certificates based on asymmetric cryptography are used to verify the integrity and authenticity of software and firmware. If the security of these certificates is compromised, malicious hackers can more easily impersonate the original manufacturer and install whatever code they desire on hardware as varied as vehicles and pacemakers (Soutar et al., 2021). Even if the certificates have in fact not (yet) been hacked, they can no longer be trusted.

2.2. The Quantum Threat to Symmetric Cryptography

Symmetric cryptography is not much threatened by quantum computing in general, and not at all by Shor's algorithm. Still, Grover's quantum algorithm (Grover, 1996) essentially decreases the time needed to break symmetric cryptography. As the runtime of this algorithm is not polynomial (as is Shor's algorithm), doubling the length of the shared key is sufficient as a mitigative measure – and even that may not be necessary according to some experts (Preuss Mattsson et al., 2021). Either way, symmetric key algorithms in general need not be replaced; as far as we know, increasing key lengths is sufficient.

3. Implications of the Quantum Threat to Cryptography and Privacy

Three of the main security and privacy guarantees that can be achieved by cryptography are confidentiality, authenticity of entities and data and integrity of personal agency. As soon as cryptographically relevant quantum computers can be built, guarantees that rely on the use of algorithms based on the hardness of the factorisation or the discrete logarithm problem will no longer hold. The failure of any of these guarantees has implications from technical, economic and legal points of view.

3.1. Technical Implications

Privacy is largely enabled by the three guarantees noted above, which are in turn guaranteed by cryptographic algorithms. Therefore, if cryptographic algorithms are compromised by quantum attackers, privacy will be compromised as well. It has been said (ETSI, 2017a) that cryptography that is secure even in the presence of quantum computers is essential for the provision of a number of important services, including 1) protecting government and military communications, 2) securing financial and banking transactions, 3) assuring the confidentiality of medical data and healthcare records, 4) safeguarding the storage of personal data in the cloud and 5) restricting access to confidential corporate networks.

Confidentiality means protecting against the disclosure of information by either ensuring that access to data is limited to those authorised to do so or by representing data in such a way that its meaning remains accessible only to those who possess certain critical information (e.g. a key for decrypting the enciphered data) (Kimmins et al., 1995). If confidentiality of data can no longer be ensured due to quantum attacks on the cryptography that protects it, but the confidentiality of those data is still required, individuals and entities such as governments and companies are put at risk.

3.1.2. Authentication

Authentication means the verification of the claimed identities of parties to a communication or transaction by means of an agreed mechanism, or of the integrity of messages (i.e. that what was sent is what has been received). Online authentication mechanisms now generally rely on cryptography that is known to be quantum-vulnerable. This means that a quantum attacker[2]

2 A quantum attacker is an attacker with access to a quantum computer. Given the expense of building or even just running a state-of-the-art quantum computer, only a few well-funded

could not only decrypt communications but also forge certificates and install fraudulent firmware updates, breaking the security of most consumer electronics, enterprise networks, the industrial IoT and critical infrastructure (Preuss Mattsson et al., 2021).

3.1.3. Back-Tracking Attacks

Another very urgent technical implication is that quantum computers will eventually enable successful 'back-tracking' attacks, also called 'harvest-and-decrypt' attacks. In such attacks, data communicated over the internet today is copied and stored ('harvested') for decryption in the future when sufficiently powerful quantum computers are available. This is a concerning attack where data – whether national security, sensitive corporate data or certain kinds of personal data – will still need to be confidential when cryptographically relevant quantum computers are available. Not only would confidentiality be compromised, but so too would the integrity of personal and corporate information if hackers are able to alter records after the fact.

3.2. Privacy Implications

3.2.1. Release of Private Information

With so much private information regarding so many areas of our lives now being conveyed and stored digitally, ensuring that this information is kept private and confidential is of the utmost importance. This usually involves encryption schemes and digital signatures, but these can often be circumvented, such as when signature schemes are broken and information is sent to an impersonator, or encryption schemes are broken and ciphertexts can be decrypted. The leakage or unauthorised release of data to the public, to certain groups of people or to a single adversary is a constant possibility, and this may be harmful to the owners or subjects of the data, depending on the circumstances.

Consider recently introduced systems that store electronic medical records or manage patient care. Releasing some kinds of data (e.g. correspondence regarding scheduling a doctor's appointment) after a few years may not be harmful or even embarrassing for patients. However, more sensitive data may need to be secure for generations; for example, if the data relate to

states, large corporations and perhaps large criminal organisations would be expected to possess the first generations of cryptographically relevant quantum computers. However, other threat actors would naturally seek to illicitly access the quantum computing capabilities of legitimate users.

chronic diseases that can be inherited or to biological relationships, this might have personal or legal implications.

3.2.2. Loss of Agency and Control Over Personal Actions
A serious threat to privacy is the loss of a person's agency or control over personal actions. To some degree, this is an extension of identity theft, where users' credentials are copied illegally, and their cars, offices or homes are subsequently accessed, vandalised or stolen. To some degree, this is also an extension of the phenomenon of 'smart' homes being accessed by threat actors hacking into the IoT. Yet it is also something new and more subtle. An example of this loss of control would be when an individual is doing something they have chosen to do, such as driving their 'smart' car, but finds that certain functions of the car have been hacked and 'rewired' from the cloud so that the car now accelerates when the driver brakes or turns left when the driver turns the steering wheel to the right.

3.3. Economic and Legal Implications

Many governments recognise the quantum threat as not just a technological issue but as a potentially serious economic and legal threat (Csenkey & Bindel, 2021). For example, beyond the problem of malicious actors' hacking operations, there are implications for business continuity if not all links in a supply chain are prepared for the quantum threat. Regulations might require all partners in the supply chain of a software or security product to take precautions against the quantum threat. Some business partners might therefore be excluded in the future, delaying the product cycle as new partners are sought or plans are implemented to create more products 'in-house'. The quantum threat will also impact other legal issues. For example, states or companies that fail to act on knowledge of the quantum threat, thereby allowing cybersecurity and thus data privacy to be compromised by quantum computing, may well violate existing regulatory requirements (ETSI, 2017a), perhaps including the European Union's General Data Protection Regulation.

4. Mitigating the Risk to Cybersecurity and Privacy

In theory, the basic ways to mitigate risk are to (a) reduce the risk by building defences against the threat, (b) transfer the risk to others (generally by outsourcing certain operations or buying insurance) or (c) cease engagement in the risky business or activity. For the purposes of this chapter, we will focus only on building defences against the threat. In this case, the threat is the quantum threat to cryptography, and the defence is essentially to migrate our systems and networks from current quantum-vulnerable cryptography to cryptography that is deemed to be quantum-safe (sometimes also called 'quantum-secure').

4.1. Migration to Quantum-Safe Cryptography

4.1.1. Post-Quantum Cryptography

For many years, researchers have been developing alternatives to current quantum-vulnerable cryptographic algorithms that can be used to underpin cybersecurity once cryptographically relevant quantum computers are available. Such 'post-quantum' cryptographic algorithms are designed to be executed on our current transistor-based computers and the corresponding infrastructure, and not on quantum computers. These algorithms are considered secure against quantum-enabled attacks because they rely on different hard mathematical problems (see Section 1.2) that cannot be solved efficiently by quantum computers as far as we know. Still, the design and software properties (e.g. the size of the keys used or the ciphertexts sent) differ considerably. So, while internet infrastructure can be upgraded to offer quantum-secure solutions, this transition will take a great deal of complex analysis and effort. The mere scale of algorithms that need to be changed, including changes to many of the current cryptographic standards, begs for joint efforts in the transition to post-quantum cryptography. Initial steps to make this transition a reality have already been taken. Most prominently, the United States National Institute for Standards and Technology (NIST) is halfway through a project to identify and standardise very strong post-quantum digital signature and public-key encryption schemes by 2024.

4.1.2. Quantum Cryptography

Quantum cryptography is an umbrella term used to describe cryptographic algorithms that make use of quantum technology, i.e. quantum devices used to store, process or communicate information. (As noted above, post-quantum cryptography is not quantum technology, even if it protects against quantum technology.) The most important and promising form of quantum cryptography currently is quantum key distribution (QKD), where a shared key is derived to then be used (e.g. in symmetric encryption as described in Section 1.1). However, in QKD the shared key is derived through the communication of bits encoded in quantum states, in practice using photons.

Any tampering or eavesdropping of the quantum states by an adversary is detectable by the legitimate parties. If the detectable disturbances – whether due to adversaries or just technological imperfections – are below some small threshold, then the legitimate parties are able to derive a shared classical secret about which any adversary would have very negligible knowledge. This property enables QKD to provide potentially very powerful security that is resilient against unexpected new mathematical or algorithmic advances in code breaking. However, the technology requires a separate communication network to enable the sending of these quantum states, as our current internet infrastructure is not suitable for this. Current methods for establishing keys over distances exceeding 100 kilometres or so would require secure/trusted relay nodes, but such nodes pose a security risk that must be considered. Emerging methods, including quantum communication satellites and quantum repeaters, would reduce or eliminate the need for such intermediate trusted nodes. However, these methods are years away from being commercially developed, certified and deployed in large-scale systems alongside the post-quantum methods discussed earlier.

4.1.3. Cryptographic Hybrids

A 'hybrid' approach to cryptography calls for two cryptographic algorithms of the same kind (e.g. two signature schemes or two key-exchange protocols) to be combined so that the combined algorithm is secure if at least one of the ingredient schemes is secure in the circumstances. These hybrid algorithms are used for various purposes.

Classical/PQC hybrids. Post-quantum cryptography solutions are very promising but are still in development. At the same time, there is an urgent need to switch to quantum-secure solutions as soon as possible. So-called 'hybrid' or 'composite' algorithms are seen as an important solution to the predicament organisations face in needing to upgrade their systems to withstand quantum attacks while maintaining the security guarantees of well-established cryptographic algorithms, such as RSA. They have been suggested as an approach during the transition by several standardisation agencies (e.g. NIST, ETSI, BSI). Originally, these hybrid approaches were seen as combining one quantum-vulnerable with one quantum-safe scheme. However, quantum-vulnerable schemes can also be combined with two or more quantum-safe schemes – whether from an abundance of caution (the 'belt-and-suspenders' approach) in the face of largely untested algorithms or to offer backward-compatible quantum-secure solutions to systems that have not yet been updated.

PQC/PQC hybrids. Eventually, when all systems are quantum-safe and quantum-vulnerable algorithms are no longer needed, there may still be good reason for organisations to use PQC/PQC hybrids to diversify the deployed base of cryptographic algorithms if no single best-at-everything post-quantum algorithm has emerged and thereby decrease the risk of a devastating attack against one of them.

PQC/QKD hybrids. Hybrid approaches can also be used to generate a shared secret key that combines a key computed using post-quantum cryptography with a key generated using QKD. This shared key can then be used to encrypt data using symmetric encryption, for example. This would increase security when the computational security of post-quantum is insufficient and/or when deploying QKD technology on its own is not preferred (e.g. to mitigate the risks of other attack vectors on QKD systems, or simply to retain existing certifications requiring post-quantum algorithms).

4.1.4. Cryptographic Agility

Migrating systems from existing quantum-vulnerable cryptography to post-quantum cryptography will eventually mean replacing classical cryptographic hardware and software with quantum-safe hardware and software. An important conceptual and technological waystation on this migration is cryptographic agility. This can be seen as an interim goal for organisations moving to upgrade their cybersecurity posture at a time when the final goal – quantum safety – is impossible to attain because standardised post-quantum algorithms are not yet available. Organisations can take advantage of the situation by starting now to make their systems cryptographically agile. In other words, organisations can make their systems forward compatible by investing in modular approaches to general cryptographic upgrades that allow for the upgrades to be easily tweaked or swapped out as technology evolves toward the point where products based on standardised post-quantum algorithms are available. Otherwise, non-strategic investments made now by decision-makers in the absence of quantum awareness can create technological dependencies that will lead to vulnerable infrastructure lock-in (Soutar et al., 2021; Quantum-Safe Canada, 2021). The use of classical/PQC hybrids can be seen as a component of cryptographic agility to the degree that they are intended specifically to facilitate both backward compatibility (so 'old' technology will still work where required) and forward compatibility (so future technology will also work when it arrives).

4.2. Timeline Considerations

It has taken almost two decades to deploy our modern public-key cryptography infrastructure. Given the amount of work that needs to be done if society is to be ready for the quantum threat, the change to quantum-secure cryptography should start very soon, even if it is unclear when cryptographically relevant quantum computers will appear. Failing to prepare for the quantum threat in time poses a huge risk to cybersecurity and thus to privacy. In essence, there are three yardsticks to keep in mind (Mosca, 2018):

(a) the number of years that information needs to be kept confidential;
(b) the number of years it will take to deploy quantum-safe cryptographic algorithms; and
(c) the number of years until a cryptographically relevant quantum computer can be built.

If (b) were to be more than (c), we would have a huge problem on our hands, since our systems could no longer be trusted to function properly, and many would likely fail altogether. If (b) were to be less than (c), but (a) and (b) together were to be more than (c), widespread systemic failure would be prevented, but many back-tracking attacks (see Section 3.1) would take place, meaning sensitive government, corporate and personal information could find its way into the public realm. For example, in our medical data scenario in Section 3.2.1, information about chronic diseases or biological relationships needs to be confidential for longer than a human lifetime (e.g. 100 years). In such cases, quantum-secure cryptography should be used as soon as possible, since experts expect large quantum computers to be built in much less than a century. On the other hand, protecting agency is often very important in the moment (e.g. when driving a smart car). In the driving scenario in Section 3.2.2, protections against back-tracking are pointless, as the only thing that matters is system integrity in the moment (i.e. (b) must be less than (c)).

4.3. Necessary Responses

Governments have access to numerous levers that may be used to encourage and even ensure that digitally enabled infrastructure – such as smart roads, smart bridges and smart cities – is designed, built and installed to be quantum-safe. These levers include approval, planning, procurement and funding powers, none of which need to be costly. A simple example would be implementing a policy that any proposal for government approval and/or funding for digital or digitally enabled infrastructure must be accompanied by a cybersecurity strategy. This strategy would necessarily include a quantum-safe strategy for infrastructure that would be expected to be in service for some decades (Mosca & Munson, 2019).

4.3.1. Standardisation

Quantum readiness demands that quantum-safe algorithms and cryptographic tools be developed to replace the tools used today for key exchange, public-key encryption and digital signatures. In 2016 NIST began a multi-year project to identify a standardised suite of viable quantum-resistant cryptographic systems by 2024. The announcement of the NIST standards should result in a global retooling of the information and communications technology infrastructure (Mosca & Munson, 2019; Preuss Mattsson et al., 2021). It can be observed that traditional allies – such as Australia, Canada, the European Union, New Zealand, the United Kingdom and the United States– tend to synchronise their standardisation efforts (Csenkey & Bindel, 2021). A recent World Economic Forum publication set out requirements regarding new international quantum-secure standards for cryptographic agility, key distribution and other infrastructure components that need to be developed collaboratively and internationally (Soutar et al., 2021).

4.3.2. Risk Assessment

Organisations and individuals should evaluate quantum risks within their existing risk-assessment processes, with quantum risk being approached like any other cyber risk. Before decisions are made on a course of action, the threat must be analysed, and mitigation measures need to be evaluated. Due to the potentially high impact and unknown timeline of the quantum threat, it is imperative that the analysis process be started sooner rather than later, with special attention being paid to addressing the risk of back-tracking attacks (Soutar et al., 2021). In particular, the quantum risk assessment should include audits of both cryptographic assets and data, with an emphasis on sensitive data, its retention requirements and location (e.g. on-premises or in the cloud), following the analysis guidelines mentioned in Section 4.2. The types of cryptographic keys used, along with their characteristics and their location in existing hardware, operating systems, application programs, communications protocols, key infrastructures and access control mechanisms, are also all relevant (Soutar et al., 2021). It is particularly important to consider the lifespan of the hardware used to execute the cryptographic algorithms, as well as if and when they can be upgraded. For example, satellites to be used for Global Positioning Systems (GPS) have a lifespan of up to 15 years and are not accessible for hardware updates once placed in orbit. Another example is vehicles offering vehicle-to-vehicle communication to raise the situational awareness of drivers or autonomous driving. Private vehicles also have a lifespan of about 15 years, and while vehicles could be available for hardware updates, the scale of such an upgrade makes it infeasible; it is estimated that there will be 100 million connected cars globally by 2025.

4.3.3. *Expanding the Quantum-Safe Skills Base*

Understanding the quantum threat, its implications for security and privacy and the ways to mitigate the threat are of the utmost importance. Therefore, the most critical investment would appear to be in the development and acquisition of knowledgeable human resources that understand the threat and the technology (Soutar et al., 2021). Going one step further, without serious measures to strengthen the skills base, cybersecurity and the protection of privacy cannot be achieved (Mosca & Munson, 2019).

Programmes and workshops to transfer knowledge from researchers to government bodies and decision-makers have started to take place (Csenkey & Bindel, 2021), the goal being to raise awareness and to include a more diverse range of actors in future expert communities. More programmes and courses offering professional training will also need to be established and directed toward more diverse groups if society is to have the necessary cadre of cybersecurity experts with the necessary quantum-safe skills at its disposal. These experts will be needed to perform cyber risk assessments and systems integration to ensure that the appropriate quantum-safe solutions have been properly installed and integrated into complex legacy systems (Mosca & Munson, 2019). As it will take several years to build up the necessary large pool of experts, two groups should be the focus of outreach efforts: higher education institutes and industry. Colleges, universities and polytechnics will need to augment their cybersecurity programmes with courses focusing on the quantum threat and the migration to post-quantum cryptography. Ideally, these institutions will collaborate to develop standard quantum-safe modules that can be incorporated into existing cybersecurity programmes. In addition, outreach to industry should be considered, as there will likely be an appetite for training courses to familiarise technical staff with quantum-safe technologies and how best to work with external quantum-safe experts. There will also need to be certification schemes through which the quality of the training and the expertise of the trainees can be evaluated (Mosca & Munson, 2019).

5. Closing Remarks

Cyber security and privacy rely on the security of cryptographic algorithms. In order to maintain that security, society needs to prepare for the appearance of powerful quantum computers that can be used to break our currently deployed cryptographic algorithms. Preparing for this quantum threat to the current cryptographic base needs to be seen as a joint effort of government, industry, research bodies and society at large. Governments can and should enable and accelerate the switch to quantum-secure cryptography by taking at least the following steps:

- introduce government policies, legislation and regulation;
- accelerate the development of a necessary large pool of experts who understand the quantum threat and how to mitigate it;
- leverage procurement, approval and funding mechanisms to demand action by the private sector;
- regulate as necessary to force compliance with national/international standards for quantum-secure algorithms, etc.;
- consider legislating to enable the above.

Migrating to post-quantum cryptography will be the largest transition ever undertaken in public-key cryptography. It will be a major challenge to plan and implement the necessary steps to respond to the quantum threat at present, when the threat's time of arrival is uncertain. Nevertheless, even in the face of such uncertainty, the work must begin.

Unfortunately, it is likely that technological advances in the coming decades (and perhaps centuries) will allow future researchers to quickly solve the very hard problems that post-quantum cryptography relies on. It is also likely that successive generations of increasingly effective quantum-safe cryptography will therefore need to be deployed and replaced over periods of years, calling for perpetual cryptographic agility and modular approaches that enable forward compatibility. These measures will continue to be necessary for the maintenance of cybersecurity and the protection of privacy.

References

Chen, L., et al. (2016). NISTIR 8105 report on post-quantum cryptography. *Technical report, National Institute for Standards and Technology (NIST)*. https://csrc.nist.gov/publications/detail/nistir/8105/final

Csenkey, K., & Bindel, N. (2021). *Post-quantum cryptographic assemblages and the governance of the quantum threat.* https://osf.io/preprints/socarxiv/3ws6p/

ETSI. (2017a). *Quantum Computing and the risk to security and privacy.* ETSI. https://www.etsi.org/technologies/quantum-safe-cryptography

ETSI. (2017b). *ETSI TR 103 570 V1.1.1 (2017-10) – Technical report: CYBER; quantum-safe key exchanges.* https://www.etsi.org/deliver/etsi_tr/103500_103599/103570/01.01.01_60/tr_103570v010101p.pdf

ETSI. (2020). *ETSI TS 103 744 v1.1.1, CYBER; quantum-safe hybrid key exchanges. Technical report, European Telecommunications Standards Institute* (ETSI). https://www.etsi.org/deliver/etsi_ts/103700_103799/103744/01.01.01_60/ts_103744v010101p.pdf

Federal Office for Information Security. (2020). *Migration zu Post-Quanten-Kryptografie Handlungsempfehlungen des BSI* [Technical report, Bundesamt für Sicherheit in der Informationstechnik, BSI]. https://www.bsi.bund.de/SharedDocs/Downloads/DE/BSI/Krypto/Post-Quanten-Kryptografie.html

Grover, L. K. (1996). A fast quantum mechanical algorithm for database search. In G. L. Miller (Ed.), *Proceedings of the Twenty-Eighth Annual ACM Symposium on the Theory of Computing* (pp. 212–219). Association for Computing Machinery.

Gueron, S., Stebila, D., & Fluhrer, S. (2022). *Hybrid key exchange in TLS 1.3* [Internet draft, technical report]. IETF Datatracker. https://datatracker.ietf.org/doc/draft-ietf-tls-hybrid-design/

Kimmins, J., Dinkel, C., & Walters, D. (1995). *SP 800-13, Telecommunications security guidelines for telecommunications management network* [Technical report, National Institute for Standards and Technology (NIST)]. https://csrc.nist.gov/publications/detail/sp/800-13/archive/1995-10-02

Mosca, M. (2018). Cybersecurity in an era with quantum computers: Will we be ready? *IEEE Security and Privacy, 16*(5), 38–41.

Mosca, M., & Munson, B. (2019). *Governing cyberspace during a crisis in trust.* Center for International Governance Innovation. https://www.cigionline.org/publications/governing-cyberspace-during-crisis-trust/

Mosca, M., & Piani, M. (2021). *Quantum threat timeline report 2021.* Global Risk Institute in Financial Services (GRI). https://globalriskinstitute.org/publications/2021-quantum-threat-timeline-report/

Preuss Mattsson, J., et al. (2021). *Quantum technology and its impact on security in mobile networks.* Ericsson Technology Review. https://www.ericsson.com/en/reports-and-papers/ericsson-technology-review/articles/ensuring-security-in-mobile-networks-post-quantum

Quantum-Safe Canada. (2021). *Thoughts on developing a national quantum strategy: Focusing on the quantum threat to cybersecurity.* The Quantum-Safe Canada Initiative. https://quantum-safe.ca/wp-content/uploads/2021/12/2021-10-14-QSC-response-to-NQS-engagement-paper.pdf

Rivest, R. L., Shamir, A., & Adleman, L. M. (1983). A method for obtaining digital signatures and public-key cryptosystems (reprint). *Communications of the ACM, 26*(1), 96–99.

Shor, P. W. (1999). Polynomial-time algorithms for prime factorization and discrete logarithms on a quantum computer. *SIAM Review, 41*(2):303–332.

Soutar, C., et al. (2021). *Quantum personas: A multistakeholder approach to quantum cyber-risk management*. World Economic Forum. https://www3.weforum.org/docs/WEF_Quantum_Personas_GFC_on_Cybersecurity_2021.pdf

4. Realistic Face Anonymisation

Håkon Hukkelås & Frank Lindseth

Abstract

Collecting and storing images has become necessary for many applications, especially for computer vision development (e.g. in the development of autonomous vehicles). However, freely collecting images violates privacy regulations in several regions, unless the data are anonymised. Traditional image anonymisation (e.g. blurring) degrades the original data, making the images unusable for many applications. Recent developments in deep generative models have enabled a new type of anonymisation: realistic anonymisation. This new technology replaces privacy-sensitive information with artificially synthesised, realistic content. These methods preserve individuals' privacy and generate visually pleasing images almost indistinguishable from the original data.

Keywords: image anonymisation; generative models; realistic anonymisation; synthetic data

1. Introduction

Collecting and sharing images is ubiquitous in modern society, everywhere from communication to the development of advanced autonomous agents acting freely in the world. Recently, however, the collection of images has become more troublesome, because legislation (e.g. the General Data Protection Regulation, GDPR, in the European Union) has limited entities' ability to collect privacy-sensitive information without consent from the individual. In some domains, collecting this consent is unfeasible, such as when recording videos in crowded streets. Anonymisation can resolve this issue by removing privacy-sensitive

Van der Sloot & van Schendel. *The Boundaries of Data.* Taylor & Francis Group, 2024
DOI: 10.5117/9789463729192_CH04

information from images, enabling actors to freely collect data without asking for consent.

Traditional image anonymisation (e.g. blurring or masking an image) is widely adopted in today's society. However, traditional anonymisation severely degrades the quality of the anonymised image, making the data unusable for many applications. For example, developing an autonomous vehicle with a dataset with blurred persons will not translate well to the real world. In addition, naïve anonymisation techniques are known to be insufficient for protecting privacy (Gross et al., 2006a; Gross et al., 2006b; Newton et al., 2005), where blurring the image can fool a human but still be recognisable by machine evaluators. This introduces the need for *realistic image anonymisation*. Figure 4.1 compares traditional versus realistic anonymisation.

Realistic image anonymisation aims to replace privacy-sensitive information with semantically equivalent information suited for the application. For autonomous vehicles, the goal might be to replace people in the image with a synthesised, realistic-looking identity. Other applications might require more specific synthesis, such as synthesising new identities with certain attributes (e.g. gender or age).

Image synthesis of realistic humans is difficult, as the anonymisation model must synthesise new identities that fit the given environment. Early methods modelled the anonymisation task as an image similarity objective: find k-similar identities to the original identity and replace the identity with the average of the k-similar faces (Gross et al., 2006a). While providing strong privacy guarantees, these images often contain 'ghosting artefacts',[1] which destroy the usability of the images. In contrast, the current state-of-the-art is based on deep learning, where the model learns to synthesise new identities by learning from thousands of examples. These techniques generate realistic images that preserve the usability of the data (see Fig. 4.2).

This chapter discusses recent advances in deep learning–based anonymisation of humans in images. First, Section 2 introduces the reader to the technology behind realistic image anonymisation, namely deep learning and generative models. Then, Section 3 presents different realistic image anonymisation techniques. Finally, Section 4 discusses the limitations of current methods.

1 Ghosting artefacts appear when the k-similar faces do not perfectly align. For example, taking the average over two faces where the eyes are at different positions will result in an image with four blurred-out eyes.

Figure 4.1. Comparison of traditional anonymisation (black-out, pixelation and blurring) versus realistic anonymisation (rightmost image).

Figure 4.2. Typical image anonymisation requires a two-stage approach: detection of privacy-sensitive areas and anonymisation of the relevant regions. The figure shows an example of anonymisation results from the DeepPrivacy (Hukkelås et al., 2019) anonymisation framework.

2. The Technology Behind Realistic Anonymisation

Realistic anonymisation methods anonymise individuals by transforming the image or completely re-synthesising parts of it (see Fig. 4.4). This is a difficult task, which requires the anonymisation method to understand how humans look and how the appearances of humans change depending on interactions with our environment. Early work (Gross et al., 2006a) relies on finding similar faces to the original identity and fusing the similar images to create an anonymised image like the original. Today most realistic anonymisation techniques generate close-to-photorealistic images and are all based on deep learning. Furthermore, most of these methods are variants of Generative Adversarial Networks (GANs) (Goodfellow et al., 2014). In the following section, we introduce the reader to deep learning and GANs.

2.1. Deep Learning

Deep learning is a type of machine learning algorithm that learns to recognise patterns in raw data by learning from examples. By recognising these patterns, deep learning algorithms can solve complex tasks, such as synthesising the appearance of a person. The foundation of deep learning is artificial neural networks – or 'neural nets', in short – which represent data as a nested hierarchical representation with an increasingly higher level of abstraction. Each representation level is expressed in terms of other lower-level representations (e.g. a combination of lower-level attributes can represent a human face), where the raw input data can be viewed as the lowest level. This representation mapping is a differentiable mathematical mapping from some input representation to an output representation. In this way, neural nets are a nested mathematical mapping from some input representation to an increasingly higher-level abstracted representation. By using machine learning, the mapping is learned from examples, often several thousand unique examples.

Understanding deep learning is not the essence of this chapter, but there are two crucial aspects to consider when using deep learning methodologies. First, neural nets are close to 'black box' models, which are difficult to interpret and explain. The current literature does not have any solution to explain why neural nets do what they do, and it is challenging to understand failure cases. In practice, ad hoc empirical methods can offer a limited explanation.[2] Secondly, neural nets learn representations based on the datasets used for training; accordingly, neural nets inherit any bias represented in the data. For example, if a dataset contains only male faces, the model will struggle to synthesise female faces.

2.2. Generative Adversarial Networks

Generative Adversarial Networks (GANs) (Goodfellow et al., 2014) are generative models that learn to model the distribution of data to synthesise new examples. GANs learn to synthesise new images by creating a competitive adversarial game between a generator and a discriminator. Commonly, the generator and discriminator are modelled as deep neural nets. The task of the generator is to generate new examples from random noise, while the discriminator tries to distinguish real examples from generated ones. In essence, the generator can be viewed as an 'art forger' that tries to convince the 'police' (discriminator) that the artificial images are real. In this way, by competing over several thousands of examples, the generator learns to generate more and more realistic examples (see Fig. 4.3).

With the introduction of GANs (Goodfellow et al., 2014) in 2014, state-of-the-art face synthesis has gone from generating low-resolution grayscale

2 For example, Grad-CAM (Selvaraju et al., 2017) can visualise regions in images that neural nets focus on by finding the region that impacted the neural network output the most.

(a) (b)

Figure 4.3. The figure shows images generated by the DeepPrivacy generator (Hukkelås et al., 2019) during training. The number in the top left corner is the number of images that the generator has trained on (in millions). Note that the image quality progressively improves as the generator trains on more and more images.

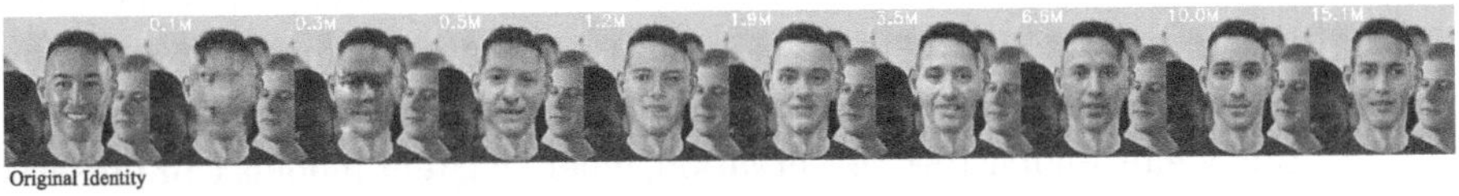

Figure 4.4. (a) Transformation-based anonymisation observes the original image/identity and transforms the person so that privacy-sensitive details are removed. (b) Inpainting-based anonymisation separates anonymisation into information removal and inpainting of missing regions. The figure illustrates anonymisation with DeepPrivacy (Hukkelås et al., 2019).

images to high-resolution photorealistic images. All methods discussed in the subsequent sections are based on GANs.

3. Realistic Image Anonymisation

The goal of realistic image anonymisation is to remove any privacy-sensitive information from the original image while generating realistic images that retain the usability of the data. Preserving utility depends on the task the data are collected for. For example, collecting data for classroom studies can require the retention of specific attributes (e.g. retaining facial expressions). Comparatively, collecting data for autonomous vehicles has softer requirements for utility preservation, where the main requirement is the realism of the generated data.

Current methods in the literature provide different guarantees with respect to privacy and utility preservation. In the following sections, we categorise the literature into two different methodologies: *anonymisation by transformation* and *anonymisation by inpainting* (see Fig. 4.4).

3.1. Anonymisation by Transformation

Anonymisation by transformation refers to methods that observe the original image and transform it to remove privacy-sensitive information (see Fig. 4.4a). Transformative anonymisation provides no formal guarantee

Figure 4.5. Example of DeepPrivacy anonymisation (Hukkelås et al., 2019). DeepPrivacy is able to generate diverse synthesised individuals from the same identity.

of privacy, as, in principle, a 'black box' model is responsible for removing privacy-sensitive information. However, quantitative experiments reflect that transformative methods can confuse humans and machine evaluators (Gafni et al., 2019; Ren et al., 2018). Furthermore, transformative anonymisation yields high utility preservation, where current models can preserve non-identifying attributes (e.g. pose, smiling, facial hair). We will briefly discuss two transformative-based systems for utility preservation.

Ren et al. (2018) propose a GAN-based transformative anonymisation model to preserve the action that the individual performs in a video sequence. The aim of the method is to generate a realistic face that is not identified as the original identity while still preserving the action performed in the sequence. Ren et al.'s results reflect that the model can preserve the actions in the video while changing other attributes, such as gender, facial expression and age.

Gafni et al. (2019) propose a system that only removes privacy-sensitive information in the face while preserving all other attributes. The method separates face attributes into privacy-sensitive and not privacy-sensitive attributes, and it anonymises the image by only adjusting the privacy-sensitive attributes. This attribute separation is learned empirically from a face recognition system. Specifically, their method learns to recognise privacy-sensitive attributes by learning what attributes a face recognition system uses for identification. Their quantitative and qualitative experiments show that the method can fool both human and machine evaluators in terms of identification. In addition, they show that the proposed method can retain attributes such as pose, expression and gender. However, as the attribute separation is learned empirically, their system encompasses the risk that the identity is still recognisable from attributes not classified as privacy sensitive.

3.2. Anonymisation by Inpainting

Anonymisation by inpainting differs from transformative-based methods in that the generative model never observes the original identity. Thus, inpainting-based methods provide stronger privacy guarantees than transformative methods. The original identity is only recognisable if an error occurs in the detection system or if the identity is recognisable outside the anonymised area. However, current inpainting-based techniques often yield poorer utility preservation than transformative-based methods.

DeepPrivacy (Hukkelås et al., 2019) is an inpainting-based anonymisation method that removes the face region and generates new identities based on the surrounding background information. DeepPrivacy can retain the general pose of the synthesised head; however, it does not enable automatic retention of specific attributes, such as facial expressions. The method can synthesise diverse identities for the same person (see Fig. 4.5), but there is no control over the attributes of the face. Thus, DeepPrivacy is efficient where the retention of specific attributes is not required to preserve the usability of the data.

CIAGAN (Maximov et al., 2020) provides more expressive synthesis control than DeepPrivacy (Hukkelås et al., 2019), where the user can specify which identity to synthesise in the anonymised image. Here the identity selection is based on a pre-defined set of different identities, where the authors use a set of 10K unique identities. Furthermore, this ability enables CIAGAN to synthesise the same identity for video sequences.

Sun et al. (2018) propose a method that inpaints the head region with the guidance of a detailed pose description of the head. In contrast to DeepPrivacy and CIAGAN, Sun et al. provide stronger privacy guarantees by inpainting a larger region covering the entire head (not only the face region, as in Fig. 4.4b). Furthermore, the dense facial pose description enables Sun et al. (2018) to generate faces with a similar pose to the original image.

3.3. Full-Body Anonymisation

The majority of realistic anonymisation methods focus on face/head anonymisation. However, the human body can be recognised from several attributes beyond the face region, such as identification from ears or the gait of the person (Sarkar et al., 2008). Thus, in most scenarios, full-body anonymisation is required to ensure privacy.

Full-body synthesis is much more challenging than head/face anonymisation, and current methods generate images that often contain annoying visual artefacts. Thus, current methods (Maximov et al., 2020; Hukkelås et al., 2023) synthesise bodies that are easily recognisable as artificial by human evaluators. However, empirical experiments reflect that the anonymisation quality provides good utility preservation for tasks such as learning computer vision models to detect the position of human bodies in images (Hukkelås et al., 2023).

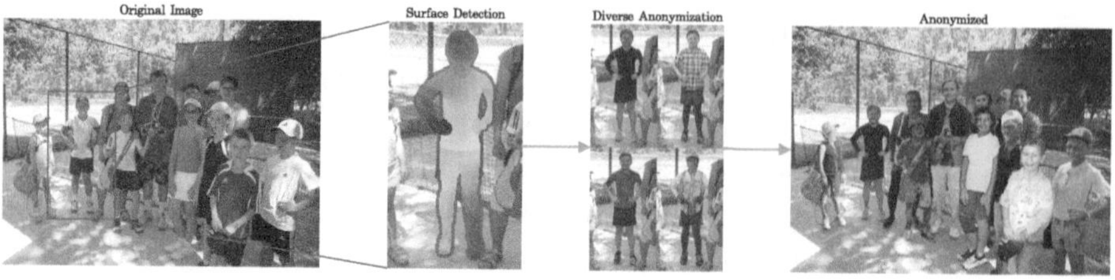

Figure 4.6. Example of full-body anonymisation (Hukkelås et al., 2023). The method individually anonymises each person with an inpainting-based anonymisation technique.

4. Limitations of State-of-the-art Anonymisation

The introduction of deep-learning-based anonymisation techniques has significantly improved the guarantee of privacy and utility preservation. However, there are several limitations to state-of-the-art methods, which we will discuss shortly below. We have categorised the most pressing issues into limitations in detection, identity leakage and limitations to synthesis quality. Due to these limitations, there are no methods that can guarantee the privacy of individuals without human supervision. Finally, we discuss the potential for these methods to be misused for malicious purposes.

4.1. Detection Limitation

Prominent anonymisation techniques rely on a two-stage system; detection of privacy-sensitive regions and anonymisation of the respective regions (see Fig. 4.2). Methods following this regime cannot guarantee the privacy of individuals, as current detection networks are far from perfect. However, current detection methods can detect most individuals in an image. For example, current state-of-the-art methods can detect up to 90% of all persons that take up a 'large' portion of the image.[3] In terms of faces, state-of-the-art methods detect well above 90% of all faces in an image (Li et al., 2019). Furthermore, detection networks are vulnerable to adversarial attacks, where malicious actors can insert objects into the physical world that can prevent the detection model from detecting individuals (Kurakin et al., 2017). However, there is currently a significant focus in the community on developing defences against these kinds of attacks (Kurakin et al., 2017).

3 For 98% of the images in the COCO dataset, this corresponds to persons that cover at least 6% of the image. Following the top-ranked COCO object detection submission as of March 2022, where a 'large' portion refers to regions larger than 96 x 96 pixels in the image.

4.2. Identity Leakage

The identity of individuals can leak through other means of recognition. State-of-the-art person anonymisation focuses primarily on the anonymisation of the face region. However, the human body is recognisable through other means than the face – for example, from the ears or the gait. The ear is a primary identifier, where technology can identify individuals with a high recognition rate from image data (Hurley et al., 2008). A more pressing limitation of current anonymisation techniques is gait recognition. A person's gait is a behavioural biometric (Sarkar et al., 2008), where the pattern of shape and motion in a video of someone walking is a discriminative feature for long-range recognition. None of the methods discussed in this chapter handle the issue of recognition from gait. Finally, it is possible to track individuals over extended periods of time and space horizons through non-identifying attributes (e.g. clothes). This enables the identification of individuals even if the detection network fails for a single frame in the video.

4.3. Synthesis Limitations

The quality of synthesised humans has substantially improved over the past few years, where current methods can generate realistic faces in varying contexts. However, current synthesis methods fail when we increase the difficulty of the synthesis task, such as synthesising the entire body instead of only the face. This results in higher data variability and reduces generated image quality significantly. As a result, current human figure synthesis methods generate images that are easily recognisable to human evaluators. Furthermore, anonymisation methods based on machine learning are restricted by the dataset used to train the model. Thus, the anonymisation model inherits any bias in the dataset. Finally, current synthesis methods have little to no control over the identity. Therefore, there is no guarantee that the synthesised person is not similar to a living person.

4.4. Potential Misuse

Realistic anonymisation methods focus on synthesising realistic humans, which creates potential for misuse. A typical example is the misuse of DeepFakes, where generative models can be used to create manipulated content to misinform. In contrast to realistic anonymisation, typical DeepFake methods observe the original identity (Zakharov et al., 2019) or perform computationally expensive finetuning on a specific individual (Thies et al., 2016).

Furthermore, there exist several solutions to mitigate the potential for misuse. The DeepFake Detection Challenge (Dolhansky et al., 2020) has increased the ability of automatic models to detect manipulated content. In addition, pre-emptive solutions – such as model watermarking (Yu et al., 2021) – can mitigate the potential for misuse, as model watermarking can embed a synthetic 'fingerprint' on the image data to identify it as fake.

5. Concluding Remarks

This chapter introduced the reader to realistic image anonymisation that uses deep learning to replace individuals in images with realistic-looking synthesised identities. Specifically, the chapter compares state-of-the-art realistic anonymisation techniques with respect to the quality of the anonymised image and the privacy guarantees provided. Realistic anonymisation offers strong privacy guarantees while generating images usable for future development that rely on the image quality of the data (e.g. the development of autonomous vehicles). Furthermore, the chapter discusses several limitations to current methods and how they cannot guarantee privacy in all scenarios. For example, current methods focus on face anonymisation, leaving the rest of the human body untouched, enabling recognition from other identifiers (e.g. recognition from gait). Finally, the progress of deep learning technology is improving at a remarkable rate, and it is reasonable to expect that realistic anonymisation techniques will improve significantly with this progress, both in terms of privacy guarantees and synthesis quality.

References

Dolhansky, B., Bitton, J., Pflaum, B., Lu, J., Howes, R., Wang, M., & Ferrer, C. C. (2020). *The DeepFake Detection Challenge (DFDC) dataset*. arXiv preprint arXiv:2006.07397.

Gafni, O., Wolf, L., & Taigman, Y. (2019). Live face de-identification in video. In *Proceedings of the IEEE/CVF International Conference on Computer Vision, Seoul, Korea (South)*, 9377–9386. IEEE. http://doi.org/10.1109/ICCV.2019.00947

Goodfellow, I., Pouget-Abadie, J., Mirza, M. Xu, B., Warde-Farley, D., Ozair, S., Courville, A., & Bengio, Y. (2014). Generative adversarial nets. *Advances in neural information processing systems*. Curran Associates, Inc.

Gross, R., Airoldi, E., Malin, B., & Sweeney, L. (2006a). Integrating utility into face de-identification. In G. Danezis & D. Martin (Eds.), *Lecture notes in computer science*, vol. 3856: *Privacy enhancing technologies* (pp. 227–242). Springer. https://doi.org/10.1007/11767831_15

Gross, R., Sweeney, L., De la Torre, F., & Baker, S. (2006b). Model-based face de-identification. In *Conference on Computer Vision and Pattern Recognition Workshop* (pp. 161–161). IEEE. http://doi.org/10.1109/CVPRW.2006.125

Hukkelås, H., Mester, R., & Lindseth, F. (2019). DeepPrivacy: A Generative Adversarial Network for Face Anonymization. In G. Bebis et al. (Eds.), *Lecture notes in computer science*, vol. 11844: *Advances in visual computing. ISVC 2019* (pp. 565–578). Springer. https://doi.org/10.1007/978-3-030-33720-9_44

Hukkelås, H., Smebye, M., Mester, R., & Lindseth, F. (2023). Realistic full-body anonymization with surface-guided GANs. In *Proceedings of the IEEE/CVF Winter Conference on Applications of Computer Vision (WACV)* (pp. 1430–1440). IEEE. http://doi.org/10.1109/WACV56688.2023.00148

Hurley, D., Arbab-Zavar, B., & Nixon, M. (2008). The ear as a biometric. In A. K. Jain et al. (Eds.), *Handbook of biometrics* (pp. 131–150). Springer. https://doi.org/10.1007/978-0-387-71041-9_7

Kurakin, A., Goodfellow, I. J., & Bengio, S. (2017). *Adversarial examples in the physical world* [Conference paper]. International Conference on Learning Representations Workshop. https://doi.org/10.48550/arXiv.1607.02533

Li, J., Wang, Y., Wang, C., Tai, Y., Qian, J., Yang, J., Wang, C., Li, J., & Huang, F. (2019). DSFD: Dual Shot Face Detector. In *2019 IEEE/CVF Conference on Computer Vision and Pattern Recognition (CVPR)* (pp. 5055–5064). IEEE. http://doi.org/10.1109/CVPR.2019.00520

Maximov, M., Elezi, I., & Leal-Taixé, L. (2020). CIAGAN: Conditional Identity Anonymization Generative Adversarial Networks. In *2020 IEEE/CVF Conference on Computer Vision and Pattern Recognition (CVPR)* (pp. 5446–5455). IEEE. http://doi.org/10.1109/CVPR42600.2020.00549

Newton, E. M., Sweeney, L., & Malin, B. (2005). Preserving privacy by de-identifying face images. *IEEE Transactions on Knowledge and Data Engineering*, *17*(2), 232–243. https://doi.org/10.1109/TKDE.2005.32

Ren, Z., Lee, Y. J., & Ryoo, M. S. (2018). Learning to anonymize faces for privacy preserving action detection. In V. Ferrari et al. (Eds.), *Lecture Notes in Computer Science*, vol. 11205: *Computer Vision – ECCV 2018* (pp. 639–655). Springer. https://doi.org/10.1007/978-3-030-01246-5_38

Sarkar, S., & Liu, Z. (2008). Gait recognition. In A. K. Jain et al. (Eds.), *Handbook of biometrics* (pp. 109–129). Springer. https://doi.org/10.1007/978-0-387-71041-9_6

Selvaraju, R. R., Cogswell, M., Das, A., Vedantam, R., Parikh, D., & Batra, D. (2017). Grad-CAM: Visual explanations from deep networks via gradient-based localization. In *2017 IEEE International Conference on Computer Vision (ICCV)* (pp. 618–626). IEEE. http://doi.org/10.1109/ICCV.2017.74

Sun, Q., Ma, L., Oh, S. J., Van Gool, L., Schiele, B., & Fritz, M. (2018). Natural and effective obfuscation by head inpainting. In 2018 IEEE/CVF Conference on Computer Vision and Pattern Recognition (pp. 5050–5059). IEEE. http://doi.org/10.1109/CVPR.2018.00530

Thies, J., Zollhofer, M., Stamminger, M., Theobalt, C., & Nießner, M. (2016). Face2Face: Real-time face capture and reenactment of RGB videos. In *2016 IEEE Conference on Computer Vision and Pattern Recognition (CVPR)* (pp. 2387–2395). IEEE. http://doi.org/10.1109/CVPR.2016.262

Yu, N., Skripniuk, V., Abdelnabi, S., & Fritz, M. (2021). Artificial fingerprinting for generative models: Rooting deepfake attribution in training data. In *2021 IEEE/CVF International Conference on Computer Vision (ICCV)* (pp. 14428–14437). IEEE. http://doi.org/10.1109/ICCV48922.2021.01418

Zakharov, E., Shysheya, A., Burkov, E., & Lempitsky, V. (2019). Few-shot adversarial learning of realistic neural talking head models. In *2019 IEEE/CVF International Conference on Computer Vision (ICCV)* (pp. 9458–9467). IEEE. http://doi.org/10.1109/ICCV.2019.00955

5. Use of Bulk Data by Intelligence and Security Services: Caught Between a Rock and a Hard Place?

Willemijn Aerdts & Ludo Block

Abstract

Bulk data and its exploitation by intelligence and security services is one of the key subjects that highlights the need to balance the powers of the services with the law and different forms of oversight. The sheer necessity for intelligence and security services to collect bulk data and exploit these data in analysis is clear, although often not well understood. Meanwhile, the exploitation of bulk data introduces a number of dilemmas for a democratic society that warrant a thorough discussion and consideration of how the law and oversight can ensure individuals' rights. This chapter aims at clarifying both the need for the exploitation of bulk data by the services and the related dilemmas.

Keywords: bulk data; oversight; uncertainty; individual rights

1. Introduction

This chapter deals with the exploitation of (bulk) data by modern intelligence and security services (hereinafter also 'the services') and focuses on how they collect and use data, the main challenges they face and how oversight of data collection and analysis powers is organised.

The workings of intelligence and security services have changed over time because of the evolving nature of threats, because of technical developments that have impacted the gathering of intelligence and, last but not least, because of the increased production of and reliance on data in society. These factors have had a major impact on the design and organisation of our

Van der Sloot & van Schendel. *The Boundaries of Data.* Taylor & Francis Group, 2024
DOI: 10.5117/9789463729192_CH05

intelligence and security services. They already are and will increasingly be data-driven, and this has implications for how they should be organised, the legal powers they can and should be allowed and, crucially, how they should be overseen.

This chapter discusses these inevitable changes. The first paragraph sets the scene by presenting a general introduction on the objectives of the services and their workings. The subsequent paragraph deals with the services' need for and use of bulk data. After that, the chapter goes into depth on the legal implications of the use of bulk data, which is followed by a discussion of the oversight on the use of bulk data. Before concluding, this chapter discusses three specific dilemmas connected to the use of bulk data by intelligence and security services.

2. What Is Intelligence, and What Is the Role of Intelligence and Security Services in a Democratic Legal Order?

Within the field of intelligence studies, there is a widespread debate about the exact definition of what constitutes intelligence (Warner, 2002; Breakspear, 2013, pp. 678–693). Most academic literature refers to intelligence within the context of its collection, analysis and dissemination. However, sometimes the concept of intelligence is also used to designate an intelligence organisation or a specific intelligence product (Lowenthal, 2017, pp. 1–2; de Valk, 2005, pp. 8–9; Scott & Jackson, 2004, pp. 141–43; de Graaff, 2012, pp. 11–14). This chapter uses the definition that considers intelligence as consisting of the organised collection of both specific public and secret information, with the overall intention of supporting the executive branch in matters of national security. Intelligence mainly focuses on understanding the intentions and capabilities of adversaries that could potentially harm or disadvantage national security and the rule of law (see Hijzen & Aerdts, 2017, pp. 521–554, and cf. Herman, 1996, pp. 49–53; Scott & Jackson, 2004, p. 154; Gill & Phythian, 2006, pp. 6–7).

The protection of national security and the rule of law directly brings us to the task of intelligence and security services. In his book *Intelligence*, Mark Lowenthal sums up the following functions of intelligence and security services:

- avoiding strategic surprise (by early warning);
- providing warnings of severe threats to national security (the prevention of terrorist attacks, for example);

- providing long-term expertise and knowledge on (national) security issues;
- providing timely intelligence to different governments bodies to help them avert these threats (Lowenthal, 2017, pp. 2–5).

A key task of the state is to provide safety and security for its citizens; in a democratic legal order, the services are two of the providers of this safety and security.[1] Therefore, as Aerdts and de Valk mention, one can speak about a form of a 'social contract' (Aerdts & de Valk, 2018, pp. 263–294) under which the services are granted coercive powers – which are a *conditio sine qua non* in order to provide security and safety – even though these coercive powers may infringe upon the individual rights of civilians. As such, a dilemma is created.

As in the academic literature on intelligence and security services, fear is sometimes voiced in public debate that these agencies can or will pose a threat to the population's privacy. Surveillance is central to contemporary governance according to Gill and Phytian (Gill & Phythian, 2008, pp. 29 and 149). However, other authors, like Mary De Rosa, make the case for a model that relies on effective oversight of the services to protect individual rights, instead of limiting the special powers to protect privacy (De Rosa, 2003, p. 27).

3. Why Do Services Need Data?

The way our societies are organised leads to ever-increasing amounts of data, and simultaneously, we are becoming increasingly reliant on these vast amounts of data ourselves. Our communication has evolved from clay tablets to handwritten letters, then telegrams, to modern-day text messages, emails and other means of digital communication. For example, every minute, 16.2 million texts messages are sent, nearly six million Google searches are executed (LocaliQ, 2022) and the SWIFT system handles 30,000 financial transactions (SWIFT, 2022).

1 In non-democratic orders, a primary task of the services in general is to keep the regime in power to which the safety and security of the population are subordinate. Therefore, in this chapter, in regard to the legal powers and oversight mechanisms, we explicitly only deal with the services that are operating in a democratic legal order. Obviously, we are aware that services from countries with other regimes also collect and interpret data on a large scale. However, these are beyond scope of this chapter.

Earlier intelligence services were able to rely on human sources – informers, diplomats and merchants – to understand threats (Iordanou, 2016, pp. 305–326), as these methods matched the pace of society at the time. The modern day is significantly different, and logically, the methodology and technology available to the services need to match the pace and challenges of our current societies that they have been tasked to protect. Allowing the services to access, acquire and retain (bulk) data is therefore, in current times, an absolute necessity if we want them to be effective and not miss threats.

A challenge for the services, particularly in our complex and dynamic open societies, is that while the general nature of some threats may be known, exactly how these will materialise is almost never known entirely. While every threat throughout time has had its unknowns, in our complex society it is the entirely unknown unknowns[2] that pose the greatest challenge. These are threats that cannot be anticipated based on past experience or research and are symptomatic of the radically uncertain world we live in. As an example, who would have thought that flying an aeroplane into a building would significantly change world politics?

This is a particularly important issue given the open character of our societies – with no boundaries on physical movement, financial transactions or communication – and the associated data allow those with nefarious aims to use denial and deception to mask their intent, capabilities and certainly their communication. Where better to hide than in plain sight? For example, Russian military intelligence operatives did just this by travelling throughout Europe posing as tourists while executing operations, such as the attempted murder on Sergei Skripal.[3] What about the International Criminal Court 'Brazilian' intern and the 'Brazilian' researcher at the University of Tromsø who both turned out to be Russian operatives (Cecco, 2022; Sabbach, 2022)?

The only way to identify these threats is by looking at data. However, without knowing exactly what data are relevant in advance, it is also not always possible to target only the very specific data that shows the threat. To identify concrete threats, security and intelligence services may need to

2 For the quote from the Pentagon press briefing by Donald Rumsfeld on 12 February 2002, see: https://archive.nytimes.com/opinionator.blogs.nytimes.com/2014/03/25/the-certainty-of-donald-rumsfeld-part-1/

3 See https://www.bellingcat.com/tag/gru/ for an overview of articles by Bellingcat in which they, by trawling through heaps of data, identified a number of GRU operatives as well as their likely missions.

trawl through large amounts of data – generally termed 'bulk data' – and apply smart queries to identify which part of the data is relevant.[4]

4. How Are These Data Acquired and Used?

So, how can intelligence and security services acquire (bulk) data? First, it is necessary to understand the context of how services use data to understand the nature and imminence of threats before we can begin discussing data collection. As noted above, neither the exact threat ('what is going to happen, where and when') nor the target ('who is going to do what') is known beforehand. On the contrary, in practice, the scope and nature of data acquisition depends on whether the target and threat are known or not.

Broadly speaking we can distinguish four situations:

– The target is known, and the (likely) threat is known.

If the target is known and the (likely) threat is also known, the services can track the target and focus data acquisition on the target and perhaps even be very precise. For example, they could intercept specific communications, as they may know where, when and how the target communicates.

– The likely target is known, but the threat is not identified exactly.

If the likely target is known but the threat has not been identified exactly, the discovery in the data is still target based. However, more data are needed to develop an understanding of the threat. In other words, what is the target going to do exactly? Intercepting communication may not suffice, and perhaps there is a need to hack into the target's laptop to look for what they have been searching or to try to get insights in the broader context and the people surrounding the target (who have they been in contact with and what do they do?).

– The target is unknown, but there is some understanding of the nature of the threat.

Obviously, matters become more complex if the target is not known. However, if there is some understanding of the nature of the threat, services could

4 Two different types of bulk data are generally distinguished: register data and behavioural data. Register data are data on identifying attributes of individuals, such as email addresses, phone numbers and bank account numbers. Behavioural data refers to data identifying specific behaviour of individuals at specific moments in time, such as phone calls made, flights taken and food ordered.

try to identify certain behaviour which would likely be displayed by the target. For example, if there are indications of an attack on a certain building, the services could try to see if they are able to discover any patterns in the mobile phone traffic around the building that could indicate reconnaissance activities. To be able to do this, the services need to initially collect large amounts of metadata, for example, from all mobile phones that were in the neighbourhood. The less the services focus on a specific target and threat, the less targeted the data collection can be in order to find the threat.

A question often asked is how effective such large data collections are. One case that gives some insight, and that has become public as a result of the Snowden revelations, is the interception of large amounts of mobile phone data by Dutch services. Originally mistakenly reported by the press as if the Dutch services were spying on Dutch citizens, the data collection turned out to relate to operations in the Gulf of Aden and the Indian Ocean against Somali pirates. The interceptions helped to identify the pirates (Derix & Modderkolk, 2014).

– Neither the exact target nor the exact nature of the threat is known. The most uncertain situations, which require the largest amounts of data, are those where neither the exact target nor the exact nature of the threat are known. A general threat may be known (e.g. hacking activities by a foreign power); however, it is unknown who is going to do what. Still, if there are indications or warnings that something is about to happen, some action must be taken. In such cases, based on hypotheses of what could happen, data can be acquired to see if any anomalies can be detected based on whether the hypotheses could be falsified, allowing the services to better focus and hopefully identify the target and threat.

Accordingly, in cases where it is impossible to target data acquisition, a wide net should be cast with the awareness that most of the data will have nothing to do with the target or the threat. However, the acquisition of non-relevant data is unavoidable, because which part of those data is relevant is uncertain and can only be determined after the data have been analysed.

Now that we have briefly illustrated what data are needed and why, we will move on to how data can actually be acquired. We discuss this question alongside the five methods defined in the Dutch Intelligence and Security Services Act 2017 (ISS Act 2017).[5] While in other jurisdictions the exact

5 See article 25 ISS Act 2017 (in Dutch, 'Wet op de inlichtingen- en veiligheidsdiensten' or 'Wiv'; for all text in ISS Act 2017, refer to Netherlands Government, 2017).

powers of the services can be different or differently organised, overall, the five distinct methodologies are similar. The five methodologies we discuss in this paragraph are:

- open sources
- general powers WIV 2017
- using agents to obtain and deliver datasets
- hacking and untargeted interception
- retrieving sets from other services

First, data can be obtained from open sources, also called OSINT.[6] Nowadays, this collection method is much more than 'just a Google search', and the amount of data that can be obtained from open sources should not be underestimated. These could be sets of commercial advertisement-based data (see Valentino-De Vries et al., 2018), leaked data – such as the recent Yandex Food data[7] – and data obtained by automatically searching multiple databases or scraping websites and repositories, also called 'automated OSINT'. The availability of and ability to obtain such data have expanded so rapidly that that the Dutch Review Committee on the Intelligence and Security Services (henceforth: 'the Review Committee') recently noted that these capabilities have outgrown the original understanding in the ISS Act 2017 of what was possible in relation to open sources (CTIVD, 2022a).

The second method by which large datasets can be collected is based on the general power of the services to request access to certain data. As an example, the services have legal access to (meta)data from telecom providers.[8]

Thirdly, the services are able to ask agents to obtain and deliver datasets.[9] These can be agents who have access to data legally, or they are able to enter the criminal world and obtain the data there.

The fourth method to collect datasets is to use special powers, such as hacking and untargeted interception.[10] The power to apply untargeted interception has caused significant debate in the Netherlands because, as is

6 Article 38 ISS Act 2017.

7 In March 2022, a dataset containing a year's work of orders from Yandex Food in Russia was leaked. The dataset, which is about 4 GB, contains names, phone numbers, email addresses and delivery notes. On this, see Roth (2022).

8 Paragraph 3.2.5.6.5 ISS Act 2017.

9 Article 41 ISS Act 2017.

10 See article 48 ISS Act 2017 for the interception powers and articles 49 and 50 ISS Act 2017 for the exploitation and analysis of the data.

argued, data from uninvolved citizens is also acquired in obtaining it. Some have argued[11] that this method results in a disproportionate infringement of human rights (Eijkman et al., 2018, p. 23). However, as discussed above, one can also argue that these powers are part of the social contract if we as a society expect the services to identify and neutralise threats in situations where both target and exact nature are unknown. We discuss this issue further in the next section.

The fifth and final method the services can use to collect datasets is to obtain these from other services.[12] This route is chosen when these services have been in a position to collect data that is potentially relevant for the Dutch services.

Now that we have explained the use and collection methods for data, in the next section we dive into the many legal questions the powers of collection may raise, especially in relation to bulk data.

5. Collection of Bulk Data and Oversight

The possible infringement of individuals' rights by the intelligence and security services should be 'balanced' by extensive oversight mechanisms, especially in relation to bulk data. In this section, we detail how the oversight on the data collection and analysis powers of the services is organised in the Dutch context.

In the case of 'Big Brother Watch v. the United Kingdom', the European Court of Human Rights (ECHR) stated that the collection of bulk data is not a violation of the Charter as such but that it should comply with the six minimum principles set by the Court. In this case, several NGOs, non-profit organisations and academics stated that the TEMPORA (surveillance) programme of the British GCHQ (the existence of which was exposed by the Snowden revelations) resulted in a violation of the right to privacy and freedom of expression, as laid down in articles 8 and 10 of the ECHR.

According to the Court, national laws dealing with bulk data must specify:

- the nature of the offences;
- a definition of the categories of people liable to interception;
- a limit on the duration of use of the special power;

11 Like civil rights organisations, such as Bits of Freedom and Amnesty International Nederland, but also journalist collectives in Germany, for example.

12 Article 25 sub 3/article 88 ISS Act 2017.

- the procedure to be followed for examining, using and storing the data obtained;
- the precautions to be taken when communicating the data to other parties, and
- the circumstances in which recordings may or must be erased or the tapes destroyed (European Court of Human Rights, 2006).

It should be noted that the first two elements focus on (criminal) investigation and are therefore not automatically applicable in the case of intelligence and security services.

In the jurisprudence of the ECHR, the Court recommends that countries install ex ante oversight mechanisms in relation to the gathering of, amongst others, bulk data. In their article on standards for oversight, Eskens, van Daalen and van Eijk state that because the abuse of data can be harmful for individuals and to democratic society, prior oversight is preferred regarding collections powers and the transfer of data to third countries (Eskens et al., 2016, p. 392).

The Court speaks about juridical oversight but leaves room for other independent oversight mechanisms. In the Netherlands, the Act of 2017 established the *Toetsingscommissie Inzet Bevoegdheden* (TIB, hereafter Investigatory Powers Commission), which bindingly reviews the lawfulness of the authorisations granted by the responsible minister in regard to some of the services' special powers, prior to the use of these powers.[13]

In the annual reports of the Investigatory Power Committee, one can see that the Committee rejected about 7% of the requests of the Military Intelligence and Security Service in 2021 (about 8% in 2020), and only just over 3% percent in 2021 (less than 2% in 2020) of the requests made to the General Intelligence and Security Service.[14]

In the Netherlands, there has been an ongoing emphasis on and criticism of the collection of bulk datasets because, as is usually argued, the majority of the data in these sets concern organisations and/or people who are not the focus of the services and probably never will be. As a result, the argument continues that the collection of bulk datasets constitutes a severe privacy

13 Article 32 of the Dutch Intelligence Acts 2017 states:
1. There shall be a Commission for the Review of the Exercise of Investigatory Powers.
2. The Investigatory Powers Commission shall be tasked reviewing the lawfulness of the authorisation granted by the Ministers concerned, as referred to in Articles 40(3), 42(4), 43(2) and (4), 45 (3), (5) and (10), 47(2), 48(2), 49(4), 50(2) and (4), 54(2) and 57(2). The decisions of the Investigatory Powers Commission shall be binding.

14 Annual reports over 2020 and 2021 of the Investigatory Powers Commission.

infringement. The Dutch population voted with a small majority against the adoption of the new Act (ISS 2017) during a referendum in March 2018. As a result, some of the provisions regarding oversight were adapted, and an evaluation of the Act was promised in two years' time, in 2020. In line with these pledges, the Review Committee has conducted several investigations that focus on these special powers (e.g. CTIVD, 2022b).

During the evaluation of this act, the evaluation committee paid significant attention to the collection and use of bulk data. In the evaluation report, they discuss the different relevant cases of the European Court of Human Rights, as well as the Court of Justice of the European Union (CJEU).[15] The committee concludes that the ISS 2017 lacks some of the necessary safeguards (the six minimum principles mentioned before) with regard to the use of bulk data and provides recommendations to improve the act (Evaluatiecommissie Wiv 2017, 2021).

In reaction to the evaluation, the Dutch government promised a revision of the Act. This is expected to be sent to parliament before the summer of 2023.[16]

6. Dilemmas

As discussed in the previous paragraph, the privacy infringements caused by the collection and use of bulk data by the services are, in essence, legally acceptable if national law has the appropriate safeguards in place. However, the devil is in the details, and more specific dilemmas related to the collection and use of bulk data by intelligence and security services exist. We discuss three.

First, we will speak about data overload. Getting access to large sets of data is one thing; being able to analyse these in a timely manner is another. Second, the cross-border sharing of unanalysed bulk data is important. How do services deal with the sharing of data that has not been analysed (yet) with other countries? The third and final dilemma that we address is the necessary special protection of persons with professional privileges. How can people in this special position be protected regarding the use of bulk datasets?

15 It should be noted that the interpretation of the EU guidelines is not applicable to the ISS 2017.

16 The evaluation was presented in January 2021. However, the alterations to the Act are expected only in 2023 because the Dutch government announced a temporary act in December to gain proper insights into the offensive cyber activities of other nations. This delayed the adjustment of the ISS 2017.

6.1. Data Overload

Not even 20 years ago, a manager could ask a researcher in the services to look into a specific topic or person on Monday. By Friday, this person could come back with an amount of data equivalent to roughly two phone directories. Nowadays, the same question could easily lead to several terabytes of data. To the untrained eye, that might seem to be an improvement, but in practice, this amount of data is a major challenge, as the capacity for timely analysis is not a given.

For the services to be effective and prevent incidents from happening, the timeliness of any analysis is paramount. However, the amounts of data available have become a challenge, if not a dilemma. As Patterson and others state, 'the sheer volume of the data creates a situation where it is difficult to determine where to look in the data field, it becomes easy to miss critical information and determining the significance of data in relation to the ongoing context is challenging' (Patterson et al., 2001, p. 17). Of course, the fact that the services have the legal power to acquire mountains of data does not automatically mean that they can exploit and analyse all of it in a timely manner.

As such, the services either try to avoid data overload or learn how to manage it. For example, the services in the Netherlands use a process of 'snapshotting' to limit the actual untargeted interception as much as possible and thereby avoid data overload.[17] Further, the Snowden revelations show that the services have not only heavily invested in data acquisition capabilities, but the technical support for data exploitation and analysis has also received significant attention (Gallagher, 2015). For example, GCHQ built up its capacity to exploit datasets through distributed processing (The Intercept, 2015). Still, while automated systems (i.e. artificial intelligence) are increasingly needed and deployed to support intelligence analysis to deal with data overload, ultimately, human analysts are still needed to interpret data in its proper context, which is something that automated systems are not capable of (yet) (Ish et al., 2021).

A very relevant aspect in relation to data overload is the discussion on the effectiveness of the use of bulk datasets. Matthias Leese discusses this dilemma in the light of privacy and data protection, arguing that research needs to take into account technical know-how to understand the workings

17 Snapshotting refers to limited interception of data over certain channels with the sole aim to assess the potential relevance of the data before full interception of a channel is executed. See CTIVD (2022b).

of algorithmic data analysis, and empirically detailed and in-depth research is necessary 'to carefully contextualise data-driven security practices' (Leese, 2022, p. 226).

Some research has been done to try to determine the effectiveness of mass surveillance. For example, Parra-Arnau and Castelluccia try to calculate the cost-effectiveness of mass surveillance by looking at the false positive paradox (Parra-Arnau & Castelluccia, 2018). Catford and Pieters interviewed different intelligence officials and identified seven criteria by which effectiveness could be measured in the eyes of the officials. Also, while 'costs' are rarely discussed, Catford and Pieters found that costs are one of the drivers behind formal evaluation of surveillance programmes (Cayford & Pieters, 2017; see also the European Union Agency for Fundamental Rights, 2017). Even though a critical approach towards the effectiveness of the use of large datasets is warranted, the question remains whether the services have much of a choice in our data-driven society. We believe this question will remain relevant for the years to come.

6.2. Sharing of Raw Data

A second important dilemma regarding the use of data by intelligence and security services is the sharing of raw intelligence. Since time immemorial, intelligence and security services have cooperated and shared information. This cooperation may be based on shared interests, or because one service has technical capabilities or access that another does not.

Available special powers and technical capabilities to collect bulk data may result in situations where the services share raw data. 'Raw' in this regard means data that has not been culled or analysed by the service that gathered the data. The reasons for sharing unanalysed data may vary depending on the urgency of the situation or a lack of capacity for analysing the data and combinations thereof.

However, sharing raw data might lead to unwanted situations, such as increased risk of using unreliable information, this information being used in legal procedures and a disproportionate infringement on individuals' privacy (Roach, 2012, p. 131).

The European Court of Human Rights also addressed this point in the case 'Big Brother Watch v. UK'. The Court stated that the international sharing of intelligence does not violate the European Charter of Human Rights because of the necessity of the flow of information between the services to combat international threats. The resulting interference with privacy rights was deemed necessary for a democratic society. Van der Sloot, however, correctly notes that the Court failed to discuss the question of oversight with respect to such cross-border sharing of data (van der Sloot & Kosta 2019).

In this case, the legitimacy of intelligence data sharing in itself is acknowledged for the first time. Importantly, it is also stressed that the minimum requirements the Court has developed for gathering data also apply to sharing data. Most pressingly, the Court explicitly pointed to the danger of circumventing legal limitations by sharing data with foreign agencies that are not subject to those rules. What is left unaddressed is the question of oversight in cross-border data sharing. Who is responsible for authorising such transfers and who audits the conditions for it? This is a challenging issue, and it would be valuable to see the Court discussing it in further detail in the future.

In the Netherlands, the legislator tried to solve this problem by weighting cooperation for the services with other countries before intelligence sharing by the use of so-called 'weighting notes'[18] and by including article 65 sub 2 in the Intelligence Act 2017. This article states that the third-party rule applies to the sharing of raw data. Furthermore, the services could add additional conditions when sharing these data (CTIVD, 2021, p. 16).

6.3 Special Protection for Persons with Professional Privileges

Another element that plays a role in relation to the acquisition of bulk data is the protection of persons with legal privileges, such as lawyers and those with journalists' privileges. The Court has ruled several times that they should be protected by prior oversight regarding the use of specials powers of the services. In the 'Telegraaf-case' of the ECHR, the Court stated that it is 'in principle desirable to entrust supervisory control to a judge', or another qualified independent body (European Court of Human Rights, 2012). In the case of 'Szabo & Vissy v. Hungary', the Court stated that this ex-ante authorisation of the use of specials powers against persons with privileged professions cannot be replaced with binding ex-post oversight (European Court of Human Rights, 2016, para. 77).

An ex-ante authorisation of the use of specials powers specifically targeted against a person with a privileged profession is nothing less than reasonable. However, this requirement in the case of undirected collection or even in

18 The Dutch services are allowed into a cooperative relationship with other services, as long as these services qualify according to the Dutch law. To qualify, the following criteria must be considered: democratic embedment of the service in the country, respect for human rights, professionalism and reliability of the service and the level of data protection (see article 88.3 of the ISS 2017). This procedure is evaluated in the report 60 of the Review Committee on the Intelligence and Security Series CTIVD in 2018.

the case the acquisition of bulk datasets from open sources would place the services in an impossible situation. After all, at the moment of collection, the services do not know exactly whose data they are collecting by definition.

In relation to bulk datasets, the Dutch services use an internal procedure (*buitenbak-binnenbakprocedure*),[19] which includes an additional authorisation step before the collected bulk data can be queried; the Netherlands oversight committee judged this procedure as legitimate (CTIVD, 2017, p. 4). While this specific procedure may not be possible in all cases, such as when anomaly detection is needed in large datasets, the principle of layered authorisation may be relevant in dealing with data from people under special protection.

7. Conclusion

In this chapter, we discussed the practices and dilemmas relevant to the use of (bulk) data by our intelligence and security services. By definition, the collection and exploitation of (bulk) data by the services entails infringing the privacy of all citizens. At the same time, if we want the intelligence and security services to be effective, they should have the powers they need to operate today. This subject has been at the centre of fierce debates in the Netherlands, where opponents argue that such coercive power is disproportionate by definition.

Nonetheless, the European Court of Human Rights seems to agree that, under certain conditions, bulk interception is allowed, and national legislators have included specific special powers in their legislation. Jurisprudence and oversight practice shows a shifting focus from discussing 'whether' the services are allowed to collect and exploit bulk data to a discussion of 'how' the services are allowed to do so. Given that the amount and role of data in society today will only increase and new technologies will emerge, we believe that this shift is understandable.

However, that does not mean that the dilemmas we discussed will be solved easily. Then again, the fact that these are seen as dilemmas is a positive feature of a democratic society in which the powers of intelligence and security services are balanced by law and different forms of oversight. That balance is precious and should be the subject of continued discussion.

19 Simply stated, the 'binnenbak-buitenbak procedure' requires the services to place collected bulk data in a repository which is only accessible after additional internal authorisation is provided. This procedure avoids unwarranted privacy infringements without a need for premature data deletion.

References

Aerdts W. J. M., & De Valk G. G. (2018). Privacy from an intelligence perspective. In B. van der Sloot B & A. de Groot (Eds.), *The handbook of privacy studies: An interdisciplinary introduction* (pp. 263–294). Amsterdam University Press.

Breakspear, A. (2013). A new definition of intelligence. *Intelligence and National Security, 28*(5), 678–693.

Cayford, M., & Pieters, W. (2017). The effectiveness of surveillance technology: What intelligence officials are saying. *The Information Society, 34*(2), 8–103.

Cecco, L. (2022). Suspected Russian spy arrested in Norway spent years studying in Canada. *The Guardian*. https://www.theguardian.com/world/2022/oct/28/russian-spy-norway-canada-brazil-academic?CMP=share_btn_link

CTIVD. (2017). *Toezichtsrapport 55 over het verwerven van door derden op internet aangeboden bulkdatasets door de AIVD en de MIVD.* Commissie van Toezicht op de Inlichtingen- en Veiligheidsdiensten. https://www.ctivd.nl/documenten/rapporten/2018/02/13/index

CTIVD. (2019). *Toezichtsrapport 60 over de wegingsnotities van de AIVD en de MIVD voor de internationale samenwerking met de Counter Terrorism Goup- en sigint-partners.* Commissie van Toezicht op de Inlichtingen- en Veiligheidsdiensten. https://www.ctivd.nl/documenten/rapporten/2019/02/06/index

CTIVD. (2021). *Toezichtsrapport 65 over het verstrekken van ongeëvalueerde gegevens aan buitenlandse diensten door de AIVD en de MIVD.* Commissie van Toezicht op de Inlichtingen- en Veiligheidsdiensten. https://www.ctivd.nl/documenten/rapporten/2019/10/15/index

CTIVD. (2022a). *Toezichtsrapport 74 over automated OSINT door de AIVD en de MIVD.* Commissie van Toezicht op de Inlichtingen- en Veiligheidsdiensten. https://www.ctivd.nl/documenten/rapporten/2022/02/08/rapport-74

CTIVD. (2022b). *Toezichtsrapport 75 over de inzet van kabelinterceptie door de AIVD en de MIVD. De Snapshotfase.* Commissie van Toezicht op de Inlichtingen- en Veiligheidsdiensten. https://www.ctivd.nl/documenten/rapporten/2022/03/15/index

de Graaff, B. G. J. (2012). *De ontbrekende dimensie: Intelligence binnen de studie van internationale betrekkingen* [Speech transcript from 2 March 2012, Utrecht). http://www2.hum.uu.nl/onderzoek/lezingenreeks/pdf/Graaff_Bob_oratie.pdf

De Rosa, M. (2003). Privacy in the age of terror. *The Washington Quarterly, 26*(3), 27–41.

de Valk, G. (2005), *Dutch intelligence: Towards a qualitative framework* [Doctoral dissertation, University of Groningen]. University of Groningen/UMCG research database.

Derix, S., & Modderkolk, H. (2014, March 8). Data uit Burum leiden naar piraten en terroristen. *NRC Handelsblad.*

Eijkman, Q., van Eijk N., & van Schaik, R. (2018). *Dutch national security reform under review: Sufficient checks and balances in the Intelligence and Security Services Act 2017?* Institute for Information Law. https://hdl.handle.net/11245.1/6973f153-3d43-4cea-9c2e-f71a375176c9

Eskens, S., van Daalen, O., & van Eijk, N. (2016). 10 standards for oversight and transparency of national intelligence services. *Journal of National Security Law & Policy 8*(3), 553–594.

European Court of Human Rights. (2006). Case of Weber and Saravia v. Germany (Application no. 54934/00). https://hudoc.echr.coe.int/fre?i=001-76586

European Court of Human Rights. (2012). Case of Telegraaf Media Nederland, Landelijke Media B.V. and others v. the Netherlands (Application no. 39315/06). https://hudoc.echr.coe.int/fre?i=001-114439

European Court of Human Rights. (2016). Case of Szabó and Vissy v. Hungary (Application no. 37138/14, Strasbourg). https://hudoc.echr.coe.int/fre?i=001-160020

European Court of Human Rights. (2018). Case of Big Brother Watch and Others v. the United Kingdom (ECLI:CE:ECHR:2018:0913JUD005817013). https://hudoc.echr.coe.int/fre?i=001-210077

European Union Agency for Fundamental Rights. (2017). *Surveillance by intelligence services: fundamental rights safeguards and remedies in the EU, Volume II: field perspectives and legal update.* http://fra.europa.eu/en/publication/2017/surveillance-intelligence-services-fundamental-rights-safeguards-and-remedies-eu

Evaluatiecommissie Wiv 2017. (2021). *Evaluatie 2020 Wet op de inlichtingen- en veiligheidsdiensten 2017.* https://www.rijksoverheid.nl/documenten/rapporten/2021/01/20/rapport-evaluatie-2020-wet-op-de-inlichtingen-en-veiligheidsdiensten-2017

Gallagher, R. (2015, September 25). From radio to porn, British spies track web users. *The Intercept.* https://theintercept.com/2015/09/25/gchq-radio-porn-spies-track-web-users-online-identities/

Gill, P., & Phytian, M. (2008). *Intelligence in an insecure world.* Polity Press

Herman, M. (2007). *Intelligence power in peace and war.* Cambridge University Press

Hijzen, C. W., & Aerdts, W. J. M. (2017). Vóór de aanslag: Terrorisme bestrijding voor inlichtingen- en veiligheidsdiensten. In E. Bakker et al. (Eds.), *Terrorisme* (pp. 521–554). Kluwer.

The Intercept. (2015). *GCHQ Analytic Cloud Challenges.* https://theintercept.com/document/2015/09/25/gchq-analytic-cloud-challenges/

Iordanou, I. (2016). What news on the Rialto? The trade of information and early modern Venice's centralized intelligence organization. *Intelligence and National Security, 31*(3), 305–326.

Ish, D., Ettinger, J., & Ferris, C. (2021). *Evaluating the effectiveness of artificial intelligence systems in intelligence analysis.* RAND Corporation. https://www.rand.org/pubs/research_reports/RRA464-1.html

Leese, M. (2022). Privacy, data protection, and security studies. In G. González, R. Van Brakel, & P. de Hert (Eds.), *Research handbook on privacy and data protection law* (pp. 214–228). Edward Elgar Publishing Limited.

LocaliQ. (2022). *What happens in an internet minute in 2022: 90 fascinating online stats.* https://localiq.com/blog/what-happens-in-an-internet-minute/

Lowenthal, M. M. (2017). *Intelligence.* Sage

Oerlemans, J., & Hagens, M. (2019). Privacy en bulkinterceptie in de Wiv 2017. *Ars Aequi*, (July/August 2019), 560–568.

Netherlands Government. (2017). Wet van 26 juli 2017, houdende regels met betrekking tot de inlichtingen- en veiligheidsdiensten alsmede wijziging van enkele wetten (Wet op de inlichtingen- en veiligheidsdiensten 2017). *Staatsblad*, 317. https://zoek.officielebekendmakingen.nl/stb-2017-317.html

Parra-Arnau, J., & Castelluccia, C. (2018). On the cost-effectiveness of mass surveillance. *IEEE Access, 6*, 46538–46557.

Patterson, E. S., Woods, D. D., Tinapple, D., Roth, E. M., Finley, J. M., & Kuperman, G. G. (2001). *Aiding the intelligence analyst in situations of data overload: From problem definition to design concept exploration.* Institute for Ergonomics/Cognitive Systems Engineering Laboratory Report, ERGO-CSEL.

Roach, K. (2012). Overseeing information sharing. In H. Born & A. Wills (Eds.), *Overseeing intelligence services: A toolkit.* DCAF.

Roth, E. (2022). *Data leak from Russian delivery app shows dining habits of the secret police.* The Verge. https://www.theverge.com/2022/4/3/23008658/data-leak-russian-delivery-app-dining-habits-secret-police-yandex-food

Sabbach, D. (2022). Russian spy caught trying to infiltrate war crimes court, says Netherlands. *The Guardian.* https://www.theguardian.com/law/2022/jun/16/russian-spy-caught-trying-to-infiltrate-war-crimes-court-says-netherlands

Scott, L., & Jackson, P. (2004). The study of intelligence in theory and practice. *Intelligence and National Security 19*(2), 139–169.

SWIFT. (2022). *Monthly FIN traffic evolution.* https://www.swift.com/about-us/discover-swift/fin-traffic-figures

TIB. (2020). Toetsingscommissie Inzet Bevoegdheden, jaarverslag 2020 [Annual report Investigatory Powers Commission 2020]. https://www.tib-ivd.nl/documenten/jaarverslagen/2021/04/30/jaarverslag-2020

TIB. (2020). Toetsingscommissie Inzet Bevoegdheden, jaarverslag 2021 [Annual report Investigatory Powers Commission 2021]. https://www.tib-ivd.nl/documenten/jaarverslagen/2022/04/22/jaarverslag-tib-2021

US Department of Defense. (2002). *DoD news briefing – Secretary Rumsfeld and Gen. Myers, 12 February 2002.* https://archive.ph/nXOnv

Valentino-DeVries, J., Singer, N., Keller, M. H., & Krolik, A. (2018, December 10). Your apps know where you were last night, and they're not keeping it secret.

The New York Times. https://www.nytimes.com/interactive/2018/12/10/business/location-data-privacy-apps.html

van der Sloot, B., & Kosta, E. (2019). Big Brother Watch and others v UK: Lessons from the latest Strasbourg ruling on bulk surveillance. *European Data Protection Law Review*, *5*(2), 252–261.

Warner, M. (2002). Wanted: A definition of intelligence. *Studies in Intelligence* 2002, *46*(3).

Wirtz, J. J., & Rosenwasser, J. J. (2010). From combined arms to combined intelligence: Philosophy, doctrine and operations. *Intelligence and National Security*, *25*(6), 725–743.

6. Farm Data Sharing: Current Practices and Principles[1]

Sjaak Wolfert, Else Giesbers, Houkje Adema & Marc-Jeroen Bogaardt

Wageningen Economic Research, Wageningen University and Research, the Netherlands

Abstract

Digital agriculture is considered one of the key technologies to address the challenges the agricultural sector is facing. As a result, agricultural processes are becoming more data-driven and data-enabled. While sharing of data can benefit some actors of the agricultural network, others are more hesitant in sharing data because of barriers and potential risks. This chapter provides insight into the current challenges and the role of data sharing in agriculture. It explains why it could be beneficial to share data but also describes obstacles to that. It is concluded that there are four potential harms for farmers that come with data sharing: image or reputation damage, financial or economic damage, loss of extra income and reclaims or fines.

Keywords: agricultural data; digital agriculture; smart farming; smart agriculture

1 This chapter is largely based on an internal report from the EU-funded project Internet of Food and Farm 2020 (IoF2020) (Giesbers et al., 2021). The objective of IoF2020 was to foster a large-scale uptake of IoT in the European farming and food sector. This was done through 33 use case projects in various subsectors (dairy, fruits, arable, vegetables, meat) all over Europe, in which multiple actors (e.g. farmers, technology providers, researchers, standardisation organisations) were co-creating digital solutions. The report describes the results from interviews with coordinators, asking them about their perspectives on current and potential future data sharing practices, the anticipated added value of data sharing, obstacles experienced when trying to get people to share data and their view on possible ways to overcome the obstacles.

Van der Sloot & van Schendel. *The Boundaries of Data.* Taylor & Francis Group, 2024
DOI: 10.5117/9789463729192_CH06

1. Introduction

Agriculture is one of the oldest human activities and has evolved into one of the main industrial activities in most developed countries. Beginning as self-sufficient farming, it has gone through a process of rationalisation, leading to specialisation, mainly driven by economies of scale. Nowadays, modern agriculture is highly productive and can be mainly divided into crop farming (e.g. grain, potatoes, fibres) and animal farming (e.g. meat, dairy, wool). Further specialisation can be seen in the growth of sectors such as horticulture, much of it taking place in greenhouses, fruit growing in orchards and fishery at sea but also in aquaculture. Despite high productivity, producing enough food – at a global level, but especially at the local level – will always be the main focus of agriculture. The global population is still growing, diets are changing and crisis situations – such as the recent COVID-19 pandemic – can easily endanger food supply because they disrupt markets, logistics and the free flow of labour (Poppe, 2020). However, there are also other challenges concerning sustainability, such as the depletion of natural resources (e.g. water, phosphorus), environmental pollution and climate change (e.g. greenhouse gas emissions, nitrogen emissions, pesticides) and public health issues (e.g. obesity). Hence, agriculture should be approached in a more integrated manner, as is done by the food systems approach. Food systems comprise all the processes associated with food production and food utilisation: growing, harvesting, packing, processing, transporting, marketing, consuming and disposing of food remains. All these activities require inputs and result in products and/or services, income and access to food, and they also have environmental effects (van Berkum et al., 2018).

Digital Agriculture is considered one of the key technologies expected to address the aforementioned challenges through providing more accurate information supply and improved efficiency (Basso et al., 2020). This means that smart machines and sensors make data grow in quantity and scope, resulting in processes becoming increasingly data-driven and data-enabled (Fig. 6.1). Rapid technological developments – such as the Internet of Things, cloud computing, blockchain technology and artificial intelligence – are propelling the phenomenon of 'Smart Farming' (Sundmaeker et al., 2016; Wolfert et al., 2017). Smart farming goes beyond concepts like precision agriculture by basing management tasks not only on location but also on data, enhanced by contextual and situational awareness, triggered by real-time events (Wolfert et al., 2014). Real-time assisting reconfiguration features are required to carry out agile actions, especially in cases of suddenly

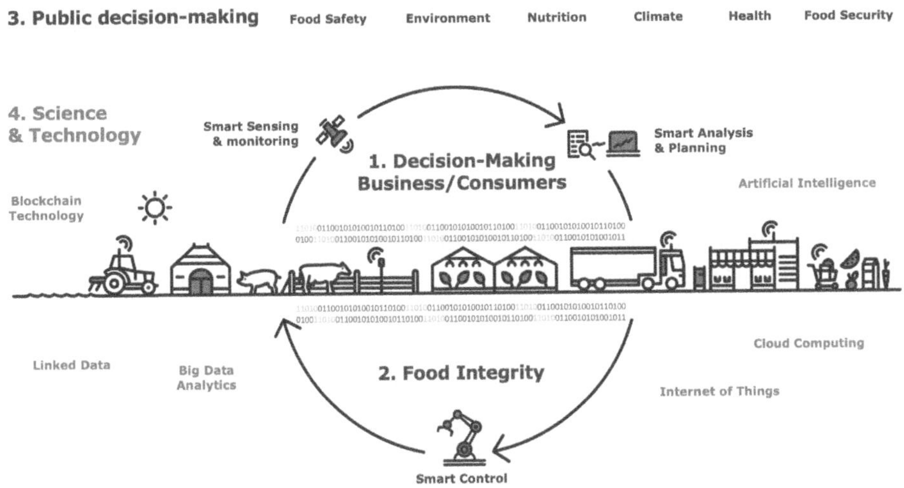

Figure 6.1 The digital transformation of agri-food coming together in four areas. The cyber-physical management cycle is intertwined with all kinds of novel technologies.

changed operational conditions or other circumstances (e.g. weather and disease alert). These features typically include intelligent assistance in the implementation, maintenance and use of the technology.

Figure 6.1 presents this as the cyber-physical management cycle, which means that smart farming devices – connected to the internet – control the agri-food production system in the middle of the picture. Smart devices extend conventional tools (e.g. rain gauges, tractors, notebooks) by adding autonomous context-awareness through all kinds of sensors and built-in intelligence, capable of executing autonomous actions or doing so remotely. In this picture, it is already suggested that autonomous robots can play an important role in control. Currently, analysis and planning are still mostly done manually, but it can be expected that this will also be increasingly assisted by machines and algorithms so that the cyber-physical cycle becomes almost fully autonomous. However, it is expected that humans will always be involved in the whole management process but at an increasingly higher intelligence level, leaving most easy, operational activities to machines.

As indicated in Figure 6.1, we distinguish between four domains in which digital transformation is expected to bring big changes and where data will play an increasingly large role:

– Digital data are becoming more important for private decision-making for businesses at any level of the agri-food supply chain: from farmers to logistic providers, for businesses and for consumers.

- The same data are essential for food integrity, assuring consumers and other stakeholders about the safety, authenticity and quality of food.
- Public decision-making for societal challenges such as food security, climate change, healthy food and nutrition could also tap into these data instead of using separate censuses and statistics, which are usually lagging.
- Finally, this digitisation is being driven by rapid developments in science and technology (S&T), such as artificial intelligence, Internet of Things and blockchain. At the same time, advancements in data science also rely heavily on data being generated by the application of data-driven research. Simply put: there is no data science without data.

In brief, the same digital objects and data can be used for multiple application areas, and consequently, these areas become increasingly intertwined. Several companies in agri-food – especially large multinationals – began to anticipate this development several years ago. The literature suggests major shifts in roles and power relations among different players in existing agri-food chains (van der Burg et al., 2019). Fierce competition for data from farm and food production can be expected (Wolfert et al., 2017).

The objective of this chapter is to provide insight into the challenges of current practices of data sharing in agriculture. Therefore, we first take a more detailed look into what kind of data in agriculture we are talking about. Then, we identify several reasons why it could be beneficial to share data. This is followed by an identification of the obstacles that explain why this is not happening, or not happening enough yet. From this, we conclude with four potential harms or damages for farmers of sharing data and raise the question of whether and how these should be addressed by additional legislation.

2. The Role of Data in Agriculture and Recent Developments

Data, transformed into useful or actionable management information, has always played an important role in all kinds of domains, and in agriculture, too. Table 1 provides a global overview of various types of data with a few illustrative examples focusing on agriculture, classified for groups of stakeholders and purposes, as listed in the first column. First of all, many data play a role in decision-making. Farmers monitor their crops, animals and so forth to see if they need attention, for example in terms of fertilising, feeding or determining whether harvest time has come. For open-air agriculture, weather data are very important for many decisions, for example assessing whether there is too much wind for spraying or when there will be dry days for cutting and harvesting the grass. Buyers and processors usually need data about the product (e.g. protein and starch content and crop variety). More specifically, some labels or certificates can be involved (e.g. organically produced), which usually requires additional data about the way food is produced (e.g. amount of pesticides, water used). Traditionally, agriculture is a heavily regulated sector, as farmers receive subsidies or are required to monitor aspects related to food quality, animal welfare and environmental concerns, which requires farmers to deliver all kinds of data about these factors (e.g. emissions, medicine use, proteins in milk). Finally, farmers must deliver a lot of financial or accountancy data to the government to estimate how much they need to pay in taxes or whether they are eligible for subsidies. Text Box 6.1 provides an illustrative example for potato production that shows how data are used and relate to each other.[2]

Table 6.1 Overview and classification of agricultural data with a few illustrative examples

Purpose/actors involved	Type of data	Examples
Farmers'/advisors' decision-making – external data – internal data	climate, market status of crops, animals, soil, etc.	weather forecast, radiation, prices biomass, animal weight, soil moisture
buyers/processors	production, quality	yield (forecasts), milk quality, starch content
certification	sustainability, labelling	pesticide use, water use, CO_2-emissions
government/public bodies	production, environmental	hectares of crop, manure production, NH_4-emission
accountancy	financial	invoice data, revenue

With the introduction of computers, several farm management information systems (FMIS) were introduced that store data digitally, but a lot of data entry is still done manually and exchanged by paper (Poppe et al., 2021). However, through FMIS, a lot of data is assembled in relatively few central information systems located at the farm, in the factory or with the certifier, government or accountancy office, and this is a relatively simple landscape to oversee. However, with the rise of digital agriculture, as described in the previous section, farm

2 For more examples we refer to the IoF2020 use case catalogue: https://www.iof2020.eu/use-case-catalogue

data have grown in quantity and scope, and farming processes are becoming increasingly data-driven and data-enabled; many other actors – besides traditional FMIS suppliers – are also getting involved, leading to an increasingly complex landscape (Wolfert et al., 2017). Data have also become less structured.

For example, a digital scan of a field by a camera-equipped drone initially provides raw data in some graphical format. It requires advanced expertise and software that usually cannot be handled by farmers themselves. If an external service provider does this job, questions can immediately be raised about whether that provider should have unlimited access to the data or only for a specific purpose. If the drone was owned and flown by farmers, one could say that the raw data can only be accessed and used by them. However, raw data hardly have any value, because they have to be transformed into actionable management information first. This transformation is expected to be done by advanced (AI) algorithms and is usually done by service providers that invest time and effort in it, resulting in new data, with added value, but based on the underlying raw data. If this is used to generate advice for the farmer who pays for it, it is likely not an issue. But what if the service provider wants to share these transformed data with other parties. Is that allowed? What if these data somehow are traceable to the farmer, which is not unimaginable when geographic coordinates are included in the data? These kinds of questions are increasingly common nowadays and have led to a higher awareness of the risks of data sharing (van der Burg et al., 2019). In the next two sections, we elaborate on this by describing why there are good reasons to share data, but also the obstacles to doing so.

Data-Driven Potato Production: An Illustrative Example

Growing a crop is typically a process from sowing to harvesting in which data play a role at various stages. It starts with the decision of what crop and variety a farmer is going to grow, depending on the market purpose. As such, market information must be obtained. For example, if you want to grow potatoes under some sustainability label for the UK market, there are all kinds of restrictions to be taken into account (e.g. use of chemicals, fertiliser, certificates). This should be matched with the information on the seed potatoes, to judge if these are suitable for this purpose. Growing potatoes requires nutrients that are taken up from the soil. Usually, organic manure is applied before sowing. Data from the soil must be acquired by laboratory analysis, or, nowadays, soil scanners can provide instant information. This must be matched with data on the quantity and composition of the organic manure. During growing, potatoes can be fertilised a few times more, usually with a chemical fertiliser based on the actual nutrient status of the potato crop. Nowadays, these data can be obtained by remote sensing, either by satellite images or other types of remote sensing (e.g. drone, handheld sensors) that estimate the biomass of the crop. Protection against diseases during growing requires local weather monitoring and forecasting data. Diseases occur in warm, humid circumstances, especially the notorious potato disease *Phytophthora*. Preventive spraying with biocides is needed, and this operation should take place under specific weather circumstances with low winds to obtain optimal results and to avoid drifting to neighbouring fields or nature. Weather information and soil moisture status are also crucial for water management to start irrigation in times of drought. Monitoring biomass also provides relevant information for yield prediction and forecasts the time of harvesting. During harvesting, the quantity of potatoes (kg/ha) and the quality (e.g. starch content) are important data for sales.

Text Box 6.1 An illustrative example of how data are used and related in agricultural production

3. Reasons for and Obstacles to Sharing Data

Persons or companies involved in digital farming networks are not always eager to share their data. Even though guidelines are shaped to improve farm data management practices and foster trust, there is still a lot of distrust in sharing farm data (van der Burg et al., 2021). The IoF2020 project, in which the development and implementation of innovative digital farming technologies were central objectives, paid a great deal of attention to data sharing practices. In this section, the reasons and obstacles to sharing data mentioned by the use cases in IoF2020 are presented.

Reasons to share data are:

- Sharing data leads to more knowledge – it helps to improve the business activities of farmers, technology developers and other actors in the value chain. The performance of digital technologies often depends on the availability of farm data and the willingness of farmers to share data with technology developers who can train algorithms. In return, advanced technology helps farmers in their decision-making by improving the planning of business activities and tackling potential problems at an early stage. Collaboration between farmers and technology developers is therefore mutually beneficial.
- Lower investment in time and money – sharing data makes paperwork and/or consulting people obsolete. For example, data can automatically provide proof of fulfilling certification standards, i.e. by sharing

data on what fertilisers are used in the field or by elaborating on the type and amount of feed for cattle. Farmers could also share data with veterinarians to enable them to monitor the health of the animals without having to visit the farm.

- Distinction from competitors – sharing data about the production process with consumers, for example, allows farmers to show that crops are grown more sustainably due to lower use of fertilisers or pesticides or that their animals have more space. Currently these types of data are often shared with certifiers and reach other actors in the supply chain via certification or labelling.
- Financial return – data can be considered as a 'product' for which, depending on the number of people using the data or the period in which the data are used, data sharers could receive financial compensation. Although this might seem like a sensible approach, there are not many initiatives in the agri-food sector facilitating these types of transactions yet. One example is Farmobile, an application that allows farmers to subscribe to a service in which their data are automatically collected from their machines and sold on the market for which farmers can get a share of the profits (Ge et al., 2015).
- Contribution to public objectives – sharing farm data with public authorities can show compliance with the law in a precise, easy and efficient way. Furthermore, it can also serve other public purposes, such as showing to what extent agricultural entrepreneurs comply with sustainability goals.
- Contribution to research – farm data can be a rich and valuable resource for scientific research. The continuous availability of data at farms allows the burden of food production on the environment to be monitored. This can enhance knowledge and provide valuable information for policymakers.
- Raise consumers' awareness – data about food production can be used to enhance consumer awareness about societal values related to food production. This may provide consumers with reasons to purchase certain foods or refrain from doing so if they disagree with choices that have been made in terms of the quality of the food, environment, animal welfare or their health and the health of the public. Data, in this sense, would allow consumers to align their choices regarding the food they wish to purchase and eat with their values as citizens.[3]

3 There are only a few initiatives (besides certification companies that indirectly provide this information) that are currently providing this information. A recent – perhaps extreme – example is the Blockchain Burger with which it is possible to trace back all separate ingredients based on blockchain technology (The New Fork, 2022).

Obstacles to sharing data are:

- Lack of knowledge about the potential benefits – benefits are not always clear to all agricultural entrepreneurs, and if they are, they might not align with the wishes and needs of the potential data sharer. Besides, some argue that the agricultural market is a low-margin market, which makes farmers reluctant to make significant investments in software with which they can share data; it is difficult to convince them of the financial gains in the long term. Some farmers mention that, despite the potential benefits, they simply do not like the idea of losing control of their data.
- Lack of trust in the data receiver – especially when many actors are involved, the overview of who has access to the data can get lost. Since digital sharing does not require physical contact, data sharing can feel like an anonymous and abstract activity that does not inspire trust. Some farmers are afraid that their data will be misused or used for other purposes than that which is agreed upon. Cultural differences can play a role here.[4] Sharing data with dominant, larger actors that have the power to influence prices of agricultural commodities can lead to hesitation because farmers can be influenced negatively. Sharing data with governmental actors also causes hesitation because farmers are afraid that data will be used for other purposes than agreed upon, such as the development of stricter regulations that will negatively affect them. Scientists are also sometimes seen as untrustworthy actors to share data with.[5]
- Technological issues – data sharing requires the availability, interoperability and connectivity of technology. In general, the technology used in the agri-food sector is lagging behind compared to other sectors (Laczkowski et al., 2018); the most up-to-date technology is not usually used on farms. This can make it more difficult to share data with other actors who work with newer software. Farmers also must cope with a

4 The IoF2020 study mentions that Spanish people generally like to keep information to themselves, which is why many Spanish farmers are reluctant to share data. On the other hand, because of the traditionally high level of trust in others in Denmark (Esteban & Roser, 2016), it is expected that the willingness to share data is higher amongst Danish farmers.

5 In April 2022, Dutch scientists presented a list of the 100 companies that have the highest nitrogen emissions in the Netherlands. However, it turned out that the data of many farms was misinterpreted, and these farms were wrongly placed on this list (NOS, 2022). It is likely that such incidents do not positively contribute to trust in scientists.

lack of standardisation in terms of software, semantics and ways of exporting data.

- Direct financial obstacles – if farmers do not have the right software (yet), they need to invest in it if they want to start sharing data. The lack of standardisation makes it hard for farmers to decide upon what software they should invest in because they do not know which software will be the most useful in the end. This is especially an issue for starting farmers or start-ups that do not have the capital needed and therefore lack flexibility to change to other software systems if necessary. Besides the one-time investment of buying the software, most software needs to be updated regularly, too. The financial benefits of sharing data are hard to estimate, and it is uncertain if and when the benefits will outweigh the costs.
- Indirect financial obstacles – if consumers have more knowledge about how a product is cultivated, produced or transported, they can respond positively as well as negatively by buying more or less of the product. This gives consumers a unique power to influence the market position of a product. For example, if consumers see that fish has been kept unrefrigerated during transport, many consumers will likely not buy it, affecting all actors in the relevant food value chain. While consumers probably want to know this information so they can make an informed decision about the food they eat, this can be a reason for farmers to think carefully about what data to share with consumers. As mentioned in the IoF2020 report, 'no one wants to share the real data with the consumer, everyone wants to share the right data with the consumer.' Another indirect risk is that some farmers believe that the value of data will decrease if more people have access to it.
- Laws and self-regulation – farmers experience difficulties complying with existing legislation because it is often unclear how it works and what they should do to act in line with it. Opposed to the General Data Protection Regulation (GDPR), the EU Code of Conduct on agricultural data by contractual agreement (EUCC)[6] focuses solely on the protection of non-personal agricultural data. It provides advice on the use and access rights of agricultural data (van der Burg et al., 2021). However, it can require lawyers to check whether a farmer is complying with the GDPR or the EUCC, which can be too expensive, especially for

6 The EUCC is developed by Copa-Cogeca (farmers' cooperatives in the EU), CEJA (European council of young farmers) and representatives of multiple agri-food organisations (Copa Cogeca et al., 2018).

smallholders. There is also a discrepancy between how the EUCC and many farmers perceive data ownership. As mentioned before, many agricultural players understand data as a possession of the owner of the land or livestock where the data originates. However, it is not always clear who the 'owner' of the data is, especially when data are processed and new data are derived from combining multiple sources. Hence, there is a need for more clarity about this ownership in regulations. However, the EUCC states that 'usage rights can be granted to an infinite number of parties, which reflects the non-physical nature of data' (Copa Cogeca et al., 2018). This reflects that the EUCC regards data not as something that can be owned by one actor but as something to which multiple actors have access at the same time. The EUCC is unclear about who has the responsibility to provide information necessary for a data sharing agreement, which makes it hard for farmers to follow this self-regulation.

It can be concluded in some cases that farmers are obliged to collect and provide data to governmental organisations – such as the national agricultural agencies who handle farmers' applications for agricultural subsidies and the national food safety authority – and to certifying bodies, their customers, food processors and their branch organisations. Farmers can also decide to voluntarily provide specific business process data to a party, such as a bank, insurance company, agricultural service/tech provider or a publically funded research institute. However, if farmers feel they have less or no control over the collected data, or if they suspect that the data will be misused, they are often less than eager or willing to share their data. Data sharing becomes even more difficult if the farmer has a dependency relationship with the data-requesting party due to its powerful position in the food value chain owing to it having a large market share or being an oligopolist.

4. Four Potential Harms for Farmers

Based on the risk considerations in the previous sections, which are clearly interrelated, we conclude with four kinds of potential harm or damage for farmers on sharing data. They are illustrated by real examples.

- Image or reputation damage. In this case, farmers are concerned that certain farm data are made public and are going to take a life of their own and possibly create a negative image of farmers. For example, in June 2021 a Dutch regional broadcasting organisation submitted two requests (according to the Dutch Public Access to Government Information Act) to the Ministry of Agriculture to obtain postal codes, house numbers and the number of animals per animal category of all livestock farms in the province of Gelderland. This was due to the ongoing public debate surrounding nitrogen emissions in the Netherlands (Heller, 2022). Several farmers objected to the disclosure of this information because they were concerned that these data were going to be used by activist groups to create a negative image of livestock farming. They argued that animal numbers did not necessarily indicate anything about a company's nitrogen emission. Several of these farmers were even concerned that malicious people would enter their farmyards and barns and take action to get media attention. However, the ministry indicated that animal numbers fall under emission data, so the ministry could not reject the requests, even if the farmers believed that animal numbers were confidential business data. The broadcasting organisation promised not to disclose any address details, but farmers felt they could not rely on that.

- Financial or economic damage. This can be illustrated by a court case in the USA on poultry farming that started in February 2017. Several poultry farmers filed a lawsuit against a few large poultry integrators (Shaffer, 2021). The poultry farmers claimed that a third party – AgriStats, which manages the data platform with which poultry farmers share their production data – had insufficiently anonymised their data. According to the poultry farmers, large poultry processors were able to find out exactly – by combining it with other data – how much money each poultry farmer was paid by the large poultry integrator to whom they deliver. That information had been shared among the poultry integrators. According to the poultry growers, that would have led to the payments being kept artificially low. The relevant legislation, in this case, is anti-cartel legislation. This US poultry case is also interesting because it raises the question of who has access to business data. To what extent do farmers have control over farm production data? To what extent should company data and location data be disconnected from each other to ensure that company data remain truly anonymous?
- Loss of extra income. One of the first indications of missing out on potential extra income came from the results of a survey by the American Farm Bureau Federation survey in 2016 (American Farm Bureau Federation, 2016). It showed that two out of three farmers believed that they should

receive a financial share from the use of their data beyond the direct value they may realise on their farm. In some use cases, IoF2020 data have been collected by private agricultural tech companies or service/input suppliers that want to profit from aggregating data into useful information with the purpose of selling back value-added products and services to the same farmers who provided the data for free. This is also being experienced in Australia, where a survey of 1,000 Australian farmers across 17 agricultural sectors showed that two out of three farmers did not feel comfortable if a service or technology provider used their data to generate profits for themselves (Wiseman et al., 2019).

- Reclaims or fines due to insufficiently reliable analysis of the data, used in models. This can play a role in the government and in interest groups. For example, in 2020 the Dutch farmers' interest organisation *Het Mesdagfonds voor de Landbouw* expressed doubts about the nitrogen calculations of the RIVM, the National Institute for Public Health and the Environment (RTL Nieuws, 2020). The RIVM measures ammonia emissions every hour with six measuring stations throughout the country; it also has 300 measuring points in 80 nature reserves. The RIVM uses these data to calculate how much of the emitted nitrogen ends up in nature. This showed that agriculture would be responsible for 45% of the nitrogen precipitation, a number that will probably be used for major policy decisions, such as buying out farmers. The Mesdag Fonds then asked external experts to recalculate the nitrogen emissions showing that agriculture was only responsible for 25% of the nitrogen emissions. However, there were serious doubts about the reliability of that result. External experts did not have access to the detailed data that the RIVM did, and according to RIVM, the external experts performed the calculations incorrectly. Accordingly, insufficient quality and reliability of emissions data and how they are used in models for policy monitoring can negatively affect farmers due to the revoking of licenses or receiving of fines. Part of the solution could be to measure emissions from each individual dairy cow in the barn and use those data instead of the 300 remote monitoring stations. However, the question is whether dairy farmers want to make those data available to policymakers or other parties.

The first three kinds of harm mainly involve business economic data used by other organisations for purposes other than originally intended. What is typical about the fourth kind of harm is that it does not concern farm data but rather data generated *off the farm* being used for public policy monitoring and evaluation with consequences for farmers. Furthermore, these four kinds of harm do not involve sensitive data in the sense of personal data according to the GDPR, but business or company data. The examples show that, in the opinion of some farmers, they should be confidential and not be accessible to everyone. However, current legislation does not prevent this. In general, farmers indicate that business-related data – such as financial data, data about the people with whom they do business and data about their yield – require more protection. Some farmers also consider the size and location of their parcels to be private, and others even see the data on the pesticides they use as private data (Kempenaar et al., 2020). The question now is how these four potential harms can be dealt with from a legal perspective. Does this mean we need additional data protection regulation? In the US, some legal scholars posed the question of whether farm data can be classified and protected as a trade secret (Ellixson et al., 2016; Ellixson et al., 2019), although this has been criticised. Alternatively, are existing legal frameworks adequate, but should the focus be more on compliance and enforcement of the legislation and self-regulation? This also includes the extent to which data processing organisations are capable of adequately assessing cases where farm business datasets are being processed that could potentially be personal data.

Conclusions

This chapter showed that the role data are playing in current agricultural practices is increasingly influenced by the digital transformation taking place in the sector. This has led to more data-driven agriculture in which data can be used for various purposes and therefore has potential value. However, to valorise data, they need to be shared with various actors in the food system. There are multiple reasons why farmers and other actors around the farm benefit from sharing data. Digitalisation is accelerating this process, but the current abundance of data and involvement of all kinds of new smart devices and new players also raise many issues that can become obstacles for sharing data, ranging from technological and financial obstacles to the core aspect of trust. We identified four kinds of potential harm or damage for farmers and raised the question of whether these can be mitigated by legislation. It is clear that data sharing in agriculture is becoming a challenging opportunity, but there are still many issues that have to be solved to guarantee sufficient protection of data where necessary without compromising the potential for innovation.

References

American Farm Bureau Federation. (2016). *Farm Bureau survey: Farmers want to control their own data*. https://wfbf.com/ag-newswire/farm-bureau-survey-farmers-want-to-control-their-own-data/

Basso, B., & Antle, J. (2020). Digital agriculture to design sustainable agricultural systems. *Nature Sustainability 3*, 254–256. https://doi.org/10.1038/s41893-020-0510-0

Copa Cogeca, et al. (2018). *EU Code of conduct on agricultural data sharing by contractual agreement*. http://www.copa-cogeca.eu/download.ashx?docID=2860242

Ellixson, A., & Griffin, T. (2016). Farm data: Ownership and protections [Conference presentation]. 13th International Conference on Precision Agriculture. July 31–August 4, St. Louis, Missouri, USA.

Ellixson, A., Griffin, T. W., Ferrell, S., & Goeringer, P. (2019). Legal and economic implications of farm data: Ownership and possible protections. *Drake Journal of Agricultural Law, 24*, 49.

Esteban, O.-O., & Roser, M. (2016). *Trust*. Our World in Data. https://ourworldindata.org/trust

Ge, L., & Bogaardt, M.-J. (2015). *Bites into the bits: Governance of data harvesting initiatives in agrifood chains*. European Association of Agricultural Economists (No. 716-2016-48655). https://doi.org/10.22004/ag.econ.229261

Giesbers, E., Adema, H., Soum, C., van der Burg, S., Beers, G., Sundmaeker, H., Berlin, A., Isakhanyan-Nuhoff, G., van de Geyte, J., Maselyne, J., Trajkovic, M., & Vlaskalin, J. (2021). *Toward broader sharing of farm data: Recommendations from the use case coordinators*. IOF. https://edepot.wur.nl/586530

Heller, A. (2022). Boeren strijden door tegen openbaar maken van gegevens: nu via de rechtbank. *De Gelderlander*. https://www.gelderlander.nl/home/boeren-strijden-door-tegen-openbaar-maken-van-gegevens-nu-via-de-rechtbank~a318f772/

Kempenaar, C., Mollema, R., Been, T., van Boheemen, K., Biewenga, G., van der Burg, S., van Wassenaer, L., van der Meij, K., Graumans, C., ter Horst, A., Janssen, S., Lokhorst, K., Sijbrandij, F., Steinbusch, M., van der Vlugt, P., & van der Wal, T. (2020). *Haalbaarheidsstudie PL4.0 data-ruimte: Knelpuntenanalyse datagebruik op boerenbedrijf en aanbevelingen om de impasse te doorbreken* (Rapport / Stichting Wageningen Research, Wageningen Plant Research, Business unit Agrosystems; No. WPR-10.18174/532701). Wageningen Plant Research. https://doi.org/10.18174/532701

Laczkowski, K., Asutosh, P., Rajagopal, N., & Sandrone, P. (2018). *How OEMs can seize the high-tech future in agriculture and construction*. McKinsey and Co. https://www.mckinsey.com/industries/automotive-and-assembly/our-insights/how-oems-can-seize-the-high-tech-future-in-agriculture-and-construction

The New Fork. (2022). Blockchain Burger. https://consumer.burgerchain.stg.thenewfork.com/

NOS. (2022). *Top-100 van ammoniakuitstoters blijkt onjuist, bedrijven onterecht op de lijst*. NOS. https://nos.nl/artikel/2424092-top-100-van-ammoniakuitstoters-blijkt-onjuist-bedrijven-onterecht-op-de-lijst

Poppe, K. (2020). Covid-19 will change the agri-food system – but how? *EuroChoices, 19*(3), 20–25. https://doi.org/10.1111/1746-692X.12276

Poppe, K., Vrolijk, H., & van Dijk, R. (2021). Design of a system for information transfer to reduce administrative burdens in the agrifood sector. *International Journal on Food System Dynamics, 12*(4), 301–313. https://doi.org/10.18461/ijfsd.v12i4.92

RTL Nieuws. (2020). *Boeren komen met alternatieve stikstofcijfers: hoe serieus zijn die?* RTL Nieuws. https://www.rtlnieuws.nl/nieuws/politiek/artikel/5029056/stikstofcijfers-boeren-mesdagfonds-stikstof-rivm

Shaffer, E. (2021). *Washington State AG files lawsuit against poultry companies*. Meat+Poultry. https://www.meatpoultry.com/articles/25710-washington-state-ag-files-lawsuit-against-poultry-companies

Sundmaeker, H., Verdouw, C., Wolfert, S., & Freire, L. P. (2022). Internet of food and farm 2020. In O. Vermesan & P. Friess (Eds.), *Digitising the industry Internet of Things connecting the physical, digital and virtual worlds* (pp. 129–151). River Publishers.

van Berkum, S., Dengerink, J., & Ruben, R. (2018). *The food systems approach: sustainable solutions for a sufficient supply of healthy food* (No. 2018-064). Wageningen Economic Research. https://edepot.wur.nl/451505

van der Burg, S., Bogaardt, M. J., & Wolfert, S. (2019). Ethics of smart farming: Current questions and directions for responsible innovation towards the future. *NJAS: Wageningen Journal of Life Sciences, 90–91*(1), 100289. https://doi.org/10.1016/j.njas.2019.01.001

van der Burg, S., Wiseman, L., & Krkeljas, J. (2021). Trust in farm data sharing: Reflections on the EU code of conduct for agricultural data sharing. *Ethics and Information Technology, 23*, 185–198. https://doi.org/10.1007/s10676-020-09543-1

Wiseman, L., Sanderson, J., Zhang, A., & Jakku, E. (2019). Farmers and their data: An examination of farmers' reluctance to share their data through the lens of the laws impacting smart farming. *NJAS: Wageningen Journal of Life Sciences, 90–91*(1), 100301. https://doi.org/10.1016/j.njas.2019.04.007

Wolfert, S., Ge, L., Verdouw, C., & Bogaardt, M. J. (2017). Big data in smart farming – A review. *Agricultural systems, 153*, 69–80. https://doi.org/10.1016/j.agsy.2017.01.023

Wolfert, S., Goense, D., & Sørensen, C. A. G. (2014, April). A future internet collaboration platform for safe and healthy food from farm to fork. In *2014 annual SRII global conference* (pp. 266–273). IEEE. https://doi.org/10.1109/SRII.2014.47

7. Microdata Access at Statistics Netherlands

Peter-Paul de Wolf, Ivo Gorissen, Michel Zaaijer & Daniël von Berg

Abstract
Microdata access at CBS is a highly valued and appreciated service. The Dutch Statistical Act has explicitly created the possibility of granting researchers access to microdata. Next to the more traditional means of public use files and scientific use files, remote access to secure use files has become the most popular way of accessing microdata at CBS. The access can only be granted while maintaining the highest possible standard in the protection of respondents' privacy. This chapter gives insight into the way microdata access is organised at CBS as well as into the dilemmas that helped in finding safe ways to grant access.

Keywords: microdata access; official statistics; remote access; five safes

1. Introduction

The main task of National Statistical Offices such as Statistics Netherlands (CBS) is to produce and publish statistical information on all aspects of society. The information needed to produce statistics is gathered by conducting sample surveys as well as by collecting administrative data. Obviously, this vast amount of data and microdata is also of interest to researchers outside CBS. Note that by a 'microdata set' we mean a set of records, where each record corresponds to a single statistical unit (person, household, company, etc.).

The production and publication of statistical information by CBS itself and research on data and microdata collected by CBS by other researchers outside CBS can only be conducted if legal grounds are present.

Regarding the first, the legal grounds are formulated on a national and on a European level. On a national, level there is the Dutch Statistics Act

Van der Sloot & van Schendel. *The Boundaries of Data*. Taylor & Francis Group, 2024
DOI: 10.5117/9789463729192_CH07

in which Article 3(1)[1] provides the legal basis for CBS to collect and process (micro)data in order to carry out its task: 'to carry out statistical research on account of the government for practice, policy and research purposes and to publish the statistics compiled on the basis of such research.' On a European level, the legal basis is formed by the European Statistics Regulation[2] accompanied by the Statistical Code of Practice.[3] To ensure that the obligations set out for CBS in the European Statistics Regulation are duly met, Article 4 of the Dutch Statistics Act[4] stipulates that CBS is responsible for the production of European statistics.

Regarding the second, the Dutch Statistics Act (Article 41 Dutch Statistics Act)[5] provides a legal basis to grant researchers access to the microdata, under strict conditions. One of the conditions is that the privacy of the statistical units should be respected. Another one is that the research should be statistical or scientific; the use of microdata for tax, administrative, auditing and judicial purposes is explicitly prohibited by law.

When giving access to microdata, we try to follow the ideas of the five 'safes': safe projects, safe people, safe settings, safe data and safe output.

1 Article 3(1) Dutch Statistics Act: 'The task of the CBS is to carry out statistical research on account of the government for practice, policy and research purposes and to publish the statistics compiled on the basis of such research.'

2 Regulation (EC) No 223/2009 of the European Parliament and of the Council of 11 March 2009 on European statistics and repealing Regulation (EC, Euratom) No 1101/2008 of the European Parliament and of the Council on the transmission of data subject to statistical confidentiality to the Statistical Office of the European Communities, Council Regulation (EC) No 322/97 on Community Statistics, and Council Decision 89/382/EEC, Euratom establishing a Committee on the Statistical Programmes of the European Communities.

3 https://ec.europa.eu/eurostat/web/quality/european-quality-standards/european-statistics-code-of-practice

4 Article 4 Dutch Statistics Act: 'The CBS is the national authority responsible for the production of European statistics.'

5 Article 41 Dutch Statistics Act:

(1) Contrary to the provisions of Section 37 the director general may, on request, provide or grant access to a set of data to a department, organisation or institution as referred to in the second subsection for the purposes of statistical or academic research where appropriate measures have been taken to prevent identification of individual persons, households, companies or institutions from those data.

(2) A set of data as referred to in the first subsection may be provided to or made accessible to:
- a university within the meaning of the Higher Education and Research Act;
- an organisation or institution for academic research established by law;
- planning offices established by or by virtue of the law;
- the Community statistical agency and national statistical agencies of the member states of the European Union;
- research departments of ministries and other departments, organisations and institutions.

Measures can be taken on each of these five safes to ensure that microdata are protected sufficiently and according to the policy of CBS. The severity of these measures may differ per safe and per situation.

In this chapter, we describe the opportunities for getting access to microdata at CBS and the dilemmas involved in doing so. We first give an overview of the different modes of access. In the subsequent section we go into more detail on the currently most popular mode of access: remote access to secure use files.

Giving access to microdata may obviously raise many practical, technical, legal and ethical dilemmas. Under 'Practical, technical, legal and ethical dilemmas', we describe some of the dilemmas CBS encountered (and still encounters). At the end we draw a number of conclusions and give our perspective on possible future developments in granting access to microdata.

2. Microdata for Statistical Purposes

The way CBS gives access to microdata sets can be characterised in (at least) two ways. The first characterisation is by means of access: releasing microdata sets that leave the premises of CBS or granting access to microdata sets that do not leave the premises of CBS. A second characterisation is by the intended users. To that end, CBS offers three flavours of microdata sets: public use file (PUF), scientific use file (SUF) and secure use file (ScUF). PUFs and SUFs are microdata sets that can leave the premises of CBS, whereas ScUFs are never allowed to leave the CBS premises.[6]

Microdata files that may leave the premises of CBS need special attention regarding the protection of information on individual units. Intuitively, this may seem an impossible mission. Indeed, microdata by definition contain information about individual units. Statistical disclosure control (SDC; see e.g. Hundepool et al., 2012) is a very active field of research that addresses the art of producing statistical information that cannot be linked to identifiable statistical units (or at least with low risk). One reason for the need for SDC stems from non-disclosure clauses incorporated in several national statistical laws in order to preserve privacy. For Europe and, more specifically, the

6 Examples of PUFs are datasets with census information (see e.g. https://international.ipums.org/international/ for international versions) or datasets on the Labour Force Survey (see e.g. https://ec.europa.eu/eurostat/web/microdata/labour-force-survey). SUFs produced by CBS can be obtained through the DANS website, https://doi.org/10.17026/dans-z5j-9bkf. For an overview of available ScUFs, see https://www.cbs.nl/en-gb/our-services/customised-services-microdata/microdata-conducting-your-own-research/microdata-catalogue.

Netherlands, in order to adhere to Article 8 of the European Convention for the Protection of Human Rights and Fundamental Freedoms (ECHR)[7] on the right to privacy, the European Statistics Regulation has defined the principle of statistical confidentiality in Article 2(1)(e) as:

> the protection of confidential data related to single statistical units which are obtained directly for statistical purposes or indirectly from administrative or other sources and implying the prohibition of use for non-statistical purposes of the data obtained and of their unlawful disclosure.[8]

The Dutch Statistics Act has adopted this in Article 37(3) as:

> The data referred to in the first subsection shall only be published in such a way that no recognisable data can be derived from them about an individual person, household, company or institution, unless, in the case of data relating to a company or institution, there are good reasons to assume that the company or institution concerned will not have any objections to the publication.

While the European Statistics Regulation speaks of single statistical units without any further elaboration, the Dutch Statistics Act defines single statistical units as being an individual person, household, company or institution. Regarding an individual person or even household, the General Data Protection Regulation (GDPR)[9] underlines statistical confidentiality in Recital 163, stating that statistical confidentiality must be upheld, as should the other principles laid out in Article 2 of the European Statistics Regulation.[10]

7 European Convention for the Protection of Human Rights and Fundamental Freedoms. Rome, 4.XI.1950.

8 Statistical confidentiality is set up as principle 5 in the Statistical Code of Practice.

9 Regulation (EU) 2016/679 Regulation (EU) 2016/679 of the European Parliament and of the Council of 27 April 2016 on the protection of natural persons with regard to the processing of personal data and on the free movement of such data, and repealing Directive 95/46/EC, General Data Protection Regulation (GDPR).

10 Recital 163 GDPR: 'The confidential information which the Union and national statistical authorities collect for the production of official European and official national statistics should be protected. European statistics should be developed, produced and disseminated in accordance with the statistical principles as set out in Article 338(2) TFEU, while national statistics should also comply with Member State law. Regulation (EC) No 223/2009 of the European Parliament and of the Council provides further specifications on statistical confidentiality for European statistics.'

SDC traditionally concentrates on two types of statistical information: aggregated information (e.g. tabular data, outputs of analyses) and microdata (PUF, SUF and ScUF). In this chapter, we focus on SDC aspects related to giving access to microdata.

The main goal of SDC is to *control* the risk of disclosing information on identifiable units. For public use files (i.e. files available to the public without further restrictions), this means a very strict aggregation of quasi-identifiers. To that end, CBS uses something related to k-anonymity, called k^m-anonymity. k^m-anonymity means that at least k individuals should score on all possible combinations of m quasi-identifiers (the so called 'keys'). For the PUFs, CBS applies k^m-anonymity and uses a huge value of k (1,000 to 200,000). Moreover, CBS does not allow any information in the PUF that would have a relatively large impact on the individual when disclosed, like income- or health-related variables. Thus, here the 'safe data' is the main control, and the 'safe output' should follow automatically.

The situation is slightly different for scientific use files. These types of microdata sets are only available to a select group of researchers. Moreover, these researchers must sign agreements on what they can and cannot do with the data. Whenever there is a breach of the agreements, sanctions are taken (e.g. their whole institute is denied access to those kind of microdata sets, with immediate effect). In addition to this legal protection, SUFs are protected to satisfy k-anonymity for certain combinations of three quasi-identifiers. Because of the legal restrictions, different keys are considered compared to the ones for PUFs and lower values of k are used. For SUFs, CBS thus lightens the burden on 'safe data' a little while increasing the control on 'safe people'.

With secure use files, the main controls that are used are the 'safe people', 'safe settings', 'safe projects' and 'safe output'. Again, only a select group of researchers can have access to these kinds of microdata sets: their project proposals are screened beforehand (questions are asked such as: is their project possible with the requested data, and is it really statistical or scientific use?), the microdata remain at the CBS premises and any output they want to bring out of the secure environment will be screened for disclosure by CBS staff. However, the microdata themselves are almost unprotected; they are only pseudonymised and limited to the datasets needed for the project. Getting access to secure use files is possible through the use of a so-called 'remote access facility'. This RA facility allows for a secure connection with CBS, where researchers can only see the data and do their analysis within the secure environment at CBS that they are connected to. In the next section, we go into more detail about the remote access facility.

3. Remote Access for Statistical Purposes

On the one hand, CBS has a public responsibility for transparency and accessibility of the data it receives. Remote access of microdata for statistical purposes is one of the ways this is being operationalised. The fact that this is highly valued is reflected in the use of the facility, with currently more than 1,100 different users and more than 600 research projects. These studies include education, labour market, housing, healthcare and pensions, as well as many other fields, often investigating interrelationships and involving users from a wide range of disciplines. This leads to a great diversity of publications, such as scientific papers, dissertations, policy reports and monitors. At the same time, however, CBS is responsible for safeguarding security and privacy.

The coexistence of these responsibilities can be found in the Dutch Statistics Act. In Article 41(1), it provides the legal ground that the director general may grant access for the purpose of statistical or scientific research to a collection of data, for which appropriate measures have been taken regarding its use to prevent the identification of individuals, households, companies or institutions.

Looking at the five safes mentioned above (safe projects, safe people, safe settings, safe data and safe output), we discuss the measures that CBS has taken to serve the public interest by giving researchers access to the collected data while protecting the private and collective interests of citizens and companies by guaranteeing security and privacy.

Safe Data

All data are pseudonymised and linkable via meaningless keys. These meaningless keys are variables that are unique for each individual unit but cannot directly be related to an identifiable unit. For example, for persons, the meaningless key is the so-called 'record identification number' (RIN); there are similar meaningless keys for addresses, companies and so forth. Three types of datasets can be distinguished. First of all, and by far the largest in volume, are the data arising from CBS' statistical processes itself. Furthermore, researchers are allowed to import additional datasets, provided that they are legally entitled to use these data and the applicable privacy and data protection legislation is respected. CBS will replace directly identifying variables (e.g. Dutch citizen service numbers or the combination of gender, date of birth, address, etc.) with the RIN. In this way, these data can be linked to the CBS microdata while the imported dataset itself is pseudonymised at the same time. Finally, under appropriate conditions, researchers can add datasets of other institutions which have made some of their datasets available for linkage (e.g. Lifelines, LISS Panel, PIAAC and SHARE).[11] These data can also be linked by using the RIN.

Safe People

Only researchers from institutions mentioned in Article 41(2) of the Dutch Statistics Act can request access to the microdata; these include universities, government research organisations (such as CPB [Netherlands Bureau for Economic Policy Analysis], SCP [The Netherlands Institute for Social Research], NIDI [Netherlands Interdisciplinary Demographic Institute]), research departments of ministries and other organisations. The main criteria for admission are that the institution conducts statistical or scientific research as its main activity, publishes its research results, has a good reputation and is located in the Netherlands or another Member State of the European Union.[12] The applicant must also have taken sufficient measures to prevent the data from being used for purposes other than statistical or scientific research. Admission is granted with a legal decision for a maximum of three years. When the validity period has expired, institutions can request an extension again of up to three years. The policy on criteria for granting access to microdata to institutions has been published in the Government Gazette on 22 July 2021.

Before researchers can access the remote access environment for the first time, researchers and their manager must sign a confidentiality statement to be renewed every three years, and researchers must answer a number of awareness questions to test their knowledge of what is and is not allowed when working with the microdata. Violations of the rules governing the use of the remote access facility may result in sanctions being imposed on

11 Lifelines is a large, multigenerational cohort study with health-related data from the northern population of the Netherlands; the LISS panel (Longitudinal Internet Studies for the Social Sciences) is an online household panel; PIAAC (Program for the International Assessment of Adult Competencies) is an OECD survey of adult skills; SHARE (Survey of Health, Ageing and Retirement in Europe) is a multidisciplinary and cross-national panel database of microdata on health, socio-economic status and social and family networks.

12 Also allowed to request access to the microdata are states party to the Agreement on the European Economic Area and countries or a part thereof for which an adequacy decision has been adopted by the European Commission under Article 45 of Regulation (EU) No. 2016/679 of the European Parliament and of the Council of 27 April 2016 on the protection of natural persons with regard to the processing of personal data and on the free movement of such data, and repealing Directive 95/46/EC (OJEU 2016, L 119).

individual users, the research project or the institution, depending on the seriousness of the breaches.

Safe Settings

The remote access environment is a separate, secure network environment run by CBS, and all microdata remain within that network; they cannot be exported by the users. Access to the remote access environment is facilitated by setting up a secure internet connection in combination with a Virtual Private Network (VPN) connection. Researchers' other internet connections are cut off during the time they spend in the environment to prevent recording of data. In addition, a hardware token with a changing numeric code as well as an SMS authentication is required. After connection to the RA environment, there is a login procedure with a username and password to set up a session on the user's own project environment.

Safe Projects

An institution must submit a separate application for project permission for each research project. The project proposals are screened beforehand, and questions are asked such as: is it possible with the requested data? Is it really statistical or scientific use? In addition, the applicable processing ground under the GDPR, the purposes of the research within the GDPR framework and the publication plan are checked. If the project is approved, only the microdata sets needed to answer the user's research questions will be made accessible (the 'need-to-know principle', or data minimisation under the GDPR).

Before a project starts, a project agreement must be signed, which specifies the conditions that must be met when conducting the research. In cases where confidentiality and/or non-disclosure has been violated, CBS may terminate this project contract with immediate effect.

Safe Output

Privacy-sensitive information is protected from unauthorised access throughout the project. If researchers wish to access their research results outside the secure environment, CBS will check whether these results pose any disclosure risks before releasing these results to the researchers. To ensure there is no direct disclosure, CBS provides rules of thumb that are constructed in such a way that research results that meet these rules can be considered safe. These rules of thumb concern the minimum number of units in a table and similar output, degrees of freedom in models, group disclosure in frequency tables and dominance in magnitude tables.

4. Practical, Technical, Legal and Ethical dilemmas

The general dilemma is the need for data confidentiality and security versus the public interest. It should be kept in mind that if CBS provides access to microdata, no matter how strict this may be, there are risks to security and privacy.

However, there is broad consensus about the high social relevance of the remote access facility and the fact that this facility should therefore, under certain conditions, be available for statistical and scientific research (as mentioned in Berg et al., 2020; Bijlsma et al., 2021). Obviously, this is not an easy feat. Essentially, the overall level of data security comes from the interplay of all the parameters involved: users, data and so forth. The report by Berg et al. (2020) was the outcome of a committee of independent scientific experts, asked by CBS to investigate possible privacy and security risks associated with providing access to microdata. In line with the committee's recommendations, CBS explored options to make some of the five safes as mentioned in the introduction more stringent and others more lenient, seeking to mitigate privacy risks and prevent data misuse while striving to facilitate statistical and scientific research in the broad interest of society in an accessible and user-friendly manner. For example, this could be achieved by being stricter in only allowing access to institutes from countries within the European Economic Area or from countries outside that area with an adequate level of data protection adopted by the European Commission.

One aspect concerns access to CBS microdata in relation to the GDPR: should pseudonymised microdata accessible via remote access be treated as personal data and should the GDPR therefore apply? The GDPR concerns the processing of personal data. Article 4.1 of the GDPR[13] concerns the definition of personal data. While there might be some room for interpretation, in the opinion of CBS, pseudonymised data are personal data, as the pseudonymisation process is reversible, although only known within an extra-secured part of CBS. A follow-up question is whether providing remote access to data without actually owning them is a form of processing. Looking at the

13 Article 4(1) GDPR:
'personal data' means any information relating to an identified or identifiable natural person ('data subject'); an identifiable natural person is one who can be identified, directly or indirectly, in particular by reference to an identifier such as a name, an identification number, location data, an online identifier or to one or more factors specific to the physical, physiological, genetic, mental, economic, cultural or social identity of that natural person.

definition in Article 4(2) GDPR[14], which mentions 'consultation' and 'use', the answer is 'yes'.

A dilemma is distinguishing between certain types of sensitive personal data, which are extra protected under the GDPR, and non-sensitive data. For practical reasons and to be on the safe side, CBS has decided to have the protection of all microdata at the same high level.

There is also a dilemma when importing additional external microdata into the environment for remote access. Linking with this kind of additional data has great value in some studies, and some studies cannot be meaningfully performed without these data. It is therefore obvious that CBS wants to make this possible. At the same time, however, the chance of recognition must be kept low. A distinction is therefore made between the types of additional data, ranging from data from organisations other than the one conducting the research to data available to the researcher themselves. At one end of the spectrum, for example, is a dataset from the Ministry of Education or the UWV (Dutch Employee Insurance Agency) that is required for research by a university. Here, the chance of recognition is considered to be just as small as that of CBS microdata. At the other end of the spectrum, you have the researcher who interviews people and wants to upload data about these people and link them to CBS microdata. Even though the data are pseudonymised, in this case, the researcher might recognise respondents because of the responses they gave. Because the chance of recognition is high, importing these data is not allowed.

Finally, there is the dilemma of maintaining the high level of security while the popularity of microdata research increases. More and more researchers and research institutions are finding their way to the CBS remote access facility. As a result, the amount of data is increasing, the number of researchers is growing, more projects must be monitored and more output has to be checked. This places a great burden on the organisation to maintain the security of this facility at the desired high level. So far, the required security level has been achieved (Berg et al., 2020). However, the growing popularity of microdata research is one of the important challenges for Statistics Netherlands for the future, and it requires further investments in technical and methodological solutions.

14 Article 4(2) GDPR:
'processing' means any operation or set of operations which is performed on personal data or on sets of personal data, whether or not by automated means, such as collection, recording, organisation, structuring, storage, adaptation or alteration, retrieval, consultation, use, disclosure by transmission, dissemination or otherwise making available, alignment or combination, restriction, erasure or destruction.

5. Conclusions

Microdata access at CBS is a highly valued and appreciated service. The Dutch Statistical Act has explicitly created the possibility of granting researchers access to microdata. Next to the more traditional means of public use files and scientific use files, remote access to secure use files has become the most popular way of accessing microdata at CBS.

However, the Dutch Statistical Act also requires CBS to maintain the highest possible standard in the protection of respondents' privacy. For personal data specifically, this is enforced by the GDPR, too. To reach this highest standard, CBS has adopted the framework of the 'five safes'. This framework aims at different angles of protection: safe people, safe settings, safe projects, safe data and safe output. This allows the organisation to balance the needed overall high level of protection by assigning different levels of protection to each of the individual five safes.

Even though our current way of granting access to microdata to researchers for scientific purposes has been reviewed and deemed sufficiently safe by a committee of independent scientific experts (Berg et al., 2020), there is no room for complacency. In light of the findings of these experts, CBS has made adjustments to the processes involving microdata access. However, the growing popularity of microdata research, the growing availability of open data at other organisations and ever-improving computational possibilities still require CBS to continuously check and update its privacy and security measures. The aim will always be to improve the possibilities for scientific research without making concessions to safety.

References

Berg, B. van den, Erkin, Z., Keymolen, E. L. O., Klievink, B., Sloot B. van der, & Steen, T. van. (2020). *Remote access to microdata: Final report*. Institute of Security and Global Affairs, Faculty of Governance and Global Affairs, Leiden University.

Bijlsma, M., Klaauw B. van der, & Knoef, M. (2021). De data-agenda van de overheid dient zich ook op de data zelf te richten. *Economisch Statisch Berichten, 106*(4800), 388–391.

Dutch Statistics Act. (2017). Wet op het Centraal bureau voor de statistiek. https://wetten.overheid.nl/BWBR0015926/2017-01-01

General Data Protection Regulation (GDPR). (2016). https://gdpr-info.eu/

Government Gazette 36083. (2021, July 22). Staatscourant van het Koninkrijk der Nederlanden. https://zoek.officielebekendmakingen.nl/stcrt-2021-36083.html

Human Rights Act, European Convention for the Protection of Human Rights and Fundamental Freedoms. (1998). https://www.legislation.gov.uk/ukpga/1998/42/contents

Hundepool, A., Domingo-Ferrer, J., Franconi, L., Giessing, S., Schulte Nordholt, E., Spicer, K., & Wolf, P. P. de. (2012). *Statistical disclosure control.* Wiley.

8. Atmospheric Profiling and Surveillance in the *Stratumseind Living Lab*: Pushing the Limits of Identifiability

Maša Galič

Abstract

The goal of many smart city projects, at least in Europe, is not to manage individuals as such but to govern them as a multiplicity, a whole sum of relationships between persons and the environment. For this purpose, individuals need not be singled out and identified. Most of the data collected within such smart city projects therefore does not concern individuals as such. Coupled with the lack of clarity and the inconsistency surrounding the notion and scope of personal data, this situation leads to an uncertain and probabilistic nature not only of the concept of identifiability but also of the regulation of such smart city initiatives. This chapter explores how surveillance studies could inform data protection law, particularly in relation to the notions of personal data and identifiability. It does so by examining a concrete example of a smart city initiative – the Stratumseind Living Lab in the Netherlands – both through the lens of Foucault's notion of security and data protection law.

Keywords: smart cities; profiling; surveillance; security; identifiability

1. Introduction

> In the absence of legislation in the Netherlands, we have drawn up our own data principles. If you want to build a house in the Netherlands, books filled with rules apply before any stone has been laid. *There is nothing that applies to the use of data.* You can reason then: it is not forbidden, so just go ahead. But that is the wrong starting point. (Rathenau Institute, 2019; emphasis added)

Van der Sloot & van Schendel. *The Boundaries of Data*. Taylor & Francis Group, 2024
DOI: 10.5117/9789463729192_CH08

These are the words of Tinus Kanters, project manager of the Stratumseind Living Lab, operating in the southern Dutch city of Eindhoven.

In Europe and elsewhere, the use of data – at least those data that fall under the broad scope of 'personal data' – is regulated by data protection law. The quote illustrates the difficulty of distinguishing between personal and non-personal data and the application of data protection law in smart city projects in Europe, like the Stratumseind Living Lab. This is a pressing issue, considering that smart city and living lab initiatives – generally referring to the extensive embedding of software-enabled technologies into the city environment, including their testing in real-time – are now a common sight in cities and towns around the world. Within the smart city discourse, such technologies serve two broad purposes: improving urban management and the quality of life in the city (such as lowering gas emissions, traffic congestion and crime) and stimulating the economic development of the city (Kitchin, 2015).

However, beyond the grand promises of the smart city and living lab discourse, data-driven monitoring practices of ICT transform cities into extraordinary apparatuses of surveillance, which try to infer and affect persons' interests, preferences, emotional states and behaviour. Yet the vast majority of data captured in smart cities relates to environmental and other contextual factors, rather than to identified or (likely) identifiable individuals. Think of data about the weather, air quality, sound and crowding levels, and the occupancy of car parks in a particular area. In fact, the aim of many recent smart city and living lab initiatives, particularly in Europe, is not to identify and target any specific individuals but to manage or nudge them as a multiplicity through a combination of the environment, persons and all their interactions (Schuilenburg & Peeters, 2018; Wray, 2021). Some smart city projects, such as Chicago's Array of Things, promise not to collect any personal or private information at all, framing their approach directly as a privacy-preserving technique: the 'technology and policy have been designed to specifically minimise any potential collection of data about individuals, so privacy protection is built into the design of the sensors and into the operating policies' (Hiller & Blanke, 2017, p. 331). It is thus unsurprising that smart city project managers do not consider the data captured within such projects to be personal, thus falling outside the scope of data protection law.[1] These practical issues relating to the application of

1 There are additional normative and practical arguments on why data protection law might have serious trouble with regulating smart city–type initiatives. See e.g. Hildebrandt (2008b); Hildebrandt & Koops (2010); Purtova (2018a); Lynskey (2019); Jasserand (2018).

data protection law in the smart city context tie into a renewed academic interest in the question of what constitutes both personal and anonymous data. According to this research, the lack of clarity and the inconsistency surrounding both notions lead to an uncertain and probabilistic nature of the concept of identifiability and, consequently, the scope of data protection law (see e.g. Finck & Pallas, 2020; Purtova, 2018b; Edwards, 2018).

This contribution ties into these discussions and critiques of data protection law by exploring how insights from surveillance studies – a multidisciplinary field examining the role and effect of particular types of surveillance (Lyon, 2001) – can inform the application of data protection law in the context of smart cities, particularly in relation to the notion of personal data and identifiability. After all, smart cities are also 'surveillance cities' (Murakami Wood, 2015; Sadowski & Pasquale, 2015; Monahan, 2018) and as such need to be imagined and framed within critical discourses, including surveillance studies (Kitchin, 2016). For this purpose, I offer a context-specific analysis of a smart city project, the Stratumseind 2.0 project and its living lab (Stratumseind Living Lab; SLL), both from a surveillance studies and data protection law perspective. Two main reasons make the SLL a worthy example to study. First of all, the SLL is a longer-lasting mid-sized project, which includes multinational and local technology companies, and was touted as a success on a national and European level (Studio 040, 2018; European Commission, 2019). As such, it serves as an illustrative example of a European smart city–type initiative. Second, within this project, persons are governed as a part of the 'atmosphere', which is understood as the whole sum of relationships between the people and the environment.

Contrary to traditional accounts of surveillance, like the panopticon or the 'Big Brother' metaphor, in which (identified or identifiable) individuals are surveilled and controlled, recent smart city projects that function on the basis of data-driven surveillance try to govern persons at an aggregate or collective level. While this type of surveillant logic operates much more in line with Foucault's concept of security (*sécurité*), according to which people's behaviour is influenced indirectly by manipulating a certain set of variables at the macro or aggregate level, smart city surveillance has not been examined through this lens yet. Yet the choice of theoretical framework through which one analyses contemporary surveillance practices can lead to very different answers to the question of whether the current legislative and regulatory framework is adequate. After all, the application of data protection law depends on the question of whether any individuals are or are reasonably likely to be identified through the data collection and processing. But smart city surveillance practices, which follow the 'atmospheric' logic of security, suggest that such a focus on the individual is insufficient and that the regulatory framework might need to be adapted.

The chapter begins with a brief description of the Stratumseind 2.0 initiative, its living lab and two of its sub-projects relating to predictive policing and nudging that employ an 'atmosphere'-centred type of surveillance: CityPulse and De-escalate. In Section 3, I discuss Foucault's concept of security and how this type of surveillance can be observed in the SLL, which tries to govern consumption by influencing the atmosphere. In the subsequent section, I discuss the notion of identifiability in data protection law, which I analyse through the lens of profiling. Based on this discussion, I then explore the type of profiling and nudging found in the SLL, proposing the notion of 'atmospheric profiling'. I conclude that the atmosphere-centred surveillance in the SLL, which leads to atmospheric profiling, puts an additional strain on the concept of personal data and renders the application of data protection law to smart cities all the more uncertain.

2. The Stratumseind Living Lab

Stratumseind is a busy nightlife street in the centre of Eindhoven, housing around 50 establishments, such as pubs, cafés, snack bars, a nightclub and a coffee shop (where marijuana is sold for personal consumption). It has been a popular nightlife destination for decades. According to the Eindhoven municipality, however, the number of visitors has dropped significantly since 2010, arguably due to the rising criminality and vandalism on the street (van Gerwen, 2013). This has led the municipality to initiate the Stratumseind 2.0 project, which officially ran from 2013 until mid-2018, although some of the projects seem to have continued with many of the same actors at least into 2020 (Oddity.ai, 2020). Stratumseind 2.0 was an umbrella project with the goal to 'long-lastingly improve the street from an economic as well as a social point of view' (van Gerwen, 2013). More concretely, the project wanted to (1) attract more visitors, (2) make them stay longer and spend more money in the establishments, (3) lower the vandalism, police and health-related costs connected to Stratumseind, (4) increase the income related to Stratumseind (and Eind)oven as a whole) and (5) create positive value of direct marketing (Kanters, 2013). These ambitious goals were planned to be achieved through a variety of means and initiatives, but primarily through 'a 365 days, 24/7 scan of all data on Stratumseind' (Kanters, 2013, n.p.). The key element and main sub-project of Stratumseind 2.0 was thus the Stratumseind Living Lab (SLL).

Living labs have been described as field labs with a variety of sensors and numerous actors, with the goal to measure, analyse and stimulate the behaviour of people in public places through technology (Ballon, 2015). In line with this description, the main goal of the SLL was to gain insight into the ways in which external stimuli can (significantly) influence escalating and de-escalating behaviour of visitors of the street (Kuindersma, 2018). The SLL was organised in the form of a public-private partnership (PPP), involving a large number of actors, including the Eindhoven municipality, the police, universities and numerous technology companies (both multinationals and small local businesses). The SLL consisted of a growing number of sub-projects with diverse but intertwined actors and goals, ranging from the prevention of crime and public disorder (CityPulse), community policing (Trillion) and community building (Stratumsepoort) to de-escalating people's behaviour using light (De-escalate). Since CityPulse and De-escalate were the largest and longest-lasting sub-projects, focused on detecting and influencing the atmosphere on the street, they merit closer examination.

2.1. The CityPulse Project: Detecting a Bad Atmosphere on the Street Through Risk Profiles

CityPulse was a project developing a system for the detection of 'deviant behaviour' (a term largely left undefined) and a 'bad' atmosphere on the Stratumseind street, which took place between 2015 and 2017. The actors involved included some of the world's biggest ICT companies, such as Atos (funded by IBM for this project) and Intel, as well as the Eindhoven municipality, the police and a few local technology companies. The goal of the project was to create 'a powerful image of the street and help authorities better predict and react to situations and de-escalate them before they would develop' (Atos, 2015).

For this purpose, the project employed numerous sensors on the Stratumseind street, as well as other data sources. In particular, the project employed video and sound cameras[2] with embedded analytical capabilities (e.g. tracking walking patterns), sound sensors, CityBeacons,[3] Wi-Fi tracking, technology for social media sentiment analysis and a weather station. These technologies continuously captured and generated data. Additional types of data were also collected and stored, including crime statistics concerning

2 These cameras have the ability to pinpoint the location of a particular sound.

3 Large poles combining the functions of cameras, information signs, signposts, antennas, advertising spaces and video screens.

the Stratumseind street and the amount of beer sold and rubbish collected per week. This resulted in the collection of a vast amount of data, including:

- image data from the video feed (where faces were blurred);
- the number of persons approaching and moving away from the Stratumseind street;
- density of people on the street;
- the total number of persons on the street;
- persons' walking patterns;
- anonymised MAC addresses resulting from Wi-Fi tracking;
- the nationality and hometown of the visitors, captured at aggregate level (based on smartphone subscription data received from Vodaphone);
- the average sound level on the street;
- general sentiment of tweets relating to Stratumseind (e.g. mentioning the street or a bar on the street), captured at aggregate level;
- petty, moderate and serious crime on the street (from official crime statistics);
- the percentage difference of beer ordered in the Stratumseind establishments (weekly);
- volume of garbage collected from the Stratumseind street (weekly);
- tonnes of glass from the street collected (weekly);
- the number of cars parked in certain car parks in the city centre;
- the rainfall and the temperature, wind speed and direction per hour (Galič, 2019).

The data were stored in a database that could be utilised through data analysis techniques.[4] It should be noted that the data on the visitors' nationality and hometown and the tweet sentiment analysis were only collected at aggregate level (e.g. classifying tweets about the Stratumseind street or particular establishment as 'negative', 'positive' and 'neutral'). The unique identifiers captured through Wi-Fi tracking were also said to be anonymised. On this basis, the SLL actors concluded that the level of aggregation was sufficient for these data to be considered anonymous (de Graaf, 2015).

The CityPulse system was designed to analyse all these types of data, looking for anomalies in data patterns, which could then be cross-referenced against other gathered data sources (e.g. a football match that took place earlier that day in the Eindhoven stadium). The system was seen as a predictive, preventative and an ancillary tool for the police in its role of crime

4 The author does not know who had access to these data or the results from their analysis.

prevention and order maintenance in the city. Put simply, the CityPulse system was primarily concerned with detecting a 'bad atmosphere' on the Stratumseind street in order to prevent crime and other deviant behaviour and deploying the police in a more efficient manner. For instance, using data analysis, the system could detect an 'escalated atmosphere', which might require police presence soon. The police could be warned of this situation through the CityPulse app (first requiring human authorisation but acting autonomously when fully developed), representing a direct link between the SLL and the police. The CityPulse app distinguished between four possible notifications (i.e. risk profiles): 'nothing wrong', 'everything alright', 'backup needed' and 'high risk situation'.[5] If the atmosphere on the street was not considered too dangerous, the CityPulse system could adapt the colour and pulsation of lights on the street – a technology developed in the related De-escalate project, discussed in the following sub-section – before calling the police. If the atmosphere on the street improved because of the lighting, the police would not need to be called to the street at all.

2.2. The De-escalate Project: Creating a Positive Atmosphere on the Street Through Nudging

De-escalate was a project developing a special lighting system with the purpose of influencing behaviour and diffusing an 'escalated' atmosphere through dynamic lighting scenarios on the Stratumseind street. This project ran from 2014 to 2018 and was led by researchers from the Technical University Eindhoven and Philips, the Dutch technology company from Eindhoven. Other actors were also involved, including the Eindhoven municipality, the police and smaller local technology companies.

The De-escalate project experimented with the effect of interactive lighting design on the 'de-escalation' of aggressive behaviour, based on psychological pathways through which exposure to dynamic lighting could defuse escalating behaviour. 'Escalated behaviour' was defined in a very broad manner, referring to all types of behaviour of persons who in some way lose self-control, including screaming, getting abusive, aggressive or crossing other behavioural boundaries that they would otherwise not cross (de Kort, 2014). The idea behind the project was based on insights from environmental psychology, which showed that directed or bright light can heighten self-awareness, whereas darkness can trigger feelings of anonymity (de Kort, 2016). The

5 It remains unclear to the author what the difference between 'nothing wrong' and 'everything all right' is, or how exactly the scenarios are delineated.

awareness of the loss of anonymity when one is in the spotlight may turn a person's attention to their inner states and traits and prompt them to examine their personal norms and engage in better self-regulation (de Kort, 2016).

Similarly, as with the CityPulse project, the De-escalate project relied on data such as incidents on the street (from crime statistics), statistics relating to the beer sold, crowding levels, weather data and Twitter sentiment analysis (den Ouden & Valkenburg, 2013). The data were analysed with the aim of finding correlations between influencing factors (e.g. bad weather or the results of a football match) and people's stress levels (den Ouden & Valkenburg, 2013). Predictions were then made about stress levels, which would engage the lighting system, aiming to proactively keep stress levels at 'acceptable levels' – although it remains unclear what constitutes 'acceptable levels' (den Ouden & Valkenburg, 2013; see also Kalinauskaitė, 2014). As such, the De-escalate system is essentially a nudging tool.

One of the key terms used in this project was 'atmosphere'. The term was seen as being of value because the police and the security staff on the Stratumseind street often referred to it, used it to evaluate the general situation on the street and to anticipate people's behaviour. Since aggression (connected to the broader concept of escalated behaviour) is behaviour that is strongly dependent on context (including crowding, noise and temperature), the socio-physical characteristics of the environment can lead to behaviour in dynamic but patterned – and thus predictable – ways (Kalinauskaitė et al., 2018). Most often, escalation and aggression occur not because they were intentionally planned but because people respond to perceived stress, become aggravated by autonomic arousal and anger and, in so doing, break personally held norms and do things they might not otherwise. De-escalate researchers thus wanted to affect the *atmosphere* on the Stratumseind street – defined as 'people's attitudes, mood, behaviour and interactions with one another as well as with their immediate environment' (Kalinauskaitė et al., 2018, p. 228) –to de-escalate aggression. Atmosphere was seen as an important indicator of risk of incidents as well as a proxy for influencing a person's behaviour. In other words, the De-escalate project was concerned with creating a 'good' atmosphere on the Stratumseind street through the effects of lighting.

3. Surveillance in the Stratumseind Living Lab: Governing Consumption Through Atmosphere

As described above, most of the data collected within the SLL focuses on environmental and other contextual factors (rather than on individuals), such as data about the weather, crowding and sound levels, the general sentiment of tweets relating to Stratumseind, the amount of rubbish collected and beer sold per week. Of course, all these data are captured in order to detect and nudge the atmosphere and thus the behaviour of persons on the Stratumseind street. However, this functions in such a way that does not – or, at least, does not need to – identify any individuals.

This approach to governing persons is indicative of a development relating to the type of surveillance taking place within smart cities. As already mentioned, smart cities depend on such a wide range of surveillance technologies that they have been dubbed 'surveillance cities'. This has led to concerns about individuals' privacy, autonomy, freedom of choice and discrimination (Finch & Tene, 2018; de Graaf, 2015). Both scholars and journalists commonly employ the prevalent but old-fashioned panopticon or Big Brother metaphors for the surveillance taking place in smart cities (see e.g. Finch & Tene, 2018; Kitchin, 2014; Dopper, 2015). However, such metaphors, which assume a centralised and continuous (hypothetical) gaze of the state focused on specific individuals,[6] are out of date for the most part. Surveillance studies research in the past decades has shown that contemporary networked surveillance practices are much more diverse and complex than the disciplinary logic of the panoptic gaze (Galič et al., 2017). Surveillance today is carried out by both public and private actors (including private individuals), in complex public-private partnerships (PPPs), for public (that is, common) and private purposes (e.g. safety and profit), over concrete suspects and the general population, and within public, semi-public and private spaces. These surveillant practices often support each other in a complex manner that is almost impossible to disentangle.

The choice of theoretical framework through which one analyses contemporary surveillance practices within smart cities is important, as it can affect what one can – and will – conclude in terms of its regulation (e.g. Galič, 2019,

6 Bentham's panopticon depicts a circular prison, with an inspector in a central tower, overseeing the activities of convicts in their cells. Through this specific architectural design, an illusion of constant surveillance is created. The prisoners are not really watched constantly, but they believe they are, or rather, they know they might be. Foucault famously projected the panopticon's operating logic onto other parts of society, such as schools, the military, hospitals and factories, in order to highlight power relations and modes of governing. The main idea behind the mode of power of the panopticon ('the panoptic gaze') is that when everybody can potentially be under surveillance, people will internalise the relevant control, morals and values. In other words, people will discipline themselves; they will become conforming, docile subjects. The goal of panoptic surveillance therefore is the internalisation of what is considered 'good behaviour', which takes place through the presence of the surveillance apparatus (e.g. CCTV cameras on the street).

pp. 226–265). As I show below, the CityPulse and De-escalate projects employ an atmosphere-centred type of surveillance, which can best be discussed through Foucault's concept of security.[7] In the following sub-sections, I thus briefly describe the surveillant logic of security, then discuss how this logic operates in the SLL. Afterwards, I show how this type of surveillance has notable implications for data protection law, since the scope of its protection depends on the question of whether any individuals are or are reasonably likely to be identified through the data collection and processing.

3.1. The Surveillant Logic of Foucault's Security

Foucault's concept of security (*sécurité*) refers to the future-oriented management of risks through the management of entire populations in particular territorial configurations. It represents a significant deviation from discipline (the logic of the panopticon), still the primary model for thinking about surveillance. Foucault's security diverges from discipline in its conceptualisation of the *object* of governance, the (conceptual) *devices* used to maximise its objective and the *means* to govern the object (Togman, 2021).

Whereas discipline focused on the individual (their physical body), security reorients the *object* of governance to the collective or multiplicity. Statistical tables, average indicators and rates of occurrence create an aggregated and anonymised construct: the 'population' (Togman, 2021, p. 233; Brighenti, 2010). Discipline requires that each and every person comply with government directives. Within the logic of security, however, the focus is no longer on absolute compliance but rather on acceptable ranges and optimal averages. As Foucault put it, the overarching question of security is 'how to keep a type of (behaviour) within socially and economically acceptable limits and around an average that will be considered as optimal for a given social functioning' (Foucault, 2009, p. 4). Security is thus based on the logic of resource-maximisation and cost-benefit analysis (Valverde, 2008, p. 23). Instead of prohibiting anything, it incentivises certain economic activities while discouraging others. Put simply, the logic of security wants to optimise consumption while simultaneously minimising labour and other expenditures through the risk management of multiplicities (Harcourt, 2014). This means that security as a mode of regulation is tolerant of minor

7 Security is not the only surveillant logic (or mode of power) operating on the Stratumseind street. Thieves, for instance, are to be identified through data analysis and excluded from the bars and street (an example of the logic of control conceptualised by Deleuze). Nevertheless, the primary mode of governance of persons on the street takes place according to Foucault's concept of security.

deviations, seeking instead to optimise, minimise or maximise rather than eliminate (Klauser et al., 2014).

Using the example of theft, Foucault explicated a new set of questions and desires, which stand at the centre of the security apparatus:

> [W]hat is the average rate of criminality for this type? How can we predict statistically the number of thefts at a given moment in a given society ... are there times, regions, and penal systems that will increase or reduce this average rate? ... [H]ow much does criminality cost society ... [and] what is the cost of repressing these thefts? Does severe and strict repression cost more than one that is more permissive ... what is the comparative cost of theft and of its repression and what is more worthwhile: to tolerate a bit more theft or to tolerate a bit more repression? (Foucault, 2009, p. 4).

These goals are to be achieved through a particular set of (conceptual) *devices*, such as statistical constructs, aggregations, averages and rates of occurrence. Today we can add AI and other complex algorithmic constructs to the list. The state and a wide variety of non-state actors (e.g. economists, the academic community and technology companies in particular) actively construct the object of the population through the collection and anonymisation of data on a macro-scale (with the census as a classic example).

Finally, there is the shift in the *means* to govern the population. Disciplinary power aims to record and survey the details of individual lives in order to control their individual behaviour. Instead, security seeks to optimise the population by 'having a hold on things that seem far removed from population but which, through calculation, analysis and reflection, one knows can really have an effect on it' (Foucault 2009, p. 72). 'The locus [therefore] shifts from knowledge of the individual itself to knowledge of environmental factors affecting the population' (Togman 2021, p. 235). People's behaviour is to be influenced *indirectly* by manipulating a certain set of variables at the macro scale. In other words, behaviour is to be affected by shaping 'the environment for decision-making' (Togman, 2021, p. 241), what would nowadays be called 'nudging' (Cass & Sunstein, 2008). This can be done by appealing to rational decision-making processes, or through manipulative practices exploiting cognitive weaknesses.

3.2. Security on the Stratumseind Street

So, how does this theoretical model operate in practice in the SLL? First of all, we see that the principles of panoptic surveillance are largely absent in the SLL. The emphasis is not on discipline: the surveilled visitors, nudged through atmosphere, are not supposed to be aware of or internalise the gaze of the SLL. The SLL is not trying to tightly control each and every one of them. On the contrary, the SLL with its 'consumption-focused use of space' (Schuilenburg and Peeters 2018, 5) is mainly interested in managing the visitors. The goal is to influence their behaviour 'just enough' to maintain an uninterrupted flow, that is, consumption on the nightlife street.

Within the SLL, security is therefore sought through control without stopping or hampering the flow of visitors on the street. Let us consider the concrete goals of the SLL: attracting more visitors to the street, making them stay longer and spend more money in the establishments and decreasing security and health-related costs connected to Stratumseind. Following the logic of security, persons are not surveilled and targeted individually. Instead, they are targeted as a multiplicity in a way that maximises consumption, while at the same time labour and other expenditures are minimised. In this sense, the logic of security can be described as inclusionary: smaller transgressions are overlooked as long as the atmosphere on the street (representing the relationships on the street as a whole) is not negatively affected.

The goal, therefore, is not to identify every single example of anti-social or escalated behaviour and intervene, for instance, through exclusion from the pub by a pub's security guard or an arrest by the police. Instead, smaller transgressions are overlooked, as long as the relationships on the street as whole can be managed in such a way so as the atmosphere is not affected in any negative way. This also means that any intervention by the police or other security actors will not be necessary, thus reducing costs. This type of surveillant logic fits rather well with the regulation of a nightlife street like Stratumseind, where a certain level of chaos (partially due to intoxication) will always be present, as it is also a part of the idea of 'nightlife' itself (Chatterton & Hollands, 2003). Research has shown that nightlife requires not only a sufficient level of safety but also a sufficient level of excitement and danger, rather than completely predictable outcomes (Brands et al., 2015; Timan, 2013). When the latter happens, people tend to move on to another, more exciting *nightscape*.[8]

This securitising logic can be illustrated more clearly with a concrete example. Imagine the following scenario:

8 The term 'nightscape' refers to a specific time (the night) and place in the city understood as a landscape, which is made of both humans and things that behave differently at night than during the day.

> Bart and Marloes are having a lovers' quarrel in front of Altstadt, their favourite rock bar on the Stratumseind street. They exhibit some type of mildly escalating behaviour, such as yelling and breaking a glass or two. The CityPulse surveillance system captures the video feed of Bart and Marloes (with blurred faces), heightened sound levels resulting from their yelling and the breaking of glass, the low crowding levels in front of Altstadt, the neutral general sentiment relating to the Stratumseind street based on tweets and weather data, which detect a clear and windless evening. The system determines that this is a 'low risk' situation on the street (i.e. 'everything all right'). As such, the police are not notified, but the special lighting scenarios developed within the De-escalate project are turned on. The slowly pulsating bright light helps Bart and Marloes become more aware of their behaviour and calm down. They make up and end up kissing in a more secluded part of the street. Activity on Stratumseind continues more or less undisturbed.

This scenario illustrates how data within the SLL are captured and analysed in order to produce risk profiles relating to the atmosphere on the street. When the risk is considered low such as in the above scenario (e.g. 'nothing wrong' or 'everything all right' situation), police intervention is not needed. The system has, however, activated lighting scenarios to 'de-escalate' the mildly transgressive behaviour, which by itself does not merit police intervention, and to prevent it from continuing and negatively affecting the consumption on the street. For this purpose, individual identification of Bart and Marloes does not and need not take place at all.

4. Atmospheric Profiling in the Stratumseind Living Lab and the Limits of Identifiability in Data Protection Law[9]

The way in which the SLL governs persons clearly has notable implications for data protection law. After all, the scope of protection depends on the question, whether any individuals are or are reasonably likely to be identified through the data collection and processing. Yet, as shown in the preceding section, for the SLL to function, individuals do not need to – and are not

9 This section is written on the basis of the author's co-authored paper and with the co-author's permission; see Maša Galič and Raphaël Gellert's 2021 article 'Data Protection Law Beyond Identifiability? Atmospheric Profiles, Nudging and the Stratumseind Living Lab' in *Computer Law & Security Review, 40*.

meant to – be identified at all. This begs the question of whether the data collected and processed within the SLL ('SLL data') can nevertheless be considered personal, thus invoking the protection of data protection law.

In this final section of the chapter, I do not conduct a detailed analysis of all the elements of the definition of personal data (1. any information; 2. relating to; 3. an identified or identifiable natural person) using the SLL example. It can quickly be determined that the SLL processes information that relates to individuals in an indirect manner (see also Galič & Gellert, 2021). While some data relating to persons directly (i.e. in content, e.g. video feed with blurred faces) is also processed, the focus lies on data relating to persons only indirectly, either in purpose or in result (see also Purtova, 2018b). After all, the data are collected with the intent to adapt the atmosphere on the street, thus indirectly influencing the behaviour of its visitors (relating in purpose).[10] We have seen this in the above scenario of the lovers' quarrel, where the goal was to de-escalate the behaviour of Bart and Marloes.[11] However, these same data also relate to other visitors of the street who might also be affected by the nudging measures of the De-escalate system. The data are thus likely to have an impact on the persons' rights and interests, where it suffices that an individual may be treated differently from others on the basis of such data (relating in result).[12] The SLL data thus seem to relate to all the visitors of the Stratumseind street at that moment in result as well.

A more complex question relates to the identifiability requirement. Even though the notion of identifiability is broad, it is questionable whether it can be concluded that persons are indeed identifiable in the SLL. The following sections therefore focus on the notion of identifiability, particularly in relation to profiling in the SLL.

4.1. Identifiability and Profiling: From Individuals to Groups

The notion of identifiability relates to a person who is not identified yet but where identification is possible, either in a direct or indirect manner. Recital 26 of the GDPR adopts a test of *reasonable likelihood* of identification by the controller or another person, referring to objective factors, such as the costs

10 Article 29WP, Opinion 4/2007, p. 10.

11 With the exception of the blurred video feed, which relates to Bart and Marloes in content, that is, directly.

12 Article 29WP, Opinion 4/2007, p. 11. A broad understanding of the reliability requirement by the former Article 29WP can be said to have been upheld by the CJEU in the Nowak judgment (Case C-434/16, Peter Nowak v. Data Protection Commissioner [2017], ECLI:EU:C:2017:994).

of and the amount of time required for the identification, and taking into account the state of technology at the time of the processing. The Article 29 Working Party (WP29) offered a longer list of factors that should be taken into consideration, including:

- the intended explicit or implied purpose or processing: when 'the processing ... only makes sense if it allows identification of specific individuals and treatment of them in a certain way,' the availability of tools of identification should be presumed reasonably likely; the risk of organisational dysfunctions (e.g. breaches of confidentiality duties) and technical breaches (e.g. data breaches);
- measures to prevent identification (i.e. to maintain anonymity).[13]

Getting back to the lovers' quarrel, one can argue that the images (with blurred faces) and the sound of Bart and Marloes yelling and breaking glass (pinpointed through sound cameras) are not direct identifiers. The same is true *a fortiori* for other data primarily relating to the environment, such as weather data, general sound and crowding levels. Indirect identifiability based on these environmental data is likely to be more difficult than data based on blurred video footage. However, and crucially, identifiability is not needed for the SLL to achieve its purposes. Even though the De-escalate lighting system is primarily aimed at Bart and Marloes, it does not target them directly and thus does not identify them. On the contrary, it affects (or at least tries to affect) everyone on the street at that particular time. In fact, the whole nudging system makes perfect sense without identification or the need for identifiability. That is, even if individuals are not identifiable, they may be nudged in this or that way, for this or that purpose. If Bart and Marloes are indeed calmed down by the lighting scenario and end up kissing in a secluded alley – that is, if the nudging works – then their identifiability is not needed at all, neither now nor later (cf. Schreurs et al., 2008, p. 243).

A similar assessment can be made regarding a higher-risk situation detected by the CityPulse system, such as a fight likely to break out, which would merit the deployment of the police on the street. In this case, the purpose of the CityPulse system is to detect a risky situation that might otherwise remain undetected through the regular CCTV operated by the police. The goal here is to detect a 'bad atmosphere' in which a fight is likely to break out so that the system can alert the police ahead of time, enabling them to arrive on the street more quickly and have a pre-emptive effect on

13 Article 29WP, Opinion 4/2007, p. 15.

the persons ready to pick a fight. To achieve this goal, CityPulse generally relies on the same types of data as mentioned in the example of the lovers' quarrel. Consequently, for the purpose of pre-empting a fight through atmosphere detection, identification is again not needed.[14]

For the operation of the SLL, identification of individuals is thus neither required nor desired. This suggests that individuals are unlikely to be identified. Nevertheless, the issue of identifiability should also be considered through the broader socio-technical lens of profiling.

The SLL functions on the basis of profiling, which relies on data mining algorithms, looking for correlations in large datasets in order to build classes or categories of characteristics. These categories can then be used to generate profiles of individuals and groups (Bosco et al., 2015). Nowadays, group (rather than individual) profiles, which represent an individual only insofar they are part of a group, are most common in practice. Such profiles serve to predict individuals' future behaviours and to take decisions affecting them on this basis (Hildebrandt, 2008a). While the question of whether and when profiling amounts to processing personal data has been hotly debated in data protection scholarship, it has not yet been definitively settled. In general, two approaches to this question can be found: one according to which profiling, which does not rely on identifying information when creating the profile, does not process personal data; and the other according to which profiling based on profiles, which do not contain identifying information, still amounts to the processing of personal data.

There are three steps that can be distinguished in profiling: (1) processing (personal and/or non-personal data), (2) creating a profile and (3) applying the profile. According to Schreurs et al. (2008, p. 243), if the first step of the profiling does not process personal data, then the remaining steps of the profiling operation cannot be considered to involve the processing of personal data either. Schreurs et al. (2008, p. 243) take the example of behavioural biometric data, such as the way in which a shopping trolley is driven in a supermarket, as a means to infer the type of customer (e.g. hurried, higher or lower purchasing power). The type of data that is processed here does not allow the identification of individuals pushing the trolley, so the profiling operation escapes the reach of data protection law. The Irish Data Protection Commissioner (2017, p. 16) has adopted a similar decision

14 The situation would be different if a fight would nevertheless break out on the street and the perpetrators would not be apprehended immediately. The police would then likely resort to its own high-resolution, non-blurred CCTV feed. However, this is a different matter and a distinct data processing operation, with which the present chapter is not concerned.

in the case of facial detection technology for advertising purposes, which is said to be able to infer mood, age or gender on the basis of facial features without actually identifying anyone.

The other approach to profiling takes a more holistic view of the profiling operation, arguing that the distinction between the creation and application of a profile is artificial. According to the 2010 Council of Europe Recommendation on profiling, for example, even when profiles are based on anonymous data, the *application* of the profile to specific individuals entails that these individuals are identifiable in themselves.[15] Put simply, one needs to be able to single out a person in order to apply the profile. Similarly, Bosco et al. define the application of a profile to individuals as 'the process of identifying and representing a specific individual or group as fitting a profile and of taking some form of decision based on this identification and representation' (Bosco et al., 2015, p. 49). This seems to be in line with the reasoning of WP29 concerning the purpose of the processing operation, which is a key parameter of identifiability.[16] If the processing only makes sense insofar as it allows for the treatment of a data subject in a certain way (which is precisely what is at stake with profiling), then the identifiability of individuals is implied by its very purpose. Or, as Barocas and Nissenbaum (2014, p. 45) famously put it, '[e]ven when individuals are not "identifiable", they may still be "reachable"', since they can be subjected to consequential inferences and predictions made on the basis of profiles. Unfortunately, there is not yet a binding legal decision confirming this position.

4.2. Atmospheric Profiles and Nudging: From Groups to Atmospheres

Based on these two perspectives on profiling, two approaches to the SLL can be taken. On the one hand, it can be argued that the profiling performed in the SLL does not process personal data, since the data used to build the profiles relates to the environment and other contextual or aggregate factors, rather than to identifiable individuals. On the other hand, it can be argued that the SLL processes data relating to identifiable individuals, since

15 Council of Europe, 'The Protection of Individuals with Regard to Automatic Processing of Personal Data in the Context with Regard to Automatic Processing. Recommendation CM/Rec(2010)13 and Explanatory Memorandum' (2010). The Recommendation from 2021 (Council of Europe, 2020) notes on p. 1 that 'a large amount of data, even anonymous data, profiling techniques can have an impact on the data subjects by placing them in predetermined categories' but does not address the question of application of the profile.

16 Article 29WP, Opinion 4/2007.

identification is implied by the very purpose of the profiling operation: to affect persons' behaviour on the Stratumseind street.

However, the possibility to argue the latter is weakened by the manner in which persons are (to be) affected: namely, persons are not to be affected as specific individuals, or even as algorithmic groups, but only indirectly as a part of the general atmosphere on the street. As Raphaël Gellert and I have argued previously (Galič & Gellert, 2021), this is an example of a new type of profiling operations in smart environments, which we call 'atmospheric profiling'. Such profiling puts an additional strain on the notion of personal data – more specifically, identifiability.

As can be seen from the description of the projects, the ideas behind the SLL are rooted in the notion of *atmosphere*. While attempts to affect the atmosphere, especially for the purpose of boosting sales, are nothing new (see e.g. Kotler, 1973), trying to affect it via sophisticated digital technologies in the (partially) public sector is a more recent development. In terms of atmosphere, the goal of the De-escalate project can be described as creating 'good atmospheres' on the Stratumseind street to de-escalate potential aggression. Similarly, the goal of the CityPulse project can be described as detecting 'bad atmospheres' on the street in order to deploy the police in a more efficient way. In the SLL, atmosphere was seen as being constituted from data relating to people's attitudes, mood, behaviours and interactions with one another, as well as with their immediate environment. The functioning of the SLL is therefore based on the detection of a positive or negative atmosphere with the intention of directly affecting this atmosphere – rather than any particular individuals – so as to reduce aggression and deviant behaviour. In terms of profiling, the SLL therefore creates profiles of atmospheres – *atmospheric profiles* – which are then translated into 'everything all right' or 'high risk' profiles within the CityPulse project. As such, persons are reduced to a constitutive element of the atmosphere on the Stratumseind street, used as a proxy to indirectly affect and nudge them.

By shifting the focus away from individuals and even groups to the broader environment and atmosphere, atmospheric profiling can be said to put an additional burden on the notion of identifiability as a constitutive element of the notion of personal data (Galič & Gellert, 2021, p. 11). If the target of the atmospheric profile is to influence the atmosphere on the street, this seems to refute arguments in favour of identifiability based on the processing, which only makes sense insofar as it allows for the treatment of a *particular* (that is, singled out) data subject in a certain way. Of course, while atmospheric profiling directly affects atmospheres, its underlying goal is to indirectly affect (or nudge) people: their mood, behaviour and interaction in a particular place. After all, the term 'atmosphere' in contemporary vernacular use refers to the distinctive 'influence' of a place on persons (Merriam-Webster, n.d.). Yet for this indirect nudging of persons' behaviour, no particular individuals are or need to be singled out. As such, no individuals are identified, and identifiability through the purpose of processing does not apply. In other words: whereas more common types of profiling practices lead to identification in terms of purpose (at least under certain interpretations), the same cannot be held regarding this new type of profiling practice. This analysis thus seems to confirm what the SLL actors have been claiming: that data protection law does not apply to the vast majority of the data processing taking place within the SLL (and similar smart city initiatives).[17]

Nevertheless, it should not be forgotten that for persons to be affected, they do not need to be identified by name or another unique identifier, or even singled out from the group, confirming once again that '[e]ven when individuals are not "identifiable", they may still be "reachable"' (Barocas & Nissenbaum, 2014). Even where nudging does not target identifiable persons, there are nonetheless important risks for rights and freedoms, which data protection is said to safeguard.[18] The most obvious risk concerns the right to private life as found in Article 8 of the European Convention on Human Rights. This is so because surveillance and nudging pose risks for identity development and autonomy, key values which privacy aims to protect and which are recognised by the European Court of Human Rights (Koops et al., 2017; Galič, 2019; Lanzing, 2019).

Perhaps luckily, then, nudging based on atmospheric profiles, which does not single out any individuals, does not seem to work very well. This seems to be the case with regard to the SLL, at least in the De-escalate project, which has not resulted in any tangible effects on aggressive behaviour. As Kanters, the SLL manager put it, 'We thought that the atmosphere could be influenced in this way [with dynamic lighting scenarios] but this was not the case in practice. In any case, it [the effect] is hardly measurable' (Hoekstra, 2017). Besides the difficulty (if not impossibility) connected to the measuring of such targets, this might also be connected – at least, partially – to the way in which manipulative nudging works: trying to covertly subvert another person's decision-making power through exploitation of the person's

17 With the mentioned exception of Wi-Fi tracking (anonymised) and video feed (blurred), the processing of which does fall under the scope of data protection law.

18 See Articles 24, 35 and Recital 75 of the General Data Protection Regulation.

cognitive weaknesses and vulnerabilities (Susser et al., 2019). This means that nudges, which are applied to everyone in the same way (such as the lighting scenarios in the De-escalate project), lack the key characteristic required to exploit someone's cognitive vulnerabilities: knowing what they are and how to leverage them.[19]

5. Conclusion

There are many practical and legal obstacles to the effective regulation of data-driven surveillance in smart cities through data protection law. The practical obstacles relate to the fact that a lot or most of the data collected within smart city projects, at least in Europe, does not concern individuals as such. Instead, it relates to the environment, such as data about the weather, air quality, sound and crowding levels. Moreover, the goal of many smart city projects is not to manage individuals as such but to govern them as a multiplicity, a whole sum of relationships between themselves and the environment, what is sometimes referred to as 'atmosphere'. For this purpose, individuals do not, in fact, need to be singled out and thus identified. The legal (and theoretical) obstacles relate to the fact that there is a lack of clarity and inconsistency surrounding the notion and scope of personal data, leading to an uncertain and probabilistic nature of the concept of identifiability and, consequently, the scope of data protection law. This is clearly an unsatisfactory solution, considering that smart city initiatives (try to) affect and reshape both places and persons, thus posing important risks to the enjoyment of our fundamental rights and freedoms, such as privacy and data protection. A clear regulatory framework that regulates such initiatives is thus needed.

In order to further this discussion, this chapter explored how surveillance studies could inform data protection law, particularly in relation to the notion of personal data and identifiability. It did so by examining a concrete example of a smart city of initiative – the Stratumseind Living Lab (SLL) in the Netherlands – both from a surveillance studies and data protection perspective. The exploration of the SLL through the lens of Foucault's notion

19 It should be noted, however, that digital technologies are well suited to facilitate nudging that would allow for 'fine-grained microtargeting' (also called 'hypernudging'), which targets and exploits individual vulnerabilities, making them much more difficult to resist. In the case of hypernudging, one could certainly speak of affecting individuals, meaning that data protection law would much more likely apply.

of security showed that the goal of the project is to manage and nudge individuals as a part of the 'atmosphere' – a combination of the environment, persons and all their interactions. As such, it is a part of a broader turn to the future-oriented management of risks through the management of entire populations in particular territorial configurations (rather than specific individuals), based on the logic of resource-maximisation and cost-benefit analysis.

Turning to the question of whether the data being processed in the SLL could be considered personal, I focused on the concept of identifiability, which I considered through the broader socio-technical lens of profiling. The particular type of profiling taking place in the SLL leads to a twofold issue. On the one hand, it adds to and further complicates the discussions around the question of whether profiling constitutes a form of personal data processing simply because of its purpose to affect individuals (in the case of the SLL, non-identified persons). This issue, which has its proponents and opponents, has not been settled yet. On the other hand, it also implies a novel type of profiling – atmospheric profiling – which tries to indirectly affect persons by affecting the general atmosphere on the street (rather than singling out individuals). As such, this type of profiling does not seem to constitute a type of personal data processing. The current reach of data protection law is thus very limited when it comes to the SLL and other smart city projects functioning according to the surveillant logic of security, based on an increasing amount of environmental data and atmospheric profiling.

So, what do the insights from surveillance studies and the discussion on atmospheric profiling suggest in terms of a possible way forward? If the identification of concrete individuals is no longer needed or relevant for the purpose of managing and nudging them, at least in the context of smart cities, then we need to consider whether the notion of personal data should not be stretched even further. This is not a novel proposal. More than a decade ago, Gutwirth and de Hert (2008) argued for a shift from personal data protection towards data protection *tout court* – that is, the application of data protection law to each processing of data that has potential negative consequences for our rights and freedoms, irrespective of whether the data processed qualify as personal or not. Perhaps it is time to revisit this idea, or to come up with another way to demarcate the scope of data protection law, going beyond or wholly abandoning the notion of 'identifiability', for instance, by focusing instead on the notion of 'identification' (Purtova, 2022; see also Urgessa, 2016).

References

Atos. (2015). *CityPulse – Using big data for real time incident response management* [Brochure]. https://atos.net/wp-content/uploads/2016/06/atos-ph-eindhoven-city-pulse-case-study.pdf

Ballon, P. (2015). Living labs. In R. Mansell & P. Hwa Ang (Eds.), *The international encyclopedia of digital communication and society* (pp. 552–556). John Wiley & Sons.

Barocas, S., & Nissenbaum, H. (2014). Big data's end run around anonymity and consent. In J. Lane, V. Stodden, S. Bender, & H. Nissenbaum (Eds.), *Privacy, big data, and the public good: frameworks for engagement* (pp. 44–75). Cambridge University Press.

Bosco, F., Creemers, N., Ferraris, V., Guagnin, D., Koops, B. J., & Vermeersch, E. (2015). Profiling technologies and fundamental rights: An introduction. In N. Creemers, D. Guagnin, & B.J. Koops (Eds.), *Profiling technologies in practice: Applications and impact on fundamental rights and values* (pp. 5–20). Wolf Legal Publishers.

Brands, J., Schwanen, T., & van Aalst, I. (2015). Fear of crime and affective ambiguities in the night-time economy. *Urban Studies, 52*(439), 439–455.

Brighenti, A. (2010). Democracy and its visibilities. In K. Haggerty & M. Samatas (Eds.), *Surveillance and democracy* (pp. 51–68). Routledge.

Chatterton, P., & Hollands, R. (2003). *Urban nightscapes: Youth cultures, pleasure spaces and corporate power.* Routledge.

Council of Europe. (2020). *Protection of individuals with regard to automatic processing of personal data in the context of profiling.* Recommendation CM/Rec(2021)8. https://edoc.coe.int/en/international-law/10670-protection-of-individuals-with-regard-to-automatic-processing-of-personal-data-in-the-context-of-profiling-recommendation-cmrec20218.html#

European Commission. (2019, June 7). *Context broker's smart services are making the city of Eindhoven a safer place* [Press release]. https://ec.europa.eu/digital-building-blocks/wikis/pages/viewpage.action?pageId=533365163

de Graaf, P. (2015, November 23). Een biertje met Big Brother erbij op Stratumseind. *De Volkskrant.*

de Kort, Y. (2014). Spotlight on aggression. *ILI.* https://www.de-escalate.nl/images/publications/De_Kort_2014_Spotlight_on_Aggression_ILI_Magazine_Volume-1.pdf

de Kort, Y. (2016). *Light on and in Context* (Inaugural lecture, Technical University Eindhoven). https://research.tue.nl/en/publications/light-on-and-in-context [13 May 2022].

den Ouden, H., & Valkenburg, A. C. (2013). Smart urban lighting. In A. Nigten (Ed.), *Real projects for real people* (Vol. 3, pp. 151–158). The Patching Zone.

Dopper, S. (2015, December 28). *Het grote Foucaultverzicht 2015: Het jaar in Michel Foucault.* Vice. https://www.vice.com/nl/article/nnaa3z/het-grote-foucaultverzicht-2015-het-jaar-in-michel-foucault-782

Edwards, L. (2018). Data protection: Enter the General Data Protection Regulation. In L. Edwards (Ed.), *Law, policy and the internet* (pp. 1–55). Hart Publishing.

Finch, K., & Tene, O. (2018). Smart cities: Privacy, transparency, and community. In E. Selinger, J. Polonetsky, & O. Tene (Eds.), *The Cambridge handbook of consumer privacy* (pp. 125–148). Cambridge University Press.

Finck, M., & Pallas, F. (2020). They who must not be identified: Distinguishing personal from non-personal data under the GDPR. *International Data Privacy Law, 10*(1), 11–36.

Foucault, M. (2009). *Security, territory, population: Lectures at the College de France 1977–78*. Palgrave Macmillan.

Galič, M. (2019). *Surveillance and privacy in smart cities and living labs: Conceptualising privacy for public space* [Doctoral dissertation, Tilburg University].

Galič, M., & Gellert, R. (2021). Data protection law beyond idientifiability? Atmospheric profiles, nudging and the Stratumseind Living Lab. *Computer Law & Security Review, 40*(1), 1–13.

Galič, M., Timan, T., & Koops, B. J. (2017). Bentham, Deleuze and beyond: An overview of surveillance theories from the panopticon to participation. *Philosophy & Technology, 30*(9), 9–37.

Gutwirth, S., & de Hert, P. (2008). Regulating profiling in a democratic constitutional state. In M. Hildebrandt & S. Gutwirth (Eds.), *Profiling the European citizen: Cross-disciplinary perspectives* (pp. 271–302). Springer.

Harcourt, B. E. (2014). Digital security in the expository society: Spectacle, surveillance, and exhibition in the neoliberal age of *Big Data*. *Columbia Public Law Research Paper*, No. 14-404. https://scholarship.law.columbia.edu/faculty_scholarship/1865

Hildebrandt, M. (2008a). Defining profiling: A new type of knowledge? In M. Hildebrandt & S. Gutwirth (Eds.), *Profiling the European citizen: cross-disciplinary perspectives* (pp. 17–45). Springer.

Hildebrandt, M. (2008b). A vision of ambient law. In R. Brownsword & K. Yeung (Eds.), *Regulating technologies* (pp. 175–191). Bloomsbury.

Hildebrandt, M., & Koops, B.-J. (2010). The challenges of ambient law and legal protection in the profiling era. *Modern Law Review, 73*(3), 428–460.

Hiller, J. S., & Blanke, J. M. (2017). Smart cities, big data, and the resilience of privacy. *Hastings Law Journal, 68*(2), 309–356.

Hoekstra, D. (2017, December 11). Netwerk van hypermoderne camera's op Stratumseind in Eindhoven gaat politie helpen. *Eindhovens Dagblad*.

Irish Data Protection Commissioner. (2017). *Annual report* [Brochure].

Jasserand, C. (2018). Law enforcement access to personal data originally collected by private parties: Missing data subjects' safeguards in directive 2016/680? *Computer Law & Security Review, 34*(1), 154–165.

Kalinauskaitė, I. (2014). *Measuring Stratumseind experience: De-escalate Stratumseind*. [PDEng report].

Kalinauskaitė, I., Haans, A., de Kort, Y., & IJsselsteijn, W. (2018). Atmosphere in an urban nightlife setting: A case study of the relationship between the socio-physical context and aggressive behaviour. *Scandinavian Journal of Psychology, 59*(2), 223–235.

Kanters, T. (2013). Living Lab, Onderdeel van Stratumseind 2.0, Smart sensors, smart interfaces, smart actors, smart lights, smart data, smart design, augmented reality, gaming. https://hetccv.nl/fileadmin/Bestanden/Onderwerpen/Grote_steden/netwerkdagen_eindhoven_living_lab.pdf

Kitchin, R. (2014). The real-time city? Big data and smart urbanism. *GeoJournal, 79*(1), 1–14.

Kitchin, R. (2015). The promise and perils of smart cities. *Society for Computers and Law.* https://www.scl.org/articles/3385-the-promise-and-perils-of-smart-cities

Kitchin, R. (2016). The ethics of smart cities and urban science. *Philosophical Transactions of the Royal Society A, 374*(2083), 1–15.

Klauser, F., Paasche, T., & Söderström, O. (2014). Michel Foucault and the smart city: Power dynamics inherent in contemporary governing through code. *Environment and Planning D: Society and Space, 32*(5), 869–885.

Koops, B. J., Newell, B. C., Timan, T., Škorvánek, I., Chokrevski, T., & Galič, M. (2017). A typology of privacy. *University of Pennsylvania Journal of International Law, 38*(483), 483–575.

Kotler, P. (1973). Atmospherics as a marketing tool. *Journal of Retailing, 49*(4), 48–64.

Kuindersma, C. (2018, November 29). De openbare ruimte als proeflab voor nudging. *Stadszaken.*

Lanzing, M. (2019). 'Strongly recommended': Re-visiting decisional privacy to judge hypernudging in self-tracking technologies. *Philosophy and Technology* 32, 549–568.

Lynskey, O. (2019). Criminal justice profiling and EU data protection law: Precarious protection from predictive policing. *International Journal of Law in Context, 15*(S2), 162–176.

Lyon, D. (2001). *Surveillance society: Monitoring everyday life.* Open University Press.

Merriam-Webster. (n.d.). Atmosphere. In *Merriam-Webster.com dictionary.* Retrieved May 13, 2022, from https://www.merriam-webster.com/dictionary/atmosphere

Monahan, T. (2018). The image of the smart city: Surveillance protocols and social inequality. In Y. Watanabe (Ed.), *Handbook of cultural security* (pp. 210–226). Edward Elgar Publishing.

Murakami Wood, D. (2015). Smart city, surveillance city. *Society for Computers and Law.* https://www.scl.org/articles/3405-smart-city-surveillance-city

Purtova, N. (2018a). Between the GDPR and the police directive: Navigating through the maze of information sharing in public-private partnerships. *International Data Privacy Law, 8*(1), 52–68.

Purtova, N. (2018b). The law of everything: Broad concept of personal data and future of EU data protection law. *Law, Innovation and Technology, 10*(1), 40–81.

Purtova, N. (2022). From knowing by name to targeting: The meaning of identification under the GDPR. *International Data Privacy Law, 12*(3), 163–183.

Rathenau Institute. (2019). *In Eindhoven herkent een algoritme vechtpartijen*. https://www.rathenau.nl/nl/digitale-samenleving/eindhoven-herkent-een-algoritme-vechtpartijen

Sadowski, J., & Pasquale, F. (2015). The spectrum of control: A social theory of the smart city. *First Monday 20*(7). https://doi.org/10.5210/fm.v20i7.5903

Schreurs, W., Hildebrandt, M., Kindt, E., & Vanfleteren, M. (2008). Cogitas, ergo sum: The role of data protection law and non-discrimination law in group profiling in the private sector. In M. Hildebrandt & S. Gutwirth (Eds.), *Profiling the European citizen: Cross-disciplinary perspectives* (pp. 241–270). Springer.

Schuilenburg, M., & Peeters, R. (2018). Smart cities and the architecture of security: Pastoral power and the scripted design of public space. *City, Territory and Architecture 5*(13), 2–9.

Studio 040. (2018). *Eindhovense innovatie is voorbeeld voor de rest van het land, Staatssecretaris brengt bezoek aan Stratumseind*. https://archief.studio040.nl/eindhovense- innovatie- is- voorbeeld- voor- de- rest- van- het- land- staatssecretaris- brengt- bezoek- aan- stratumseind/content/ item?1109883

Susser, D., Roessler, B., & Nissenbaum, H. (2019). Online manipulation: Hidden influences in a digital world. *Georgtown Law Technology Review, 4*(1), 1–45.

Thaler, R., & Sunstein, C. (2008). *Nudge: Improving decisions about health, wealth, and happiness*. Penguin.

Oddity.ai. (2020). *The Stratumseind pilot*. Oddity.ai. https://oddity.ai/blog/stratumseind-pilot/

Timan, T. (2013). *Changing landscapes of surveillance: Emerging technologies and participatory surveillance in Dutch nightscapes* [Doctoral dissertation, University of Twente].

Togman, R. (2021). Foucauldian security and the threat to democratic policy-making. *Critical Review of International Social and Political Philosophy, 24*(2), 230–252.

Urgessa, W. G. (2016). The protective capacity of the criterion of identifiability under EU data protection law. *European Data Protection Law Review, 2*(4), 521–531.

Valverde, M. (2008). Police, sovereignty, and law: Foucaultian reflections. In M. M. Dubber & M. Valverde (Eds.), *Police and the liberal state* (pp. 15–32). Stanford University Press.

van Gerwen, E. (2013). *Stratumseind 2.0: Plan van aanpak* [Brochure].

Wray, S. (2021). Why the city of Amsterdam developed its own crowd monitoring technology. *Cities Today*. https://cities-today.com/why-the-city-of-amsterdam-developed-its-own-crowd-monitoring-technology/

9. Data Used in Governmental Automated Decision-Making and Profiling: Towards More Practical Protection

Sascha van Schendel

Abstract

The chapter uses the examples of SyRI and OxRec to illustrate challenges pertaining to governmental automated decision-making and profiling, regarding: data used in a different context than the one in which they were gathered originally or in a specific context with its own unique aspects; bias in data; group profiles in a legal landscape of regulation of data towards individuals; and the assumption of the low risk of non-personal data. The chapter recommends that the regulatory framework be contextual enough to take all the above-discussed factors into account and pay attention to the importance of groups in data and the importance of non-personal data. This short chapter offers examples and arguments to further this discussion.

Keywords: profiling; automated decision-making; data protection; group data; SyRI; OxRec

1. Introduction

A variety of data are used in profiling and automated decision-making tools. These data range from non-personal data (such as aggregated data) to static personal data (such as age) to dynamic personal data (such as behavioural data). While the increase of available data and algorithms to detect patterns in such data can enhance the efficiency of decision-making processes and create new opportunities for enacting government policy, there are risks to fundamental rights involved in the use of new technologies. There is

Van der Sloot & van Schendel. *The Boundaries of Data*. Taylor & Francis Group, 2024
DOI: 10.5117/9789463729192_CH09

continuous academic debate about the risks of the use of automated decision-making and profiling. These risks include discrimination and stigmatisation, as well as false positives and false negatives potentially leading to erroneous decisions.[1] Another aspect that must be taken into account is the data that underpin the use of such tools: the data used in developing the tools and in specific analyses, along with what challenges follow from various types of data used for creating profiles further down the road. The great variety of data underpinning automated decision-making and profiling begs the question of whether each data type is equally suited for those purposes, and what that means for the fundamental protection rights of those to whom the data pertain or those who are confronted with the data in other ways. To analyse this situation, this chapter uses two short examples from practice to illustrate what data are used by governmental actors in automated decision-making and profiling. The examples are described in Section 2: the first is System Risk Indication (hereinafter: SyRI),[2] which is a fraud detection system deployed in the context of digitised social welfare by the Dutch government; the second is the OxRec,[3] which is a risk assessment tool for advising in trial and probation decisions used in the Netherlands. One example comes from the administrative branch of government and the other from the criminal justice branch. Each comes with its own specific contextual factors; however, together the examples illustrate the different types of data used and their challenges.

Following a short description of SyRI and OxRec, Section 3 provides an analysis, in which I use the case studies to illustrate several challenges pertaining to the data used in governmental automated decision-making and profiling. In the analysis, I discuss the following points: data used in a different context than the one in which they were gathered or in a specific context with its own unique aspects; bias in data; group profiles in a legal landscape of regulation of data towards individuals; and the assumption of the low risk of non-personal data.

Although the chapter is aimed more at illustrating practices revolving around data, it also has a legal dimension, as I assess whether the regulatory framework aligns with the practical reality. I examine these challenges in light of the current provisions for profiling and automated decision-making under EU data protection law: Article 22 of the General Data Protection Regulation (hereinafter: GDPR) and Article 11 of the Law Enforcement

1 For a brief description, see van Schendel (2019).

2 For a description see District court The Hague (2020) (English version).

3 For an overview of OxRec, see https://oxrisk.com/oxrec-nl-2-backup/.

Directive (hereinafter: LED).[4] Pursuant to these arguments, in Section 4, I propose that we take a different view on profiling and automated decision-making than we do under current data protection law, with Article 22 GDPR and Article 11 LED, which are more adaptive to the current reality and take the group dimension of data and the use of non-personal data into account.

2. Case studies: SyRI and OxRec

2.1. SyRI

SyRI is a project-based system used under the authority of the Dutch Ministry of Social Welfare and Employment. It is used to prevent and combat fraud relating to social security and income-dependent schemes, taxes and social security and labour laws. SyRI is a system that can have different collaborative public sector partners for each project that it is used in; several governmental actors together can launch a request with the Ministry to use SyRI. SyRI is a collaborative environment in which actors share data and work with a predetermined risk model for each different collaborative project. Data are run through the system, and SyRI flags which individuals are high-risk or low risk for one or more of the three types of fraud. The results for low risk are deleted, and the citizens that are labelled as high-risk can be investigated further.[5]

In the past, SyRI was used without a specific legal basis: it functioned on a nationwide structure of intervention teams. In 2003 the bodies involved in this structure completed a Cooperation Agreement for Intervention Teams. The agreement created a two-level structure: a National Intervention Teams Steering Group (called the LSI) and projects carried out at the regional level by Anti-Fraud Regional Platforms. In 2004 a legal basis was provided for the linking of data in the Work and Social Assistance Act (District court The Hague, 2020, paras. 3.5–3.8). It was not until 2014 that a specific legal basis for SyRI was adopted in the Work and Income (Implementation Organisation Structure) Act, more commonly called the SUWI Act. More detailed provisions were provided in the SUWI Decree, following the SUWI Act.

4 For detailed legal analysis of data protection instruments or notions, see chapters 10 through 15 of this book.

5 For an elaborate description of SyRI in English see District court The Hague (2020) (English version). Or, in Dutch, see also van Schendel (2020).

According to the SUWI Decree, SyRI works with large databases consisting of many sources, all outlined in law:[6]

- labour data (data that can determine labour performed by an individual);
- data concerning administrative measures and sanctions imposed on an individual or company;
- tax data (e.g. which income taxes an individual has to pay);
- property data;
- data concerning refusal grounds for social benefits;
- trade data;
- housing details;
- identifying data (name, residential address, postal address, date of birth, gender, or data of administrative characteristics in case it pertains to an organisation rather than an individual);
- data concerning the integration process (data that can determine whether an individual has certain integration requirements to comply with, such as language certificates);
- legal compliance data (e.g. outstanding fines);
- education data (data that can determine the need for financial support in paying for education);
- pension data;
- data concerning reintegration into the labour market;
- data about debts;
- data concerning social benefits;
- data about permits and legal exemptions;
- healthcare insurance data.

However, in February 2020, the District Court of the Hague (District court The Hague, 2020) determined that the current legal provisions underpinning the SyRI system (Section 65 SUWI Act and Chapter 5a SUWI Decree) violated Article 8 of the European Convention of Human Rights. Meanwhile, a new legal basis (Eerste Kamer, 2020) is being developed by the Dutch legislature.

Over the years, SyRI has been deployed in 27 projects. One of the most notable ones, and a good illustration for this chapter, is the Waterproof project from 2005. In the Waterproof project, to verify the living situation of recipients of social benefits in 65 municipalities, records pertaining to the consumption figures of water companies were compared to living details and pollution units of the water boards. After some criticism

6 Article 5a.1 paragraph 3 SUWI Decree.

from the Dutch DPA, a black box environment was set up for the record sharing; this was ended in 2010 (District court The Hague, 2020, para. 3.8). The Minister responsible for the use of the SyRI system referred to it as a 'neighbourhood-oriented approach', meaning that addresses in a particular neighbourhood of a municipality were investigated by the intervention team in the context of fraud, and the purpose of these projects was to contribute to the improvement of living conditions in such neighbourhoods. According to the Minister, these projects also paid specific attention to offering care and support to persons exhibiting 'care-avoiding behaviour'.[7]

2.2. OxRec

The three Dutch probation authorities[8] use the RISc (recidivism estimation scale) as a risk classification tool to help them with the estimation of recidivism risk. The RISc is used in all stages of the criminal trial: in arraignment before the Examining Magistrate, in the criminal trial, in decision-making in penitentiary programmes, in decision-making about 'placement at the discretion of the state'[9] and in decision-making on the conditions of probation (Probation Netherlands, n.d.). OxRec is used as an actuarial risk assessment tool within the RISc system relying on both static and dynamic risk factors.[10] OxRec was originally developed by Oxford University and designed to make statistical analyses of the risk of general recidivism and recidivism for violent crimes. In 2017 OxRec was adapted for the Dutch criminal justice system using data from Statistics Netherlands, the research and documentation centre and data from the three Dutch probation authorities (Probation Netherlands, n.d.). Actuarial risk assessment tools can be best described as tools that focus on the correlations between the characteristics of a specific individual and recidivism data, generating an indication of the recidivism of groups of people with the same characteristic as the specific individual in question (Probation Netherlands, n.d.). Thus, group risk profiles are applied to individuals to be assessed. In the use of

7 Parliamentary Papers II 2014/15, 17050, 508; see also District court The Hague (2020), para. 3.9.

8 Reclassering Nederland, Leger des Heils jeugdbescherming & reclassering and Stichting Verslavingsreclassering GGZ.

9 In Dutch this is referred to as 'TBS'. It is a hospital order that a court can impose if an offender has a serious psychiatric disorder.

10 Static factors are factors that cannot be changed by the suspect or offender, such as age or criminal history. Dynamic factors are factors that are prone to change, such as employment status, address, financial situation and so forth.

OxRec in the Dutch system, probation officers draft an advisory report about the situation in question in addition to the advice from the OxRec system. The probation officer's recommendation can deviate from the one provided by OxRec (Probation Netherlands, n.d.). Through the RISc, the results from the risk analysis per aspect – such as finances, relationships and substance use – are shown in a traffic light model, ranging from green to orange to red, next to the risk estimation from the OxRec (Probation Netherlands, n.d.).

As one of the goals of the criminal justice system is to ensure a safe society, the use of risk classification tools is important. The tools are used to identify and classify dangerous individuals who pose a risk to society and to remove them from society for as long as they pose a significant risk, e.g. by imprisonment (van Wingerden et al., 2011, p. 9). In recent years, this risk management function has come to the fore in the criminal justice system, leading to an increase in automated tools to perform the risk assessments (van Wingerden et al., 2011; de Vries et al., 2021). Risk assessment tools, such as OxRec, are generally labelled as assisting tools, meaning that they are not fully automated decision-makers but merely advisory in the decision-making process. This advisory function raises the question of how the tools' use relates to the decision-making process of, for example, judges and probation authorities.

According to a study on the use of risk assessment in sentencing in the Netherlands, there are three non-mutually exclusive ways in which results from tools like OxRec can be used. The first is that a judge relies on the report of the probation authority, which is based on the RISc assessment. The second is that a judge makes their own risk assessment based on static risk factors (e.g. gender, age, criminal history), which are not the most prominent aspects in RISc assessments; the third is that a judge makes their own risk assessment based on dynamic risk factors, which are risk factors related to the social circumstances (e.g. employment status, substance use) and are also the prominent factors of the RISc assessment (van Wingerden et al., 2011). In this way, the RISc (and thus OxRec) can play a role of varying prominence in each case.

There are three legal frameworks at play here. First, there are principles from the Dutch Code of Criminal of Procedure that apply if the OxRec analysis is used in a criminal trial. Second, there is the landscape of legal instruments applying to the probation authorities, who are responsible for the use of the tools. Third, there are provisions from the Police Data Act and the Judicial Data and Criminal Records Act that apply to data analysis.[11] In

11 Which both implement the EU Law Enforcement Directive.

the Dutch Code of Criminal of Procedure, we can find provisions, which regulate that the Public Prosecution Service can call in the assistance of a probation institution and can commission a pre-sentence report; the same power is assigned to the examining magistrate or the judge to call in the assistance of probation authorities for advice.[12] Thus, the Dutch Code of Criminal Procedure does not regulate how the probation authorities conduct their assessment in any way. If a report from a probation authority is used by the court to determine the type or severity of the sanction that will be imposed, general principles of sentencing apply. The court is required to motivate its verdict and to explain which reasons have led to choosing the sanction in question.[13] Thus, the court must motivate why it follows or does not follow a recommendation from the probation authorities including the OxRec assessment and why a certain sanction is justified. This requirement of explanation does not stipulate in any way what type of advice from the probation authorities can or cannot be used, or what this advice must look like.

For the second category of legislation specific to probation authorities, the most prominent instruments are the 1995 Probation Regulation (Reclasseringsregeling, 1995) and the 2005 Probation Implementation Act (Uitvoeringsregeling reclassering, 2005). These instruments regulate the organisational aspects of the probation authorities and determine when a recommendation or report must be or can be drafted. However, neither of these instruments specifies how risk assessment tools can be used in probation advice or otherwise mentions the use of risk assessment tools. More specifically, the law does not regulate or prescribe which factors or data points should or should not be used in the assessment, under what conditions the assessment should be performed – such as whether an algorithm can be used or how factors should be weighed – nor what the accuracy of the risk assessment tool should be. Internally, there can be guidance documents from the probation authorities on how to use OxRec, which outline which data can go into the assessment, what the rates are for false positives and negatives and guidelines on technical control measures and other methodological safeguards (Maas et al., 2020). These guidelines are not a part of the regulatory framework.

Third, where personal data are processed, data protection legislation applies. In the context of criminal prosecution, this is the Police Data Act and, more importantly, the Judicial Data and Criminal Records Act. We can

12 Article 147 CCP articles 177 and 310 of the CCP.

13 Article 359 paragraph 5 and 6 CCP.

distinguish two different scenarios here: on the one hand, systems like OxRec can be used to make automated decisions, such as determining sentences; on the other, they can also be used in an advisory context for the court. For automated decisions, extra safeguards apply, pursuant to the Police Data Act and the Judicial Data and Criminal Records Act, following EU data protection legislation. In the case of OxRec, following the reports from the probation authorities, OxRec is only used in an advisory capacity; the advice on the sentence is always determined by the 'human decision-maker', i.e. the probation officer. In turn, the report is presented to the court, but the court still takes its own decision on the sentence. It is thus not very likely that such systems entail automated decision-making. Nonetheless, for both scenarios, the data protection framework does not specifically determine which data points can be used in profiling or automated decision-making; in terms of types of data, there are only extra safeguards for the use of special categories of data which are deemed more sensitive.

Overall, unlike for SyRI, for OxRec the regulatory framework does not determine whether AI can be used or not, which types of data can be used, how different types of data are weighted or any other similar lines of inquiry.

3. Analysis

3.1. Context

When data are collected, they are collected in a specific context, which is characterised by at least the following elements. First of all, there is a specific purpose for which the data are collected at the moment of collection. Second, there is a specific perspective on the subject of the data. This is not to be confused with the data protection term 'data subject', because outside the scope of data protection law, the subject of the data can also be a group of individuals or a person that cannot be identified in said data. Third, there is a specific actor gathering the data, bringing its own perspective or bias and capabilities to the collection. In automated decision-making and profiling applications, this context tends to get lost or abandoned.

In data protection legislation, we can find the term 'profile' being used to refer to images or representations of people through data:

> profiling means any form of automated processing of personal data consisting of the use of personal data to evaluate certain personal aspects

> relating to a natural person, in particular to analyse or predict aspects concerning that natural person's performance at work, economic situation, health, personal preferences, interests, reliability, behaviour, location or movements. (Article 4[4] GDPR)

Profiling is thus focused on evaluating aspects, which is useful in decision-making. However, profiling consists of more than just evaluation. To get to that point, one needs to take several steps, such as defining categories, labelling characteristics as belonging to specific categories and grouping individuals into the categories based on their apparent characteristics. In this sense, profiles are a type of image that can be used to identify and represent someone (Hildebrandt & Backhouse, 2005). Profiles include an assumption that an individual has all the characteristics attributed to them in the profile. This assumption, together with the possibility of comparing different individuals and groups easily, enables the mastery of large quantities of data. Profiling is essentially a way to cope with information overload. As exponentially more data become available, it provides the means necessary to work with that quantity of data and extract meaningful information (Hildebrandt & Gutwirth, 2008, p. 1). Processing data in this way does not necessarily imply that the analysis results in meaningful information; correlations do not require a causal relationship between different characteristics, nor a meaningful relation between data points.

Thus, in profiles there will be data points connected that were originally in different contexts. We can see an example of this in the case of SyRI. In some instances, data about water consumption and water billing were the main data in a risk profile on fraud. The use of data in a different context than what they were originally gathered for raises issues from a privacy perspective. For example, people tend to have a general expectation that data about their water usage will be used mainly for purposes like determining the water bill, efficiently running the drinking water system, fairly dividing drinking water or efficiently running the sewage system. Generally speaking, water data being used to determine instance of fraud is not what most people would expect. This is partially why projects like Waterproof under SyRI were received with such scepticism: people felt surveilled after it became publicly known that these kinds of data was being used for these kinds of purposes. In the court case against the legislation that regulated the SyRI system, claims were put forward owing to privacy violations and the chilling effects of data-driven social welfare systems (District court The Hague, 2020). The idea that people have a certain assumption about data collection within a particular context is not new. Nissenbaum raised awareness of this issue with her theory on privacy as contextual integrity:

> Contextual integrity ties adequate protection for privacy to norms of specific contexts, demanding that information gathering and dissemination be appropriate to that context and obey the governing norms of distribution within it. (Nissenbaum, 2004)

Nonetheless, the issue of context still plays a role today in digitised and datafied government systems.

Concerns surrounding the introduction of more data-driven systems in the context of social welfare were also voiced by the United Nations Special Rapporteur on extreme poverty and human rights in a report in 2019 on the digital welfare state. Under the concept 'digital welfare state', he describes the following developments:

> new forms of governance are emerging which rely significantly on the processing of vast quantities of digital data from all available sources, use predictive analytics to foresee risk, automate decision-making, and remove discretion from human decision-makers. (OHCHR, 2019b)

The Special Rapporteur mentions challenges of risk scoring and classification, such as enforcing individual rights when groups are targeted, a lack of transparency surrounding the process and risk classification reinforcing or exacerbating existing inequalities and discrimination (OHCHR, 2019b). The Special Rapporteur offered a separate analysis of the Dutch SyRI risk profiling system in view of the court case against the use of SyRI and submitted his analysis to the court in an amicus brief (OHCHR, 2019a). According to the Special Rapporteur, such a system requires assurances that particular groups are not being unfairly singled out, and SyRI can have a hugely negative impact on the rights of poor individuals without affording them due process (OHCHR, 2019a). This is another part of the contextualisation of data collection illustrated by SyRI: the data collected are gathered about a specific subject, namely groups in society that receive social benefits. This is a context that creates its own specific challenges that should be taken into account, as it includes a potentially vulnerable group within society. As such, it is even more crucial not to blur the boundaries of that context. Nonetheless, as stated before, one of the hopes behind SyRI projects like Waterproof was to improve care and support provisions to persons exhibiting 'care-avoiding behaviour'. This ambiguous phrasing is different from fraud detection, which is more a criminal, or at least administrative, justice goal. Offering governmental support is something entirely different than fraud detection.

All three aspects of context in which data are gathered are illustrated through the SyRI example: the purpose for which data are collected, the subjects about whom data are collected and the perspective of the actor who is gathering the data. It is important to align all three of these aspects to prevent privacy, opacity, discrimination and stigmatisation problems. In practice, all factors of context matter; the question is to what extent the legal framework is able to take full account of the context of data, as legal norms or classifications can be too rigid or binary.

3.2. Bias

Data are not as objective or clear cut as they might first appear. A point of concern that is often put forward in discourse on automation, Big Data and profiling is that of bias in data (Vogiatzoglou, 2019; Friedman & Nissenbaum, 1996; Kitchin, 2013; Mittelstadt et al., 2016). Bias, in this context, could be described as an inclination or prejudice that does not (completely) reflect an objective state of affairs but that plays a role through choices made by humans in the process, usually not consciously. Bias could, for example, be present in training data, in the data collected for analysis, in selecting the input data and in inferring new data (Bennet Moses & Chan, 2014, p. 648; Van Brakel, 2016). Since data are usually the start of the process and only one of the components, these choices echo throughout the process and the outcomes. In addition, bias is not only an issue in itself, but it is a problem throughout the process, also manifesting itself in machine learning systems through rules, training inputs, hypotheses and assumptions introduced in the designing of algorithms (Vogiatzoglou, 2019; Bennett Moses & Chan 2018).

When we look at the example of applications like OxRec, which is used in the criminal justice and policing sector, there is the additional complexity that comes with police data. For example, as Shapiro explains, the data in policing applications suffer from their own particular issues with bias:

> In the context of law enforcement and 'predictive policing' applications, the focus has been on the data used to train predictive algorithms. Data that are limited, incomplete, inaccurate, or biased due to discriminatory policing practices stand to reinforce disparate treatments for already marginalized communities. (Shapiro 2019)

An important point to keep in mind concerning the use of law enforcement data is that these data are limited. Law enforcement data can be influenced by underreporting of crimes or by a focus on certain crimes or groups over others (Barrett 2017; Joh 2017). Crime data are not real time data of actual crime; they simply reflect the rate of crime that was caught or reported and recorded (Barrett 2017; Joh 2017). So, not only is crime data not a perfect mirror of crime occurring, but the police also make choices regarding their data, which influences the data through the way they observe, notice, act upon, collect, categorise and record them (Joh 2017). Another issue to take into account is that data are also impacted by the act of policing itself (Bennett Moses & Chan 2018). This effect is especially visible in predictive policing targeting locations. Predictive policing involves officers being sent to a specific area based on predictive policing algorithms. The increased presence of police in these areas can increase the recording of crimes there. In turn, this can create the illusion or assumption that actual crime in that area is increasing, while it is just the recording of crime that has increased. It can also perpetuate a bias in the model by promoting the assumption that there is crime in an area so that crime is increasingly recorded. Facts can become self-perpetuating: what might seem to be an objective process can become a means of perpetuating historic discrimination or bias (Bennett Moses & Chan, 2018). A system like OxRec is focused less on policing and more on advising in probation and sentencing. Nonetheless, even in OxRec, crime data and criminal justice data play a role in the assessment.

Bias in data also plays a role in governmental profiling and automated decision-making outside the policing context. For example, factors such as postal code, gender, age, education level or income can be really good predictors (for example, to determine the likelihood that someone will commit crimes), but they can also be indicators for ethnic profiling (van Dijck, 2020; Frase, 2009). We see a similar problem in profiling and automated decision-making in the context of social welfare in systems, such as SyRI, where interventions can be location- or neighbourhood-based and thus indirectly target specific societal groups who become overrepresented in the system. For all data, it should be considered that they are gathered in a certain way and that data are always a representation of reality. When we talk about governmental decision-making that is not automated, there is also something to be said for bias in human thinking and decision-making. Nonetheless, a crucial point is that the more data-driven systems become, the more difficult it is to disentangle the biased data from decision-making, making the bias more hidden and exacerbating the inequalities.

It should be kept in mind that data in governmental automated decision-making and profiling are part of a system: design choices and limitations in a system influence what data are gathered and how. Although this is a complex matter to disentangle, there should be more consideration of issues like bias and the objectivity granted to data in its regulation.

3.3. Effects of Group Profiles

Profiles often involve some component of aggregation: data from individuals are combined to detect patterns and correlations. Together, these correlations can form a profile that represents an idea of an individual, such as a profile reflecting a group of people with a shared interest or shared behaviour. Thus, this kind of profile is about a group of individuals who share data points rather than information about one specific individual. For group profiles, there is an assumption that the creation and use of them is less harmful than profiles about specific individuals: the legal framework tends to offer protection only if the profile is applied to an individual or if the profile is comprised of traits of specific (identified) individuals. For example, in data protection law, safeguards are attached to the use of profiles and decision-making only on the individual level. Article 22 of the GDPR and Article 11 of the LED both limit automated decision-making and profiling, but only when it comes to a decision concerning a data subject, thus an individual.

Article 22(1) GDPR determines:

> The data subject shall have the right not to be subject to a decision based solely on automated processing, including profiling, which produces legal effects concerning him or her or similarly significantly affects him or her.

Article 11(1) LED determines:

> Member States shall provide for a decision based solely on automated processing, including profiling, which produces an adverse legal effect concerning the data subject or significantly affects him or her, to be prohibited unless authorised by Union or Member State law to which the controller is subject and which provides appropriate safeguards for the rights and freedoms of the data subject, at least the right to obtain human intervention on the part of the controller.

The headings of Article 22 GDPR and Article 11 LED make clear that both provisions apply only to decisions about individuals. The text of the provisions further emphasises this by mentioning the data subject in singular form. The scope of the LED and GDPR applying only to the processing of personal data and the focus on natural persons demonstrate that these instruments are tailored to the individual. Over the years, there have been more and more discussions about the strong individual emphasis of data protection legislation at the expense of attention for groups and collectives.[14] This point of criticism on instruments like the GDPR and the LED becomes painfully clear in relation to profiling. While the protection offered by data protection, such as in Article 22 GDPR and Article 11 LED, focuses on the individual, algorithmic harms in profiling arise from how systems classify groups or compare individuals, creating a mismatch between profiling practices and the legal safeguards. Some scholars argue that this issue with groups versus individuals has been an issue in data protection and privacy legislation for some time (de Hert & Papakonstantinou, 2021; Taylor et al., 2017, p. 238) and that the issue remains underexplored in the context of automated decision-making and explanations (Edwards & Veale, 2017, p. 22). The creation of groups and categories of individuals for the purposes of creating or applying profiles means that profiling practices and decision-making can have risks or harmful effects that go beyond the individual or are not even applicable at the individual level. This concern also applies to automated decision-making, where scenarios are possible in which a decision has an effect that goes beyond the individual and therefore Article 22 GDPR or Article 11 LED does not apply to the situation, or the provisions only apply to one individual while the actual scope of the decision is much broader. Collective decisions affecting multiple individuals or groups can, for example, be based on the shared characteristic of living in a certain area, such as is the case with automated decisions taken by the police to increase police surveillance in a certain geographical area, affecting all data subjects living in it (Brkan, 2019, p. 100).

The use of profiles also means that information about categories or groups becomes the most prominent data, sometimes more so than personal data of an individual. As Edwards and Veale explain, profiles can be seen as belonging to a group rather than to an individual (Edwards & Veale, 2017, pp. 35–36). The merit of the use of profiles is not so much the identification of characteristics of individuals but rather the comparison with other individuals in the dataset (Edwards & Veale, 2017, pp. 35–36). For example, using an example from criminal justice, an individual who has committed a string of burglaries is more likely to commit another burglary than someone

14 For the field of data protection, see for example Mantelero (2016) and Taylor et al. (2017).

who has a record of traffic violations. To apply this to a more complicated scenario, the knowledge of interest is what makes one individual more likely to commit a certain type of crime compared to another, more so than identifying the individual characteristics of a person. Mittelstadt talks of algorithmically assembled groups, to which data protection (and privacy) legislation would not be attuned and do not offer protection, since the focus of legislation is on the individual. In algorithmically assembled groups, individuals are linked through patterns and correlations based on behaviour, preferences and other characteristics using offline identifiers (e.g. age, ethnicity, geographical location) and new behavioural identity tokens, allowing for predictions and decisions to be taken at a group level (Mittelstadt, 2017, p. 476).

The provisions on profiling under the GDPR and LED are thus limited in scope since they only protect against automated decision-making if a decision is applied on an individual level and only towards that individual. In addition to this limitation in *ratione personae*, a possible threshold can also be found in the requirement of processing personal data. Decision-making systems not involving the processing of personal data but focusing on the aggregate or the group could fall outside the scope of this legislation (Bygrave, 2020).[15] Hildebrandt argues that even if we claim that a profile itself becomes personal data once it is applied to an individual, this still does not offer protection to the group and group profile in question (Hildebrandt, 2015). Following this line of reasoning, neither Article 11 LED nor Article 22 GDPR cover a decision impacting only groups, or a collective decision. Edwards and Veale reason that excluding collective automated decisions from the scope of protection creates an imbalance in how individual and collective automated decisions are treated, which could lead to the circumvention of the prohibition of individual automated decisions by adopting collective decisions. Therefore, they propose considering a collective or group decision as a bundle of individual decisions (Edwards & Veale, 2017). This would, however, lead to the protection of individuals still, focusing on individual harm. As such, it can be questioned whether this kind of approach would solve all the problems surrounding the scope of protection of individual decision-making.

Legal safeguards do not protect groups or take into account the effects of group profiles, but more pressingly, the legal framework also fails to acknowledge that evaluative profiles are not solely comprised of data about that specific person. As the profile is an estimation of the traits an individual

15 See further e.g. Mantelero (2016) and Mittelstadt (2017).

possesses, that estimation comes from patterns, extracted from the data of multiple individuals. This does not seem to be acknowledged in the GDPR or LED. Again, if we look at the example of OxRec, we can see this clearly: OxRec gives an indication of the recidivism risk of groups of people with certain characteristics.[16]

The legal regime focuses on the application of profiles to individuals, but it does not clearly regulate how these profiles come to be, nor does it take into account that group representations are applied to individuals as if all individuals in a group are always exactly the same. The legal regime does not match up with the practical reality, as the legal perspective focuses on the individual, while in practice, groups are often more important than individuals in terms of collecting data and creating profiles.

3.4. Assumptions About Lower Fundamental Rights: Risks of Non-Personal Data and Other Types of Data

A final problem is related to the assumptions behind the use of non-personal data. As data protection legislation only applies to personal data, this limited scope demonstrates the assumption that there is only a need to regulate data from a fundamental rights perspective. However, as data-driven processes (such as profiling and automated decision-making) are so dependent on non-personal data (such as statistics and aggregated data), non-personal data play an equally important role. Arguably, aggregated data and statistics actually fuel the constructions of models and compilations of categories. Ultimately, this means that the use of non-personal data affects groups and individuals when profiles are applied to them and/or lead to decisions impacting them. The EU legislator has opted to only focus on the application of profiles on individuals with data protection legislation by focusing on human intervention as a safeguard and by setting requirements for when profiling and automated decision-making can be deployed. However, in this approach the EU legislator leaves the door wide open for the gathering of statistical and aggregated data and for the creation of profiles.

Correlations and patterns also create new meaning, and thus seemingly insignificant personal data can become highly significant (Hildebrandt, 2008). The same is true of non-personal data: they can be deemed not to contain sensitive or important information but, if combined with other data, can actually reveal a lot of traits, behaviours and other valuable information. This raises questions for legislators about how to protect individuals against

16 See also van Dijck (2020).

privacy infringements caused by the generation of information in unseen ways or ways that are not covered by existing data protection legislation and privacy safeguards.

In practice, it is difficult to draw strict boundaries between what data can or cannot be used in governmental profiling and automated decision-making. Data can be assumed not to be important while actually being much more sensitive than other types of personal data. A good example of this can be found in processes conducted by the Dutch Tax Administration that were deemed unlawful by the Dutch Data Protection Authority (DPA). In July 2020, the Dutch DPA determined that the benefits office of the Dutch Tax Administration should not have processed the nationality of childcare benefit applicants in the way it had been doing for years. According to the results of the DPA's investigation, this practice was unlawful and discriminatory.[17] This example of using nationality as an important factor in a profile shows that the value and sensitivity of a type of data are very much dependent on their situation or context.

4. Conclusion

This chapter offers food for thought on the various types of data that play a role in profiling and automated decision-making as used by public actors, ranging from personal to aggregated or statistical data. In practice, in the use of governmental profiling and automated decision-making systems, various issues arise in terms of the practical realities of data vis-à-vis the regulatory framework: the legal framework regulating these practices, which is most prominently the data protection framework, does not seem to take into account all aspects of practical reality. We can see examples of these issues in the use of systems like the Dutch SyRI and OxRec. More specifically, the legal framework does not seem to take into account that data are often gathered in a different context than that for which they are used in profiling and for automatic decision-making, or that this context comes with its own complexities. It could be argued that the regulatory framework should make reference to this and acknowledge more of this contextuality. While there was little room to fully explore contextuality in the data protection legal framework, a few important issues are highlighted here. When data are collected, they are collected in specific contexts, which

17 See https://autoriteitpersoonsgegevens.nl/en/news/methods-used-dutch-tax-administration-unlawful-and-discriminatory.

are characterised at the very least by a specific purpose for collection, a specific perspective on the subject of the data and a specific actor gathering the data. In automated decision-making and profiling applications, this context tends to get lost or abandoned. We can see this reflected in bias in data bound to a specific context almost as a subset of that overarching problem. In addition, profiles and automated decision-making in practice have a very group-oriented nature, while the legal framework focuses very much on the individual level. This creates a risk of nuances and context getting lost in the translation from the group level to the individual level. Lastly, in practice, data that are labelled as 'non-personal data' by the regulatory framework, such as aggregated data and statistical data, play a key role in the creation of profiles, putting another strain on the regulatory framework focusing its protection on personal data instead. Similarly, we can also see examples where data are expected to be less important and deserving of legal protection, while this is not the case in reality. Or there are examples where data are deemed usable in governmental profiling, but for the context in which they were collected, they are actually too sensitive for that purpose.

All in all, to maintain a perspective on data used in governmental automated decision-making and profiling in tune with reality, the regulatory framework needs to be able to be contextual enough to take all the factors discussed into account and pay attention to the importance of groups in data and the importance of non-personal data. This short chapter has offered examples and arguments to further this discussion.

References

Barrett, L. (2017). Reasonably suspicious algorithms: Predictive policing at the United States border. *New York University Review of Law & Social Change, 41*(3), 327–366.

Bennet Moses, L., & Chan, J. (2014). Using big data for legal and law enforcement decisions: Testing the new tools. *University of New South Wales Law Journal, 37*(2), 643–678.

Bennett Moses, L., & Chan J. (2018). Algorithmic prediction in policing: Assumptions, evaluation, and accountability. *Policing and Society, 28*(7), 806–822.

Brkan, M. (2019). Do algorithms rule the world? Algorithmic decision-making and data protection in the framework of the GDPR and beyond. *International Journal of Law and Information Technology, 27*(2), 91–121.

Bygrave, L. (2020). *Machine learning, cognitive sovereignty and data protection rights with respect to automated decisions.* University of Oslo Faculty of Law Legal

Studies Research Paper Series No. 2020-35. [Version 1.1; final version published in Ienca, M., et al. (Eds.). (2022). *Cambridge handbook of life sciences, information technology and human rights*. Cambridge University Press.]

de Hert, P., & Papakonstantinou, V. (2021). Framing Big Data in the Council of Europe and the EU data protection law systems: Adding 'should' to 'must' via soft law to address more than only individual harms. *Computer Law & Security Review, 40*. https://doi.org/10.1016/j.clsr.2020.105496

de Vries, M., Bijlsma, J., Mackor, A. R., Bex, F., & Meynen, G. (2021). AI-risicotaxatie: nieuwe kansen en risico's voor statistische voorspellingen van recidive. *Boom Strafblad, 2*, 58–66.

District court The Hague. (2020, February 5). ECLI:NL:RBDHA:2020:1878.

Eerste Kamer. (2020). *Wet gegevensverwerking door samenwerkingsverbanden* [Draft bill]. https://www.eerstekamer.nl/wetsvoorstel/35447_wet_gegevensverwerking_door

Edwards, L., & Veale, M. (2017). Slave to the algorithm? Why a 'right to an explanation' is probably not the remedy you are looking for. *Duke Law & Technology Review, 16*(1), 35–36.

Edwards, L. (2016). Privacy, security and data protection in smart cities: A critical EU Law perspective. *European Data Protection Law Review 2*(1), 28–58.

Frase, R. S. (2009). What explains persistent racial disproportionality in Minnesota's prison and jail populations? *Crime and Justice: A Review of Research, 38*, 201–280.

Friedman, B., & Nissenbaum, H. (1996). Bias in computer systems. *ACM Transactions on Information Systems 14*(3), 330–347.

Hildebrandt, M. (2008). Profiles and correlatable humans. In D. E. Price & B. Weiler (Eds.), *Who owns knowledge? Knowledge and the law* (pp. 265–284). Routledge.

Hildebrandt, M. (2016). *Smart technologies and the end(s) of law: Novel entanglements of law and technology*. Edward Elgar.

Hildebrandt M., & Backhouse J. (2005). *Descriptive analysis and inventory of profiling practices. FIDIS Project Deliverable 7.2.* http://www.fidis.net

Hildebrandt M., & Gutwirth, S. (2008). General introduction and overview. In M. Hildebrandt & S. Gutwirth (Eds.), *Profiling the European citizen: Cross-disciplinary perspectives* (pp. 1–13). Springer.

Joh, E. E. (2017). Feeding the machine: Policing, crime cata, & algorithms. *William & Mary Bill of Rights Journal, 26*(2), art. 3. https://scholarship.law.wm.edu/wmborj/vol26/iss2/3

Kitchin, R. (2013). Big data and human geography: Opportunities, challenges and risks. *Dialogues in Human Geography, 3*(3), 262–267.

Maas, M., Legters, E., & Fazel S. (2020). Professional en risicotaxatieinstrument hand in hand: Hoe de reclassering risico's inschat. *Nederlands Juristenblad, 28*, 2055–2058.

Mantelero, A. (2016). Personal data for decisional purposes in the age of analytics: From an individual to a collective dimension of data protection. *Computer Law & Security Review, 32*(2), 238–255.

Mittelstadt, B. From individual to group privacy in big data analytics. *Philosophy & Technology, 30*, 475–494.

Mittelstadt, B. D., Allo, P., Taddeo, M., Wachter, S., & Floridi, L. (2016). The ethics of algorithms: Mapping the debate. *Big Data & Society, 3*(2). https://doi.org/10.1177/2053951716679679

Nissenbaum, H. (2004). Symposium, privacy as contextual integrity. *Washington Law Review, 79*(1). https://digitalcommons.law.uw.edu/wlr/vol79/iss1/10

OHCHR. (2019a, September 26). Brief by the United Nations Special Rapporteur on extreme poverty and human rights as Amicus Curiae in the case of NJCM c.s./De Staat der Nederlanden (SyRI) before the District Court of The Hague (case number: C/09/550982/HA ZA 18/388). https://www.ohchr.org/Documents/Issues/Poverty/Amicusfinalversionsigned.pdf

OHCHR (2019b, October 11). Report of the Special Rapporteur on extreme poverty and human rights, A/74/48037, p. 3. https://www.ohchr.org/Documents/Issues/Poverty/A_74_48037_AdvanceUneditedVersion.docx

Probation Netherlands. (n.d.). *RISC*. Reclassering Nederland. https://www.reclassering.nl/over-de-reclassering/wat-wij-doen/risc

Reclasseringsregeling. (1995). No. 455985/94/6. Overheid.nl. https://wetten.overheid.nl/BWBR0007120/2019-06-26

Shapiro, A. (2019). Predictive policing for reform? Indeterminacy and intervention in big data policing. *Surveillance & Society, 17*(3–4), 456–472.

Taylor, L., Floridi, L., & van der Sloot, B. (Eds.). (2017). *Group privacy. New challenges of data technologies*. Springer.

Uitvoeringsregeling reclassering. (2005). No. DDS 5378751. Overheid.nl. https://wetten.overheid.nl/BWBR0019016/2005-11-25.

Van Brakel, R. (2016). Pre-emptive Big Data surveillance and its (dis)empowering consequences: The case of predictive policing. In B. van der Sloot, D. Broeders, & E. Schrijvers (Eds.), *Exploring the boundaries of Big Data*. Amsterdam University Press.

van Dijck, G. (2020). Algoritmische risicotaxatie van recidive: Over de Oxford Risk of Recidivism tool (OXREC), ongelijke behandeling en discriminatie in strafzaken. *Nederlands Juristenblad, 95*(25), 1784–1790.

van Schendel, S. (2019). The challenges of risk profiling used by law enforcement: Examining the cases of COMPAS and SyRI. In L. Reins (Ed.). *Regulating new technologies in uncertain times* (pp. 225–240). T.M.C. Asser Press. https://doi.org/10.1007/978-94-6265-279-8_12

van Schendel, S. (2020). *Noot bij Rb. Den Haag, 5 februari 2020 (De rechtbank komt tot het oordeel dat de SyRI-wetgeving in haar huidige vorm de toets van artikel 8 lid 2 EVRM niet doorstaat). 2020/87.* [Case note on: Rechtbank Den Haag, 5/02/20, C-09-550982-HA ZA 18-388, ECLI:NL:RBDHA:2020:865 Computerrecht, 2020(3), 183-188]

van Wingerden, S. G. C., Moerings, M., & van Wilsem, J. A. (2011). *Recidiverisico en straftoemeting, 3*(7). Sdu Uitgevers.

Vogiatzoglou, P. (2019). Mass surveillance, predictive policing and the implementation of the CJEU and ECtHR requirement of objectivity. *European Journal of Law and Technology, 10*(1). https://ejlt.org/index.php/ejlt/article/view/669/903

10. Data: A Very Short Introduction to the EU Galaxy and to Five Potential Paths Forward

Bart van der Sloot

Abstract
The General Data Protection Regulation is essentially the same as the 1995 Data Protection Directive, which was based to a large extent on the Council of Europe Convention 108 from 1981 and two resolutions from 1973 and 1974. Societal and technological changes undermine the fundaments of the GDPR. Additional EU data and technology regulation only makes matters more complex and increases the gap between the legal paradigm, on the one hand, and technological practice and societal reality, on the other. That is why this chapter discusses a number of regulatory alternatives, each of which has potential advantages as well as disadvantages.

Keywords: General Data Protection Regulation; EU data & technology regulation; AI; open data; de-anonymisation; regulatory alternatives

1. Introduction

The goal of this chapter is unambitious. It is to describe the basic anchor points for the regulation of data within the EU (for a great starting point, see Bygrave, 2002). What are the factors that play a role in determining which rules apply, to whom do they apply and what they entail? This chapter will focus primarily on the General Data Protection Regulation (GDPR) to provide a blueprint for the approach to data regulation taken in the EU (Section 2). Subsequently, it will provide the questions and challenges with respect to the approach adopted by the EU, especially in light of modern processing techniques (Section 3). Then, it will suggest that these questions and challenges are deepened by the fact that the EU takes different

Van der Sloot & van Schendel. *The Boundaries of Data*. Taylor & Francis Group, 2024
DOI: 10.5117/9789463729192_CH10

approaches to data regulation in legislative instruments other than the GDPR, which complicates the picture and may undermine the regulatory effectiveness of each of the instruments (Section 4). Finally, a sketch for alternative regulatory frameworks will be provided, taking into account the developments that have been sketched elsewhere in this book (Section 5).

2. GDPR

The basic topic this section covers regards the who, what, where, when and how of the data protection regime, in particular the GDPR. By going through the basic fundaments from a bird's-eye view, this section will not only arrive at a basic blueprint for how the EU approaches the regulation of data. It will also indicate what choices have not been made, what aspects are left outside the scope of the GDPR and what activities are not dealt with in detail.

2.1. Where

Location plays an important role in terms of the applicability of the data protection regime (for more in general, see Kohl, 2010). The GDPR either applies to the processing of personal data where the processing activities are executed in the context of an establishment in the EU or where the data concern the activities of citizens in the EU (Article 3 GDPR). Practically speaking, the EU cannot protect EU citizens' data when they physically travel to areas outside the EU, as it would require jurisdictional competence in every other territory in the world (however, see Bradford, 2020). What seems to be the linking pin of the data protection regime is where the processing takes place, either in light of having an establishment in the EU or in light of activities outside the EU, when data are gathered from EU citizens in a digital EU space and being directed at an EU audience, such as setting up a digital website in German directed at the German market instead of owning a physical shop in Germany.

Location also plays a role with respect to the household exemption, although it did not initially (Article 2 GDPR). The exemption stresses that, where personal data are processed for purely personal or household activities, the data protection regime does not apply (on the household exemption, see inter alia Chen et al., 2020). This could include gathering personal data from the public sphere and making that data available to third parties, as long as the activities themselves were considered purely personal or related to household. The Court of Justice, however, through its Lindqvist and Rynes cases, reinterpreted the provision in a way in which location has become a determining factor. It has stressed that, where data are gathered from the public domain and where processing entails transferring data from the private to the public domain, the household exemption, in principle, cannot apply.

There are few rules on where data are gathered. From the household exemption, even after its reinterpretation by the Court of Justice, it may be gathered that, when data are gathered in the private domain and stay in the private domain, they will normally fall under the exemption (although this does not include data gathered in the private domain of others). The household exemption was initially a question of 'why', while the CJEU reinterpreted it to primarily refer to 'where'. This means, perhaps intuitively contradictory, that data processing in the private domain is regulated less than outside the private domain. This confirms the mild preference in the EU to use the notion of locationality, connected to where the processing takes place. In addition, when a person has actively disclosed sensitive data about themselves in public (Article 9 para. 2 sub. e GDPR), these data may be processed, provided that the requirements of necessity, proportionality and related principles are met (Dove & Chen, 2021).

Under the GDPR, it is noteworthy that there are additional rules that specifically target data processing in the public domain. When data processing concerns 'a systematic monitoring of a publicly accessible area on a large scale', the data protection regime now holds that a data protection impact assessment must be made:

> A data protection impact assessment is equally required for monitoring publicly accessible areas on a large scale, especially when using optic-electronic devices or for any other operations where the competent supervisory authority considers that the processing is likely to result in a high risk to the rights and freedoms of data subjects, in particular because they prevent data subjects from exercising a right or using a service or a contract, or because they are carried out systematically on a large scale. (Recital 91 GDPR)

2.2. Who

The GDPR essentially distinguishes between two parties: data subjects and data controllers, the party whose data are processed and the party processing the data. There is a third player, the data processor, but that is essentially the person or organisation that processes data about the data subject on behalf of the data controller and is thus essentially a subordinate of the data controller (see inter alia Hintze, 2018).

The data protection regime does not give a definition of the data subject. It gives a definition of personal data, from which the definition of the data subject can be derived. Since personal data means any information relating to an identified or identifiable natural person (i.e. the data subject), the data subject must mean the natural person that can be identified on the basis of personal data. This means that data are not provided protection as such, but only in so far as they are linked to a living person. Although the ePrivacy regime extends its scope of protection to legal persons, the data protection regime does not. In addition, it does not provide protection to groups; at most, various data subjects that have been affected by the same data processing initiative can bundle their complaints. The processing of aggregated data or data about categories as such, however, in principle falls beyond the scope of the GDPR. This also means that, on this point, the data protection regime provides protection to private interests and not or only marginally to general interests (Taylor et al., 2017).

With respect to the party processing the data, the main focus is on the data controller, that is, the person or organisation that determines the purposes and means of processing. This means that determining who has the principle obligation to ensure that the data protection regime is adhered to is decided on the basis of the why and the how. It is possible to have multiple data controllers (joint controllers), for example, if more than one party determines the purposes for processing or when one party determines the means and the other determines the purposes for processing (WP29, 2010). The GDPR also distinguishes the position of data processors from that of controllers, with processors being the party that processes data on behalf of the data controller. Although processors are said to be relieved from many data protection obligations, they in fact have to conform to the GDPR fully, but it is the data controller's obligation to ensure that they do so. With regard to the data controller, the GDPR takes a holistic approach: it looks at the party or parties responsible for the whole process and does not, for example, make subdivisions between different types of processes or activities, for which parties may be responsible.

Formally, the data controller can be both a natural person and a legal person, but the data protection regime seems to be primarily written with legal persons in mind. Although previous data protection regimes have sometimes applied different rules to public sector organisations and private sector organisations (Council of Europe, 1973; CoE, 1974) and the initial proposal for the data protection directive did so as well (COM, 1990), the choice was made for the Data Protection Directive and the GDPR to apply the basic regime to all parties alike. Still, three types of parties are excluded from the general data protection framework, namely EU institutions, law enforcement authorities and intelligence agencies. Although the former two are regulated through a GDPR-like (Regulation 2018/1725) and a GDPR-light (Directive 2016/680) regime, respectively, intelligence agencies fall outside EU competence as such (Article 2 GDPR). The difference between public and private sector organisations remains relevant in the GDPR with respect to one aspect specifically: the grounds for the processing of non-sensitive personal data and sensitive personal data (Article 6 and 9 GDPR).

2.3. What

The object of protection, or perhaps more precisely, the mode of regulation in the data protection instrument, is (perhaps unsurprisingly) through data. Two distinctions guide the application of the data protection instrument. First is the distinction between personal and non-personal data. When data relate directly or indirectly to a natural person, the data protection regime applies. When data do not, the regime does not apply. This is a binary categorisation (on this topic, see inter alia Graef et al., 2018). Second, there is the distinction between sensitive data and non-sensitive personal data, which is also a fixed and binary categorisation (Jasserand, 2016). The same basic regime applies to both categories, the major difference being the legitimate processing grounds.

Although both categorisations are presented as binary, reality is more fluid. For example, there are at least three reasons why the distinction between sensitive and non-sensitive data is not as sharp as sometimes suggested.

- First, the difference in processing grounds in practice makes a small difference. The GDPR provides that sensitive data can, in principle, not be processed unless there is a legitimate exemption. Consequently, the question is whether the data controller can rely on a legitimate ground for processing all the same. The exemptions for sensitive and the grounds for non-sensitive personal data mostly resemble each other (e.g. consent or public interest), with the only essential difference being that, for processing non-sensitive personal data, the controller can rely on its own interests for processing the data, while this is not allowed for processing sensitive personal data (WP29, 2014). Otherwise, instead of consent, the

GDPR requires explicit consent for the processing of sensitive personal data; instead of a public interest, it requires a substantial public interest for processing sensitive personal data, and so forth.

- Second, the same basic regime applies to all processing of personal data, irrespective of whether the data being processed are sensitive and the obligations imposed on the data controller mostly contain a contextual element. For example, the obligation to keep registers and documentation on data processing within an organisation is linked, inter alia, to the question of whether the processing it carries out is likely to result in a risk to the rights and freedoms of data subjects (Article 30 GDPR). The obligation to establish a data protection policy is linked to the sensitivity of the data processing, meaning that the more sensitive the processing operations are, the more comprehensive the policy should be (Article 24 GDPR). The requirement to implement data protection by design and default standards (Article 25 GDPR) and technical and organisational security requirements are linked to the nature, scope, context and purposes of the processing, in particular the risks at stake (Article 32 GDPR). The data protection impact assessment is linked to the risks involved (Article 35 GDPR). To provide a final example, there is an obligation to appoint a data protection officer, inter alia, when the data controller processes sensitive data on a large scale (Article 37 GDPR). Consequently, the sensitivity of the data processing operation is an element implicit in many of the provisions of the GDPR, in a non-binary way.
- Third, although not following from the data protection framework itself, the way in which the EU Court of Justice treats sensitive data seems to imply fluidity. On the one hand, the court often seems to avoid assessing the applicability of the regime of sensitive data when it regards large-scale data processing operations (e.g. CJEU, 2014). On the other hand, the court makes a hierarchical difference in terms of the types of sensitive data listed in the GDPR, suggesting, inter alia, that health data are to be considered especially sensitive (CJEU, 2011).

The data protection framework focuses on regulating the processing of personal data in general, making the definition of processing so wide that it includes virtually everything. This means that the GDPR does not, for example, regulate specific technologies, which could be an alternative approach. What is finally important to note is the dual relationship in the EU's attitude toward a sectoral approach, which is typically associated with the United States (further on this topic, see Hirsch, 2011; Hirsch, 2013. The

US distinguishes between the regulation of data processing in different sectors, such as the healthcare sector, the financial sector and the online sector (e.g. HIPPA and COPPA). The EU clearly does not take this approach. Instead, it lays down one general regime for all data processing operations. Still, at least one sector is regulated differently, namely the law enforcement sector. In addition, the EU encourages sector-specific regulation, either by Member States or by sectors themselves, by adopting codes of conduct that must be approved by data protection authorities (Article 40 GDPR). These codes should specify in detail how the rather general and abstract rules in the GDPR should be interpreted in practice and make the sector itself primarily responsible for the oversight and enforcement of the rules. So far, however, neither the Member States nor the sectors have been specifically active on this point (EDPB, 2023).

2.4. Why

In a certain sense, 'why' is the most important aspect of the data protection regime, as it is perhaps with the whole human rights framework. The why is partially connected to the who. The classical human rights framework was focused on public organisations. When they interfere with human rights, they must do so to serve a public interest, like preventing disorder and crime, or ensuring the economic well-being or the health of the population. The competence to interfere with a human right should be laid down in law. Finally, the interference should be necessary in a democratic society, proportionate to the aim pursued and meet the subsidiarity requirement, meaning that there are no less intrusive alternatives available for reaching the same goal (Greer, 1997). Under the GDPR, basically, this same structure is copied and made explicit: public organisations (private organisations may sometimes be tasked with processing personal data in light of a public interest) should, in principle, only process data on the basis of a law and when the processing serves a public interest (Article 6 sub. 1 and 2 GDPR).

There is a separate rule for private organisations. In principle, they can only process personal data when serving the interests of the data subject. A data subject can express what they deem to be in their best interest through consent or a contract. Alternatively, when they are not capable of expressing their interests, but it should be clear that it is in their vital interests to process their data, data controllers may also do so. There is one exception to this rule, which only applies to the processing of non-sensitive personal data. This is the infamous clause that allows for processing personal data when the interests of the data controller or a third party override the interests of the data subject. This is used so infrequently in practice that even data protection authorities have suggested using it more often (WP29, 2014). Private sector organisations generally prefer to base their processing on the consent of the data subject.

The 'why' is obviously the linking pin of the purpose specification and the purpose limitation principles (Article 5 para. 1 sub. b GDPR). In addition, the other principles, such as the data minimisation and storage limitation principles, are directly linked to the purpose for processing (von Grafenstein, 2018). These GDPR requirements are, in fact, reformulations of the general principles of human rights law, namely that any interference with a human right should be necessary and strictly proportionate to the aim pursued and that there should be no other means available to achieve the same aim without interfering with a human right or to a lesser extent (Christoffersen, 2009).

There are no content limits to specific 'why's' or purposes, as long as processing does not conflict with the law. This means that, in principle, any 'why' consented to by the data subject or laid down in law by the democratic legislator would be deemed legitimate under the framework. Consequently, the data protection framework provides that there are two basic modes of arriving at the 'why' and leaves the rest open; it adopts a proceduralist standard rather than a substantive one.

2.5. When

Time plays an important role in the data protection regime in the sense that most data protection principles kick in when data are first gathered. It is at that moment when the ground for the processing must be determined and the purpose specified. Both the purpose limitation principle and storage limitation principle link back to that moment. The duration of data processing and the reasons for processing are limited to what is necessary in light of that original purpose. The data minimisation and storage limitation principles relate back to the goal set out when gathering the personal data (Article 5 para. 1 GDPR). The obligation of transparency and providing information to the data subject is also principally linked to the moment that the data are first processed: information should be provided at that moment when the data are gathered, or when the data are obtained not from the data subject directly, the information has to be provided no later than a month after the data have been obtained (Wachter, 2018). The moment data are gathered is also the moment that the security and confidentiality principle and the data quality principle kick in, although these requirements play a role throughout the process. Also, their role and meaning may change in time, as, among other things, the techniques available for third-party hacking evolve (Cunningham, 2012).

There are very few rules in the data protection framework that apply to other moments than the initial gathering and storage of personal data. Perhaps this is an artifact of the development of the data protection rules in the 1970s, where the question of whether data were gathered and stored was deemed the quintessential question (Westin & Baker, 1972). There are virtually no rules on the analysis of data and no rules on the use of data, perhaps with the exception of one provision on the prohibition of automated decision-making. This provision, however, plays virtually no significant role, both because it may be exempted when there is a legal basis and consent and because it speaks of *solely* automated processing, while in practice, there is almost always some human element embedded in the processing operation (Hildebrandt, 2009).

Finally, the element of time is relevant in the sense that there is a time element implicit in the definition of personal data. The notion of 'identifiability' entails that even when data cannot be used to identify a person now, but might in the future, it still qualifies as personal data (see e.g. Shabani & Marelli, 2019):

> To determine whether a natural person is identifiable, account should be taken of all the means reasonably likely to be used, such as singling out, either by the controller or by another person to identify the natural person directly or indirectly. To ascertain whether means are reasonably likely to be used to identify the natural person, account should be taken of all objective factors, such as the costs of and the amount of time required for identification, taking into consideration the available technology at the time of the processing and technological developments. (Recital 26 GDPR)

Interestingly, this kind of time element is not present in the definition of sensitive personal data. Sensitive data refers to data that reveal a specific aspect of a person, thus linking sensitive data to the notion of 'when' only if at the moment of processing the data reveal anything sensitive.

2.6. How

The GDPR applies independent of how the data are processed. Processing is defined in such a way that it includes any operation. The only exception is that manual, unstructured processing of personal data is left outside the scope of the data protection regime. This used to be a relevant distinction, excluding a substantial number of processing operations when the data protection regime was drafted in the 1990s. Now, however, it is quasi-irrelevant, as almost all data processing, even keeping personal notes or a call list, is digitised.

Perhaps the only exception to the technology neutrality of the GDPR is its specific mention of profiling, which is defined as any form of automated processing of personal data consisting of the use of personal data to evaluate certain personal aspects relating to a natural person, in particular to analyse or predict aspects concerning that natural person's performance at work, economic situation, health, personal preferences, interests, reliability, behaviour, location or movements. Profiling is not prohibited per se, but it might be a relevant element for determining the need for an impact assessment (Binns & Veale, 2021).

3. Questions

With each of the approaches taken in the GDPR, questions arise, especially in light of the evolving technological capacities, such as through Big Data, artificial intelligence, large language models, facial recognition and, potentially, quantum computing (Hoofnagle & Garfinkel, 2022).

With respect to the applicability of the GDPR, it is clear that the territoriality principle is increasingly difficult to apply. Although the EU claims competence over organisations based outside the EU when processing personal data about EU citizens, this creates a significant enforcement problem, and the tendency toward complex partnerships with stakeholders in various jurisdictions increases the legal complexity (Kuner, 2021). In addition, the spheres of processing personal data are not as clear-cut as they were 30 years ago, let alone 50 years ago, when the data protection regime was designed. Data gathered and processed in the private sphere can be disseminated to a worldwide audience with the push of a mouse button; people carry their smart phone, giving access to their most private photos, videos and ancillary data in public; commercial and professional meetings are held at home, while private activities take place in public or semi-public settings (see e.g. West et al., 2009).

With respect to the norm addressee of the data protection regime, it is clear that, due to the multi-party partnerships (Liu et al., 2021), increasing numbers of organisations have an influence on what data are processed, how and why, either with respect to the whole process or parts of it. This makes the difference between processors and controllers, joint controllers and the division of responsibilities and liability increasingly difficult to establish. This also applies to the distinction between public and private sector organisations and organisations that process personal data for national security, for law enforcement and for other purposes. Due to the focus on public-private partnerships in the law enforcement sector, for example, it is increasingly difficult to assess which legal regime applies to what part of the process at which stage and how the fact that different rules apply to different parties affects the partnership (Masciandaro, 2017). More importantly, with the move to group profiling and the analysis of aggregated data for predictive and probabilistic statistical correlations, the question is whether the data protection regime should not also cover those data processing initiatives, either by reformulating the definition of personal data or by extending the protective scope of the data protection regime to include not only data subjects defined as natural persons but also data about groups and/or categories of people (Floridi, 2017; Loi & Christen, 2020). Finally, the difference between data controller and data subject is blurred when data subjects (e.g. influencers) share the most intimate details about their own lives on the internet, also adopting the role of data controller (van der Sloot, 2020).

With respect to the object being regulated, two things stand out. First, the data protection framework is focused on fixed and relatively binary categories of data, especially with respect to the distinction between non-personal data – to which the GDPR does not apply – and personal data – to which it does. In addition, there are separate rules for pseudonymous data and sensitive data. It is questionable to what extent these distinctions are viable in an age where the status and use of data can change from aggregated data to identifiable data in a split second (Fluitt et al., 2019). There is a time element involved in the current definition of personal data, so the data's likely future state will determine how they are to be considered and categorised at this moment in time; given the fact that data techniques evolve rapidly, it is questionable whether this approach can be maintained, as it is increasingly likely that at some point in time, non-personal data may be turned into identifiable data and that non-sensitive data becomes sensitive, for example through merging datasets or connecting previously unrelated datapoints. Essentially, this would mean that all data should be treated as personal data (van der Sloot, 2017; Purtova, 2018).

The motivations for processing personal data are also increasingly fluid. Data tend to get reused for new purposes, which is said to be one of the great advantages of modern data processing techniques (Moerel & Prins,

2016). The EU also explicitly encourages the reuse of data, for example, by requiring public sector organisations to make their data available for reuse for commercial purposes through the Open Data Directive (Directive 2019/1024). In addition, because of the speed with which data technologies evolve, parties often do not know what possibilities there will be for harvesting the data in their possession in two or three years' time. The emphasis placed in the GDPR on obtaining consent for the reuse of personal data (Article 6 para. 4 GDPR) seems ill-conceived, both because data subjects are already overwhelmed by the number of consent requests and because they are often not in a position to understand the possibilities generated by the new technologies available (Solove, 2012; Sloan & Warner, 2014; Schermer et al., 2014; Susser, 2019).

With regard to the time element involved in the data protection framework, it is remarkable how many rules apply or are triggered when data are collected and stored and how few rules there are for analysing and further processing personal data, while the analysis of (aggregated) data is considered the heart of data processing in artificial intelligence (AI) systems and other complex information analytics technologies (see e.g. Zhu, 2020; Yang et al., 2021; Barja-Martinez et al., 2001). In addition, perhaps with the exception of the prohibition on automated processing and ancillary rules on profiling, there are no rules on the use of data and technologies other than those connected to the moment of data gathering (see e.g. van Hoboken, 2016).

4. Other Regimes

As several regulations have already been adopted and the Commission is proposing even more acts for the data-driven environment, the EU hopes to lay down a detailed and comprehensive legislative package for the 21st century.[1] The extensive corpus now on the table should make Europe fit for the digital age, allowing enterprises to flourish and governmental organisations to operate more effectively while providing a high level of protection to EU citizens at the same time. Each of these instruments contains valuable provisions, prohibitions and rights, meaning that, taken separately, their introduction should be welcomed. One thing the EU has invested in little, however, is the consistency between these and other legal instruments and

1 https://commission.europa.eu/strategy-and-policy/priorities-2019-2024/europe-fit-digital-age_en

the consistency between the laws applicable to the data-driven environment. There are at least three relevant examples.

First, ever since the EU started to adopt laws that move away from the socio-economic realm and enter the realm of human rights law, little effort has gone into harmonising these with the more established European Convention on Human Rights of the Council of Europe and the jurisprudence by the European Court of Human Rights (ECtHR). Often EU law simply mentions that account should be made of the case law of the ECtHR on, for example, the concepts of necessity and proportionality, while leaving open what that exactly means for the interpretation of EU laws and legal principles (Article 53 Charter of Fundamental Rights of the European Union). This is important because the EU's legal corpus, including the European Court of Justice (ECJ) judgments, is not entirely consistent with the approach taken within the Council of Europe. Examples include, but are not limited to:

- the difference between the protection of privacy under Article 8 of the European Convention on Human Rights and the EU's data protection regime under the General Data Protection Regulation and the Law Enforcement Directive (Kokott & Sobotta, 2013);
- the differences between the prevention of discrimination under Article 14 ECHR and the EU laws on specific forms of discrimination, such as on grounds of race and ethnic origin (Directive 2000/43/EC); discrimination at work on grounds of religion or belief, disability, age or sexual orientation (Directive 2000/78/EC); equal treatment for men and women in matters of employment and occupation (Directive 2006/54/EC); equal treatment for men and women in the access to and supply of goods and services (Directive 2004/113/EC); and discrimination based on age, disability, sexual orientation and religion or beliefs beyond the workplace (Directive Proposal [COM(2008)462]) (Besson, 2008; Tobler, 2014);
- the difference between the EU's approach to liability of internet intermediaries, focusing on safe harbours and a notice and takedown or notice and action regime, and the ECtHR's focus on the freedom of expression and the obligations of publishers (van der Sloot, 2015).

Because of the discrepancy between both legislative corpuses, it matters for the outcome of a legal dispute whether it is treated under EU law or the European Convention on Human Rights, or whether it is judged by the ECJ or the ECtHR.

Second, the EU adopts so much legislation, in such broad terms, that it will be almost impossible for national legislators to bring their full legislative corpus in compliance with EU national law. At least two points should be underlined here:

- One is the scope of EU laws, such as the GDPR; being an EU regulation, it will prevail over national law of Member States. National laws of Member States need to be brought in conformity with the GDPR. But nearly every law will entail some form of data processing, e.g. when referring to the requirement to keep or produce 'documents', 'files', 'registers' or 'information', and virtually all the specific documents, files, registers or information will or may contain personal data. No Member State has assessed its entire legislative corpus and revised it in full to bring it in conformity with the GDPR; rather, they have chosen to update a handful of laws central to data processing practices and stressed that all other laws must be interpreted 'in light of the GDPR' (van der Sloot, 2019).
- Another is that the EU often takes a similar approach when it comes to determining the relationship between various EU laws. It does not provide clarity on how various EU laws should be interpreted in light of each other. Instead, the GDPR is 'without prejudice to the application of Directive 2000/31/EC' (Article 2 para. 4 GDPR), while the e-Commerce Directive shall not apply to 'questions relating to information society services covered by' the ePrivacy Directive and the GDPR (Article 1 para. 5 sub. b e-Commerce Directive). In similar vein, the Open Data Directive finds, 'This Directive is without prejudice to Union and national law on the protection of personal data, in particular Regulation (EU) 2016/679 and Directive 2002/58/EC and the corresponding provisions of national law' (Article 1 para. 4 Open Data Directive). These types of formulations leave it to Member States to harmonise the various legal regimes, which will often entail complicated legal interpretations. For example, the Open Data Directive requires Member States to make public sector information publicly available for reuse, which will often contain personal data; in principle, the GDPR prohibits reuse of personal data for purposes other than that for which they were initially processed, emphasises confidentiality rather than openness and obliges the data controller to inform the data subject who had access to her data, while such information may often be unknown to the data controller in open data environments (Scassa, 2014; Borgesius et al., 2015). The fact that Member States, having to decide on the right interpretation of these seemingly conflicting requirements, make choices that are sometimes explicitly condemned by the European Court of Justice makes things even more complicated (CJEU, 2022).

Third, the EU itself is often not consistent in its approach and terminology. Not only are these inconsistencies left intact and smoothened out by magic formulas, such as suggesting that certain instruments are 'without prejudice' to another, but different instruments often also take different regulatory approaches, lay obligations on different actors and distinguish between different types of data.

- For example, the GDPR applies different levels of protection to personal data, sensitive data, anonymous and aggregated data; places pseudonymous data somewhere in between anonymous and personal data; and recognises several types of sensitive data, such as genetic data, biometric data and data concerning health. Many of the proposed acts now on the table use different terminologies. The proposed ePrivacy Regulation distinguishes between various kinds of metadata, including location and traffic data, electronic communications data, electronic communications content and electronic communications metadata. The proposed AI Act defines and regulates still different types of data, such as training data, validation data, testing data and input data. The Digital Markets Act (DMA) yet emphasises the difference between aggregated and non-aggregated data and between personal and anonymised data. It also refers to data, both in contrast to the definition of personal data, for which reference is made to the GDPR, and to that of non-personal data, for which reference is made to the Regulation on the transfer of non-personal data. Interestingly, the Regulation on the free flow of non-personal data does not give a definition of non-personal data itself, but of data which is seen as encompassing all data but personal data. The DSA refers to illegal content as a special category of data, the Data Governance Act, like the DMA distinguishes between three types of data – although not between data, personal data and non-personal data, but between data, non-personal data and metadata. The proposed Data Act only refers to data, and the Open Data Directive refers to dynamic data, research data and high-value datasets as categories of data that are specifically regulated. How these various categories of data and the partial overlaps and contrasts between them interact is left open.
- In addition, parties involved with data handling are categorised differently in each legal regime, with different roles and responsibilities being attributed. The GDPR differentiates between the data subject, the data processor and the data controller. The Regulation on the free flow of non-personal data speaks of service providers, users and professional users. The DSA refers to information society services, recipients of

services, consumers, traders, intermediary services and online platforms. The DMA in turn differentiates between gatekeepers, core platform services, cloud computing services, software application stores, online intermediation services, online search engines, ancillary services, online social networking services, identification services, video-sharing platform services, number-independent interpersonal communication services, operating systems, end users, business users and undertakings. The Data Governance Act makes reference to data holders and data users. The Data Act refers to users, data holders, data recipients and data processing services. The AI Act, to give a final example, has rules for providers, small-scale providers, users, importers, distributors and operators.

– The various instruments also mention different types of processing techniques and applications. The GDPR distinguishes between automated and non-automated processing, between data that are a part of a filing system and those that are not and between structured and unstructured data processing. In addition, it makes special mention of profiling. The Digital Service Act (DSA) defines and separately regulates the dissemination of data to the public, of content moderation as well as recommender systems. The DMA refers to ranking; the ePrivacy Regulation distinguishes between electronic mail, direct marketing communications, direct marketing voice-to-voice calls and automated calling and communications systems. The AI defines a set of different processing operations and systems, such as an artificial intelligence system, biometric categorisation system, remote biometric identification system, real-time remote biometric identification system and post remote biometric identification system. Then there are a range of activities, such as reuse, data sharing and data altruism as defined in the Data Governance Act (DGA), and reuse, which is defined differently in the DGA than in the Open Data Directive.

5. Analysis and Alternatives

Given the questions posed in Section 3 and the additional complexities triggered by the new EU legal instruments discussed in Section 4, the question is whether alternative modes of regulation can be considered. This chapter will provide a sketch for five such alternative regulatory approaches: treating all data alike (Section 5.1), adopting a fully contextual data protection regime (Section 5.2), making smaller changes to the current data protection regime (Section 5.3), adopting a sector or technology-specific approach to data regulation (Section 5.4) or regulating several stages of data processing operations, especially adding rules for the analysis of data (Section 5.5). Not all these alternative regulatory approaches necessarily exclude each other; some could thus potentially be applied in combination with one another.

5.1. One Regime for All Data

There is an ambiguous approach to the right to data protection and the scope of 'personal data' in particular.

On the one hand, the European Union is set on maintaining a strict separation between personal and non-personal data, as well as other categories of data. While personal data are protected under arguably the world's strictest regime, non-personal data are free from regulation, or to be more precise, the EU has adopted a regulation on non-personal data in which it dissuades public and private sector organisations from adopting any restrictions on or creating barriers to the free flow of non-personal data. This choice fits in a broader tradition within the EU for opting for separate, demarcated types of data that each have their own level of protection. On the other hand, the concept of 'personal data' has been extended in the various data protection instruments adopted over the decades. In case law, courts have also given a broad interpretation to the definition.

The approach of defining several types of data, each with their own scope of protection, is being increasingly criticised. Broadly speaking, three arguments can be put forward.

- First, it is argued that working with well-defined and delimited definitions of different types of data only works if the status of data is relatively stable, if a 'datum' falls into one category in a relatively stable way. This is increasingly less so. The nature of the data in Big Data processes is not stable, but volatile. A dataset containing ordinary personal data can be linked to and enriched with another dataset so as to derive sensitive data. The data can then be aggregated or stripped of identifiers and become non-personal, aggregated or anonymous data. Subsequently, the data can be de-anonymised or integrated into another dataset to create personal data. All this can happen in a split second. The question is, therefore, whether it makes sense to work with binary categories if the same 'datum' or dataset can literally fall into a different category from one second to the next and into still another the very next second.

- Second, it is increasingly difficult to determine the status of data precisely. As the Working Party 29 already stated:

  - the assessment of whether the data allow identification of an individual, and whether the information can be considered as anonymous or not depends on the circumstances, and a case-by-case analysis should be carried out with particular reference to the extent that the means are likely reasonably to be used for identification. (WP29, 4/2007).

  - This refers to the phrase in the GDPR, holding that, to determine whether a datum is to be considered 'personal', account should be made of the means that can reasonably be expected to be used for identification. Therefore, to determine the current status of a datum or dataset, the expected future status of the data must be considered. Given the democratisation of technologies and the stark reduction of costs, it is increasingly likely that when a database is shared or otherwise made available, there will be a party who will combine it with other data, enrich it with data scraped from the internet or merge it into an existing dataset. It is thus increasingly likely that if an anonymised dataset is made public, there will be a party that will de-anonymise it or combine it with other data to create personal profiles; that if a set of personal data is shared, there will be a party that will use that data to create a dataset containing sensitive personal data; and so on. On the other hand, there will be other parties who have access to that data but will not engage in such activities; there will be parties who will not use the data, use it as they are provided or even de-identify a database containing personal data. Who will do what is not clear in advance. The legal category to which the data belongs is therefore no longer a quality of the data themselves, but a product of a data controller's efforts and investments.
- Third, the question is whether the distinction made between different categories of data is still relevant. The underlying rationale is that the processing of personal data has an effect on natural persons, while the processing of non-personal data does not. The idea is that the processing of sensitive personal data may have significant consequences (greater than the processing of 'ordinary' personal data normally has), so the latter are subject to the most stringent regime. Personal data fall under the 'normal' protection regime, and the processing of non-personal data

> is not subject to any restrictions. Pseudonymisation does not ensure the full protection of individuals, but it does reduce the number of people and organisations that can link data to specific individuals, which is why pseudonymous data are put in an intermediate category of protection. The question is to what extent this rationale is still tenable in the 21st century. Information about the content of communication can be distilled from metadata, identifying data can be inferred by combining two datasets holding no personal data, etc. Modern data processing on the basis of aggregated data, for example, can also have very large individual and social consequences. Profiling, by definition, targets groups rather than individuals. The consequences of profiling can be negative for groups, without the damage being directly relatable to individuals, such as when the police, using predictive policing, decide to patrol certain neighbourhoods more often than others. The possible arrests made in these neighbourhoods may all be justified in and by themselves, while the general problem of stigmatisation of deprived neighbourhoods and blind spots on the part of the police with regard to 'better' neighbourhoods may be significant. The same applies to profiles used in smart cities. One can therefore question the idea that the more sensitive the data are and the more directly they can be linked to a person, the more strictly their processing should be regulated.

On the one hand, the second regulatory approach – to continue stretching the notion of personal data and of sensitive personal data so that more and more data fall under those categories – is also criticised, as it would effectively make data protection law applicable to virtually all processes in an increasingly data-driven society. In addition, by accepting that more and more personal data may indirectly disclose sensitive personal data, more and more data processing initiatives will be put under the strictest regulatory regime. This approach may stifle innovation, reduce economic growth and block data processing initiatives that serve personal and societal interests and thus undermine the very purpose of the EU data protection regime, which was to enable the processing of personal data for legitimate purposes, provided that a number of procedural safeguards were taken into account (see also the dual purpose of the GDPR as reflected in Article 1 GDPR).

One option to solve this tension would be to dissolve the categories of data and simply apply one regime to all 'data' alike or, alternatively, to regulate non-personal data through a GDPR-lite regime as well. Two core provisions could be applicable to the processing of non-personal data, which are inspired by the GDPR. There is no direct reason why these principles, which do not relate to data subject rights and serve societal interests as well as personal ones, could not be applied mutatis mutandis to the processing of non-personal data. Rather, given the increased importance of non-personal, aggregated and anonymous data in the data environment and given the fluidity of data status, such may be necessary.

Principles
Non-personal data shall be:

- processed lawfully, fairly and in a transparent manner ('lawfulness, fairness and transparency');
- collected for specified, explicit and legitimate purposes and not further processed in a manner that is incompatible with those purposes ('purpose limitation');
- adequate, relevant and limited to what is necessary in relation to the purposes for which they are processed ('data minimisation');
- accurate and, where necessary, kept up to date; every reasonable step must be taken to ensure that non-personal data that are inaccurate, having regard to the purposes for which they are processed, are erased or rectified without delay ('accuracy');
- kept for no longer than is necessary for the purposes for which the personal data are processed ('storage limitation');
- processed in a manner that ensures appropriate security of the non-personal data, including protection against unauthorised or unlawful processing and against accidental loss, destruction or damage, using appropriate technical or organisational measures ('integrity and confidentiality').

Obligations
To the extent reasonable and proportionate, every natural and legal person processing non-personal data has to:

- adopt a data protection policy that specifies how the rules in this regulation shall be implemented and respected within its organisation ('data protection policy');
- implement the policy decisions in its technical infrastructure by design or by default ('data protection by design and default');
- maintain records specifying the data that are processed, the source of the data, the purpose for processing the data, the period for which the data are stored, the natural and legal persons with whom the data are

shared and the technical and organisational measures applied ('records of processing activities');

- conduct a data protection impact assessment before engaging in specific processing activities, taking into account the likely effects on citizens, groups and society at large and developing strategies for mitigating those effects ('data protection impact assessment');
- designate a data protection officer, who shall be fully independent, trained and have access to necessary resources to adequately fulfil their tasks; the data protection officer is responsible for ensuring that all relevant principles are upheld ('data protection officer'); and
- process data transparently, meaning that the public is informed through a website of the data that are processed, the source of the data, the purpose for processing the data, the period for which the data are stored, the organisations with whom the data are shared, the technical and organisational measures applied and whether any data breach has occurred ('transparency').

5.2. A Fully Contextual Approach

A second option to solve the tensions described in Section 5.1 would be to make the data protection framework more contextual. There are already several provisions that foreshadow this approach. For example, a data protection policy should be set up in proportion to the processing activities. Data protection by design and by default efforts should be undertaken and technical and organisational security measurements implemented according to the state of the art, the costs of implementation and the nature, scope, context and purposes of processing as well as the risk of varying likelihood and severity for the rights and freedoms of natural persons. In addition, both the data protection impact assessment and the requirement to appoint a data protection officer are connected to data processing initiatives that are considered especially sensitive. Lastly, the obligation to keep registers of the data processing initiatives does not apply to small organisations that engage in processing, which is unlikely to result in a risk to the rights and freedoms of data subjects, when the processing is occasional, and the processing does not include sensitive personal data.

A solution to the problem of defining personal data is, building on these contextual elements in the GDPR, to simply to make all obligations contextual. This means that the more data are gathered, the more sensitive these data; thus, the higher the potential impact of the processing activities, the more parties having access to the data, etc., and the rules in the data protection framework should be interpreted more strictly. For example, the more sensitive the processing operations, the more precise and limited the definition of the purpose should be; the higher the potential impact, the more effort should be put into ensuring that the data are correct and up to date; the more sensitive the data are, the higher the security measures should be; the riskier the processing operations, the more strictly the processing grounds should be interpreted; the higher the potential impact of the a data breach, the more quickly and elaborately relevant parties should be informed.

Instead of defining personal data, sensitive data and other types of data, the data protection framework could consist of two main provisions:

Obligations and principles:

1. Proportional to the state of the technological art, the costs of implementation, the nature, scope, context and purposes of processing, the nature and sensitivity of the data, the likelihood and severity of the impact of data processing on the rights and freedoms of natural persons and the number of parties having access to the data, the data controller shall ensure that:

- data are processed lawfully, fairly and in a transparent manner in relation to the data subject;
- data are collected for specified, explicit and legitimate purposes and not further processed in a manner that is incompatible with those purposes;
- data are adequate, relevant and limited to what is necessary in relation to the purposes for which they are processed;
- data are accurate and, where necessary, kept up to date;
- data are kept in a form that permits the identification of data subjects for no longer than is necessary for the purposes for which the personal data are processed;
- a data protection policy is adopted;
- data protection by design and by default measures are implemented;
- an assessment of the impact of the envisaged processing operations is carried out;
- the person, group or category affected is informed of the data processing initiative;
- data are only processed if and to the extent that at least one of the following applies:
  - the data subject has given consent, either directly or indirectly through a contract;
  - processing is in the public interest and is necessary for compliance with a legal task or obligation to which the controller is subject;

2. Proportional to the state of the technological art, the costs of implementation and the nature, scope, context and purposes of processing, the nature and sensitivity of the data, the likelihood and severity of the impact of data processing on the rights and freedoms of natural persons and the number of parties having access to the data, the controller and, where applicable, the processor shall ensure that:

- appropriate technical and organisational measures are implemented;
- in case of a data breach, the relevant (joint) controller is informed, as are the data subject and the data protection authority;
- a record of processing activities under its responsibility is kept;
- a data protection officer is appointed.

5.3. Changing the Definitions in the GDPR

A third alternative could be to make relatively small changes to the definitions contained in the GDPR while leaving the general structure intact.

First, broadening the scope of the entities provided protection could be considered, including groups, legal persons and potentially unborn and deceased persons. The current definition of personal data is again seemingly black and white, excluding data about deceased persons (see e.g. Harbinja, 2017), the unborn (e.g. Pormeister & Drozdzowski, 2018) and legal persons (see also the interesting discussion in: Mokrosinska, 2020), while in reality the picture is one of grey tones. Including a reference to aggregated data in the definition could be considered as well. The technological advancements make it possible to use the data of deceased persons, e.g. bringing them back to life through deepfake technology, in a highly intrusive way, and to link the data of unborn people to natural persons once they are born. This definitional change would do justice to those developments. The link to aggregated and group data, if included, will have a particularly big impact on the scope and interpretation of the data protection regime, as it would come close to the variant discussed in Section 5.1.

Another option would be to remove the temporal element from the definition of personal data and the explanation given in the recital regarding anonymous data or, alternatively, to include it in the definition of sensitive personal data, so as to harmonise the data protection framework on this point. The element of time adds a layer of complexity to the data protection framework and to the fact that non-personal data that in the future may be turned into personal data will, at this point in time, fall under the data protection regime. In practice, this means that increasing numbers of datasets containing non-personal and aggregated data will fall under the protective scope as well. This, in part, has the effect that the distinction between the various categories of data is increasingly redundant. At the same time, it ensures that a level of protection is offered before data processing becomes potentially harmful to data subjects or groups, so that for either option there are arguments in favour or against. Leaving aside which option is chosen, it would make sense to adopt the same approach with respect to the definition of personal data as with respect to the definition of sensitive personal data: either include a time-element or not.

There are questions as to whether the focus on the strictly defined categories of data still holds in this day and age, inter alia because the processing of other types of data, not included in Article 9 GDPR, may also have a significant impact. That is why a third option may be to consider extending the scope of the list of sensitive personal data to include children's data, financial data and data about socio-economic status, for example. An alternative could be to include a residual category in the definition provided in Article 9 GDPR, similar to Article 14 ECHR.

5.4. Sectoral and/or Technology-Specific Approach

Although the EU is the world leader in the regulation of data technologies, technology regulation in the EU seems like a game of musical chairs at times. While the EU's legislative proposals are avant-garde and extensive, they lack specificity. Take the GDPR. What does it actually say? Not much more than the obvious. Only gather data that you need, specify a purpose before you gather data, delete the data when you no longer need them and store the data safely and confidentially. It does not provide clear standards (how long data can be stored; when data can be shared with third parties; which security standards should be adopted and how high should they be; etc.), and as a consequence, the GDPR, in and of itself, is unable to give much guidance on modern data processing operations in concrete circumstances. Even the proposed Artificial Intelligence Act, which is not technology neutral, as it addresses specifically one technology and also mentions specific applications (such as deepfakes), suffers from a lack of specificity. Article 52 para. 3, for example, specifies:

> Users of an AI system that generates or manipulates image, audio or video content that appreciably resembles existing persons, objects, places or other entities or events and would falsely appear to a person to be authentic or truthful ('deep fake'), shall disclose that the content has been artificially generated or manipulated.

This provision is representative of the EU's approach to regulation; it does not set clear prohibitions or standards but lays down general and open norms. If it does refer to specific technologies; it lays down procedural and bureaucratic requirements. This means that a technology or application is allowed, providing it adheres to these standards. The act does not prohibit deepfakes, nor does it, for example, set a moratorium on the use of facial recognition systems in public places (EDPS, 2021).

The choice for open norms and ex post regulation is not a problem in and of itself. The EU could very well adopt general principles, abstract duties of care and procedural requirements if national legislators would provide further detail as to the meaning and interpretation of these vis-à-vis specific technologies, applications or contexts. But the national implementation acts have generally refrained from doing so, although there are specific prohibitions and clear red lines here and there. This again would not be a problem in and of itself if Data Protection Authorities (DPAs) were to take up that role. But DPAs are generally hesitant to adopt concrete guidelines and adopt moratoria on their own. They often point to the European Data Protection Board (EDPB), as most legal questions play a role in other countries as well and there should be a level playing field throughout the Union. In addition, DPAs often do not have the manpower to give detailed advice to companies or institutions with questions about what is and what is not legitimate; rather, they sanction illegitimate data processing operations ex post, using the stick rather than the carrot. The EDPB has adopted quite a number of opinions, but these mostly regard frameworks proposed by the EU, legal agreements for the transfer of data or the lists for mandatory Data Protection Impact Assessments adopted by the DPAs. There are only a few opinions that discuss concrete applications or technologies and how the general principles should be interpreted in those concrete contexts. However, again, this would not be a problem in and of itself, if the possibility to set up codes of conducts by sectors would be regularly used. Through such codes, sectors can agree on specific rules and standards for their own sector, such as the national association of universities. These kinds of codes could specify standards for, inter alia, international consortia, consortia with private sector partners, obtaining a legitimate ground, sharing data between the consortia partners, data storage terms and so on. However, very few sectors have so far adopted these kinds of codes of conduct because, among other reasons, they are weary of the paperwork and the fact that they will be responsible for the oversight of and compliance with the rules, and they have to set up an independent institution that is responsible for issuing judgements on complaints by data subjects or on other disputes that may arise. Rather than taking up that role themselves, they stress that the national or EU regulator should set up clearer guidelines and rules for specific sectors.

The loser in this game of musical chairs is legal certainty. Data controllers often do not know whether their internal policies and activities will be deemed to conform with the GDPR by the DPA. Data subjects do not know concrete standards either and are thus left in the dark about whether the processing of their data in concrete circumstances is legitimate, until they have heard the decision of the DPA or judge on their specific case. Because there are no ex ante prohibitions or concrete rules and guidelines for concrete technologies and contexts, DPAs are overwhelmed by requests and cases. The EU Commission also often loses cases against internet companies because the EU Court of Justice adopts another interpretation of the rules than it did.

This problem could be addressed through two approaches, either alone or in combination. Let go of taking 'data' as anchor for regulation and instead focus on the different sectors within which data are processed, or on the technologies used for processing data. For example, a sectoral approach could be considered. Europeans used to mock Americans for their sector-specific approach to data protection; they had informational privacy standards for specific domains, such as laws for the protection of online privacy of children, laws concerning privacy protection in the health care sector, laws regarding data processing in light of credit reporting, etc. Europe, instead, had an omnibus law that applied to all data processing activities irrespectively. Thus, there were no legislative gaps and no discrepancies between the various legal instruments. European data protection legislation is, of course, still miles away from any other legislative regime around the world, and the EU and the Court of Justice have taken immense steps to ensure that citizens are protected against large internet companies. However, the more diverse the types of data processing techniques become, the more diverse the parties that have access to the technologies and the more diverse the goals for which they are put to use, and the less an omnibus regulation seems the right type of regulation. In the 1990s, there were still relatively few data processing techniques available, and there were relatively few parties with access to them. Now not only big corporations and governmental organisations but virtually all have access to advanced data processing technologies. These technologies may serve a variety of purposes. Medical institutions that do total genome analysis, for example, are in no way comparable to citizens that use drones and spy products. Similarly, the way in which private-public partnerships in smart cities use data analytics for nudging is in no way comparable with how companies extract information from public sector information that has be made available for reuse in aggregated form.

The more disparate the data processing landscape becomes, the more the question becomes relevant: should we not rather work with sector-specific regulation? Adopting specific frameworks that are tailor-made for these sectors could be considered, instead of applying the basic GDPR rules with slight variations, such as is the approach taken in the Law Enforcement Directive. Sectors that would deserve their own regulation include, but are not limited to, the health care sector, the financial sector, the advertising sector, the energy sector, the agrifood sector and the transportation sector.

5.5. Regulating Stages of Data Processing

A final approach may be to focus on the stages of data processing instead of the data itself. Either these principles could apply to the current categorisations, having the benefit that there will be additional rules for analysing and using data, or alternatives could be developed for broadening or altering the definitions of the different types of data along the lines suggested in Section 5.1, 5.2 or 5.3. The largest added benefit would be when the scope of the data processing framework would include aggregated data as well, which are currently mostly left outside its scope, while it is increasingly possible to act on these data, without directly linking them to specific persons or delineated groups.

The rules included in the current data protection regime could remain intact, regulating specifically the moment of data gathering. Additional rules could be developed for analysing data. When developing these rules, inspiration could be sought from the instruments for processing of statical data (Eurostat, 2017). Finally, rules could be designed for using data. The most obvious approach would be to greylist or blacklist certain applications.

Article 1 Gathering and storing data
The following rules should be adhered to:

- data are gathered lawfully, fairly and in a transparent manner in relation to the data subject;
- data are collected for specified, explicit and legitimate purposes;
- data that are gathered should be adequate, relevant and limited to what is necessary in relation to the purpose for which they are processed;
- data that are stored should remain accurate and up to date;
- data are kept in a form that permits identification of data subjects for no longer than is necessary for the purposes for which the personal data are processed;

- data must be stored safely and confidentially;
- data are only gathered if and to the extent that at least one of the following applies:
  - the data subject has given consent, either directly or indirectly through a contract;
  - processing is in the public interest and is necessary for compliance with a legal task or obligation to which the controller is subject;

Article 2 Analysing data

When data are analysed, the following rules should be adhered to:

1. *Statistical principles*
   - Before analysing data, it must be ensured that the data are gathered in a neutral and objective manner.
   - Data must be updated, and updating data must be done in a neutral and objective manner and accord to the original research design.
   - Categorisation of data must be done in a neutral and objective manner.
   - Algorithms used to analyse the data must be objective and neutral.
   - Data may only be used for the purpose for which they were gathered.
2. *Transparency and oversight*
   - The methods of research and analysis should be recorded.
   - Those methods should be made public.
   - Any changes in the methods should be recorded and made public; errors and biases should be corrected and made public.
   - Internal audits should be conducted to analyse the correctness and efficacy of the methods – before, during and after the analysis of data.
   - External audits by experts or other organisations should be allowed and promoted – before, during and after the analysis of data.
3. *Comparability and compatibility*
   - Metadata on the database and analysis process should be kept.
   - Gathering, classifying and categorising data should follow the rules and procedures commonly used by other organisations.
   - Research methods and tools should align with those commonly used by other organisations.
   - There should be an equal spread in data about parts of the population.
   - When databases are integrated or merged, categorisation and analysis should ensure the reliability of the merged dataset and the data analysis following from it.

Article 3 Using data
When data and the outcomes of data analysis are used, the following shall be prohibited:
- e.g. profiling and nudging in public and private spaces.
- e.g. the use of medical and biometric data other than by professional healthcare organisations.
- e.g. personalised advertisements shown to children.
- ....

References

Official Documents
The Children's Online Privacy Protection Act of 1998 (COPPA).
CJEU, C-101/01 Criminal proceedings against Bodil Lindqvist, 6 November 2003, ECLI:EU:C:2003:596.
CJEU, Judgment of the Civil Service Tribunal (First Chamber) of 5 July 2011. V v European Parliament. Case F-46/09. ECLI:EU:F:2011:101.
CJEU, Case C-212/13, František Ryneš V Úřad pro ochranu osobních údajů, 11 December 2014, ECLI:EU:C:2014:2428.
CJEU, Judgment of the Court (Grand Chamber), 13 May 2014. Google Spain SL and Google Inc. v Agencia Española de Protección de Datos (AEPD) and Mario Costeja González. Case C-131/12.
CJEU, WM (C-37/20), Sovim SA (C-601/20) v Luxembourg Business Registers, 22 November 2022, ECLI:EU:C:2022:912.
COM(90) 314 final ~SYN 287 and 288 Brussels, 13 September 1990.
Council of Europe: Resolution (73) 22 on the protection of the privacy of individuals vis-à-vis electronic data banks in the private sector (Adopted by the Committee of Ministers on 26 September 1973 at the 224th meeting of the Ministers' Deputies).
Council Directive 2000/43/EC of 29 June 2000 implementing the principle of equal treatment between persons irrespective of racial or ethnic origin.
Council Directive 2000/78/EC of 27 November 2000 establishing a general framework for equal treatment in employment and occupation.
Council Directive 2004/113/EC of 13 December 2004 implementing the principle of equal treatment between men and women in the access to and supply of goods and services.
Directive 2000/31/EC of the European Parliament and of the Council of 8 June 2000 on certain legal aspects of information society services, in particular electronic commerce, in the Internal Market (Directive on electronic commerce).

Directive 2002/58/EC of the European Parliament and of the Council of 12 July 2002 concerning the processing of personal data and the protection of privacy in the electronic communications sector (Directive on privacy and electronic communications).
Directive (EU) 2016/680 of the European Parliament and of the Council of 27 April 2016 on the protection of natural persons with regard to the processing of personal data by competent authorities for the purposes of the prevention, investigation, detection or prosecution of criminal offences or the execution of criminal penalties, and on the free movement of such data, and repealing Council Framework Decision 2008/977/JHA.
Directive (EU) 2019/1024 of the European Parliament and of the Council of 20 June 2019 on open data and the re-use of public sector information.
EDPS, 2021. https://edps.europa.eu/press-publications/press-news/press-releases/2021/artificial-intelligence-act-welcomed-initiative_en
EDPB, 2023. https://edpb.europa.eu/our-work-tools/our-documents/topic/code-conduct_en
European Statistics Code of Practice for the National Statistical Authorities and Eurostat (EU statistical authority). Adopted by the European Statistical System Committee, 16 November 2017.
The Health Insurance Portability and Accountability Act of 1996 (HIPAA).
Proposal for a Council Directive on implementing the principle of equal treatment between persons irrespective of religion or belief, disability, age or sexual orientation {SEC(2008) 2180} {SEC(2008) 2181}.
Proposal for a Regulation of the European Parliament and of the Council concerning the respect for private life and the protection of personal data in electronic communications and repealing Directive 2002/58/EC (Regulation on Privacy and Electronic Communications).
Proposal for a Regulation of the European Parliament and of the Council on harmonised rules on fair access to and use of data (Data Act).
Proposal for a Regulation of the European Parliament and of the Council laying down harmonised rules on artificial intelligence (Artificial Intelligence Act) and amending certain union legislative acts.
Regulation (EU) 2016/679 of the European Parliament and of the Council of 27 April 2016 on the protection of natural persons with regard to the processing of personal data and on the free movement of such data, and repealing Directive 95/46/EC (General Data Protection Regulation).
Regulation (EU) 2018/1725 of the European Parliament and of the Council of 23 October 2018 on the protection of natural persons with regard to the processing of personal data by the Union institutions, bodies, offices and agencies and on the free movement of such data, and repealing Regulation (EC) No. 45/2001 and Decision No. 1247/2002/EC.

Regulation (EU) 2018/1807 of the European Parliament and of the Council of 14 November 2018 on a framework for the free flow of non-personal data in the European Union.

Regulation (EU) 2022/868 of the European Parliament and of the Council of 30 May 2022 on European data governance and amending Regulation (EU) 2018/1724 (Data Governance Act).

Regulation (EU) 2022/1925 of the European Parliament and of the Council of 14 September 2022 on contestable and fair markets in the digital sector and amending Directives (EU) 2019/1937 and (EU) 2020/1828 (Digital Markets Act).

Regulation (EU) 2022/2065 of the European Parliament and of the Council of 19 October 2022 on a single market for digital services and amending Directive 2000/31/EC (Digital Services Act).

Resolution (74) 29 on the protection of the privacy of individuals vis-à-vis electronic data banks in the public sector (Adopted by the Committee of Ministers on 20 September 1974 at the 236th meeting of the Ministers' Deputies).

WP29, Opinion 4/2007 on the concept of personal data, 01248/07/EN WP 136, 20 June 2007.

WP29, Opinion 1/2010 on the concepts of 'controller' and 'processor', 00264/10/EN WP 169, 16 February 2010.

WP29, Opinion 06/2014 on the notion of legitimate interests of the data controller under Article 7 of Directive 95/46/EC, 844/14/EN, WP 217, 9 April 2014.

Academic literature

Ausloos, J. (2019). *GDPR transparency as a research method* [Working paper]. Institute for Information Law. https://hdl.handle.net/11245.1/59f63de3-9197-46f9-b322-c2689ee0aad2

Barja-Martinez, S., Aragüés-Peñalba, M., Munné-Collado, Í., Lloret-Gallego, P., Bullich-Massague, E., & Villafafila-Robles, R. (2021). Artificial intelligence techniques for enabling Big Data services in distribution networks: A review. *Renewable and Sustainable Energy Reviews, 150*, 111459.

Besson, S. (2008). Gender discrimination under EU and ECHR Law: Never shall the twain meet? *Human Rights Law Review, 8*(4), 647–682.

Binns, R., & Veale, M. (2021). Is that your final decision? Multi-stage profiling, selective effects, and Article 22 of the GDPR. *International Data Privacy Law, 11*(4), 319–332.

Borgesius, F. Z., Gray, J., & van Eechoud, M. (2015). Open data, privacy, and fair information principles: Towards a balancing framework. *Berkeley Technology Law Journal, 30*(3), 2073–2131.

Bradford, A. (2020). *The Brussels effect: How the European Union rules the world.* Oxford University Press.

Bygrave, L. A. (2002). *Data protection law: Approaching its rationale, logic and limits.* Kluwer Law International.

Chen, J., Edwards, L., Urquhart, L., & McAuley, D. (2020). Who is responsible for data processing in smart homes? Reconsidering joint controllership and the household exemption. *International Data Privacy Law, 10*(4), 279–293.

Cimina, V. (2021, January). The data protection concepts of 'controller', 'processor' and 'joint controllership' under Regulation (EU) 2018/1725. *ERA Forum, 21*(4), 639–654.

Christoffersen, J. (2009). *Fair balance: Proportionality, subsidiarity and primarity in the European Convention on Human Rights* (Vol. 99). Brill.

Cunningham, M. (2012). Privacy in the age of the hacker: Balancing global privacy and data security law. *George Washington International Law Review, 44.* https://papers.ssrn.com/sol3/papers.cfm?abstract_id=2138307

Dove, E. S., & Chen, J. (2021). What does it mean for a data subject to make their personal data 'manifestly public'? An analysis of GDPR Article 9 (2)(e). *International Data Privacy Law, 11*(2), 107–124

Floridi, L. (2017). Group privacy: A defence and an interpretation. In L. Taylor, L. Floridi, & B. van der Sloot, *Group privacy: New challenges of data technologies* (pp. 83–100). Springer.

Fluitt, A., Cohen, A., Altman, M., Nissim, K., Viljoen, S., & Wood, A. (2019). Data protection's composition problem. *European Data Protection Law Review, 5*(3). https://ssrn.com/abstract=3450650

Gil González, E., & de Hert, P. (2019, April). Understanding the legal provisions that allow processing and profiling of personal data – An analysis of GDPR provisions and principles. *Era Forum, 19*(4), 597–621.

Graef, I., Gellert, R., & Husovec, M. (2018). Towards a holistic regulatory approach for the European data economy: Why the illusive notion of non-personal data is counterproductive to data innovation. *TILEC Discussion Paper No. 2018-029.* https://doi.org/10.2139/ssrn.3256189

Greer, S. C. (1997). *The exceptions to Articles 8 to 11 of the European Convention on Human Rights.* Human rights files No. 15. Council of Europe Publishing

Harbinja, E. (2017). Post-mortem privacy 2.0: Theory, law, and technology. *International Review of Law, Computers & Technology, 31*(1), 26–42.

Haverkort-Speekenbrink, S. (2012). *European non-discrimination law: A comparison of EU Law and the ECHR in the field of non-discrimination and freedom of religion in public employment with an emphasis on the Islamic headscarf issue.* Intersentia.

Hintze, M. (2018). Data controllers, data processors, and the growing use of connected products in the enterprise: Managing risks, understanding benefits, and complying with the GDPR. *Journal of Internet Law* (*Wolters Kluwer*). http://dx.doi.org/10.2139/ssrn.3192721

Hildebrandt, M. (2009). Who is profiling who? Invisible visibility. In S. Gutwirth, Y. Poullet, P. Hert, C. Terwangne, & S. Nouwt, *Reinventing data protection?* (pp. 239–252). Springer.
Hirsch, D. D. (2011). The law and policy of online privacy: Regulation, self-regulation, or co-regulation. *Seattle University Law Review, 34*(2), 439–480.
Hirsch, D. D. (2013). In search of the holy grail: Achieving global privacy rules through sector-based codes of conduct. *Ohio State Law Journal,74*(6), 1029–1070.
Hoofnagle, C. J., & Garfinkel, S. L. (2022). *Law and policy for the quantum age.* Cambridge University Press.
Jasserand, C. (2016). Legal nature of biometric data: From generic personal data to sensitive data. *European Data Law Protection Law Review, 2*(3), 297–311.
Jasserand, C. (2018). Law enforcement access to personal data originally collected by private parties: Missing data subjects' safeguards in directive 2016/680? *Computer Law & Security Review, 34*(1), 154–165.
Kohl, U. (2010). *Jurisdiction and the Internet: Regulatory competence over online activity.* Cambridge University Press.
Kokott, J., & Sobotta, C. (2013). The distinction between privacy and data protection in the jurisprudence of the CJEU and the ECtHR. *International Data Privacy Law, 3*(4), 222–228.
Kuner, C. (2021). Territorial scope and data transfer rules in the GDPR: Realising the EU's ambition of borderless data protection. *University of Cambridge Faculty of Law Research Paper 20/2021.* http://dx.doi.org/10.2139/ssrn.3827850
Loi, M., & Christen, M. (2020). Two concepts of group privacy. *Philosophy & Technology, 33*(2), 207–224.
Liu, T., Mostafa, S., Mohamed, S., & Nguyen, T. S. (2021). Emerging themes of public-private partnership application in developing smart city projects: a conceptual framework. *Built Environment Project and Asset Management, 11*(1), 138–156.
Masciandaro, D. (Ed.). (2017). *Global financial crime: terrorism, money laundering and offshore centres.* Taylor & Francis.
Moerel, L., & Prins, C. (2016). Privacy for the homo digitalis: Proposal for a new regulatory framework for data protection in the light of Big Data and the Internet of Things. https://dx.doi.org/10.2139/ssrn.2784123
Mokrosinska, D. (2020). Why states have no right to privacy, but may be entitled to secrecy: A non-consequentialist defense of state secrecy. *Critical Review of International Social and Political Philosophy, 23*(4), 415–444.
Pormeister, K., & Drozdzowski, L. (2018). Protecting the genetic data of unborn children: A critical analysis. *European Data Protection Law Review, 4*(1), 53–64.
Purtova, N. (2018). The law of everything. Broad concept of personal data and future of EU data protection law. *Law, Innovation and Technology, 10*(1), 40–81.
Scassa, T. (2014). Privacy and open government. *Future Internet, 6*(2), 397–413.

Schermer, B. W., Custers, B., & van der Hof, S. (2014). The crisis of consent: How stronger legal protection may lead to weaker consent in data protection. *Ethics and Information Technology, 16*(2), 171–182.

Shabani, M., & Marelli, L. (2019). Re-identifiability of genomic data and the GDPR: Assessing the re-identifiability of genomic data in light of the EU General Data Protection Regulation. *EMBO Reports, 20*(6), e48316. https://doi.org/10.15252/embr.201948316

Sloan, R. H., & Warner, R. (2014). Beyond notice and choice: Privacy, norms, and consent. *Journal of High Technology Law, 14*(2), 370.

Solove, D. J. (2012). Introduction: Privacy self-management and the consent dilemma. *Harvard Law Review, 126*(7), 1880.

Susser, D. (2019). Notice after notice-and-consent: Why privacy disclosures are valuable even if consent frameworks aren't. *Journal of Information Policy, 9*, 37–62.

Taylor, L., Floridi, L., & van der Sloot, B. (Eds.). (2016). *Group privacy: New challenges of data technologies* (Vol. 126). Springer.

Tobler, C. (2014). Equality and non-discrimination under the ECHR and EU Law. A comparison focusing on discrimination against LGBTI persons. *Zeitschrift für ausländisches öffentliches Recht und Völkerrecht, 74*(3), 521–561.

van der Sloot, B. (2015). Do privacy and data protection rules apply to legal persons and should they? A proposal for a two-tiered system. *Computer Law & Security Review, 31*(1), 26–45.

van der Sloot, B. (2015). Welcome to the jungle: The liability of Internet intermediaries for privacy violations in Europe. *Journal of Intellectual Property, Information Technology and E-Commerce Law, 6*(3), 211–228.

van der Sloot, B. (2017). Do groups have a right to privacy and should they? In L. Taylor, L. Floridi, & B. van der Sloot (Eds.), *Group privacy* (pp. 197–224). Springer.

van der Sloot, B. (2017). *Privacy as virtue*. Intersentia.

van der Sloot, B. (2018). Beyond the access-use debate. In S. Goslinga et al. (Eds.), *Tax and trust*. Eleven International Publishing.

van der Sloot, B. (2019). 'Legal consistency after the General Data Protection Regulation and the Police Directive. *European Journal of Law and Technology*, 9(3). http://ejlt.org/article/view/620

van der Sloot, B. (2020). Regulating non-personal data in the age of Big Data. In M. Tzanou (Ed.), *Health data privacy under the GDPR: Big data challenges and regulatory responses*. Routledge.

van der Sloot, B. (2021). Editorial. *European Data Protection Law Review, 7*(3), 351–357.

van der Sloot, B. (2022). Editorial. *European Data Protection Law Review, 8*(1), 1–6.

van Hoboken, J. (2016). From collection to use in privacy regulation? A forward looking comparison of European and US frameworks for personal data processing.

In B. van der Sloot, D. broeders, & E. Schrijvers, *Exploring the boundaries of Big Data* (pp. 231–259). Amsterdam University Press.

von Grafenstein, M. (2018). *The principle of purpose limitation in data protection laws.* Nomos Verlagsgesellschaft mbH & Co. KG.

Wachter, S. (2018). The GDPR and the Internet of Things: A three-step transparency model. *Law, Innovation and Technology, 10*(2), 266–294.

West, A., Lewis, J., & Currie, P. (2009). Students' Facebook 'friends': Public and private spheres. *Journal of Youth Studies, 12*(6), 615–627.

Westin, A. F., & Baker, M. A. (1972). *Databanks in a free society: Computers, record-keeping, and privacy.* Quadrangle Books.

Yang, Y., Zhuang, Y., & Pan, Y. (2021). Multiple knowledge representation for big data artificial intelligence: Framework, applications, and case studies. *Frontiers of Information Technology & Electronic Engineering, 22*(12), 1551–1558.

Zhu, H. (2020). Big data and artificial intelligence modeling for drug discovery. *Annual Review of Pharmacology and Toxicology, 60*, 573–589.

11. The Regulation of Access to Personal and Non-Personal Data in the EU: From Bits and Pieces to a System?

Thomas Tombal & Inge Graef

Abstract

For years, the nature of data has influenced the rhetoric used and the priorities set in EU debates about regulating access to data. Interestingly, the scope of the proposal for a Data Act no longer depends on whether data qualify as personal or not. Against this background, the chapter discusses how different types of data and policy objectives become intertwined and how different regimes regulating access to data can be aligned – despite the current piecemeal regulatory approach. We discuss the relationship between the GDPR's right to data portability and the Data Act's IoT data access right as well as how forms of data access beyond the initiative and control of individuals can be brought in line with the GDPR.

Keywords: data access, data economy, data sharing, legislative coherence, Data Act, personal data

1. Introduction

As early as 2014, the European Commission began considering the adoption of legislative and non-legislative measures to stimulate the European data economy by promoting access and reuse of data (European Commission, 2014, p. 3). The dividing line between personal and non-personal data has been a recurrent issue in these debates. This dichotomy between the two types of data originally stems from the fact that the scope of application of data protection law (now contained in the General Data Protection Regulation, or GDPR) is limited to personal data. As a result, the processing of data beyond personal data largely remained unregulated until the EU

Van der Sloot & van Schendel. *The Boundaries of Data*. Taylor & Francis Group, 2024
DOI: 10.5117/9789463729192_CH11

legislator adopted the Regulation on the free flow of non-personal data in 2018 (FFNPDR). In the debates about access to data, the nature of the data has influenced the rhetoric used and the priorities set.

While the need for restrictions to create trust and control for individuals has been emphasised in the context of personal data, there has been a much stronger focus on openness and reuse as mechanisms to promote data-driven growth for non-personal data (see European Commission, 2020a, p. 1). In February 2022, the European Commission published its proposal for a Data Act[1] that introduces a data access targeted at the 'Internet of Things' (IoT) (European Commission, 2022a). Interestingly, the scope of this legislative initiative no longer depends on whether data qualifies as personal. Instead, it is 'data generated by the use of a product or related service' that triggers the application of the rules (European Commission, 2022a, Art. 1.1). Nevertheless, when personal data are included in such a dataset, additional conditions apply for data access in the sense that a valid lawful ground under the GDPR needs to be present if the request for data access does not come from the data subject themselves (European Commission, 2022a, Arts. 4.5 and 5.6). The distinction between personal and non-personal data will thus still impact the extent of data access.

Against this background, the chapter discusses how different types of data and different policy objectives in the area become intertwined and how different regimes regulating access to data can be aligned – despite the current piecemeal regulatory approach. For the purpose of this chapter, we interpret the concept of data access broadly, including portability, which consists of physically moving data to another provider, as well as (in situ) access, where the data remain with the original provider that will act as intermediary between the party invoking data access and the new provider (Van Alstyne et al., 2021, pp. 34–35). As we will show, overlap between different data access regimes is common, so several regimes can apply in parallel to the same situation.

Section 3 discusses the relationship between the GDPR's right to data portability and the data access right created by the Data Act proposal. These two legal mechanisms overlap in scope, considering that an individual may invoke the GDPR portability right to move personal data between IoT devices but may also choose to rely on the data access right created by the Data Act proposal. Beyond such user-initiated requests, access to personal data may be desirable to stimulate data-driven innovation even if no consent is or can be obtained from the individual. While sector-specific data access regimes – such as the Data Act proposal for the IoT sector and the Payment

1 For a detailed comment of this proposal, see Drexl et al. (2022).

Services Directive 2 (PSD2) for the payment sector – only facilitate access at the request of the user, the Digital Markets Act contains a form of data access between a gatekeeping platform and businesses without the need for individual users to take any action.

Section 4 discusses how forms of data access beyond the initiative and control of individuals can be brought in line with the GDPR. Even though the scope of the mechanisms for data access contained in more recently proposed legislation, like the Digital Markets Act and the Data Act proposal, no longer depend on whether data are personal, the nature of the data still plays a role in the implementation of the data access. We show that creating upfront guidance on how to balance considerations of data protection (inherent to personal data) with considerations of competition and innovation (typically prevailing in the case of non-personal data) can help these new legislative instruments reach their objectives and limit the discretion of market players to balance these considerations themselves in a way that promotes their own commercial goals. Before diving into these issues, Section 2 provides a background of the policy and academic debate regarding the distinction between personal and non-personal data.[2]

2. Distinction Between Personal and Non-Personal Data

Personal data are defined in the GDPR as 'any information relating to an identified or identifiable natural person (data subject)' (Article 4.1 GDPR). Information can relate to an identified or identifiable natural person either in content, purpose, result or impact (Article 29 Working Party, 2007, pp. 9–12; Graef et al., 2019, p. 609). According to the GDPR, an identifiable natural person is one who can be identified, directly or indirectly, in particular by reference to an identifier (Article 4.1 GDPR). In order to determine whether a person is identifiable, account must be taken of all the reasonable means likely to be used, either by the data controller or by a third party, to identify, directly or indirectly, the person (Recital 26 GDPR). In other words, a person is identifiable if they can be singled out (Article 29 Working Party, 2007, pp. 12–15). To ascertain the likeliness of the re-identification of the person, account must be taken of a series of objective factors, such as the costs of and the amount of time required for re-identification, in light of the available technology and technological developments at the time of processing (Recital 26 GDPR).

2 Note that the analysis is based on the Commission's proposal of the Data Act, as the final text was not yet available at the time of finalising the chapter.

In policy documents, it has been acknowledged that personal data can be gathered in various ways. Accordingly, we further sub-divide personal data into four categories, depending on the way they are collected. These sub-categories are not purely trivial, as they have relevance for determining the scope of application of the right to data portability, as will be discussed in Section 3. The first category is 'data actively and knowingly provided by the data subject' (Article 29 Working Party, 2017, p. 10). This includes, but is not limited to, any information provided by completing an online registration form, posts on social media, etc. This category is also sometimes referred to as 'volunteered data' (OECD, 2019, p. 30). The second category is 'observed data provided by the data subject by virtue of the use of the service or the device' (Article 29 Working Party, 2017, p. 10). Examples include the search history of a data subject, the history of the websites they have visited, traffic and location data generated by the use of a mobile application or other types of data, such as the average pulse rate or the number of steps taken by a data subject, which would be collected by a connected watch. The third category is 'inferred data and derived data created by the data controller on the basis of the data "provided by the data subject"' (Article 29 Working Party, 2017, p. 10). This refers to data resulting from a subsequent analysis carried out by the controller on the basis of data provided (actively or observed) by the data subject. Examples are user profiles created by the controller on the basis of the analysis of data provided by the data subjects, or the results of an assessment of the data subject's health based on the health data collected by their smart watch. This is also sometimes presented as 'second generation data', which is created, inferred or derived from 'first generation data' (Kemp, 2019, p. 8). The fourth category is 'acquired data', which is personal data obtained from third parties on the basis of a voluntary data sharing mechanism (e.g. data acquired from data brokers; OECD, 2019, p. 31) or on the basis of a compulsory data sharing mechanism. For instance, PSD2 grants to the providers of a payment initiation service and the providers of an account information service the right to acquire the payment account information of the users of their services (the consumers), if the latter have explicitly consented to it (Articles 64–67 PSD2).

Non-personal data, on the other hand, are usually residually defined as all data other than personal data (Article 1 FFNPDR), either because they have never been personal data in the first place (such as industrial data generated by the IoT, e.g. sensors installed on industrial machines that provide data on maintenance needs), or because they have been anonymised[3] (e.g. through

3 'Process by which personally identifiable information (PII) is irreversibly altered in such a way that a PII principal can no longer be identified directly or indirectly, either by the PII controller alone or in collaboration with any other party' (ISO, 2011, point 2.2).

mathematical and statistical operations) and therefore no longer qualify as personal data since the data subject is no longer identifiable (Recital 26 GDPR; European Commission, 2019, p. 6). In this regard, anonymised data should not be confused with pseudonymised data, which remain personal data subject to the GDPR, given that the data subject can still be re-identified by using additional information (Article 4.5 GDPR). Importantly, determining whether specific data should be considered as anonymised or pseudonymised will always be a function of the specific circumstances of each individual case (European Commission, 2019, p. 6).

This choice of a residual definition for non-personal data has been criticised, as it presumes that the scope of what constitutes personal data can be clearly defined (Somaini, 2020, pp. 88–89; Graef et al., 2019, pp. 608–610). The criticism does not relate to the existence of the dichotomy between personal and non-personal data as such, which originates from the fact that the GDPR's reach is limited to personal data, but it is up to the European legislator to adopt a separate regulatory framework built on the notion of non-personal data. The FFNPDR, among others, prohibits Member States from imposing data localisation requirements according to which processing of data would have to take place in their own territory – with the exception of requirements justified on grounds of public security (Article 4.1 FFNPDR). The intention of the legislator to complement the free movement of personal data, already regulated by the GDPR, with provisions on the free movement of non-personal data (contained in the FFNPDR), seems logical. However, it gives rise to the situation that stricter free movement obligations apply to non-personal data. This is because the GDPR does not prohibit Member States from imposing restrictions on the free movement of personal data for reasons other than data protection. As a result, Member States could try to bypass the stricter free movement obligations under the FFNPDR by claiming that data are personal (Graef et al., 2019, p. 613).

Indeed, it might not be easy to determine whether specific data should be considered as personal in practice. This is due to the broad definition of personal data, making it a dynamic, fluid and open-ended concept, as the possibilities of re-identification evolve with the technology, increasing the scope of what should be considered as personal data over time (Somaini, 2020, pp. 88–90; Graef et al., 2019, p. 609). This is because 'technological and other developments may change what constitutes "unreasonable time, effort or other resources" ... to re-identify the data subject' (Council of Europe, 2018, p. 4).

This has led some authors to call for a more holistic approach, because it is impossible to govern and regulate personal data and non-personal data separately due to the constant flow between each category (Graef et al., 2019; Taylor, 2013). From a normative perspective, there is no reason to believe that non-personal data constitutes a more important input for innovation than personal data (Wendehorst, 2017, pp. 330–331). Similarly, the scope of application of other legal regimes relevant to data innovation beyond data protection does not depend on whether data are personal. Innovation is at the heart of intellectual property and competition law, where the personal or non-personal character of data has never been a relevant consideration (Graef et al., 2019, pp. 617–618).

Moreover, the dichotomy is also complex to apply in practice because, in most cases, datasets will be 'mixed', i.e. composed of both personal and non-personal data (European Commission, 2019, pp. 4 and 7; Graef et al., 2019, pp. 610–611). In its guidance on the FFNPDR, the Commission clarified that the GDPR will have to be applied to the entirety of a dataset if personal and non-personal data are 'inextricably linked', even if personal data only represent a small part of it (Article 2.2 FFNPDR; European Commission, 2019, p. 9). Although this concept of 'inextricably linked' is not defined, it should be understood as encompassing situations where it would be impossible, economically inefficient or technically infeasible to separate the personal data from the non-personal data in the set (European Commission, 2019, p. 10).

Like the assessment of whether personal data have been anonymised or merely pseudonymised, we argue that 'account should be taken of all objective factors, such as the costs of and the amount of time required …, taking into consideration the available technology at the time of the processing and technological developments' (Recital 26 GDPR). For instance, it would be economically inefficient for a company to multiply its software costs if it had to purchase separate software to manage personal data, on the one hand, and non-personal data, on the other (European Commission, 2019, p. 10). There might also be cases where separating the data generated a significant decrease in the value of the dataset, making it economically inefficient (European Commission, 2019, p. 10). Regarding the assessment of the technical infeasibility of separating the mixed datasets, the changing nature of the data might reinforce the difficulty of striking a clear distinction between personal and non-personal data (European Commission, 2019, p. 10). In sum, because most datasets are mixed and 'inextricably linked', there is a risk that 'in the near future everything will be or will contain personal data, leading to the application of data protection to everything' (Purtova, 2018, p. 40).

To some extent, this call for a holistic approach seems to have been heard by the European legislator, as more recent legislative initiatives, such as the Data Governance Act (DGA) and the Data Act proposal, cover both personal and non-personal data, while taking personal data protection considerations into account where relevant. In Section 3, we illustrate how this holistic approach in the Data Act corresponds with the GDPR in terms of user-initiated requests for data access.

3. User-Initiated Requests for Data Access: The GDPR Versus the Data Act

One of the novelties contained in the Data Act proposal is the 'Internet of Things data access right' (European Commission, 2022a, p. 13), which makes it compulsory for providers of IoT products[4] and of related services,[5] including virtual assistants,[6] to share some of their data with their users[7] or with private third parties at the request of their users (European Commission, 2022a, Arts. 3–7). In a nutshell, the Data Act proposal provides that 'products shall be designed and manufactured, and related services shall be provided, in such a manner that data generated by their use are, by default, easily, securely and, where relevant and appropriate, directly accessible to the user' (European Commission, 2022a, Art. 3.1). If these IoT-generated data are not directly accessible to the user, the provider of IoT products or related services will have to make it available to the user upon request (B2U data sharing) (European Commission, 2022a, Art. 4.1). Furthermore, the provider of IoT products or related services will also have to make this IoT-generated data available to a third party (B2B data sharing), upon request by a user or by a party acting on behalf of a user (European Commission, 2022a, Art. 5.1).

4 '"Product" means a tangible, movable item, including where incorporated in an immovable item, that obtains, generates or collects, data concerning its use or environment, and that is able to communicate data via a publicly available electronic communications service and whose primary function is not the storing and processing of data' (European Commission, 2022a, Art. 2[2]). See also Recitals 14 and 15.

5 '"Related service" means a digital service, including software, which is incorporated in or inter-connected with a product in such a way that its absence would prevent the product from performing one of its functions' (European Commission, 2022a, Art. 2[3]). See also Recital 16.

6 '"Virtual assistants" means software that can process demands, tasks or questions including based on audio, written input, gestures or motions, and based on those demands, tasks or questions provides access their own and third party services or control their own and third party devices' (European Commission, 2022a, Art. 2[4]). See also Recital 22.

7 '"User" means a natural or legal person that owns, rents or leases a product or receives a services' (European Commission, 2022a, Art. 2[5]). See also Recital 18. According to some, this definition is too restrictive, as 'persons that use the product without having such legal title will not be vested with the right' (Drexl et al., 2022, 24).

While we will detail this right further below, the above already makes it reminiscent of the data portability right contained in Article 20 of the GDPR.[8] One might therefore wonder whether the latter would remain relevant in situations where both legislative instruments could apply in parallel. Accordingly, this section aims to clarify to what extent these two legal mechanisms overlap and/or differ in terms of objectives, scope, beneficiaries and sharing modalities and in terms of factoring the interests of others.

3.1. Objectives

Before outlining the specific objective of the IoT data access right, it is first relevant to understand the broader objective of the Data Act proposal in which the right has been inserted. In short, the goal of this proposal is to address issues slowing down the development of the European data economy, such as the insufficient availability of data for reuse, by aiming to create a legal instrument, which would enable wider data use across the economy (European Commission, 2022b, pp. 1 and 7). In this context, the objective of the IoT data access right is to ensure fairness in the allocation of value from data among actors in the data economy and to foster access to and use of data in order to increase innovation and competition (European Commission, 2022a, p. 2).

Indeed, the proposal outlines that the provider's exclusive de facto or de jure control over the use of data generated by IoT products or related services typically contributes to lock-in effects, which hinder the development of aftermarket services by alternative players (European Commission, 2022a, Rec. 19). Accordingly, this kind of an IoT data access right would allow for the development of a more competitive offer for aftermarket services, such as repair and maintenance of connected objects, as the users would no longer depend on the manufacturer's services only (European Commission, 2022a, Rec. 28; European Commission, 2022c).[9]

Article 20 GDPR, on the other hand, aims at strengthening the control that data subjects have over 'their' personal data (Recital 68 GDPR). In reality, this objective is translated into two sub-objectives. First, this right to data portability 'represents an opportunity to "re-balance" the relationship between data subject and data controllers' 'by affirming individuals' personal rights

8 For a detailed analysis of the portability right in the GDPR, see Tombal (2022, pp. 134–151).

9 Some, however, argue that the economic justification of this IoT data access right remains unclear, especially the rationale for permitting the reuse of the data to develop products/services that do not compete with the data holder's (Drexl et al., 2022, pp. 15–19).

and control over the personal data concerning them' (European Commission, 2012, p. 9). This objective is transversal in the GDPR and goes beyond the right to data portability (Tombal, 2018, pp. 555–556; Somaini, 2018, p. 172). Second, this right to data portability aims at breaking down the power of powerful data controllers by making it easier for the data subject to change service providers through the prevention of 'lock-in' situations (Article 29 Working Party, 2017, p. 4). In the first version of its guidelines on the right to data portability, the Article 29 Working Party (today the European Data Protection Board, EDPB) even indicated that this was the 'primary aim' of this new right, as it should facilitate the creation of new services (Article 29 Working Party, 2016, p. 4). This echoes the statement made by the Council regarding its position at first reading, where it outlines that the right to portability 'also encourages competition amongst controllers' (Council, 2016, p. 89). However, in what seems to be a move to position this right as a fundamental rights tool rather than as a tool aiming to address competition issues, the indication that this constituted the 'primary aim' of the right was deleted in the revised version of the guidelines from April 2017. They now state that the main objective of this right is to promote 'data subject empowerment' and that the GDPR aims to regulate the processing of personal data and not to deal with competition issues (Article 29 Working Party, 2017, p. 4).

These distinct objectives underlying the GDPR's right to data portability and the Data Act's data access right illustrate their complementary nature but also raise questions about how the two legal mechanisms can be applied in parallel.

3.2. Scope

A key element to understand whether the IoT data access right and the GDPR portability right potentially overlap and/or differ is the determination of the scope of these rights. In this regard, we aim to clarify their respective scope by answering two fundamental questions: who can be targeted by an access/portability request, and which types of data are covered?

3.2.1. Who Can Be Targeted by an Access/Portability Request?

An important difference between the GDPR portability right and the IoT data access right is that the GDPR potentially applies to any type of data controller that processes personal data by automated means, independently of the type of (economic or societal) activity it pursues (Article 20.1 GDPR).

Comparatively, the Data Act only applies to providers of IoT products and of related services, including virtual assistants. While this scope might appear quite limited at first sight, the definition of 'IoT products' is in fact quite broad, as it covers any type of 'connected object' equipped with sensors generating or collecting data about its performance, use or environment and able to communicate data through the IoT (European Commission, 2022a, Rec. 14). This is especially true today as objects that we use in our daily life are increasingly 'connected' or 'smart', such as 'vehicles, home equipment and consumer goods, medical and health devices[10] or agricultural and industrial machinery' (European Commission, 2022a, Rec. 14).

Nevertheless, the proposal outlines that providers of products that are primarily designed to display, play, record or transmit content should, on the contrary, not be covered by the IoT data access right (European Commission, 2022a, Rec. 15). The Commission argues that this is because such products, which would include 'personal computers, servers, tablets and smart phones, cameras, webcams, sound recording systems and text scanners', require human input to produce various forms of content, such as text documents, sound files, video files, games and digital maps (European Commission, 2022a, Rec. 15). The proposal thus makes a difference between products that generate data and those that generate content. While this distinction is appealing in theory, it might not always be as straightforward in practice. For instance, when is a text file content or data? Disagreements can be expected about this issue. Moreover, some have criticised this distinction by outlining that 'there is no reason why a user of a smart watch can rely on the [IoT data access right] to get the watch repaired by a third-party service provider while such right would not be recognised with respect to a camera or a smartphone. Complete exclusion of such devices is not at all warranted' (Drexl et al., 2022, p. 24).

The proposal also clarifies that the IoT data access right should apply to providers of digital services, including software, which are incorporated in or connected with products in such a way that their absence would prevent the products from performing one of their functions (European Commission, 2022a, Art. 2.3 and Rec. 16). Furthermore, this right should also apply to virtual assistants because they can act as a single gateway to record significant amounts of relevant data on how users interact with IoT products, notably in 'smart houses' (European Commission, 2022a, Rec. 22).

10 Regarding medical and health devices, the European Data Protection Board (EDPB) and the European Data Protection Supervisor (EDPS) have expressed concerns about the fact that sensitive data could thus be covered and that insufficient safeguards to protect such highly sensitive information are currently provided in the proposal (EDPB-EDPS, 2022, pp. 2 and 8).

Finally, an important limitation to the scope of the IoT data access right is that it does not apply to providers of IoT products or related services that qualify as micro or small enterprises (European Commission, 2022a, Art. 7.1),[11] while no such size limitation exists for the GDPR portability right. Although such exclusion is criticised (Drexl et al., 2022 pp. 35–36), this can be linked to the objectives of each of these tools. Indeed, as the GDPR portability right aims at rebalancing the relationship between the data subjects and the data controllers, it is logical that it also applies to smaller undertakings. On the other hand, since the IoT data access right aims at stimulating innovation and competition, it makes sense to avoid burdening smaller undertakings (European Commission, 2022a, Rec. 37). This shows how the underlying objectives of data access regimes influence their scope of application.

In conclusion, the scope of the GDPR portability right is thus broader than the scope of the IoT data access right. The GDPR's right to data portability applies to all forms of personal data processing, also beyond IoT, and does not have a carve-out for smaller undertakings. That being said, it is important to underline that the GDPR portability right only applies to data controllers that process personal data on the basis of the data subjects' consent or of a contract (and thus not, for instance, to controllers processing data based on public or legitimate interests; see Articles 6.1.e) and f) GDPR; European Commission, 2022b, p. 16), while the IoT data access right applies irrespective of the lawful ground of processing (European Commission, 2022a, Rec. 31).

3.2.2. *Which Types of Data Are Covered?*

Another important difference between these two rights is that while the GDPR portability right only applies to personal data, the IoT data access right applies to both personal and non-personal data (European Commission, 2022a, Recs. 30–31). Focusing on personal data, both rights seem to apply to the same sub-categories of personal data presented in Section 2, namely 'actively provided' and 'observed' personal data.

Indeed, the IoT data access right applies to personal and non-personal data generated by the use of a product or related service, which includes data intentionally provided by the user (actively provided), as well as data 'generated as a by-product of the user's action, such as diagnostics data, and without any action by the user, such as when the product is in "standby mode", and data recorded during periods when the product is switched off' (observed data) (European Commission, 2022a, Rec. 17).

11 Micro and small enterprises are defined in European Commission (2003, Art. 2).

Similarly, the GDPR portability right is limited to personal data 'provided' by the data subject (Article 20.1 GDPR). While the GDPR itself does not explain the meaning of the word 'provided', the Article 29 Working Party has clarified that it includes 'data actively and knowingly provided by the data subject', as well as 'observed data provided by the data subject by virtue of the use of the service or the device' (Article 29 Working Party, 2017, p. 10). However, the fact that 'observed data' are also covered by Article 20 GDPR is uncertain and has been criticised by some, who argue that it goes beyond what has been envisaged by the European legislator (European Commission, 2022b, p. 16; Meyer, 2017). This might explain why the Commission outlined in its Data Act proposal that, contrary to the GDPR data portability right, there is no doubt as to whether the IoT data access right also applies to 'observed data' (European Commission, 2022a, Rec. 31).

On the other hand, none of these two rights apply to data that have been derived or inferred from this 'actively provided' or 'observed' data (inferred/derived data) (European Commission, 2022a, Rec. 14; Article 29 Working Party, 2017, p. 10). This prevents potential competitors of the data holders from accessing their most strategic data, as the true value of their services lies precisely in this second generation data, generated on the basis of the actively provided/observed data (e.g. user profiles that can be monetised to advertisers) (Graef et al., 2018, p. 1375). Accordingly, exempting inferred/derived data from the scope of these rights protects the innovation, investment and collection incentives of the data holders and thus reaches an appropriate balance between the benefits for the users/data subjects and the preservation of the business interests of the data holder (European Commission, 2022a, p. 3; Article 29 Working Party, 2017, pp. 11–12; Krämer et al., 2020, p. 9; OECD, 2020, p. 45).[12]

3.3. Beneficiaries and Sharing Modalities

A common point between the GDPR data portability right and the IoT data access right is that they should both benefit data subjects/users, as well as third parties.[13] However, there are differences in terms of eligible third parties as well as regarding data sharing modalities.

12 For the same reasons, the IoT data access right does not apply to inferred non-personal data either. Nevertheless, some argue that the Data Act proposal should also apply to such inferred/derived data, as otherwise it risks being inefficient (Drexl et al., 2022, pp. 10–15).

13 At least in theory, as it must be acknowledged that, so far, such rights have not been used much in practice.

3.3.1. *The Data Subject/User of the IoT Product Itself*

On the one hand, the data holder should make the data available to the data subject (Article 20.1 GDPR) or the user of the IoT product itself (European Commission, 2022a, Art. 4.1). While this is quite straightforward in the context of the GDPR (e.g. a person moves their pictures from a social network server to their own laptop), it must be reiterated that the user of the IoT product can be a natural person or a legal person (e.g. a farmer asking to obtain data generated by their use of their smart tractor, or a car manufacturer asking to obtain data generated by the use of an industrial machine on an assembly line) (European Commission, 2022a, Art. 2[5]). In the latter case, the legal person could be asking to obtain not only IoT-generated non-personal data but also IoT-generated personal data pertaining to data subjects (e.g. the workers responsible for the industrial machine in the assembly line). Accordingly, the Data Act proposal provides that if a user asks to obtain personal data generated by the use of a product or related service and is not itself the data subject, such data shall only be made available by the data holder to the user if a valid lawful ground under the GDPR exists – such as the consent of the data subject or legitimate interest (European Commission, 2022a, Art. 4.5).[14] In this regard, the EDPB and the European Data Protection Supervisor (EDPS) outline that, as far as possible, such data should be anonymised and data subjects should be clearly informed about this transfer in order to be able to exercise their rights (EDPB-EDPS, 2022, pp. 2–3 and 14–15). This shows that the nature of data still influences how the data access right of the Data Act proposal is to be implemented, even though the scope of the new right no longer depends on whether the data are personal.

Regarding data sharing modalities, the GDPR and the Data Act proposal both provide that this should be done free of charge, without undue delay and on the basis of a simple request through electronic means where technically feasible (Articles 12.3 and 12.5 GDPR; European Commission, 2022a, Art. 4.1). However, these two rights differ in terms of the technical modalities of the sharing. Indeed, while the Data Act proposal remains silent regarding the format in which such data should be shared, the GDPR provides that the data should be provided 'in a structured, commonly used and machine-readable format' (Article 20.1 GDPR).

14 Interestingly, the proposal adds that this provision does not create a lawful ground under the GDPR for the data holder to provide access to personal data when requested by a user that is not a data subject (Recital 24). On the use of contracts as a lawful ground, see EDPB-EDPS (2022, pp. 10–11).

Another distinction between the GDPR portability right and the Data Act's data access rights relates to the temporality of the sharing. Indeed, the IoT data access right explicitly provides that, where applicable, the data should be shared continuously and in real-time (European Commission, 2022a, Art. 4.1). On the other hand, although the formulation of Article 20 GDPR leaves no doubt about the fact that the right to personal data portability is not merely a 'one shot', it is more uncertain whether this provision could be used as a basis to establish a continuous portability of personal data (Krämer et al., 2020, p. 81; European Commission, 2022b, p. 16; Tombal, 2022, pp. 149–151). This is because this right has been designed to enable switching between service providers rather than to enable data reuse in a wider digital ecosystem (European Commission, 2020a, p. 10). However, the fact that such a possibility has likely not been considered by the drafters of the GDPR nor by the Article 29 Working Party in its guidelines does not mean that the text of Article 20 could not be read as allowing such continuous portability. Nevertheless, due to this uncertainty, some authors argue that Article 20 in its current form does not allow for the continuous porting of personal data and that this limits its effectiveness and the potential benefits that can be derived from it (Krämer et al., 2020, p. 13; European Commission, 2020a, p. 10). The Data Act's data access right is thus more prescriptive than the GDPR portability right in this regard.

3.3.2. Third Parties

On the other hand, both the GDPR and the Data Act provide that the subject/user can share the data it obtained from the data holder with a third party (indirect sharing; Article 20.2 GDPR; European Commission, 2022a, Rec. 28) and can even request the data holder to share data directly with that third party (direct sharing; Article 20.2 GDPR; European Commission, 2022a, Art. 5.1).[15] However, the GDPR provides that the data holder must only enable such direct sharing 'where technically feasible' (Article 20.2 GDPR), which means that the data holder has no obligation to ensure this technical feasibility. On the contrary, under the Data Act, this possibility for direct data sharing with a third party at the request of the user is no longer a mere possibility but an obligation, and the data must be of the same quality as

15 Our understanding of the Data Act Proposal is that Article 5 only pertains to the direct sharing of data between a data holder and a third party, while the indirect sharing with a third party would occur through Article 4 (i.e. the data holder shares the data with the user on the basis of Article 4 of the Data Act Proposal, and the user then shares these data with a third party).

is available to the data holder (European Commission, 2022a, Art. 5.1 and Rec. 31). Importantly, if the user is a legal person, IoT-generated personal data pertaining to data subjects can only be shared with a third party if a valid lawful ground under the GDPR is present (European Commission, 2022a, Art. 5.6). Furthermore, the data should be anonymised to the greatest extent possible, and the data subjects should be informed about this transfer (EDPB-EDPS, 2022, pp. 2–3 and 14–15). Third parties should also keep in mind whether the data to be accessed are personal, even though the new right is equally applicable for accessing personal as well as non-personal data.

Another relevant difference between the two regimes is that while any third party (public or private) could receive data through Article 20 GDPR, the Data Act identifies the third parties that are eligible to receive data through the IoT data access right, namely undertakings, research organisations and non-profit organisations (European Commission, 2022a, Rec. 29). Moreover, any undertaking that would be designated as a gatekeeper under Article 3 of the Digital Markets Act (European Commission, 2020b; European Parliament 2022) is not an eligible third party (European Commission, 2022a, Art. 5.2). The justification for their exclusion is that 'given the unrivalled ability of these companies to acquire data, it would not be necessary to achieve the objective of this Regulation, and would thus be disproportionate in relation to data holders made subject to such obligations' (European Commission, 2022a, Rec. 36).[16]

Accordingly, a gatekeeper may not receive data directly from the data holder nor indirectly receive data from a user that the latter has obtained through the IoT data access right (European Commission, 2022a, Art. 5.2.c). It also cannot solicit or commercially incentivise in any manner, including through (monetary) compensation, a user to share the data indirectly with it, or by requesting the direct sharing from the data holder (European Commission, 2022a, Art. 5.2.a–b). Furthermore, a third party cannot transmit data that it has received through the IoT data access right to a gatekeeper, for instance through sub-contracting the service provision to a gatekeeper (European Commission, 2022a, Art. 6.2.d and Rec. 36).[17] This should prevent gatekeepers from circumventing their ineligibility to receive data.

However, since gatekeepers can receive data through the GDPR portability right, this would allow them to by-pass this restriction to some extent.

16 Some however argue that there are several arguments that can be made against such an exclusion (Drexl et al., 2022, pp. 34–35).

17 Nevertheless, 'this does not prevent third parties from using data processing services offered by a designated gatekeeper' (Recital 36).

This is acknowledged in the Data Act proposal itself, as it provides that 'this Regulation does not prevent these companies from obtaining data through other lawful means' (European Commission, 2022a, Rec. 36). That being said, this is not as advantageous for gatekeepers. First, it would only allow gatekeepers to get access to personal data but not to non-personal data. Second, the GDPR portability right only applies to data controllers that process personal data on the basis of the data subjects' consent or of a contract. Third, gatekeepers will only get access to the data directly from the data holder 'where technically feasible' and will thus often have to request these data from the data subject herself. Fourth, it is uncertain whether Article 20 GDPR would allow for a continuous and real-time portability of personal data. As a result, this remains less appealing for gatekeepers than if they could rely on the IoT data access right. Nevertheless, it will be interesting to see whether the disqualification of gatekeepers as eligible third parties under the Data Act gives rise to a dynamic whereby big tech firms start to plead for an expansive interpretation of the GDPR's right to data portability, against which they were opposed up to now (Egan, 2019), to ensure the technical feasibility of direct data transfers and to facilitate continuous and real-time portability under the GDPR.

In terms of modalities, the GDPR and the Data Act proposal both provide that sharing with third parties should occur without undue delay and that it should be free of charge for the user (Articles 12.3 and 12.5 GDPR; European Commission, 2022a, Art. 5.1). On the other hand, while the GDPR does not provide for any type of remuneration between the third party and the data holder, the Data Act outlines that the data holder could request a reasonable compensation to the data holder (European Commission, 2022a, Art. 9.1 and Rec. 31). Importantly, while it is certain that the third party will need to remunerate the data holder if the data are directly shared between them, it is unclear whether such remuneration is also due if the third party only indirectly receives the data through the user (i.e. the data holder shares the data with the user on the basis of Article 4 of the Data Act Proposal, and the user then shares these data with a third party). In any case, it cannot be excluded that this remuneration requirement will indirectly affect the users, as the price paid by third parties to access the data could be passed on to them in the cost of the product or service. Therefore, some argue that the data holder should not be remunerated by third parties either (Drexl et al., 2022, p. 29).

More concretely, and in light of the principle of contractual freedom, the data holder and the third party will have to conclude a data sharing agreement to determine the fair, reasonable and non-discriminatory terms under which the data will be shared (European Commission, 2022a, Art. 8

and Rec. 39).[18] One wonders whether more specific and prescriptive rules regarding the conditions of the Data Act's data access right would have been desirable to prevent negotiation problems and disputes, in particular in instances where imbalances in bargaining power may otherwise result in limited data access (Kerber, 2022, pp. 11–12). For instance, determining whether the data access will occur through the transmission of a copy of the data to the third party (the data goes to the algorithm) or through 'in-situ access' by the third party to the data holder's databases (the algorithm comes to the data) is important, as the control exercised by the data holder and the potential limits this might create for the third party are much greater in the latter scenario (Kerber, 2022, pp. 8–9; Drexl et al., 2022, p. 26). In fact, the Data Act proposal seems to favour 'in-situ' access (European Commission, 2022a, Rec. 8 and 21), while the proposal's impact assessment refers to 'data access and portability' (European Commission, 2022b, p. 67).

The conclusion of such a contract is thus a precondition for the sharing according to the Data Act proposal, while the GDPR does not contain a similar requirement. Once again, while it is certain that such a contract will need to be concluded if the data are directly shared between the holder and the third party, it is unclear whether such contract is also necessary if the third party only indirectly receives the data through the user. If such a contract is also requested for indirect sharing, this implies that users cannot share data obtained from the data holder through the Article 4 IoT access right with a third party unless the latter and the data holder have concluded such a contract (Kerber, 2022, p. 6). This could significantly hamper data sharing possibilities. However, the Data Act provides that if the data holder and the third party do not find an agreement in this regard, this should not hinder, prevent or interfere with the GDPR data portability right (European Commission, 2022a, Art. 5.7 and Rec. 31).

This seems to indicate that the Commission views the GDPR as containing a de minimis data portability right with a broad scope of application, on top of which more specific and narrower, but arguably more 'powerful', portability rights (such as the IoT data access right) can exist. At the same time, the degree to which the Data Act's data access right will be more powerful than the GDPR portability right also seems to depend on the outcome of contractual negotiations between the parties as to the precise conditions of data access (Kerber, 2022).

18 According to the EDPB and the EDPS, the fact that the data subject, whose data might be shared, plays no role in the elaboration of such contract 'risks to severely compromise the effectiveness of data protection rights' (EDPB-EDPS, 2022, p. 17).

3.4. Factoring the Interests of Others

Like any other data sharing initiative, both the GDPR portability right and the IoT data access right entail balancing exercises (Tombal, 2022; von Grafenstein, 2022). Indeed, the benefits that the data subject, the user or the third party will derive from receiving the data must be articulated with the interests of the data holder, in order to preserve his data collection and processing incentives, as well as with the rights and freedoms of other data subjects (European Commission, 2022a, p. 3; Article 29 Working Party, 2017, pp. 11–12).

3.4.1. Factoring the Interests of the Data Holders

The GDPR explicitly outlines that the data portability right should not affect the data holder's intellectual property (IP) rights or trade secrets (Article 20.4 and Rec. 63 GDPR). While the GDPR does not provide much more guidance on how this should be done in practice, the Article 29 Working Party has outlined that the potential risks that data portability might entail for the data holder's business interests and (IP/trade secret) rights cannot themselves serve as the basis for a refusal to apply such a right (Article 29 Working Party, 2017, p. 12). Rather, a concrete analysis of the adverse effects that portability could entail for the data holders' IP/trade secrets rights must therefore be carried out, and some suggest that the standard for rejecting portability requests should be higher than when there is a mere 'interference' with these rights (Graef et al., 2018, p. 1379).

The Data Act proposal, on the other hand, is more explicit regarding the articulation between the IoT data access right and the data holders' IP and trade secret rights. Indeed, it outlines that in order not to hinder the exercise of the IoT data access right, the application of the data holder's sui generis database right (Database Directive: Directive 96/9/EC, Art. 7) on 'databases containing data obtained from or generated by the use of a product or a related service' should be excluded (European Commission, 2022a, Art. 35). Regarding the data holder's trade secrets, the Data Act provides that they should only be disclosed if all the specific necessary measures are taken to protect their confidentiality (European Commission, 2022a, Arts. 4.3 and 5.8). Moreover, they can only be disclosed with third parties 'to the extent that they are strictly necessary to fulfil the purpose agreed between the user and the third party' (European Commission, 2022a, Art. 5.8). The balance with the data holder's database rights is thus struck in favour of the users and third parties, while the balance with its trade secrets is struck in favour of the data holder. This has the merit of being clearer than the

GDPR regime, although the exact outcome of any balancing with the data holder's trade secrets is left up to contractual negotiations between parties to a large extent (Kerber, 2022, pp. 11–2). Moreover, some argue that the Data Act overlooks the fact that 'it is often highly uncertain whether the legal requirements of trade secrets are fulfilled, or to put it differently, whether at a later stage a court will confirm trade secrets protection' (Drexl et al., 2022, p. 100). In this regard, any disputes regarding trade secret protection and confidentiality agreements must be settled by competent authorities or courts at the Member State level and do not benefit from the speedier mechanism of dispute settlement within 90 days that the Data Act sets up for the determination of fair, reasonable and non-discriminatory terms of data access (European Commission, 2022a, Arts. 10 and 31).

The interests of the data holder can also be preserved through the limitation of the authorised data reuses. In this regard, the Data Act provides that a third party shall not 'make the data available it receives to another third party, in raw, aggregated or derived form, unless this is necessary to provide the service requested by the user' (European Commission, 2022a, Art. 6.2.c), although it cannot prevent the users themselves from doing so (European Commission, 2022a, Art. 6.2.f). This echoes the GDPR's purpose limitation and data minimisation principles and makes similar considerations relevant for other data beyond personal data under the Data Act's data access right (Articles 5.1.b–c GDPR). It does not seem immediately logical to extend the reach of these data protection principles to non-personal data, where the predominant focus – unlike for personal data – has so far been on promoting reuse and sharing of data. As a result, the decision of the Commission to impose considerations similar to purpose limitation and data minimisation on non-personal data in the Data Act proposal may indicate the importance it attaches to protecting the investments of original data holders in collecting data. While this is a valid policy choice, it shows that the Commission's approach to the Data Act proposal ultimately does not prioritise the reuse and sharing of non-personal data as much as its earlier policy documents may have suggested.

More fundamentally, while the GDPR portability right does not put any kind of restriction on the type of use that the data subjects and the third parties can make of the ported data (providing it complies with personal data protection rules), the IoT data access right prevents the users and the third parties from developing a product that competes with the product from which the data originates (European Commission, 2022a, Arts. 4.4 and 6.2.e). The reasoning behind this is that the Data Act wishes 'to avoid undermining the investment incentives for the type of product from which the data are obtained, for instance, by the use of data to develop a competing product' (European Commission, 2022a, Rec. 28). Beyond this restriction, users and third parties remain free in how they use the obtained data. In particular, users and third parties are not prevented from developing competing services or new and innovative (complementary) products or services (European Commission, 2022a, Rec. 28 and 35). Recital 28 of the Data Act proposal even explicitly states that users are free to provide the data to a third party offering an aftermarket service that may be in competition with a service provided by the original data holder. As such, the Data Act prevents imitation of products that lie at the basis of data collection while leaving open competition for new products and for services more generally – irrespective of whether the services compete with the services offered by the original data holder.

To illustrate, we can picture a farmer using firm A's sensors that collect data about the quality of the soil, which allows firm A to provide the farmer with personalised smart farming services (e.g. advice on when to plant seeds, water, harvest, etc.). Arguably, the farmer could use the IoT data access right to share the soil quality data with a third party, and this third party could either use these data to develop his own competing smart farming services or to build complementary products (e.g. smart tractors that rely on the use of this soil quality data). However, the farmer could not use these data to develop their own sensors that collect data about the quality of the soil, as this would compete with firm A's product. Although it could once again be argued that this restriction could be circumvented by the third parties if they acquire the data through the GDPR data portability right instead, this might not be as advantageous in practice, as outlined above. Beyond this, it may be tricky in practice to determine when a product is sufficiently 'new' to no longer be regarded as competing with the product of the original data holder for the purposes of the Data Act.

3.4.2. Factoring the Data Protection Rights of Others

Finally, both the GDPR and the Data Act provide that the data portability right and the IoT data access right should not adversely affect the data protection rights of others (Article 20.4 GDPR; European Commission, 2022a, Art. 5.9). Regarding the GDPR, while the Regulation itself does not provide more detail on this articulation, the Article 29 Working Party suggests that the processing of these other data subjects' personal data should be authorised only insofar as these data remain under the sole control of the data subject at the origin of the sharing and that they should only be processed for the purposes determined by this data subject (Article 29

Working Party, 2017, p. 12). From this perspective, if the data are shared with a third party, it could therefore not process the other data subjects' personal data for purposes that have not been defined by the data subject at the origin of the data sharing, such as marketing purposes (Article 29 Working Party, 2017, p. 12).

Interestingly, these limits seem to have been explicitly included, to some extent, in the Data Act proposal. Indeed, if the user is a legal person, IoT-generated personal data pertaining to data subjects can only be shared with the user or a third party if there is a valid lawful ground under the GDPR (European Commission, 2022a, Arts. 4.5 and 5.6). However, it must be underlined that the Data Act does not mention the need to factor the rights of other data subjects in a B2U sharing situation where the user itself is a natural person anywhere, while such a situation is covered by Article 20.4 GDPR.

Moreover, the Data Act provides that third parties should only process the data 'for the purposes and under the conditions agreed with the user, and subject to the rights of the data subject insofar as personal data are concerned' (European Commission, 2022a, Art. 6.1 and Rec. 33 and 34) and that they shall not use the data for profiling[19] purposes 'unless it is necessary to provide the service requested by the user' (European Commission, 2022a, Art. 6.2.b). This again shows the key role that the contractual agreements between the data holder and third parties will have on the extent of data access.

According to the EDPB and the EDPS, the Data Act should also explicitly remind that any further personal data processing must comply with Article 6.4 GDPR and should include clearer limitations or restrictions of reuse for 'purposes of direct marketing or advertising, employee monitoring, credit scoring or to determine eligibility to health insurance, to calculate or modify insurance premiums' (EDPB-EDPS, 2022, pp. 3 and 15–16). Furthermore, the EDPB and the EDPS add that all the above should not only apply to third parties accessing data through Article 5 but also to business users, who are not data subjects, accessing data through Article 4 (EDPB-EDPS, 2022, p. 16).

Finally, it is worth noting that the Data Act proposal goes a step further than the GDPR in the context of attempting to address the complex issue of

19 '"Profiling" means any form of automated processing of personal data consisting of the use of personal data to evaluate certain personal aspects relating to a natural person, in particular to analyse or predict aspects concerning that natural person's performance at work, economic situation, health, personal preferences, interests, reliability, behaviour, location or movements' (Article 4.4 GDPR).

dark patterns employed by digital actors to collect (excessive amounts of) data from the users of their services (on dark patterns, see: Nouwens et al., 2020; Pielaet, 2020). Indeed, it outlines that third parties shall not 'coerce, deceive or manipulate the user in any way, by subverting or impairing the autonomy, decision-making or choices of the user, including by means of [dark patterns built in their] digital interface with the user' (European Commission, 2022a, Art. 6.2.a and Rec. 34).

4. Beyond User-Initiated Requests for Data Access: The Digital Markets Act

It follows from the previous section that the Data Act strengthens the data access already facilitated by the GDPR's right to data portability. Both legal mechanisms require a request from the user before data can be exchanged. For instance, a request of an individual to share their electricity consumption profile obtained by a smart thermostat with a comparison service triggers the exchange of data between their electricity provider and the provider of the comparison service. The same is true for other data access regimes such as the PSD2. Upon the explicit consent of the payer, PSD2 enables third-party providers to access the payer's bank account to offer payment initiation services and account information services (Articles 66–67 PSD2). These services, defined in Articles 4.15 and 4.16, are delivered at the request of the user, so it is logical to limit the data access to instances where users ask for it. At the same time, there will also be occasions where data access is desirable beyond any request of the user in order to stimulate data-driven innovation in the form of the development of new products and services. The Digital Markets Act (DMA) provides an example of such a scenario regarding the sharing of search query data, which this section will explore. It is likely that we will see more of these scenarios in the future, so it is useful to reflect on how these requests for data access beyond the initiative of the user can be aligned with the GDPR considering that the dataset to be shared will often also involve personal data.

4.1. Objectives

The DMA aims at harmonising rules to ensure 'contestable and fair markets in the digital sector across the Union where gatekeepers are present' (Art. 1.1 DMA). It does so by imposing obligations on particularly powerful providers of core platform services, which include (among others) search engines, social network services, cloud computing services and advertising services (Art. 2.2 DMA). The providers of core platform services covered by the DMA are referred to as 'gatekeepers'. Whether a provider of a core platform service qualifies as a gatekeeper is to be determined according to three criteria: (1), (2) the control of an important gateway for business users towards final consumers and (3) an (expected) entrenched and durable position (Art. 3.1 DMA).[20] The notion of gatekeeper as the key trigger for the application of the DMA indicates that it is a form of asymmetric regulation. It imposes obligations only on the selected market players that meet the thresholds. As a result, market players in the same sector will be subject to different levels of regulatory control. For instance, while Google is a target of the DMA, other search engines like DuckDuckGo and Ecosia do not fall under its scope of application. The asymmetric nature of the DMA is a difference from the approach of the GDPR and the Data Act, although the latter excludes, to some extent, micro or small enterprises from the scope of application of its provisions – as discussed in the previous section.

Another difference is that the DMA does not target the individual relationship between a user and a provider as much as the GDPR's data portability and the Data Act's data access regimes do. The latter two instruments focus on empowering individual consumers and businesses by providing them with rights to access data, while the DMA mainly addresses problems at the overall level of the market. These perspectives do overlap. A clear example of this overlap is the obligation of the DMA regarding data portability for business users and end users. Article 6.10 of the DMA requires gatekeepers to facilitate the portability of aggregated and non-aggregated data provided or generated through the activity of a business user or end user, including in a continuous and real-time manner. As such, this obligation interacts with the relevant provisions of the GDPR and the

20 Three main cumulative quantitative criteria apply for providers to be presumed a gatekeeper under Article 3.1 and 3.2 of the DMA: (1) the existence of a significant impact on the internal market: this is presumed to be the case if the company achieves an annual Union turnover equal to or above € 7.5 billion in each of the last three financial years, or where its average market capitalisation or its equivalent fair market value amounted to at least € 75 billion in the last financial year, and it provides the same core platform service in at least three Member States; (2) the control of an important gateway for business users towards final consumers: this is presumed to be the case if the company operates a core platform service that, in the last financial year, had at least 45 million monthly active end users established or located in the EU and at least 10,000 yearly active business users established in the EU; (3) an (expected) entrenched and durable position: this is presumed to be the case if the company met the previous two criteria in each of the last three financial years.

Data Act, even though the objectives of the overall legislative instruments differ. Beyond this, the DMA also mandates the sharing of search data outside the control and initiative of the user and therefore goes beyond the GDPR and the Data Act.

Article 6.11 of the DMA requires gatekeepers to provide any third-party providers of online search engines 'with access on fair, reasonable and non-discriminatory terms to ranking, query, click and view data'. The motivation behind this obligation is described in the recitals to the DMA where the argument is made that the access by gatekeepers to search data 'constitutes an important barrier to entry and expansion, which undermines the contestability of online search engine services' (Rec. 61). By enabling access to these data, third-party providers of search engines are expected to be able to 'optimise their services and contest the relevant core platform services' (Rec. 61 DMA). This refers to an objective of creating competitive and contestable markets, which goes beyond the approach of the GDPR's data portability and the Data Act's data access rights. Individual users can invoke their right to data portability under the GDPR to move their profile to another search engine provider. These individual requests can increase competition in the search engine market, but the extent of such competition depends on how actively users at the aggregate invoke their right to data portability. It is therefore unlikely that user-initiated requests for data access are a sufficient measure for the purpose of stimulating a competitive and contestable search engine market on their own. While the DMA's duty on gatekeepers to share search data is thus to be welcomed, it does raise the question of how such a form of data access beyond user-initiated requests can be brought in line with the requirements of data protection law, considering that users have no control over such sharing of search data.

4.2. Alignment With the GDPR

Article 6.11 of the DMA makes access to search data subject to anonymisation where the data constitutes personal data, such as in cases where the data include information about personal characteristics or locations of searches that can be linked to an individual. However, it is well reported that the effectiveness of anonymisation techniques constantly keeps improving to the extent that previously anonymised personal data risk becoming de-anonymised at some point (Article 29 Working Party, 2014). It therefore seems unlikely that search data can always be fully anonymised. The recitals to the DMA require a gatekeeper to 'ensure the protection of the personal data of end users, including against possible re-identification risks, by appropriate means, such as anonymisation of such personal data, without substantially degrading the quality or usefulness of the data' when providing access to its search data (DMA). This points at a balancing exercise between protecting personal data and ensuring that a sufficient amount and extent of search data is available to enable third parties to optimise their search engines and compete with the gatekeeper. It is likely that there will be disagreement among gatekeepers, third-party providers of search engines and the regulator about how to conduct this balancing.

Article 6.11 of the DMA can be seen as a legal obligation for the processing of personal data, so there is a lawful ground as required by Article 6.1 GDPR. However, even in the presence of a lawful ground for processing, the principles of purpose limitation and data minimisation also still apply and can lead to questions about how to minimise the extent of data sharing and the uses of the search data by third parties (Articles 5.1b–c GDPR).

The DMA does not provide any clarity about the practical implementation of the duty regarding access to search data. There are indications showing how gatekeepers sometimes rely on privacy or data protection as a justification for keeping their datasets closed for third parties and potential competitors. For instance, the UK Competition and Markets Authority required commitments from Google to address the competition concerns resulting from its decision to remove third-party cookies and other functionalities from its Chrome browser (Competition & Markets Authority, 2022). While Google's browser changes protect users' privacy, they also promote Google's own commercial interest in restraining anyone else but itself from following users across services and devices (Geradin et al., 2021). In such situations, there is a tension between the objectives of data protection and competition. A higher level of data protection implies a more closed system, giving competitors less ability to contest the position of the incumbent provider. Increasing competition would mean accepting a lower level of data protection, because third parties require some extent of access to the personal data of users in order to compete with the incumbent provider. Similar considerations will come up in the implementation of Article 6.11 of the DMA where a balance needs to be found to ensure both a sufficient level of competition and a sufficient level of data protection. Upfront guidance is welcome to prevent gatekeepers themselves from holding the full discretion to make this trade-off.

The need for alignment with the data protection framework illustrates the challenges that forms of data access beyond user-initiated requests pose. Considering that user-initiated requests for data access can hardly be seen as a sufficient measure to stimulate a flourishing data economy on their own, these challenges will come up in the future in other areas beyond the DMA as well – for instance in the context of the sectoral data spaces the Commission wishes to establish (European Commission, 2018). Beyond this, the data access right contained in the Data Act proposal and the Digital Markets Act's obligation on gatekeepers to share access to search data indicate that the distinction between personal and non-personal data may no longer be so vital in delineating the scope of data access mechanisms. This will bring the law closer to reality, where no such distinction between personal and non-personal data indeed exists in extracting value from data for the purposes of enhancing competition and innovation in data markets. Nevertheless, data holders may still invoke the personal nature of data as an argument to keep their datasets closed (e.g. in the context of the sharing of search data under the Digital Markets Act) or to obtain overly beneficial terms for data access from third parties (for instance in the context of the contractual negotiations between the original data holder and the third party under the Data Act proposal). To prevent such situations, proactive guidance is needed from policymakers and regulators on how to effectively implement more holistic data access mechanisms that no longer strictly separate personal and non-personal data from each other.

5. Conclusion

Stimulating the European data economy requires a mix of strategies combining the regulation of user-initiated requests for data access, as facilitated by the GDPR's data portability and the Data Act's data access rights, with forms of data access beyond the control of users, such as in the context of the DMA's obligation to provide access to search data held by gatekeepers. This implies that a variety of regimes will exist next to each other. While these regimes can complement one another in their scope in useful ways, it is important to prevent the regulation of access to data in the EU from becoming an inconsistent patchwork of different provisions and approaches. Whether the bits and pieces of the regulation of data will be capable of acting as a coherent system of law not only depends on the substance of the rules but also on how market players implement and regulators enforce the various regimes. The future relationship between the GDPR's right to data portability and the Data Act's data access provisions can serve as an example or test case in this respect.

We believe that it could be argued that, while the GDPR data portability right and the Data Act's IoT data access right partially overlap, the former remains relevant even in situations where they might apply in parallel. In this regard, we believe that the GDPR could be viewed as containing a de minimis data portability right with a broader scope of application, on top of which more specific and narrow forms of data access (such as the IoT data access right) can exist. The Data Act's IoT data access right has the potential to be more 'powerful' than the GDPR, but its exact implementation also depends on the outcome of contractual negotiations between the data holder and third parties regarding the conditions of data access.

As outlined above, the scope of the GDPR portability right is broader than the scope of the IoT data access right, as it is not limited to providers of IoT products or related services but rather applies independently of the type of (economic or societal) activity that is pursued by the data controller. It also does not exclude from its scope micro or small enterprises. Moreover, any third party (public or private) could receive data through Article 20 GDPR, while only undertakings (excluding gatekeepers), research organisations and not-for-profit organisations are eligible third parties under the Data Act. Furthermore, while the GDPR portability right does not put any kind of restriction on the use that the data subjects and the third parties can make of the ported data (as long as it complies with personal data protection rules), the IoT data access right prevents the users and the third parties from developing a product that competes with the product from which the data originates.

Because the scope of the GDPR is broader, these limits to the more specific and narrower IoT data access right can arguably be circumvented by resorting to the former rather than to the latter. However, this is not as advantageous, as the former tool is not as 'powerful' as the latter. First, it would only allow access to personal data but not to non-personal data, as the GDPR portability right only applies to personal data, while both personal and non-personal data are covered by the IoT data access right. Second, it only applies to data controllers that process personal data on the basis of the data subjects' consent or of a contract. Third, third parties will only get access to the data directly from the data holder 'where technically feasible' and will thus often have to request these data from the data subject herself. Fourth, it is uncertain whether Article 20 GDPR would allow for a continuous and real-time portability of personal data. That being said, it will be interesting to see whether the disqualification of gatekeepers as eligible third parties under the Data Act gives rise to a dynamic whereby big tech firms start to plead for an expansive interpretation of the GDPR's right to data portability, against which they were opposed up to now, to ensure the technical feasibility of direct data transfers and to facilitate continuous and real-time portability under the GDPR.

Even though newer legislative instruments like the Digital Markets Act and the Data Act proposal formally no longer distinguish between personal and non-personal data and therefore form a more realistic reflection of current data markets where datasets are typically mixed, the legal qualification of data is still likely to influence the extent of data access they create. To prevent data holders from invoking the personal nature of data extensively as an argument to unjustifiably limit data access to their advantage for alleged data protection purposes, proactive guidance from policymakers or regulators on how to conduct the balancing exercise between the need for data protection and the need for competition and innovation in data markets is welcome. The implementation of these new and more holistic data access instruments needs to be steered to ensure that they can reach their respective objectives and contribute to completing the system of regulating data access in the EU, instead of fragmenting it even more.

Acknowledgements

This work was undertaken in the context of the Digital Legal Studies research initiative, which is funded through the Law Sector Plan of the Dutch Ministry of Education, Culture and Science (OCW).

References

Article 29 Working Party. (2007). *Opinion 4/2007 on the concept of personal data*, WP 136, 20 June 2007.

Article 29 Working Party. (2014). *Opinion 05/2014 on anonymisation techniques*, WP 216, 10 April 2014.

Article 29 Working Party. (2016). *Guidelines on the right to data portability*, WP 242, 13 December 2016.

Article 29 Working Party. (2017). *Guidelines on the right to data portability*, WP 242 rev.01, 13 April 2017.

Competition & Markets Authority. (2022, May 17). *Investigation into Google's 'Privacy Sandbox' browser changes*. https://www.gov.uk/cma-cases/investigation-into-googles-privacy-sandbox-browser-changes

Council. (2016). *Position (EU) No 6/2016 of the Council at first reading with a view to the adoption of a Regulation of the European Parliament and of the Council on the protection of natural persons with regard to the processing of personal data and on the free movement of such data, and repealing Directive 95/46/EC (General Data Protection Regulation)*, Brussels, 3 May 2016, OJ C 159/1.

Council of Europe. (2018). Explanatory report to the protocol amending the Convention for the Protection of Individuals with regard to Automatic Processing of Personal Data. *Council of Europe Treaty Series no. 223*, Strasbourg.

Directive (EU) 2015/2366 of the European Parliament and of the Council of 25 November 2015 on payment services in the internal market, amending Directives 2002/65/EC, 2009/110/EC and 2013/36/EU and Regulation (EU) No. 1093/2010, and repealing Directive 2007/64/EC, *OJ L 337/35*, 23 December 2015.

Directive 96/9/EC of the European Parliament and of the Council of 11 March 1996 on the legal protection of databases. 27 March 1996, OJ L 77/20.

Drexl, J., et al. (2022, May 25). *Position statement of the Max Planck Institute for Innovation and Competition on the Commission's proposal of 23 February 2022 for a regulation on harmonised rules on fair access to and use of data (Data Act)*. Max Planck Institute for Innovation and Competition. https://www.ip.mpg.de/en/research/research-news/position-statement-on-the-eu-data-act.html

EDPB-EDPS. (2022, May 4). *Joint Opinion 2/2022 on the Proposal of the Proposal of the European Parliament and of the Council on harmonised rules on fair access to and use of data (Data Act)*. European Data Protection Board. https://edpb.europa.eu/our-work-tools/our-documents/edpbedps-joint-opinion/edpb-edps-joint-opinion-22022-proposal-european_en

Egan, E. (2019). *Data portability and privacy: Charting a way forward* [White paper]. Facebook. https://about.fb.com/wp-content/uploads/2020/02/data-portability-privacy-white-paper.pdf

European Commission. (2003). *Annex to the Commission Recommendation 2003/361/EC of 6 May 2003 concerning the definition of micro, small and medium-sized enterprises*, 20 May 2003, OJ L 124/36.

European Commission. (2012). *Proposal for a Regulation of the European Parliament and of the Council on the protection of individuals with regard to the processing of personal data and on the free movement of such data (General Data Protection Regulation)*, Brussels, 25 January 2012, COM/2012/011 final.

European Commission. (2014). *Communication from the Commission to the European Parliament, the Council, the European Economic and Social Committee and the Committee of the Regions 'Towards a thriving data-driven economy'*, Brussels, 2 July 2014, COM(2014) 442 final.

European Commission. (2018). *Communication from the Commission to the European Parliament, the Council, the European Economic and Social Committee and the Committee of the Regions 'Towards a common European data space'*, Brussels, 25 April 2018, COM/2018/232 final.

European Commission. (2019). *Communication from the Commission to the European Parliament and the Council 'Guidance on the Regulation on a framework for the free flow of non-personal data in the European Union'*, Brussels, 29 May 2019, COM(2019) 250 final.

European Commission. (2020a). *Communication from the Commission to the European Parliament, the Council, the European Economic and Social Committee and the Committee of the Regions 'A European strategy for data'*, 19 February 2020, COM(2020) 66.

European Commission. (2020b). *Proposal for a Regulation of the European Parliament and of the Council on contestable and fair markets in the digital sector (Digital Markets Act)*, Brussels, 15 December 2020, COM(2020) 842 final.

European Commission. (2022a). *Proposal for a Regulation of the European Parliament and of the Council on harmonised rules on fair access to and use of data (Data Act)*, 23 February 2022, COM(2022) 68 final.

European Commission. (2022b). *Commission Staff Working Document 'Impact assessment report accompanying the document Proposal for a Regulation of the European Parliament and of the Council on harmonised rules on fair access to and use of data (Data Act)'*, Brussels, 23 February 2022, SWD(2022) 34 final.

European Commission. (2022c). *Data Act: Commission proposes measures for a fair and innovative data economy* [Press release, 23 Februrary 2022]. https://ec.europa.eu/commission/presscorner/detail/en/ip_22_1113

Geradin, D., et al. (2021). GDPR myopia: How a well-intended regulation ended up favouring large online platforms – The case of ad tech. *European Competition Journal*, *17*(1), 47–92.

Graef, I., et al. (2018). Data portability and data control: Lessons for an emerging concept in EU law. *German Law Journal*, *19*(6), 1359–1398.

Graef, I., et al. (2019). Towards a holistic regulatory approach for the European data economy: Why the illusive notion of non-personal data is counterproductive to data innovation. *European Law Review*, *44*, 605–621.

ISO. (2011). ISO 29100:2011. International Organization of Standardization. https://www.iso.org/obp/ui/#iso:std:iso-iec:29100:ed-1:v1:en

Kemp, R. (2019). *Legal aspects of managing data* [White paper]. Kemp IT Law. http://www.kempitlaw.com/legal-aspects-of-managing-data/

Kerber, W. (2022). *Governance of IoT data: Why the EU Data Act will not fulfill its objectives* [Working paper]. SSRN. https://papers.ssrn.com/sol3/papers.cfm?abstract_id=4080436

Krämer, J., et al. (2020). *Making data portability more effective for the digital economy.* CERRE. https://www.cerre.eu/publications/report-making-data-portability-more-effective-digital-economy

Meyer, D. (2017, April 25). *European Commission experts uneasy over WP29 data portability interpretation.* IAPP. https://iapp.org/news/a/

european-commission-experts-uneasy-over-wp29-data-portability-interpretation-1/

Nouwens, M., et al. (2020). Dark patterns after the GDPR: Scraping consent pop-ups and demonstrating their influence. *CHI Conference on Human Factors in Computing Systems*. https://doi.org/10.48550/arXiv.2001.02479

OECD. (2019). *Enhancing access to and sharing of data: Reconciling risks and benefits for data re-use across societies*. OECD Publications. https://www.oecd.org/publications/enhancing-access-to-and-sharing-of-data-276aaca8-en.htm

OECD. (2020, June). *Consumer Data Rights and Competition – Background note*. DAF/COMP(2020)1. http://www.oecd.org/daf/competition/consumer-data-rights-and-competition.htm

Pielaet, P.-O. (2020). La *privacy by design* à l'épreuve des 'dark patterns', *R.D.T.I.*, *80*, 33–45.

Purtova, N. (2018). The law of everything. Broad concept of personal data and future of EU data protection law. *Law, Innovation and Technology*, *10*(1), 40–81.

Regulation (EU) 2016/679 of the European Parliament and of the Council of 27 April 2016 on the protection of natural persons with regard to the processing of personal data and on the free movement of such data, and repealing Directive 95/46/EC (General Data Protection Regulation), 4 May 2016, OJ L 119/1.

Regulation (EU) 2018/1807 of the European Parliament and of the Council of 14 November 2018 on a framework for the free flow of non-personal data in the European Union, 28 November 2018, OJ L 303/59.

Regulation (EU) 2022/868 of the European Parliament and of the Council of 30 May 2022 on European data governance and amending Regulation (EU) 2018/1724 (Data Governance Act), 3 June 2022, OJ L 152/1.

Regulation (EU) 2022/1925 of the European Parliament and of the Council of 14 September 2022 on contestable and fair markets in the digital sector and amending Directives (EU) 2019/1937 and (EU) 2020/1828 (Digital Markets Act), 12 October 2022, OJ L 265/1.

Somaini, L. (2018). The right to data portability and user control: Ambitions and limitations. *MediaLaws: Rivista di Diritto dei Media*, *3*, 164–190.

Somaini, L. (2020). Regulating the dynamic concept of non-personal data in the EU: From ownership to portability. *EDPL*, *1*, 84–93.

Taylor, L. (2013). *Hacking a path through the personal data ecosystem*. Linnet Taylor. https://linnettaylor.wordpress.com/2013/12/12/hacking-a-path-through-the-personal-data-ecosystem/

Tombal, T. (2018). Les droits de la personne concernée dans le RGPD. In C. de Terwangne & K. Rosier, *Le Règlement general sur la protection des données (RGPD / GDPR) – Analyse approfondie* (pp. 407–557). Larcier.

Tombal, T. (2022). *Imposing data sharing among private actors: A tale of evolving balances*. Kluwer Law International.

Van Alstyne, M. W., et al. (2021). 'In situ' data rights. *Communications of the ACM, 64*(12), 34–35.

von Grafenstein, M. (2022). Reconciling conflicting interests in data through data governance: An analytical framework (and a brief discussion of the Data Governance Act Draft, the AI Regulation Draft, as well as the GDPR). *HIIG Discussion Paper Series 2022-2*. https://doi.org/10.5281/zenodo.6457735

Wendehorst, C. (2017). Of elephants in the room and paper tigers: How to reconcile data protection and the data economy. In S. Lohsse et al. (Eds.), *Trading data in the digital economy: Legal concepts and tools* (pp. 327–356). Nomos/Hart Publishing.

12. Regulating 'Non-Personal Data': Developments in India

Rishab Bailey & Renuka Sane

Abstract

This chapter provides an overview of the proposals to regulate non personal data (NPD) in India as distinct from proposals to regulate personal data under a draft data protection law. It identifies the motivations for regulation and outlines and analyses proposals for a new regulatory framework for non-personal data proposed in 2020. Despite certain positive aspects in the recommendations of the committee, the chapter highlights how the scope of the recommendations may be impractical. The chapter also points to recent developments in proposed personal data legislation which suggest expanding the scope of the draft law to cover both personal and non-personal data. Thus, the future of the regulatory framework applicable to NPD remains uncertain.

Keywords: non-personal data; data sovereignty; community data; data legislation

1. Introduction

The growth of the digital economy propelled by the spread of the internet, the 'Internet of Things' and development of artificial intelligence has made regulating the use of data central to discussions on economic and geo-strategic policy in the 21st century. While states initially focused on preventing harm to citizens by regulating the processing of 'personal data',[1]

1 This is commonly understood as data that relates to or through which an individual can be identified. For instance, Article 4 of the EU's General Data Protection Regulation defines 'personal data' as 'any information relating to an identified or identifiable natural person ("data subject")'. Similarly, the California Consumer Privacy Act, 2018, defines 'personal information' as 'information that identifies, relates to, describes, is reasonably capable of being associated with, or could reasonably be linked, directly or indirectly, with a particular consumer or household'.

Van der Sloot & van Schendel. *The Boundaries of Data*. Taylor & Francis Group, 2024
DOI: 10.5117/9789463729192_CH12

in recent times there has been an increasing focus on the need to regulate the non-personal data (NPD) ecosystem as well. This need largely arises due to the dominance of big technology companies in the data ecosystem. The fear is that by monopolising data collection and processing (of both personal and non-personal data), these companies will be able to exclude other entities from market entry while also extending their dominance into adjacent markets. Traditional competition law is seen as unsuitable to deal with these issues, as it would intervene only on a case-by-case basis, based on evidence of harm caused to consumers by the 'abuse of [a] dominant position' (Mayer-Schönberger et al., 2018).

Many jurisdictions are therefore increasingly viewing data as being akin to an 'essential facility' or an 'essential infrastructure', with preferential access to data seen as an enabler of market dominance (OECD, 2015).[2] There appear to be three primary motivations for the need to regulate NPD: (a) economic benefits of the reuse of non-rivalrous data, (b) incentive effects in regard to investing in data and innovation and (c) addressing distributional questions about fairness in regard to the sharing of the benefits of the data (Kerber, 2017).

In India the discussion of data governance has been relatively recent. The issue of data protection began to receive mainstream attention around 2017, following the Cambridge Analytica incident and the Supreme Court's decision in *K. S. Puttuswamy v. Union of India*, where privacy was recognised as a fundamental right under the Indian Constitution (K. S. Puttaswamy v. Union of India, 2017). Pursuant thereto, the government appointed a committee to suggest a framework to regulate personal data (Srikrishna et al., 2018). This process eventually led to a draft Personal Data Protection Bill in 2019 (PDP Bill) being introduced in parliament (Personal Data Protection Bill, 2019).[3]

At the same time, other government initiatives, such as the 2018 consultation paper on the national strategy for AI and the draft e-commerce

2 This position can be seen for instance in the German Act Against Restraint of Competition. The EU's Digital Markets Act also applies the essential facilities doctrines to require dominant companies to provide competitors with access to essential data (Herbers & Nieuwmeyer, 2021). The report of the US Congress's House Judiciary Antitrust Sub Committee also suggests numerous measures to enable easier access to data collected by dominant companies, including the imposition of interoperability mandates as well as measures to strengthen the essential facilities doctrine (Nadler et al., 2020).

3 While the PDP Bill was clear in extending only to 'personal data', it nevertheless included Section 91(2), which empowered the central government to call for any non-personal data from any individuals or entities in the pursuit of its governance and policymaking functions. Non-personal data was understood as comprising data that are not personal data.

policies of 2018 and 2019, have identified the issue of data access by Indian firms as being critical for developing a start-up and AI ecosystem in India. Competition concerns, especially vis-à-vis foreign multinationals, became the primary motivation behind data governance related policies. This view is concerned that the dominance of foreign monopolies will create an unequal society, where data resources obtained from the people of India will enrich stakeholders outside the country (Singh, 2019). This would not only stunt economic development in India but also pose strategic problems for the state. The value of data to enable various state functions (such as policymaking) was also an important motivation. Together, these lead to the 'data sovereignty' perspective: data generated in India should first of all benefit India (Basu, 2021).

These motivations, together with the progress on regulating the personal data space, saw the Ministry of Electronics and Information Technology (MEITY), Government of India, establish a committee of experts chaired by a co-founder of the Indian technology giant Infosys, Kris Gopalakrishnan, to suggest a regulatory framework for non-personal data in 2019 (the NPD Committee). The NPD Committee submitted two reports, and while the recommendations in each report are different, they adopt a similar position on the need for regulation of NPD and seek to achieve similar objectives. Simply stated, these boil down to: (a) enabling easier access to and sharing of NPD, particularly for Indian businesses, (b) empowering communities to control the use of and benefit from NPD and (c) protecting against harm that may arise from the processing of NPD. The final recommendations of the NPD Committee include designating certain datasets as 'high-value datasets' (HVDs), setting up the institution of a 'data trustee' to manage the datasets, a framework through which the HVDs could be accessed, and setting up a regulator (the NPD Authority) to oversee the process. A central theme behind this regulation is that of 'public good' – not only are HVDs viewed as being 'public goods', but obligations applying to them are premised on their use for the benefit of the community or the public at large.

The NPD Committee brought various new rationales and proposals to the data governance discourse. For instance, it went beyond mere competition concerns as a reason for regulation of NPD. While most jurisdictions focus on granting rights to individuals, the Committee introduced the concept of community benefit to deal with the diffused NPD ownership structures. This is seen as both preventing harm and promoting fairness in the data ecosystem by limiting how corporations can profit off individuals or groups of people. Thus, it would not be inappropriate to call the regulatory framework proposed by the NPD Committee both well intentioned and ambitious.

That said, in a final analysis, the NPD Committee's recommendations, while certainly advancing the discourse on NPD regulation, may prove impractical and underdeveloped.

Following the release of the NPD Committee's final recommendations, a joint parliamentary committee (JPC) tasked with examining the PDP Bill suggested that the proposed personal data protection law be revised to a general data protection law, governing both personal and non-personal data. Subsequently, the government has withdrawn the PDP Bill from parliament while indicating that a revised version will be introduced at a future date. At this point in time, it is unclear what kind of law will finally be presented to parliament and the extent to which non-personal data will be regulated through statute.

In this chapter, we provide an overview of the proposals to regulate NPD in India. We identify the motivations for regulation and outline and analyse proposals for a new regulatory framework. The chapter is structured as follows: In this section, Section 1, we have laid out the background of the data governance discourse in India and provided an overview of the chapter. Section 2 describes the proposals to regulate NPD in India, with a particular focus on the recommendations of the Committee. Section 3 provides an analysis of the Committee's proposals. Section 4 presents the interplay between the personal data and the non-personal data regulatory proposals, and Section 5 concludes.

2. Developing a Comprehensive Regulatory Framework for NPD

In this section, we first examine the developing rationale for regulation of NPD in India. We then provide an overview of the primary set of proposals for a regulatory framework in the form of the recommendations proposed by the NPD Committee.

2.1. Why Regulate NPD?

As mentioned, economic concerns have been at the forefront of the need for data governance–related interventions. For instance, the report of an e-commerce task force released in 2018 identified the need to nurture domestic digital innovation and stimulate domestic digital economy as a primary goal of data policy (Government of India, 2018). This report viewed data as a resource and identified data access as a barrier to market entry in India, especially for start-ups. To this end, it suggested enabling data sharing (by dominant firms) with Indian start-ups.[4] The draft 2019 e-commerce policy reiterated this perspective. While recognising the central role of data as a resource for economic development, the report once again highlighted concerns arising from the dominance of certain companies over the data economy (Department of Industrial Policy & Promotion, 2019). Notably, the 2019 policy likened data to a 'societal commons', noting that 'India and its citizens have a sovereign right to their data', just as it would over other resources within its territory (such as oil). Accordingly, it articulated the need for a level playing field aimed at promoting growth of indigenous innovation. To this end, it suggested streamlining access to data (while protecting privacy), as a win-win scenario for all stakeholders.[5] The NITI Aayog, too, in its 2018 consultation paper on the national strategy for AI identified the issue of data access by Indian firms as a key barrier in achieving the goal of 'AI for all'. It therefore identified the need to develop large foundational annotated datasets to 'democratise data' and to 'create multi-stakeholder marketplaces' across the AI value chain to create a level playing field in the data space.

This discourse led the MEITY to constitute an eight-member committee in 2019 tasked with devising a regulatory framework to govern NPD (since a law pertaining to personal data had already been drafted).[6] The NPD Committee released its first report in July 2020 ('First Report') (Gopalakrishnan et al., 2020a).[7] Following the receipt of comments from over 1,500 individuals and organisations, a second report was issued in December 2020 (in Gopalakrishnan et al., 2020b, hereafter cited as 'Final Report').

The MEITY identified two reasons for constituting the Committee: first, NPD, unlike personal data, were seen as having diffused ownership structures that were not amenable to an individual rights–based framework (i.e. rights-based frameworks that typically place the individual as the locus of rights). Second, the increasing economic and governance implications of NPD meant that it was necessary to implement some form of regulation in this space.

4 In addition, the report sought to restrict cross-border flows of data, especially of data generated by Indian social media or search engine users or of data collected by IoT devices in public spaces. The report also recognised the need to enable government access to data for security and policymaking purposes.

5 The draft policy has not yet been finalised.

6 The Committee comprised three individuals from the government, two from the private sector (including the chair), one from academia and two from civil society. The reasons for selection of these individuals were not provided to the public, a common occurrence (Ministry of Electronics and Information Technology, 2019).

7 The public was invited to comment on this report, for which a time period of about a month was provided (Ministry of Electronics and Information Technology, 2020).

The perspectives first articulated in the draft e-commerce policies appear to have shaped the NPD Committee's views to a large extent. Thus, the Committee emphasised that the data economy was dominated by large foreign players, largely Chinese and American companies. This was put down to, amongst other factors, an early mover advantage, economies of scale and network effects. The privileged access to data these companies enjoy was said to raise entry barriers to new and domestic players, creating an imbalance in the market. The objective of the NPD Committee was therefore to try and reduce the ability for data to act as a differentiator of firms and limit the possibility for greater vertical integration. Enhancing access to data was seen as enabling further development of the data economy by 'unlocking' the value of resources which would otherwise be closed to all but a few big corporations. This perspective views data as an infrastructural element or a public good, upon which multiple data-driven businesses can build and innovate, given that data are a non-rivalrous resource (Singh, 2020). By seeking to reduce the dominance of big tech firms, the NPD Committee sought to open up the data economy to new (Indian) businesses while also securing Indian geopolitical interests.

The NPD Committee was motivated by three additional factors: first, the need for the government and public authorities to access data to perform their functions, in particular policymaking, crime/fraud prevention and targeted resource allocation; second, to limit harm arising from the processing of NPD either in the form of harm arising due to the de-anonymisation of data derived from personal data or certain collective harms (such as discrimination on the basis of group identities). Finally, the NPD Committee was motivated by the need to ensure equity or fairness in the use of data derived from Indian citizens.

To this end, it recognised that the benefits of processing NPD should not accrue 'only to the organizations that collect and process such data, but also equally to India and the community that typically produces the data that is being captured' (Para. 3.6 Final Report). Interestingly, the NPD Committee relied on a directive principle enshrined in Article 39(b) of the Indian Constitution to buttress its position.[8] This principle requires the state to distribute material resources of the community for the common good.[9]

8 Directive Principles are non-enforceable (non-justiciable) obligations of the State prescribed in the Constitution. Generally speaking, they require the State to act for the welfare of citizens in enacting laws and policies.

9 Note that in *State of Karnataka v. Ranganatha Reddy*, a case cited by the Committee, the Supreme Court of India noted that the phrase 'material resources' includes anything of value or use in the material world. The Committee therefore argued that this extends to data. This interpretation is reportedly under challenge before a nine-judge bench of the Supreme Court (Venkatesan & Mishra, 2021).

Thus, one can identify five interlinked themes that provide the rationale for regulation of the NPD space:

- Data are a vital resource, required by the private sector and state. However, these data are currently monopolised by a few foreign companies to the exclusion of others.
- India must protect sovereignty over its data and protect its strategic interests.
- By democratising access to data, one can boost innovation and domestic economic growth. The idea is to enhance competition at layers above data (i.e. at the algorithm, service delivery, UX layers, etc.) rather than by enabling incumbents to benefit from the data they are in a unique position to leverage.
- There is a need to prevent harm to individuals and groups due to the processing of NPD.
- There must be a degree of equity and fairness in processing NPD by giving individuals and communities some measure of control over how NPD derived from them are used and enabling benefits of processing their data to be shared with them.

2.2. Proposed Regulatory Framework

The primary recommendation of the NPD Committee was to enact a single, comprehensive law to govern NPD, which would complement the proposed personal data protection law. The NPD law would be overseen and enforced by a Non-Personal Data Protection Authority (NPD Authority). The NPD Committee provides the broad contours for the proposed law, with the detail left to be worked out at a later stage – either in the text of the law or in the form of regulations to be laid down by the NPD Authority.[10] The proposed law would govern the processing of all 'non-personal data', defined quite simply as data that is not 'personal data' under the PDP Bill.[11] Broadly,

10 The Committee argues that a new regulator is required in view of the need for specialised knowledge, and since the nature of tasks to be performed by this institution will be different to other regulators such as those concerning personal data (which focuses on preventing privacy harms), the Competition Commission of India (which largely takes post facto action and is not suited to decide on data sharing obligations) or sectoral regulators (who cannot take horizontal or cross-cutting views or have economy-wide expertise).

11 The PDP Bill (2019) in Section 1(28) defines 'personal data' as 'data about or relating to a natural person who is directly or indirectly identifiable, having regard to any characteristic, trait, attribute or any other feature of the identity of such natural person, whether online or

this implies that any data that does not contain personally identifiable information or that cannot be related to an individual would be governed by the NPD framework.[12]

Somewhat similar to the conception of a 'data subject' and a 'data controller' in personal data protection laws,[13] the Committee introduced the concept of a 'data principal' and a 'data custodian'. Data principals refer to the individual(s), entities or communities from which NPD are collected from or relate to.[14] The term 'community' is used to refer to a group of individuals 'bound by common interests and purposes, and involved in social and/or economic interactions' (Para. 7.2 Final Report). Data custodians are entities engaged in collecting or processing NPD.[15]

With a view to enhancing the sharing of and access to NPD, the Committee suggested establishing a mandatory data sharing framework, the contours of which changed drastically from the First to the Final Report.

The First Report envisaged a very broad data sharing requirement. All 'Data Businesses' – that is, entities from the public or private sector that harness or exploit data as part of their functioning – would have to register with the NPD Authority. Upon reaching certain (undefined) data thresholds, these entities would be required to submit metadata about the NPD that

offline, or any combination of such features with any other information, and shall include any inference drawn from such data for the purpose of profiling.'

12 The Final Report clarifies the interface between the PDP Bill and the proposed NPD law. Anonymised data are to be regulated under the proposed NPD law, while personal data and mixed datasets are regulated under the PDP Bill. To this end, the Committee also recommends deleting provisions in the PDP Bill that empower the union government to regulate non-personal data. See Section 91(2), PDP Bill (2019).

13 The PDP Bill uses the terms 'data principal' and 'data controller'.

14 The First Report recognises 3 types of NPD: (a) *Public NPD*, referring to NPD generated or collected by governments or in the course of publicly funded work. This could include for instance land records, public health information, pollution data, etc. (b) *Community NPD*, referring to anonymised personal data or NPD whose source or subject pertains to a 'community' of natural persons. This could include raw datasets collected by municipalities, datasets from mobility apps, etc. (c) *Private NPD*, referring to NPD collected or produced by private entities, the source or subject of which relates to assets/processes that are privately owned. This type of data also includes derived, inferred or observed data created using proprietary or private efforts. The Final Report however eschews this classification and merely explains that NPD can be of two broad types – data that were never related or relatable to individuals (such as weather pattern data, data from public infrastructure or industrial machines) and data that are derived from personal data but processed so as not to contain personally identifiable information.

15 The Committee also defines 'data processors' as entities who process data on behalf of a data custodian. No specific obligations are cast on data processors, other than to act as a data custodian for data it collects, stores or processes as part of its business operations.

they collect and process to the NPD Authority.[16] This metadata would be made openly accessible to third parties (Indian entities and individuals), who could then submit requests to the Data Business to access the underlying 'raw' data collected/stored by the Data Business. Access requests could be made for three broad purposes: (a) for sovereign and state functions, (b) for public interest purposes[17] or (c) for economic purposes, that is, to encourage competition and reduce entry barriers into a Data Business, or for fair monetary consideration as part of a data market.

Data Businesses would only need to share the raw/factual data that they collect, enabling them to keep any proprietary information, such as algorithms, confidential. However, they would not be able to charge fees for providing access to this raw/factual data, except in cases where they have added value to the raw dataset, in which case fair, reasonable and non-discriminatory compensation could be required. The NPD Authority would adjudicate disputes pertaining to data access requests by evaluating the 'genuineness' of the request based on social/public/economic good.

The Final Report significantly restricted this broad data sharing mandate. While it retained the requirement for Data Businesses[18] to populate metadata directories,[19] it restricted the data sharing requirement to datasets designated (by the NPD Authority) as being of 'High Value' (HVDs). The data sharing requirement was extended only to raw/underlying data, in accordance with formats to be developed by the NPD Authority.[20] Proprietary information (i.e. information protected by intellectual property laws), trade

16 They will need to disclose the types of data being collected, the purpose and method of collection, types of data services being developed, amongst other information.

17 The Committee describes these as being 'for community benefits or public goods, research, policymaking, for better delivery of public services, etc.'.

18 The Final Report clarifies that the threshold for classification of an entity as a Data Business will be based on factors such as its revenues, number of consumers, percent of revenue derived from processing consumer information, etc.

19 Metadata directories are to be openly accessible (but not downloadable) by any organisation registered in India.

20 This position is broadly based on the understanding that underlying/raw data are not subject to intellectual property protection, such as through copyright. The Committee recognises that copyright would vest in a database where some measure of skill or creativity has been used in compilation. However, it notes that a copyright cannot vest in the underlying data, for instance in cases where there is only one way to express the underlying data. Further, by limiting the data sharing mandate to HVDs, pertaining to which the NPD Authority will specify predetermined fields that are subject to data sharing, the Committee argues that the data sharing mandate would not violate copyright. This position has, however, been criticised by some on the grounds that 'the principle of non-copyrightability of underlying information in a dataset may not be absolute' (Venkatesan & Mishra, 2021).

secrets and data that could violate privacy of individuals or communities were excluded from the scope of the sharing requirement.

Any public authority or private entity could request that the NPD Authority designate a dataset as an HVD and offer to be the data trustee with respect to that dataset.[21] Datasets were to be classified as HVDs based on whether they could benefit 'the community at large' (Para. 7.8 Final Report). The NPD Authority would prescribe regulations for identification of an HVD, although the Committee outlined indicative types of HVDs such as data 'that is useful for policymaking and improving public services and citizen engagement', that 'helps create new and high-quality jobs', that 'helps in research and education', that helps in 'creating newer innovations, newer value added services/applications' or help in 'achieving a wide range of social and economic objectives including poverty alleviation, financial inclusion, agricultural development, skill development, healthcare, urban planning, environmental planning, energy, diversity and inclusion, and others' (Para. 7.6 Final Report).

Should a dataset be deemed an HVD, the data trustee would collect the underlying raw/factual data from the data custodian and store it in distributed, secure databases. Third parties (private or public entities registered in India, but not individuals) could seek access to HVDs by submitting requests to a data trustee (with whom they would have to first register themselves). Upon receiving a valid access request, the data trustee would have to provide access to the data through secure application protocol interfaces (APIs).

Data access requests could only be made on the ground of public interest, that is, where processing of the HVD would benefit the public or community at large.[22] As HVDs are seen as public goods, the data trustee could only levy a nominal charge for access. The Committee noted that the additional grounds for access specified in the First Report (sovereign/state functions and economic reasons) need not be covered under the proposed NPD law because: (a) the government already has powers to

21 The First Report envisages data trustees as (public or private) entities that act to combine and curate NPD from multiple sources with a view to enable easy access thereto. The Final Report clarifies that they are entities who will be responsible for 'creation, maintenance, data-sharing of High-value Datasets'.

22 Explaining this concept, the Committee notes that HVDs must 'benefit the society at large'. Such datasets could be useful for policymaking, improving public services, or 'in general, supporting a wide range of social objectives, including science, healthcare, urban planning, etc.' The Committee also highlights certain types of datasets that it views as priority domains for creation of HVDs, notably, agriculture, education, skill development, MSME support and logistics. The use of HVDs to promote research (by both the private and public sector) is also seen as a primary goal (Para. 8.2 Final Report).

access data it requires and (b) data sharing mechanisms between private entities already exist. These changes, in particular the latter, appear to have been made in response to the significant criticism received by the NPD Committee from the business community. The exception created for sharing proprietary datasets or datasets that are considered trade secrets is another clarification that was likely implemented to secure greater buy-in from the business community.

The NPD Committee also sought to establish certain rights over NPD that are derived from or relate to a 'community'. In this context, the data trustee would have to act as a fiduciary towards the community from whom the data were derived. Thus, this type of NPD can only be used 'in the interests' of the relevant community.

Further, the NPD Committee attempted to recognise the concept of 'collective privacy' by specifying that no harm should occur to the community through the processing of NPD. This could imply, for instance, that data about a community should not be used to discriminate against members of the community or the community itself. Accordingly, data custodians and trustees must use appropriate standards of anonymisation of personal data and take other technical steps to prevent the misuse of such data. Data trustees are also required to establish a grievance redress mechanism to take complaints from members of the relevant community.

To protect individuals from the risk of misuse of NPD derived from their personal data, the NPD Committee recommends first that individuals' consent be taken for anonymisation and use of their data and second that data custodians (entities who process the NPD) should ensure no harm occurs to persons or groups of persons by re-identification of NPD. Further, the Committee suggests implementing a graded system of cross-border data transfer restrictions. This system borrows from the classification adopted in the PDP Bill by restricting the transfer of NPD derived from 'critical' and 'sensitive personal data' to locations outside India.[23]

23 The PDP Bill recognises a subset of personal data as 'sensitive personal data' based on the enhanced privacy risks processing of such data poses to an individual. Per Section 3(36) of the PDP Bill, sensitive personal data includes financial and health data, official identifiers, sexual orientation, genetic data, caste or tribe and religious or political affiliations, amongst others. Critical personal data are undefined in the PDP Bill but are understood as relating to data having strategic or national security implications. Section 33 of the PDP Bill prohibits cross-border transfer of critical personal data. Further, sensitive personal data can be transferred but not stored outside India. Even a transfer of such data can only occur subject to various conditions specified in Section 34. These include the need for adoption of an approved intra-group scheme, or certification, by the central government of the adequacy of data protection in the foreign country, or for emergencies, etc.

3. Analysing the Proposed Regulatory Framework

In this section, we analyse and critique the regulatory framework proposed by the Committee. While noting certain positive aspects in the Committee's recommendations, we highlight how the absence of a clear problem statement, lack of proper evidence of harm and the use of ambiguous concepts have led to a somewhat impractical set of recommendations.

The NPD Committee was clearly grappling with an issue of increasing salience, both in India and abroad. The issue of how to ensure greater competition in the digital economy is important from geopolitical and economic development perspectives, as well as to limit harm to individuals and society more generally. A number of jurisdictions have therefore proposed new regulations to deal with big technology firms' dominance of the data economy.[24] The NPD Committee locates these broader conversations in the Indian context and also adds new perspectives to the discourse, such as by looking beyond mere competition concerns as a rationale for regulation of NPD.

Notably, the introduction of the 'community benefit' concept is an interesting development, even if it is not properly fleshed out. While most jurisdictions focus on granting rights to individuals, the fact that the concept of community benefit was introduced to deal with the diffused ownership structures of NPD represents an innovative development, particularly in a country where individuals are often unable to properly exercise their rights for a variety of structural reasons. One must also keep in mind that the Indian Constitutional framework also imposes welfare obligations on the state. By seeking to empower individuals to act as a collective (through the mechanism of data trustees), the NPD Committee seeks to provide individuals and communities with greater bargaining power and thus greater control over the use of their data. The fact that the NPD Committee goes beyond merely equating corporate gain with benefit to India (as seen in the

24 Notably, Germany has implemented the Act Against Restraint of Competition in 2021, which inter alia revises German competition law to enable imposition of data sharing mandates on dominant digital entities. The UK and US are also considering new pro-competition legislation. The Competition and Markets Authority's 2020 report suggests various measures requiring entities with strategic market status to share their data with competitors. Similarly, The EU's Digital Markets Act envisages data sharing requirements on 'core platforms services' classified as 'gatekeepers'. In the US, the 2020 report(s) of the House Judiciary Committee have led to the introduction of a number of bills in Congress that seek to introduce more competition in the digital sector. The ACCESS Act, for instance, seeks to enable user-mandated interoperability of platforms and in this context promotes data sharing. See generally (Bailey & Misra, 2022).

older e-commerce policies of 2018 and 2019) is also noteworthy. In addition, the introduction of the concept of collective (privacy) harm to the broader privacy discourse in India is, as some have mentioned, 'overdue' (Rathi et al., 2020). It is argued that there is an excessive focus of privacy discourse on individual rights, while data processing business models often thrive on the collection and processing of aggregate information.

Thus, the proposed regulatory framework can be seen as a novel attempt to deal with problems arising from the monopolisation of data in the digital economy. However, any regulatory proposal should ideally have evolved from an analysis of the root cause of the problem, including an analysis of the reasons why the market for data sharing does not work. This should have been followed by a thorough cost-benefit analysis of possible approaches, such as (alternative) soft-touch or sector-specific regulatory interventions. Such a cost-benefit analysis may have revealed that the proposed recommendations may be tough to implement (OECD, 2008). This kind of analysis would be important to identify the root cause of the problem the Committee is trying to solve and also provide alternatives that may solve the problem in more effective ways. For example, mandatory data sharing may skew incentives to make investments in data collection methods, or it may hurt smaller firms because of larger compliance costs or enable larger firms to access data that give a smaller firm a competitive advantage. The Committee also fails to adequately explain why some of the concerns raised cannot be addressed by revising existing sectoral or other laws pertaining to competition or intellectual property. This is a route being taken by numerous other jurisdictions, with many seeking to bring about substantive and institutional changes to their competition law frameworks. The mere ineffectiveness of present competition law to deal with the digital economy cannot in itself be a reason to justify the creation of a new law and regulatory structure, and in this context, further analysis of the ability to reform present legal and institutional frameworks (or the lack thereof) in India may be appropriate (Bailey et al., 2020).

This lack of rigorous analysis is also demonstrated by the fact that the NPD Committee does not provide sufficient evidence that the lack of data is the binding constraint in development of data-related businesses in India. Notably, it fails to provide any evidence or data to support its assumptions pertaining to the presence or effects of monopolisation across the digital economy as a whole. In this context, one may note, for instance, that the UK's Competition Markets and Authority provides specific evidence of harm caused by monopolisation of data by online service providers, such as dominant social media companies, in order to recommend implementation of data sharing (interoperability) and related obligations on select entities (UK Competition & Markets Authority, 2020).

The proposed framework is guided by the principle that 'India has rights over data of India, its people and organisations' and that 'benefits of data must accrue to India and its people' (Section 3.4 Final Report). There is little to argue, in theory, about the importance of data and the rights of and benefits from the data pertaining to India. Without delving further into the merits of emphasising only national identities in a globalised world, translating this into practice becomes difficult. The NPD Committee's emphasis on ensuring a level playing field for only Indian actors instead of providing a non-discriminatory platform (irrespective of the country/nationality of the actor) has the potential to violate India's trade obligations under the WTO (Rathi et al., 2020). It is important to point out that a level playing field in any sector is determined by many factors – including taxation, regulation and the general business environment. In the Indian context especially, it is possible that these factors could have an equal or greater implication for Indian firms than simply access to data.

The NPD Committee requires Data Businesses to register themselves in India and open up their metadata. This, it is presumed, will lead Indian entities to access this metadata and create innovative products/services by combining the underlying data of different entities. The framework provides for a process to (a) assign designate certain datasets as HVDs, (b) hand custody of those datasets to data trustees and (c) allow Indian firms to request access of these datasets from the trustees. Access to HVDs is limited to those that can justify need based on public interest or benefit to the community/society at large. The scope of what can constitute an HVD as well as the reasons for which this can be accessed are fairly ambiguous and widely worded. The notion of public interest, for example, is susceptible to a number of different interpretations. Even the indicative examples provided by the NPD Committee are broad in nature. For instance, any data that can be used to 'create new and high quality jobs' can be deemed an HVD. Similarly, datasets that help in 'agricultural development', 'healthcare' and with 'poverty alleviation' can be designated as HVDs (Para. 7.6 Final Report). HVDs are to be used for the benefit of the community – but whether and how this benefit is to be actualised is unclear. While the NPD Committee suggests that jurisprudence will develop around these phrases and concepts, for clarity it may be preferable for definitions to be provided in the legal framework so as to avoid regulatory uncertainty and disputes. It must also be kept in mind that regulatory capacity in India is not exactly high, which may lead to the misuse of the vast discretion afforded to the proposed regulatory authority in designating datasets as HVDs or adjudicating disputes.

The NPD Committee's proposals therefore present several challenges, many of which arise from the lack of specificity in its recommendations. Two of these are closely related: the role of the 'community' and the institution of a 'data trustee'. In the proposed framework, any group of people could qualify as a community without any regard for whether they identify as such or have the means or willingness to assert their identity as a community. Defining communities may be particularly complex in the context of the digital economy, where communities may be spread across geographies, transient or context-specific creations. In addition to problems with identifying communities appropriately, problems may also arise from contestations of power or a lack of alignment of interests within or between community groups, particularly in contexts where a single dataset relates to multiple communities (Bailey et al., 2020). It may also be possible that the interests of a specific community (or sub-community) may come into conflict with what the state or other dominant members of the Committee perceive to be the broader public interest. This becomes important given the requirement for data trustees to act 'only in the interests' of the community (to whom the data relate) and to ensure no harm occurs to individuals or the community.

If the very existence of a 'community' is nebulous, then forcing a data trustee to 'always act in the interests' of a community may not be a practical standard to adopt.[25] It may often be the case that a data trustee collects and shares anonymised data pertaining to a community to enable a third party to draw inferences and make decisions that would be applied to the benefit of another community. Giving such a duty to data trustees would therefore significantly limit the scope of the data sharing requirement.

25 In this context, it must also be kept in mind that as has been argued elsewhere in the context of regulating personal data, all relationships of information exchange are not ipso facto fiduciary in nature (Khan & Pozen 2019; Bailey & Goyal, 2019). It is unclear on what basis it is assumed that all relationships where NPD are exchanged arise from or create a significant vulnerability or power differential between the parties, sufficient to deem all data custodians or data trustees as fiduciaries (Khan & Pozen, 2019; Bailey & Goyal, 2019). Extending the concept of a fiduciary relationship to the large number of relationships where non-personal data are exchanged therefore goes against existing jurisprudence on fiduciary relationships. Others point to various other problems with using fiduciary mechanisms (such as data trusts) to resolve issues of data governance. For instance, some point to how creating data trusts would not always reduce the power asymmetries between individuals and big corporates (Delacroix & Lawrence, 2019). Establishing and maintaining data trusts could also prove expensive and impractical, in addition to which it may be difficult for individuals to appropriately exercise agency even within the framework of a data trust–based system (McDonald, 2019; Delacroix & Lawrence, 2019).

The NPD Committee also suggests that any entity can apply to be a data trustee. This raises questions about the suitability of the entity to act as a data trustee, especially if the entity has little to do with the community the data relate to.[26] This suggestion also presumes that the relevant trustee will always act in the interests of the community whose data is in question. Public choice theory, however, would question this assumption, as actors may be influenced by factors such as an expansion of their own sphere of influence and other such internal considerations (Bailey et al., 2020). This may be true of government agencies/public authorities being appointed as data trustees, who may be influenced by factors such as budgetary interests or appointments and promotions. It is also true of private entities, who, in addition to prioritising revenue maximisation, are not subject to a constitutional mandate to act dispassionately towards competing interests, not being bound by equality requirements under the constitution.

Another practical challenge in this framework is the interplay between personal and non-personal data (Section 5 Final Report). The NPD Committee recognises that the PDP Bill is intended to regulate personal data and limits the scope of the NPD framework to only focus on data not derived from individuals or that have been anonymised and are hence no longer personal. It also makes a provision for non-personal data that get re-identified to be treated as personal data once again. However, in reality it may not be possible to define data in such a strictly binary way. Data are personal or not depending on context – the same data may constitute personal data when processed by one party but be non-personal when processed by another (Marda, 2020). Equally, whether data are personal or not cannot be solely based on their provenance (Bailey, Lashkari & Aneja, 2022).

Similarly, the NPD Committee's recommendation that only raw/factual data need to be shared may prove difficult to actualise. Collecting and curating any dataset requires some work/value addition, and in this sense, data represents a valuable resource to a firm. Meta-data can also reveal a lot about the strategic direction in which a company is moving, making firms vulnerable to competitors (Hasgeek, 2021). While the NPD Committee notes that copyright protection would not extend to a database where there is no exercise of skill or creativity in its creation (as India does not recognise copyright in databases but only protects them as literary works), this position has been challenged by some commentators (Venkatesan & Misra, 2021; Esya Centre, 2021). The entire data sharing mandate therefore becomes

26 The Final Report does away with the need for the data trustee to be 'the closest and most appropriate representative body', as envisaged in the First Report.

subject to the vagaries of intellectual property protection over databases, leading to further uncertainty. This issue also indicates the difficulties in balancing business interests with broader community or social interests. While some questioned the wide data sharing mandate proposed by the First Report, others have criticised the limitation of the data sharing mandate in the Final Report, and specifically the need to exempt all copyrighted material from the scope of data sharing mandates (Ramachandran, 2021; Pahwa, 2020; Hasgeek, 2021).

Finally, there is not enough clarity pertaining to the proposed regulatory apparatus, which has implications on the overall cost of compliance to firms (Bailey et al., 2020; Esya Centre, 2021). For instance, maintaining data on the scale envisaged by the NPD Committee could involve significant costs to organisations (Hasgeek, 2021). The creation of standards for data sharing and access is also not a trivial task, particularly when required across industries and while adhering to appropriate security and other standards. These processes will therefore pose a significant cost to the ecosystem.[27] The inability of a data trustee to charge more than a 'nominal fee' also raises questions about the incentive structures being created. This also limits the possibility of non-state actors or other wealthy entities acting as such. Finally, the proposal of creating two regulators in adjacent areas – particularly where the boundaries between NPD and personal data are so fluid – is also likely to lead to significant confusion for both firms and the regulators themselves (Esya Centre, 2021). Achieving appropriate levels of regulatory co-ordination between the different arms of government (including those designated as data trustees and data custodians) and different horizontal and sectoral regulators may prove difficult.

Overall, the NPD Committee suggests the adoption of a broad-based framework that is riddled with ambiguity. While introducing certain innovative and interesting ideas to the data governance discourse, it fails to adequately analyse the regulatory options available or provide an adequate evidence base for the actions proposed. By seeking to adopt a 'silver bullet' solution in the form of a single, centralised law governing all NPD (something that is also questionable, given the federal division of competencies prescribed by the Indian Constitution), the NPD Committee seeks to regulate a vast field covering a multiplicity of sectors, businesses and relationships in a fast-changing ecosystem (Bailey et al., 2020). While certainly advancing the conversation on the regulation of NPD, the final recommendations of

27 See for example the discussion around the costs of standards to enable interoperability mandates (OECD, 2021).

the NPD Committee may be viewed as underdeveloped. Instead, attempting to implement iterative, needs-based regulation may have been preferable (Bailey et al., 2020; Rathi et al., 2020).

4. More Recent Developments: Developing a Comprehensive Data Protection Law

In this section, we describe developments pursuant to the NPD Committee's report and opine on the future of NPD regulation in India.

Following publication of the Committee's Final Report, it was widely expected that a draft law would also be published. However, this has not occurred. After the release of the Final Report, a Joint Parliamentary Committee (JPC) tasked with scrutinising and suggesting revisions to the PDP Bill, 2019, released its report in December 2021 (Joint Committee on Personal Data Protection Bill 2019, 2021). In a rather unexpected turn of events, the JPC suggested that the proposed personal data protection law be revised to a general data protection law, governing both personal and non-personal data. Explaining this change, the JPC noted that NPD and personal data are inextricably connected, not least as large chunks of NPD are derived from PD. This is regarded as making it difficult to distinguish between the two, although the JPC nevertheless recommends that personal and non-personal data should receive 'different layers of protection or security'. The JPC also highlights that a single regulatory system with a unified data regulator would establish a simpler and more cohesive regulatory framework.

However, despite making some cosmetic changes to the draft law, the JPC fails to actually engage with the issue of NPD regulation in any meaningful way. Notably, it fails to even mention the work done by the Committee or refer to either of its two reports. The lack of engagement with the regulation of NPD is demonstrated by the fact that the JPC only makes two substantive changes to the PDP Bill in this regard. First, it extends provisions pertaining to personal data breaches to non-personal data.[28] Second, it extends an existing provision that empowered the central government to frame policies on the digital economy to the ability to also frame policies on NPD and anonymised PD. Interestingly, despite acknowledging the risks that may arise from de-anonymisation of anonymised data, the JPC retains a provision in the PDP Bill that empowers the central government to call for any NPD

28 These relate to the need to notify the regulator of a breach, the actions to be taken by the regulator subsequent to notification and so on.

or anonymised personal data from any entity, for purposes of targeting or delivery of services or formulation of evidence-based policies, subject only to regulations to be laid down by the regulator.[29]

Thus, the suggested changes do not actually implement any statutory rights and obligations with respect to NPD (with the exception of provisions concerning data breach). In fact, the revisions appear to leave it entirely to the government to create a governance framework for NPD. The retention of the power of the government to call for any NPD on broad grounds is also cause for concern. The absence of any meaningful limitations or checks on exercise of this power imply that, should any sets of NPD be prone to de-anonymisation, the government would find it easy to carry out surveillance of citizens and communities (Bailey et al., 2019). This provision therefore fails to find a meaningful balance between the state and individual/community interests.

In the absence of a proper explanation, one can only surmise as to the reasons behind the revisions suggested by the JPC. On the one hand, the Committee's recommendations regarding mandatory data sharing caused controversy, with many arguing that this would prove disastrous to data reliant businesses (Bhalla, 2020; Ramachandran, 2021; Esya Centre, 2021).[30] Together with the absence of clarity in the Committee's recommendations, the JPC may have just found it easier to avoid the Committee's recommendations in toto. The JPC therefore merely made cosmetic changes to the PDP Bill as a response to public discourse on the issue of NPD, while giving the government sufficient power to frame relevant policies at a later point in time.

On the other hand, to take an even more uncharitable view, one could surmise that the JPC's report could be designed to muddy the waters and delay the passage of a personal data protection law. Such a law would require significant restructuring of the data economy. This would impose costs on the Indian economy and, in particular, Indian businesses, which are currently free to process personal data with relative impunity given the absence of any proper data protection regulations in India. Further, a strong data protection law could also limit the state's broad powers to process personal data of individuals.

29 Refer to Section 91(2) of the PDP Bill renumbered as Section 92(2) in the JPC's version of the draft law.

30 Some even referred to the First Report as mandating the 'nationalisation' of data, which, it is argued, would be disastrous to innovation and the development of a data economy (Pahwa, 2020).

Subsequently, the government has withdrawn the PDP Bill from parliament. It is however expected that a fresh version will be introduced in the near future, though it is still unclear what kind of law will finally be adopted in Parliament – whether the proposals of the Joint Parliamentary Committee, which suggested that both personal and non-personal data be governed by a single data protection law, will be accepted as a whole or in part (possibly with more substantive provisions being added pertaining to regulation of NPD) or whether Parliament will revert to a law specifically covering personal data.

More recently, in another step that appears to indicate the government's intent to distance itself from the recommendations of the Gopalakrishnan Committee while doubling down on the imperative of using 'Indian' data to enable economic growth of the domestic digital ecosystem, the Ministry of Electronics and Information Technology has proposed establishing a policy framework known as the National Data Governance Framework Policy (Ministry of Electronics and Information Technology, 2022). This policy explicitly aims to promote domestic innovation by enabling Indian businesses and researchers to access NPD held by government entities through a platform managed by a new institution known as the India Data Management Office. Data access will be permissioned, but fees charged will be nominal. The policy has been criticised on various grounds, including its failure to adequately consider the harms that may arise from the recombination of datasets released by the government, the excessive focus on economic outcomes as opposed to citizen empowerment and government accountability (which are typically the focus of open government programmes the world over) and the excessive discretion afforded to the proposed India Data Management Office (Bailey, Shah et al., 2022; Aapti Institute, 2022; D'Cunha & Mohamed, 2022). This document is currently under review and will likely be finalised in the course of the year.

5. Conclusion

The discussions on regulating non-personal data in India are driven primarily by competition concerns, especially vis-à-vis foreign multinationals, as well as issues of 'fairness' and equity in the distribution of the benefits of the data economy, which derive from a view that links regulation of data to India's sovereignty. This view encompasses questions of who has access to data, who captures its value and how these benefits get distributed as critical elements of the Indian digital economy as well as society. To this end, the

NPD Committee, established by the Government of India, adopted a design that includes designating certain datasets as HVDs, setting up the institution of a 'data trustee' to manage the datasets, determining a framework through which the HVDs could be accessed and establishing a regulator, the NPD Authority, to oversee the process. The recognition of a community's right to benefit from the data economy and the mention of group privacy rights are notable additions to the data governance discourse in India.

The proposed regulatory framework is aspirational in its goal of opening access to NPD and brings novelty by recognising the community as a distinct stakeholder in the data governance debate. However, the framework seeks to regulate a vast field covering a multiplicity of sectors, businesses and relationships in a fast-changing ecosystem, which may prove to be impractical. While certainly advancing the conversation on the regulation of NPD, the final recommendations of the NPD Committee may be viewed as underdeveloped.

Following submission of the NPD Committee's Final Report, a Joint Parliamentary Committee to scrutinise and revise the PDP Bill suggested enacting a general data protection law to cover both personal and non-personal data. The JPC completely ignores the recommendations of the NPD Committee but is nonetheless short on substantive regulations pertaining to NPD. After the JPCs recommendations, the PDP Bill has been withdrawn from parliament, ostensibly to enable revision thereof. At this point in time, it is unclear what kind of law will finally be adopted in parliament and if or when such a law will be passed. More recently, the government has moved to open up access to NPD held by government departments for use by Indian businesses and researchers. As with previous policies, the draft National Data Governance Framework Policy seeks to make 'Indian' data accessible for domestic economic development – indicating the focus of the government on promoting domestic businesses in the development of the Indian data economy.

References

Aapti Institute. (2022). Comments on the National Data Governance Framework Policy. https://thedataeconomylab.com/wp-content/uploads/2022/06/Aapti-submission_National-Data-Governance-Framework-Policy.pdf

Bailey, R., Bhandari, V., Parsheera, S., & Rahman, F. (2019). Comments on the (draft) Personal Data Protection Bill, 2019. *Comments submitted to the Lok Sabha's Joint Parliamentary Committee on the PDP Bill, 2019*. https://papers.ssrn.com/sol3/papers.cfm?abstract_id=4051127

Bailey, R., & Goyal, T. (2019). *Fiduciary relationships as a means to protect privacy: Examining the use of the fiduciary concept in the draft Personal Data Protection Bill, 2018* [Working paper 04]. Data Governance Network. https://www.datagovernance.org/report/fiduciary-relationships-as-a-means-to-protect-privacy

Bailey, R., Lashkari, B., & Aneja, U. (2022). Comments on the draft India Data Accessibility and Use Policy, 2022. https://papers.ssrn.com/sol3/papers.cfm?abstract_id=4080917

Bailey, R., & Misra, P. (2022). *Interoperability of social media platforms: An appraisal of the regulatory and technical ecosystem*. IT for Change. https://papers.ssrn.com/sol3/papers.cfm?abstract_id=4095312

Bailey, R., Sane, R., & Parsheera, S. (2020). Comments on the 'Report by the Committee of Experts on Non-Personal Data Governance Framework'. *National Institute of Public Finance and Policy*. https://papers.ssrn.com/sol3/papers.cfm?abstract_id=3724184

Bailey, R., Shah, A., Naik, A., & Lashkari, B. (2022). Comments on the National Data Governance Framework, 2022. https://papers.ssrn.com/sol3/papers.cfm?abstract_id=4144213

Basu, A. (2021). Sovereignty in a 'datafied' world. *Observer Research Foundation* [ORF Issue Brief No. 501]. https://www.orfonline.org/research/sovereignty-in-a-datafied-world/

Bhalla, K. (2020). *Start-ups, tech bodies red flag non personal data framework*. Inc42 Media. https://inc42.com/buzz/startups-tech-bodies-red-flag-non-personal-data-framework/

California Consumer Privacy Act. (2018). California Civil Code [1798.100 – 1798.199.100]. https://leginfo.legislature.ca.gov/faces/codes_displayText.xhtml?division=3.&part=4.&lawCode=CIV&title=1.81.5

D'Cunha, J., & Mohamed, B. (2022). *Comments to MEITY on the draft National Data Governance Framework Policy*. Centre for Communication Governance at National Law University, Delhi. https://ccgdelhi.s3.ap-south-1.amazonaws.com/uploads/ccg-nlu-comments-to-meity-on-the-draft-national-framework-policy-300.pdf

Department of Industrial Policy & Promotion. (2019). *Draft National E-Commerce Policy*. Government of India. https://dipp.gov.in/sites/default/files/DraftNational_e-commerce_Policy_23February2019.pdf

Draft Privacy Bill. (2011). Government of India. https://cis-india.org/internet-governance/draft-bill-on-right-to-privacy

Delacroix, S., & Lawrence, N. D. (2019). Bottoms-up data trusts: Disturbing the one-size fits all approach to data governance. *International Data Privacy Law, 9*(4), 236–252. https://academic.oup.com/idpl/article/9/4/236/5579842

Esya Centre. (2021). Response to the second draft report by the committee of experts on non-personal data governance framework. Issue No. 105. https://tinyurl.com/y8xb5rda

General Data Protection Regulation. (2016). European Union (2016/679). https://eur-lex.europa.eu/legal-content/EN/TXT/PDF/?uri=CELEX:32016R0679

German Federal Ministry of Justice. Act Against Restraint of Competition (Competition Act – GWB). https://www.gesetze-im-internet.de/englisch_gwb/

Gopalakrishnan, K., et al. (2020a). *Report by the Committee of Experts on Non-Personal Data Governance Framework*. Ministry of Electronics and Information Technology, Government of India. https://static.mygov.in/rest/s3fs-public/mygov_159453381955063671.pdf

Gopalakrishnan, K., et al. (2020b). *Report by the Committee of Experts on Non-Personal Data Governance Framework*. Ministry of Electronics and Information Technology, Government of India. https://static.mygov.in/rest/s3fs-public/mygov_160922880751553221.pdf

Government of India. (2018). Electronic commerce in India: Draft national policy framework. https://www.medianama.com/wp-content/uploads/Draft-National-E-commerce-Policy.pdf

Hasgeek. (2021). *Non-personal data regulatory framework: Community recommendations from India's startup and investor ecosystem*. Hasgeek Learning. https://drive.google.com/file/d/1Z8OGQ88_L19kyyTxIQ3WRPxbDpqZKc8G/view

Herbers, B., & Nieuwmeyer, R. (2021). *Friends of an effective Digital Markets Act, part 2 – France, Germany and Netherlands publish second joint position paper with proposals to amend the DMA*. CMS Law-Now. https://bit.ly/3IeU285

Joint Committee on Personal Data Protection Bill, 2019. (2021). *Report of the Joint Committee on the Personal Data Protection Bill, 2019*. 17th Lok Sabha, Lok Sabha Secretariat. http://164.100.47.193/lsscommittee/Joint%20Committee%20on%20the%20Personal%20Data%20Protection%20Bill,%202019/17_Joint_Committee_on_the_Personal_Data_Protection_Bill_2019_1.pdf

K. S. Puttaswamy v. Union of India. (2017). 10 SCC 1.

Kerber, W. (2017). Rights on data: The EU communication 'Building a European data economy' from an economic perspective. *MAGKS Joint Discussion Paper Series in Economics, No. 35-2017*. http://hdl.handle.net/10419/174331

Khan, L., & Pozen, D. (2019). A skeptical view of information fiduciaries. *Harvard Law Review, 133*, 497. https://scholarship.law.columbia.edu/faculty_scholarship/2451/

Manjunatha, M. (2017). *Privacy and data protection laws in India* (*Part 1*). Commercial Law Blog, Agama Law Associates. https://agamalaw.in/2017/05/25/privacy-and-data-protection-laws-in-india-part-i/

Marda, V. (2020) *Non-personal data: The case of the Indian Data Protection Bill, definitions and assumptions*. Ada Lovelace Institute. https://www.adalovelaceinstitute.org/blog/non-personal-data-indian-data-protection-bill/

Mayer-Schönberger, V., & Ramge, T. (2018). A big choice for big tech: Share data or suffer the consequences. *Foreign Affairs*, *97*(5), 48–54.

McDonald, S. M. (2019). *Reclaiming data trusts*. Centre for International Governance Innovation. https://www.cigionline.org/articles/reclaiming-data-trusts/

Ministry of Electronics and Information Technology. (2019). Office Memorandum No. 24(4)/2019-CLES. Government of India. https://www.meity.gov.in/writereaddata/files/constitution_of_committee_of_experts_to_deliberate_on_data_governance_framework.pdf

Ministry of Electronics and Information Technology. (2020). *Expert committee invites public comments on Non-Personal Data Framework*. Press Information Bureau, Government of India. https://pib.gov.in/PressReleseDetailm.aspx?PRID=1640701

Ministry of Electronics and Information Technology. (2022). *Draft National Data Governance Framework Policy*. Government of India. https://www.meity.gov.in/content/draft-national-data-governance-framework-policy

Nadler, J., et al. (2020). *Investigation of Competition in Digital Markets, Majority Staff Report and Recommendations*. Subcommittee on Antitrust, Commercial and Administrative Law of the Committee on the Judiciary. United States Congress. https://judiciary.house.gov/uploadedfiles/competition_in_digital_markets.pdf?utm_campaign=4493-519

OECD. (2008). *Introductory handbook for undertaking regulatory impact analysis (RIA)*. https://www.oecd.org/gov/regulatory-policy/44789472.pdf

OECD. (2015). *Data-driven innovation: Big data for growth and well-being*. OECD Publishing. http://dx.doi.org/10.1787/9789264229358-en

OECD. (2021). Data portability, interoperability and digital platform competition. *OECD Competition Committee Discussion Paper*. http://oe.cd/dpic

Pahwa, N. (2020). Nationalisation of data will destroy value for businesses investors. *Times of India*. https://timesofindia.indiatimes.com/blogs/toi-edit-page/nationalisation-of-data-will-destroy-value-for-businesses-investors/

Personal Data Protection Bill (PDP). (2019). Government of India. http://164.100.47.4/BillsTexts/LSBillTexts/Asintroduced/373_2019_LS_Eng.pdf

Ramachandran, T. V. (2021). Mandate to share non-personal data may hinder startups. *Financial Express*. https://www.financialexpress.com/opinion/mandate-to-share-non-personal-data-may-hinder-start-ups/2339729/

Rathi, A., et al. (2020). *Inputs to the Report on the Non-Personal Data Governance Framework*. The Centre for Internet and Society, India. https://cis-india.org/raw/inputs-to-report-on-non-personal-data-governance-framework

Shah, Justice A. P., et al. (2012). *Report of the Group of Experts on Privacy.* Planning Commission, Government of India. https://cis-india.org/internet-governance/blog/report-of-group-of-experts-on-privacy.pdf

Singh, P. J. (2019). *Data and digital intelligence commons: Making a case for their community ownership* [Working Paper No. 02, 2019]. Data Governance Network. https://datagovernance.org/files/research/ITFC_Parminder_Data_Commons_-_Paper_2.pdf

Singh, P. J. (2020). *Treating data as commons.* IT for Change. https://itforchange.net/index.php/treating-data-as-commons

Srikrishna, Justice B. N., et al. (2018). *A free and fair digital economy: Protecting privacy, empowering indians.* Committee of Experts Under the Chairmanship of Justice BN Srikrishna, Government of India. https://tinyurl.com/y4a08t9s

State of Karnataka v. Ranganatha Reddy. (1978). AIR 1978 SC 215.

UK Competition & Markets Authority. (2020). *Online platforms and digital advertising.* Government of UK. https://bit.ly/3KcLJvn

Venkatesan, S., & Mishra, P. (2021). Govt now accepts value of IPR in non-personal data, but its recommendations pose new problems. *The Print.* https://theprint.in/opinion/govt-now-accepts-value-of-ipr-in-non-personal-data-but-its-recommendations-pose-new-problems/594112/

13. Data Protection Without Data: Informationless Chilling Effects and Data Protection Law

Dara Hallinan

Abstract
Individuals make assumptions about information processing concerning them based on environmental cues. These assumptions may lead to behavioural adaptations which constitute harms to fundamental rights – for example, certain acts of self-censorship. A set of such adaptations, where individuals refrain from engaging in legitimate activities, are called chilling effects. Given, however, that behavioural reactions to cues underlie chilling effects, chilling effects can occur in contexts where the relevant cues are presented but where no information is ever processed: 'informationless chilling effects'. The aim of this article is to introduce and elaborate the concept of informationless chilling effects and to sketch the argument for looking to EU data protection law to provide protection in relation to these effects.

Keywords: data protection; chilling effects; informationless chilling effects; EU law; fundamental rights

1. Introduction

The prevalence of information processing in modern societies means that individuals may make presumptions about information processing concerning them based on cues in their environment. For example, one might assume that accepting advertising cookies would lead to one's internet usage information being processed for targeted advertising. In this regard, one form of harm to fundamental rights relating to certain forms of information processing is that individuals may problematically adapt their behaviours – for example, by self-censoring – in reaction to the presentation of cues that this processing will take place: these are called 'chilling effects'.

Van der Sloot & van Schendel. *The Boundaries of Data.* Taylor & Francis Group, 2024
DOI: 10.5117/9789463729192_CH13

Since behavioural reactions to cues cause chilling effects – as opposed to the information processing itself – one may imagine the existence of chilling effects in relation to systems and contexts in which the relevant cues are presented but in which no information is ever actually processed: 'informationless chilling effects'.

EU data protection law can be considered as a key area of law aimed at protecting individuals from harms to fundamental rights posed by third-party activities relating to information processing concerning those individuals. Informationless chilling effects only exist in contexts where information processing is already embedded and prevalent, i.e. in relation to contexts where individuals have already learned to recognise cues and their implications. Accordingly, informationless chilling effects may be regarded as a form of rights harm related to information processing. An unusual and perhaps counterintuitive question therefore emerges: is EU data protection law relevant to protect individuals from the systems and contexts that engender informationless chilling effects?

This article offers a sketch of the argument for looking to EU data protection law to provide protection in relation to informationless chilling effects. It highlights: (i) correspondence between the purpose of EU data protection law and the form of harm caused by informationless chilling effects and (ii) the potential for systems and contexts engendering informationless chilling effects to fall within the bounds of the scoping concepts of data protection law.

The article begins by considering the purpose of EU data protection law. It offers general observations concerning a range of factors that might be considered in determining the purpose of an area of EU law. In light of these general observations, the article then proposes a broad, flexible and open-ended conceptualisation of the purposes of EU data protection law (sections 2–3). Building on this, the article considers the boundaries of scoping concepts in EU data protection law, taking the concept of personal data as an exemplar. The article highlights the possibility of conceptualising personal data in a flexible and open-ended manner, with boundaries linking it to the purpose of data protection law (sections 3–4).

Next, the concept of informationless chilling effects is introduced and described. The article first introduces the general concept of chilling effects, then elaborates informationless chilling effects as a specific sub-category related to information processing (sections 5–6). The article then combines the preceding sections and observes how: (i) informationless chilling effects can be seen as constituting a form of harm to rights in relation to which EU data protection law seems a logical candidate to provide protection, and (ii) systems and contexts engendering informationless chilling effects may fall within the flexible and open-ended scoping concepts of data protection law, where the boundaries of these concepts are related to the purposes of the law (section 7).

Finally, the article considers three objections that may be raised against the idea of systems and contexts that engender informationless chilling effects within the scope of EU data protection law. These are the positive objection, the utility objection and the conceptual integrity objection. Each is elaborated on and countered (sections 8–10).

Prior to diving into the discussion, some observations on what this article is and what it is not should be made. This article should be read as a first conceptual exploration of an interesting question and idea. It should not be read, however, as an immediate call for correction of law or for legal recognition of the argument. Nor should it be read with the presumption that it intends to provide a complete and final analysis of this issue. Such concrete propositions require considerably more research and thought.

2. Determining the Purpose of an Area of Law: A Multifaceted Consideration

To start, I would like to offer the background observation that the determination of the purpose of a particular area of EU law requires a multifactorial consideration – within which only certain factors directly relate to the valid positive law.

Legislation and jurisprudence form the core of valid law in the EU. Accordingly, the range of meanings that can be ascribed to legislative texts and their judicial interpretations are key to framing the range of possible purposes that might be attributed to an area of EU law. Where legislative texts are ambiguous and there is no jurisprudence to alleviate uncertainty, assistance can be sought by reliance on various gap-filling concepts. One of the most important of these – and the one which will be used in subsequent analysis in this article – is the 'will of the legislator'. Legislation is enacted through law-making processes representing the translation of the communicative power of citizens, through the legislator, into legal form. Thus, the concept provides a useful anchor to maintain clear and consistent links between the political and legal systems.[1]

These approaches alone, however, are not always sufficient to determine the purpose of an area of EU law. Legal texts emerging from a legislative

1 For a more elaborated discussion of the idea of the translation of communicative power via the political process into law, see Habermas (2017, pp. 1–42).

process are unlikely to fully grasp and describe the world they seek to regulate and, accordingly, will seldom be entirely clear. Equally, reality changes following the legislative process. As a result, the world as modelled in legislation may no longer correspond to reality, leading to uncertainty in how a text should apply (see, for example: Bennet Moses, 2007). Jurisprudence may, in certain circumstances, address problems of uncertainty. In others, however, it may not. Some cases of uncertainty may never be clarified. It seems fair to posit that the significance of such uncertainties will grow with increases in the abstraction and scope of an area of law, as well as with the speed and unpredictability of changes in the phenomena requiring regulation.[2] Looking to approaches like the 'will of the legislator' may provide clear answers to address uncertainties in some instances. Often, however, such concepts will not provide the answers desired – the will of the legislator, for example, will often simply not be accessible in a way that can provide the answers sought.[3]

Equally, appeals to valid law alone ignore a significant feature in the determination of the purpose of an area of EU law: namely the reliance

2 The idea that societies as a whole are becoming more complex and indeterminate is a common strand of thought in the social sciences. While increasing social complexity and indeterminacy have deep historical roots, modern discussions have highlighted the significance of the developments in information processing technologies in their acceleration. Castells, for example, provides an extensive sociological elaboration of the ways in which information processing technologies have proliferated, allowing the possibility to form greater quantities of social connections, novel forms of social connections and social connections of greater flexibility. On top of these observations, he charts the emergence and utility of new forms of social structure – built on new connective possibilities – and the encompassing changes in social systems these structures have spurred. Eventually he proposes the emergence of a new form of society: the network society. This social form appears as one in which the breadth and pace of change make accurate predictions of the future, based on stable models of the world, increasingly difficult. Castell's ideas are brought together in his three-volume work on the information age: (Castells, 2010; Castells, 2004; Castells, 1998). Castells' work is now over 20 years old. While some of the content is dated, I find the work still pertinent, cogent and accessible in offering a framework within which to perceive modern information flows and their social consequences.
The idea of increasing social complexity and indeterminacy has also permeated discussions of law. Recognitions have taken different forms, emerge from different conceptual foundations and accordingly propose different ways forward in the construction of legal systems functional in response. See, for instance, the following three examples: Ladeur (2013); Pradini (2013); Ruhl (2008).

3 This is true for several reasons. Following the enactment of legislation, the 'will of the legislator' can no longer be directly accessed where this is not explicitly clear from available legislative materials – who, given 'the legislator' will usually be a body of numerous representatives of shifting membership and shifting politics, would even be asked. Second, the separation of powers requires that legislative bodies, following the legislative process, are excluded from providing direct input into proceedings determining valid law within the legal system.

on the law by its users to fulfil perceived needs or interests. Various parties (individuals, corporations, NGOs, etc.) may look to convert needs and interests they seek to have fulfilled into justiciable claims – or arguments to claims – under areas of law they feel are suitable. The legal system is then required to consider and address these claims. In addressing claims, alterations to the range of legal information relevant to the determination of the purpose of an area of law occur. In other words, there is a reflexive interplay between valid, positive law and the use of law relevant for the determination of the purpose of an area of law (see, for example: Luhmann, 2012, pp. 76–211). From this perspective, the purpose of an area of EU law might also be considered from two other perspectives: (i) in light of possibilities to translate needs and interests into concrete legal claims, i.e. the degree to which the structure of an area of law permits the translation and success of different forms of potential claim, and (ii) in light of the availability and utility of other alternative areas of law under which such claims might also be made, i.e. the degree to which users are likely to appeal to one area of law over another.

The above constitutes a set of general observations concerning the determination of the purpose of an area of EU law. These can now be specified in relation to the purpose of EU data protection law.

3. The Broad, Flexible and Open-Ended Purpose of EU Data Protection Law

Building on the previous section, I now suggest that the purposes of EU data protection law be considered in a broad, flexible and open-ended manner.

The function of EU data protection law, as mentioned in its text, is extremely broad.[4] Article 1 of the General Data Protection Regulation (GDPR) is indicative of this, stating:

- This Regulation lays down rules relating to the protection of natural persons with regard to the processing of personal data and rules relating to the free movement of personal data.

4 There are naturally other legislatives texts that are relevant in the area of EU data protection law. The General Data Protection Regulation, however, is undoubtedly the most important text, and accordingly, the discussion here focuses on this text.

– This Regulation protects fundamental rights and freedoms of natural persons and in particular their right to the protection of personal data. (Regulation [EU] 2016/679, 2016, Article 1)

From this, one might draw certain limited conclusions as to the purpose of the area of law, such as that EU data protection law is intended to function in relation to information processing concerning individuals and that data protection concerns the protection of rights and freedoms in relation to this phenomenon. There is good reason, however, to be cautious about being any more specific.

In the first instance, there is little jurisprudence that provides further clear delineations of the of the boundaries of the purpose of EU data protection. For example, while there are jurisprudential references to the purpose of data protection in relation to the protection of specific fundamental rights, these are liable to be followed by recognition that the full range of rights – potentially the subject of protection – may remain open. The Article 29 Working Party, for example, stated:

> the scope of 'the rights and freedoms' of the data subjects primarily concerns the right to privacy but may also involve other fundamental rights such as freedom of speech, freedom of thought, freedom of movement, prohibition of discrimination, right to liberty, conscience and religion. (Article 29 Working Party, 2014, p. 8).

In turn, looking to legislative documentation to determine the 'will of the legislator' tends only to reveal top-level clarifications pertaining to the need to protect individuals' rights in relation to information processing (see, for example, European Commission, 2012, pp. 1–7).

Efforts to delimit the purposes of EU data protection law by looking to the likely use contexts of the law reveal an equally broad range of future possibilities. The possible range of harms to rights emerging from future developments in information processing remains highly uncertain. In principle, there are few structural limitations to how future information processing concerning individuals may impact rights (see, for example, the discussion in: Floridi, 2015, pp. 1–17). Accordingly, there is no apparent way, ex ante, of delimiting the range or form of rights claims that might be brought under data protection law in the future. Equally, efforts to delineate the range of future rights claims that might fall under data protection law, as opposed to under other areas of law, reveal limited results. There is a paucity in comparable areas of law which seem capable of encompassing potential future harms to rights relating to information processing concerning individuals.

In light of the above, building on the GDPR's wording on the purposes of data protection law, the open-ended nature of harms to rights that may eventuate as a result of information processing concerning individuals in future and the paucity of comparable areas of law, I propose that the purposes of EU data protection law should only be formulated in a broad, flexible and open-ended way. The following formulation might be taken forward: the purpose of EU data protection law is to provide protection in relation to (i) harms to fundamental rights, (ii) which eventuate in relation to systems and contexts of information processing concerning individuals, (iii) while not, in advance, exhaustively defining either the forms of harms to rights encompassed or the forms of systems and contexts relating to information processing concerning individuals, which are encompassed under this purpose (see also in this regard: Dalla Corte, 2020).

The elaboration of the logic of considering the purpose of EU data protection law in a broad, flexible and open-ended manner has consequences for the conceptualisation of the boundaries of scoping concepts in EU data protection law.

4. Broad, Flexible and Open-Ended Scoping Concepts in EU Data Protection Law

The above conceptualisation of the purposes of EU data protection law supports an equivalent broad, flexible and open-ended conceptualisation of scoping concepts. This area of law includes a range of scoping concepts. Each is defined by different criteria and can be considered with more specificity in relation to the subject matter of the article. For the argument in this article, it seems sufficient, however, to take arguably the most important scoping concept in EU data protection law as an exemplar: that of personal data.

The concept of personal data is pivotal for determining the scope of EU data protection law. EU data protection law only applies if personal data are processed. It appears as a scoping concept at all levels of EU data protection law – from the right to the protection of personal data in Article 8 of the Charter of Fundamental Rights through secondary EU data protection law (Charter of Fundamental Rights, 2012, art. 8). A detailed definition of the concept is found in Article 4(1) of the GDPR:

> 'personal data' means any information relating to an identified or identifiable natural person ('data subject'); an identifiable natural person is one who can be identified, directly or indirectly, in particular by reference to an identifier such as a name, an identification number, location data, an online identifier or to one or more factors specific to the physical, physiological, genetic, mental, economic, cultural or social identity of that natural person.

In most analyses, efforts to delineate the boundaries of the concept of personal data focus on establishing a relationship between the concept as elaborated in legislation and jurisprudence and some form of specific class of substance with an objective existence in the world – in other words, a substance whose existence is detached from the individual whose rights may be harmed and the third party whose activities in relation to the substance may cause the harm (see, for example, the breakdown offered in: Article 29 Working Party, 2007, pp. 6–24). Such analyses make sense in terms of defining the concept's scope to understand whether the law should apply in relation to specific phenomena and thus to apply the law in practice. More in-depth efforts, however, highlight the uncertainties surrounding the concept's boundaries and its fluidity in relation to the real world of information processing (see, for example: Purtova, 2018).

However, there may be other ways to conceptualise the boundaries of the concept. There is a line of jurisprudential recognition that the boundaries of the concept of personal data ought to be regarded, at least in part, in light of the purposes of the law. This highlights that the concept's boundaries can be regarded as being defined, at least in part, by the boundaries of the general subject matter of the law, and the boundaries of the general set of harms in relation to which the law should provide a response. From this perspective, a reflexive interplay between the purpose of the area of law and the practical scoping concepts of the law is foreseen.[5] Accordingly, personal

5 See, for example, the statement of the Article 29 Working Party under the head of 'General Considerations and Policy Issues' concerning the scope of personal data: 'Articles 1 of Directive 95/46/EC and of Directive 2002/58/EC clearly state the ultimate purpose of the rules contained therein: to protect the fundamental rights and freedoms of natural persons and in particular their right to privacy, with regard to the processing of personal data. This is a very important element to take into account in the interpretation and application of the rules of both instruments... and it may caution against any interpretation of the same rules that would leave individuals deprived of protection of their rights' (Article 29 Working Party, 2007, p. 4). Equally, the Court of Justice of the European Union has observed: 'The Court has already held that the provisions of Directive 95/46, in so far as they govern the processing of personal data liable to infringe fundamental freedoms, in particular the right to privacy, must necessarily be interpreted in

data need not be reductively understood as limited to something with an objective material existence. Rather, it might be understood – in line with the broad, flexible and open-ended purpose of the law – in a broad, flexible and open-ended manner.

Considering the concept of personal data from this perspective enables us to unpack the concept in a novel way: the concept of personal data is the legal concept that (i) describes the subject matter of the relationship (ii) between an individual and a third party engaging in an activity relating to information processing concerning an individual, (iii) where the activity in question harms individual rights (iv) while not necessarily being determinate as to the form of subject matter of relationship, nor necessarily being determinate as to the range of harms, which may be subsumed within the scope of the concept.

The prior sections suggested that the purpose and scoping criteria in EU data protection law might be understood in a broad, flexible and open-ended way. I now move way from EU data protection law to provide an introduction and explanation of informationless chilling effects.

5. Chilling Effects and Information Processing

It seems logical to introduce the concept of informationless chilling effects by providing an introduction to chilling effects and their relevance to information processing.

In principle, the concept of chilling effects in relation to fundamental rights rests on the idea that knowledge of actions by third parties – for example the state – may provoke certain reactions from individuals or groups. Some forms of such behavioural response – such as self-censorship in relation to the right to freedom of speech – may be conceptualised as harms to rights or other values. For example, harms may be identified if behavioural responses take a form that indicate individuals are being dissuaded from exercising rights. In certain cases, these harms may mean that an action (i) cannot be regarded as legitimate or (ii) may only be regarded as legitimate subject to the implementation of supplemental safeguards aimed at mitigating the likely occurrence or impact of chilling effects.

the light of fundamental rights, which, according to settled case-law, form an integral part of the general principles of law whose observance the Court ensures and which are now set out in the Charter' (Case C-131/12, 2014, para. 68). For a more extensive discussion on the issue, see also Demetzou (2020, pp. 129–132).

The concept of chilling effects has been used at various levels of European jurisprudence concerning fundamental rights. It has a long history in the case-law of the European Court of Human Rights, particularly in relation to the right to freedom of expression – see, for example, the discussion of relevant case-law in Pech's work on the concept (Pech, 2021, pp. 8–15). The concept also appears more recently in the case law of the Court of Justice of the European Union. Pech, for example, discuses its relevance in the Court's case-law and points to the logic of the concept being used, such as in the recent case of *Commission v. Poland* (Pech, 2021, p. 21; Case C-791/19, 2021, para. 82). The concept also appears in national constitutional jurisprudence. The German Constitutional Court, for example, has worked with comparable concepts.[6]

The concept has found specific use in relation to information processing and fundamental rights. The concept has been explicitly used, for example, in the Council of Europe's 'Declaration of the Committee of Ministers on Risks to Fundamental Rights stemming from Digital Tracking and other Surveillance Technologies'. In the Declaration, the Committee of Ministers observes:

> Legislation allowing broad surveillance of citizens can be found contrary to the right to respect of private life. These capabilities and practices can have a chilling effect on citizen participation in social, cultural and political life and, in the longer term, could have damaging effects on democracy. (Declaration of the Committee of Ministers, 2013)

In academic literature, the concept is used in relation to an even broader range of forms and contexts of information processing. Consider, for example, the recent contribution on algorithmic profiling and chilling effects by Büchi et al. (2020).

This brief introduction to the general concept of chilling effects provides the background against which to introduce the concept of informationless chilling effects.

6 The Court observed, for example: 'Denn die Verurteilung zur Zahlung von Schmerzensgeld führt nicht nur zu einer Genugtuung für eine in der Vergangenheit liegende Ehrverletzung. Sie entfaltet unvermeidlich präventive Wirkungen, indem sie das Äußern kritischer Meinungen einem hohen finanziellen Risiko unterwirft; dadurch kann sie die Bereitschaft mindern, in Zukunft Kritik zu üben, und auf diese Weise eine Beeinträchtigung freier geistiger Auseinandersetzung bewirken, die an den Kern der grundrechtlichen Gewährleistung rühren muß' (BVerfG, 1980, para. 29).

6. The Concept of Informationless Chilling Effects

The concept of informationless chilling effects describes, as the name might suggest, a sub-category of chilling effects relating to information processing.

The previous section highlighted that chilling effects emerge as a result of individuals' behavioural responses prompted by reaction to certain cues. In this regard, a specification as to when chilling effects are engendered might be made. Actions – to which cues sparking behavioural responses relate – are not actually a prerequisite for chilling effects to eventuate. Rather, only the cues relating to actions, and the behavioural responses these cues might prompt, are relevant to the materialisation of chilling effects. One might observe that chilling effects relate to doxastic relationships (relationships of belief) as opposed to substantial relationships (relationships where specific actions actually occur). In other words, chilling effects only require an individual to believe a given action will occur.

Accordingly, in contexts where information processing is prevalent, systems that aim to elicit a behavioural response from individuals based on prompting the belief that information processing will occur, while not ever actually processing information, may still engender chilling effects. More specifically, these chilling effects will likely manifest in relation to a system or context where (i) individuals have learned to recognise cues that information processing will take place; (ii) individuals have developed mental models about what will happen with their information pursuant to these cues; (iii) individuals are likely to engage in behavioural responses in relation to these cues; (iv) cues can be presented by a third party to provoke behavioural responses which serve their own purposes and (vi) the behavioural responses themselves might be regarded as a harm to rights. This special form of chilling effect can be referred to as informationless chilling effects.[7]

7 It would seem expedient to offer a brief comment on the relationship and distinction between nudges and informationless chilling effects. The two concepts certainly relate and overlap in certain cases. One can imagine, for example, instances in which certain online nudges might provoke informationless chilling effects. Even where nudges concern information processing, however, there are differences. The following three seem particularly pertinent. First, nudges can be considered as design causes that relate to certain responses, while informationless chilling effects are specific forms of legal consequences that may eventuate off the back of design causes and associated responses. Second, nudges do not need to provoke the forms of action with which informationless chilling effects are concerned – e.g. certain forms of nudge may actively encourage behaviours which are the opposite of informationless chilling effects. Third, nudges are usually associated with subtle and often clandestine efforts to encourage actors to make specific choices, while there is no need for systems and contexts which aim to

While the concept of informationless chilling effects may seem esoteric and theoretical, there are examples of systems in operation that may already engender these effects. Perhaps the most obvious example is dummy camera systems. These are systems that seek to influence behaviour based on the pretence of surveillance and information processing. In turn, given the ever-increasing significance of information processing in modern societies, it seems likely that the possibility and utility of manipulating individuals based solely on the presentation of cues that information processing will occur will only rise. It is possible to imagine the identification of standard online patterns in relation to the presumption of information processing. This might be used in website design capable of engendering informationless chilling effects. Accordingly, there is a possibility that the range of systems and contexts in relation to which informationless chilling effects are engendered will grow over time.

One obvious question emerging from the discussion of informationless chilling effects is what options are offered in law in terms of the provision of protection. Bringing the discussion in all the preceding sections together, I now highlight the logic of looking at EU data protection law as potentially providing protection.

7. Informationless Chilling Effects and EU Data Protection Law

In light of the discussions above, one might argue that (i) informationless chilling effects constitute a form of harm to rights that falls within the purview of EU data protection law and (ii) scoping concepts in data protection law offer the potential to encompass systems and contexts engendering informationless chilling effects.

Section 4 provided a three-point elaboration of the purpose of EU data protection law. In relation to each of these points, it makes sense to consider EU data protection law as a logical legal response to informationless chilling effects that (i) constitute harms to fundamental rights; (ii) can be said to relate to information processing operations and systems concerning individuals, as informationless chilling effects are forms of harm that are parasitic to the prevalence of information processing concerning individuals, without which no recognition of cues which spark problematic behaviour could eventuate; and (iii) while they constitute a form of harm to rights that has not hitherto been recognised as corresponding to purpose of data

provoke informationless chilling effects to be subtle in this way. In this regard, it would seem an unusually broad use of the term nudge as a descriptor for the operation of dummy camera systems.

protection law, the broad, flexible and open-ended nature of this purpose means this need not be an issue.

An argument can thus be made that systems and contexts engendering informationless chilling effects may fall within the boundaries of the scoping concepts of EU data protection law. In Section 5, the concept of personal data was taken as an exemplar of such a scoping concept. A four-point unpacking of the boundaries of this concept was then offered.[8] In relation to each of these points, systems and contexts engendering informationless chilling effects might be subsumed within the concept: (i) the subject matter of the relationship is the belief that information will be processed; (ii) the relationship concerns an individual and the third party controlling the system or context engendering the informationless chilling effect – which, as above, relates to information processing concerning individuals; (iii) the informationless chilling effects constitute the harm to rights; and (iv) while the idea of including doxastic relationships within the concept of personal data is novel and unusual, it may be justified owing to the flexible and open-ended boundaries of the concept of personal data, their connection to the purposes of EU data protection law and the rationale that informationless chilling effects constitute a harm that falls within the purview of the purposes of data protection law.

To support the above, I would highlight that there is jurisprudence that recognises the logic of connecting EU data protection law with the protection of individuals against informationless chilling effects. The Court of Justice of the European Union's decision in the *Digital Rights Ireland* case highlighted the relevance of chilling effects in relation to EU data protection law.[9]

8 For ease: 'the concept of personal data is the legal concept which i) describes the subject matter of the relationship, ii) between an individual and a third party engaging in an activity relating to information processing concerning an individual, iii) where the activity in question harms individual rights, iv) whilst not necessarily being determinate as to the form of subject matter of relationship, nor necessarily being determinate as to the range of harms, which may be subsumed within the scope of the concept.'

9 '[T]he fact that data are retained and subsequently used without the subscriber or registered user being informed is likely to generate in the minds of the persons concerned the feeling that their private lives are the subject of constant surveillance' (Case C-293/12, 2014, para. 37). A more explicit reference is made in the opinion of Advocate General in relation to the case: 'First of all, it is true that it must not be overlooked that the vague feeling of surveillance which implementation of Directive 2006/24 may cause is capable of having a decisive influence on the exercise by European citizens of their freedom of expression and information and that an interference with the right guaranteed by Article 11 of the Charter therefore could well also be found to exist...The collection of such data establishes the conditions for surveillance which, although carried out only retrospectively when the data are used, none the less constitutes a permanent threat throughout the data retention period to the right of citizens of the Union to confidentiality in their private lives. The vague feeling of surveillance created raises very

In turn, there are certain national data protection laws that specifically address systems that function on the pretence of information processing while never actually engaging in information processing. Norwegian data protection law, for example, includes provisions dealing with dummy camera systems and equipment designed to give the impression that an area is under surveillance (see, for example: Opdahl & Gjerde Lia, 2021; Hvidsen & Weitzenboeck, 2021). Certain data protection authorities in other EU jurisdictions have also touched on the topic of dummy camera systems, albeit without confirming the applicability of data protection law to them (Die Landesbeauftragte für Datenschutz und Informationsfreiheit).

Should there be other relevant areas of law that obviously offer protection in relation to informationless chilling effects, it would perhaps make no less sense to look to EU data protection law. In relation to specific cases in specific jurisdictions, there are undoubtedly other areas of law and other legal principles that are relevant for offering protection. In Germany, for example, courts have found that general personality rights may be impacted by dummy camera systems (see, for example: AG Frankfurt/Main, 2015). To my knowledge, however, beyond data protection, there are no other areas of law that might obviously be looked to as offering a general, accessible, elaborated scheme of protection relevant in relation to systems and contexts engendering informationless chilling effects in the EU. Accordingly, should cases emerge where informationless chilling effects are at issue and a legal response is called for, it is conceivable that claims under EU data protection law, to bodies concerned with data protection law, will be made. From here, jurisprudential clarification that EU data protection law applies to such systems and contexts is merely a decision away.

The argument outlined above highlights the logic of looking to EU data protection law as an area of law that might provide protection in relation to informationless chilling effects. There are, however, several objections imaginable that might be posed to exploring this idea further. Three particularly pertinent objections are defined and addressed in the following sections.

8. Objection 1: The Positive Boundaries of Scoping Concepts

The first objection highlights that scoping concepts in data protection law are defined by specific legal definitions and criteria and that these can neither

acutely the question of the data retention period' (Opinion of Advocate General Cruz Villalón, 2013, paras. 52 and 72).

be ignored nor can they encompass systems and contexts that engender informationless chilling effects. These scoping criteria cannot simply be ignored. It is difficult to imagine a theory of legal interpretation in which the terms and meanings of legal texts could simply be ignored while still retaining a legal system's integrity (see, for a discussion of methodological options: Ladeur, 2013, pp. 170–179). It is also true that scoping concepts in EU data protection law are defined by specific legal definitions and criteria, which appear to make it awkward for them to encompass systems and contexts engendering informationless chilling effects. One critical example is the criterion of 'information' in relation to the concept of personal data. Personal data can only be seen to exist, and EU data protection law can only apply if 'information' is somehow present (see, for example, in this regard: Case C-434/16, 2017, para. 34). How then could the concept of personal data possibly extend to doxastic relationships? There is weight to this objection. Nevertheless, it is not necessarily a definitive objection. This can be demonstrated with a deeper discussion of the criterion 'information'.

A look at how the boundaries of the concept of 'information' – as a scoping criterion for EU data protection law – have been defined in jurisprudence reveals the significance of the concept of harms to rights. In this regard, the conceptual boundaries of the criterion have been linked to the purpose of data protection law (also see the discussion in Section 3, and the discussion in: Hallinan & Gellert, 2020, pp. 280–282). In light of this link, the question ceases to be whether a vernacular or limited legal-positivistic understanding of the concept of information might encompass doxastic connections, but rather, whether it would (i) make sense in terms of the protection of fundamental rights that claims concerning informationless chilling effects are subsumed within the scope of EU data protection law, and (ii) whether a concept of information could be feasibly imagined in law – whether a sui generis concept or a concept that draws on other inspirations – which would allow this subsumption to proceed while not ignoring the text of the law.

It might be argued that such a creative interpretation of 'information' in law is impossible, or at least very difficult. In response, it should first be highlighted that the concept of information – as Raphael Gellert and I have discussed at greater length elsewhere – enjoys a healthy existence in which it takes a variety of different forms depending on the disciplinary context in which it is used, where each form has different defining criteria (Hallinan & Gellert, 2020, pp. 275–279; see also Bygrave, 2015). This recognition undermines the logic of presuming restrictive limitations to the scope of the concept of 'information' as a scoping criteria in EU data protection law. Equally, it should be highlighted that there is a very lively jurisprudence in the area of EU data protection law, which has already shown the inclination to go beyond straightforward interpretations of the legal text. Consider, as an example, the apparent willingness of the European Data Protection Board to express a position on the limitations imposed by the GDPR on the use of personal data as consideration, despite this issue scarcely being addressed in the GDPR itself.[10]

9. Objection 2: The Disutility of the Provisions of EU data Protection Law

The second objection suggests it would be misguided and counterproductive to apply the substantive principles of EU data protection law to systems and contexts engendering informationless chilling effects. This objection revolves around the fact that the substantive principles of data protection law were not designed for this form of harm to rights and, accordingly, are unlikely to constitute a suitable response. This objection might be broken down into two different sub-objections: (i) that the set of substantive principles in data protection law will fail to provide a framework capable of providing protection for individuals in relation to informationless chilling effects, and (ii) applying the set of substantive principles in data protection law to systems and contexts in which informationless chilling effects may be relevant will mean applying principles to contexts in which they make no sense, and in which their application may lead to negative side-effects. While these are well-founded objections, again, I do not see them as necessarily monolithic.

In relation to the first sub-objection, it may indeed be the case that certain concrete provisions in data protection law may not provide adequate and suitable protection. I would highlight, however, that there are also flexible substantive principles in data protection law that require that controllers ensure suitable safeguards are in place such that individuals are adequately protected from the specific harms engendered in a specific context. Examples of such provisions include: (i) the principle of data protection by design and default – elaborated in Article 25 of the GDPR – requires that systems are designed such that individuals are adequately protected in relation to all

10 'As data protection law is aiming at the protection of fundamental rights, an individual's control over their personal data is essential and there is a strong presumption that consent to the processing of personal data that is unnecessary, cannot be seen as a mandatory consideration in exchange for the performance of a contract or the provision of a service' (European Data Protection Board, 2020, p. 10).

risks to rights, and (ii) the requirement to conduct a data protection impact assessment – elaborated in Article 35 of the GDPR – obliges controllers to evaluate all possible impacts on rights and to implement context-appropriate mitigation measures prior to engaging in processing (see, for example: Bieker & Bremert, 2020). Indeed, some of these flexible provisions, including both principles discussed in this paragraph, are already relevant prior to any information ever being processed.

In relation to the second sub-objection, several current data protection principles would simply be irrelevant in relation to systems and contexts engendering informationless chilling effects. What would it mean to suggest, for example, that personal data be held accurately – as required under Article 5(1)(d) of the GDPR – when no information capable of being accurate will ever be held?[11] In such cases, however, irrelevancy will mean that negative consequences will likely be reduced to bureaucratic consequences (e.g. costs of documenting the lack of action in relation to a principle). There are, however, circumstances imaginable in which the applicability of substantive provisions may have more direct and significant negative consequences. One could imagine, for example, circumstances in which the imposition of information obligations such as those in Articles 13, 14 and 15 of the GDPR, under some interpretations, would completely undermine the intended function of dummy camera systems. In relation to such cases, it should be highlighted that there is jurisprudence that foresees the possibility to adapt or restrict the application of specific principles of data protection law such that they make sense in context (see, for example: Article 29 Working Party, 2007, p. 5).

10. Objection 3: The Conceptual Integrity of Data Protection Law

The third objection concerns the idea that EU data protection law is conceptually connected to a specific class of activities and that this class includes only activities done on information conceptualised as a form of substance with an objective existence. The objection suggests that to maintain the conceptual integrity and therefore the clarity of the area of law, this connection should not be broken. In this regard, the objection asserts that including systems and contexts engendering informationless chilling effects would disrupt this connection and endanger the conceptual

11 See also the comparable discussion of the irrelevancy of certain data protection provisions and their lack of problematic impact in relation to the processing of genomic data in the form of biological samples in biobanking in Hallinan (2021, pp. 229–230).

clarity of the area of law. There can be no doubt that the extension of EU data protection law to systems and contexts engendering informationless chilling effects would constitute a novel and creative expansion of the range of phenomena that fall within the scope of the area of law. Despite this, and despite recognising legitimacy in the objection, I do not regard this as a monolithic obstacle.

The basic idea that the conceptual integrity of EU data protection law would be undermined by the inclusion of systems and contexts that engender informationless chilling effects seems doubtful. There is a conceptual connection between informationless chilling effects and the purpose of data protection law – see the extensive elaboration of this connection in Section 7. In this regard, there seems to be no reason that the conceptual integrity of data protection law must, in principle, come under threat from an inclusion of systems and contexts engendering informationless chilling effects, although it cannot be ruled out that possible subsequent choices regarding the substantive approach taken in dealing with such systems and contexts could endanger the conceptual integrity of the area of law.

In turn, the objection paints the connection between EU data protection law and the forms of phenomena to which it relates in a way which belies the dynamic development of the area of law. Data protection remains a relatively new area of law, no more than a few decades old. In this brief timespan, its history has become one in which change and development are the norm, hallmarks of an area of law at the epicentre of legal efforts to address a burgeoning information society of increasing complexity and indeterminacy. In this brief history, both the range of social activities to which the law has related and the range of risks with which the law has been connected have never ceased to shift. The reader is referred here to authors such as Viktor Mayer-Schönberger and Gloria González Fuster, who present excellent overviews of the changes in the scope and approach of data protection laws over this period (Mayer-Schönberger, 1997, pp. 219–242; González Fuster, 2014, pp. 55–252). Compare, for example, the focus of some of the first data protection laws on specific technologies and use contexts, with the technologically neutral and encompassing scope of the GDPR (Mayer-Schönberger, 1997, pp. 219–242).

8. Conclusion

This article outlined the argument that EU data protection law could be looked to as a relevant area of law to provide protection to individuals in relation to systems and contexts which engender informationless chilling effects, chilling effects which emerge when individuals make presumptions that information about them will be processed and thus problematically change their behaviour, despite the fact that no information will ever actually be processed.

The article highlighted that the purpose of EU data protection law might be elaborated in a broad, flexible and open-ended manner. The following description was offered: the purpose of EU data protection law is to provide protection in relation to (i) harms to fundamental rights, (ii) which eventuate in relation to systems and contexts of information processing concerning individuals, (iii) while not pre-emptively exhaustively defining either the forms of harms to rights which are encompassed or the forms of systems and contexts relating to information processing concerning individuals, which are encompassed under this purpose.

The article further suggested that the boundaries of scoping concepts in EU data protection law might also be considered as broad, flexible and open-ended and as being defined – at least in part – in relation to the purpose of data protection law. The concept of personal data was used as an exemplar for which the following description was offered: the concept of personal data is the legal concept that (i) describes the subject matter of the relationship (ii) between an individual and a third party engaging in an activity relating to information processing concerning an individual, (iii) where the activity in question harms individual rights (iv) while not necessarily being determinate as to the form of subject matter of relationship, nor necessarily being determinate as to the range of harms, which may be subsumed within the scope of the concept.

Building on the above, the article highlighted that informationless chilling effects might be seen as harms to rights which relate to information processing concerning individuals, albeit as a form of emergent risk parasitic to the general prevalence of information processing technologies. Accordingly, the article made the observations that (i) informationless chilling effects constitute a form of harm to rights, which falls within the purview of the purposes of EU data protection law and (ii) scoping concepts in data protection law offer the potential to encompass systems and contexts engendering informationless chilling effects.

The article then finished by considering three objections that could be raised against the idea that EU data protection law might constitute a logical response to provide protection in relation to systems and contexts engendering informationless chilling effects: (i) the objection that the specific legal criteria defining the scoping concepts in EU data protection law exclude such a possibility, (ii) the objection that there would be disutility in the application of the substantive provisions of EU data protection law and (iii) the objection that an extension of scope of EU data protection law to such systems and contexts would endanger the conceptual integrity of the area of law. While each objection carries weight, it was argued that none of them constitute a monolithic obstacle.

References

AG Frankfurt/Main Az: 33 C 3407/14. (2015).

Article 29 Working Party. (2007). *Opinion 4/2007 on the concept of personal data* (WP 136, 2007), 4–5, 6–24. https://ec.europa.eu/justice/article-29/documentation/opinion-recommendation/files/2007/wp136_en.pdf

Article 29 Working Party. (2014). *Statement on the role of a risk-based approach in data protection legal frameworks* (WP 218, 2014) 8. https://ec.europa.eu/justice/article-29/documentation/opinion-recommendation/files/2014/wp218_en.pdf

Bennet Moses, L. (2017). Recurring dilemmas: The law's race to keep up with technological change. *Journal of Law, Technology and Policy*, 239–285.

Bieker, F., & Bremert, B. (2020). Identifizierung von Risiken für die Grundrechte von Individuen. Auslegung und Anwendung des Risikobegriffs der DS-GVO. *Zeitschrift für Datenschutz*, *10*(1), 7–14.

Büchi, M., Fosch-Villaronga, E., Lutzc, C., Tamò-Larrieux, A., Velidi, S., & Viljoen, S. (2020). The chilling effects of algorithmic profiling: Mapping the issues. *Computer Law & Security Review*, *36*, 105367.

BVerfG. (1980). Beschluss vom 13.05.1980 – 1 BvR 103/77.

Bygrave, L. (2015). Information concepts in law: Generic dreams and definitional daylight. *Oxford Journal of Legal Studies*, *35*(1), 91–120.

Case C-131/12. (2014). *Google Spain SL, Google Inc v AEPD, Mario Costeja González*, ECLI:EU: C:2014:317.

Case C-293/12. (2014). *Digital Rights Ireland Ltd*, ECLI:EU:C:2014:238.

Case C-434/16. (2017). *Peter Nowak v Data Protection Commissioner*, ECLI:EU:C:2017:994.

Case C-791/19. (2021). *Commission v Poland*, ECLI:EU:C:2021:596.

Castells, M. (1998). *The information age: Economy, society and culture*, Vol. 3: *End of millenium*, 1st ed. Blackwell.

Castells, M. (2004). *The information age: Economy, society and culture*, Vol. 2: *The power of identity*, 2nd ed. Wiley-Blackwell.

Castells, M. (2010). *The information age: Economy, society and culture*: Vol. 1: *The rise of the network society*, 2nd ed. Wiley-Blackwell.

Charter of Fundamental Rights of the European Union. (2012). OJ C 326/391, Article 8.

Dalla Corte, L. (2020). A right to a rule: On the substance and essence of the fundamental right to personal data protection. In D. Hallinan, R. Leenes, S. Gutwirth, & P. De Hert (Eds.), *Data protection and privacy: Data protection and cemocracy* (pp. 27–58). Hart.

Declaration of the Committee of Ministers on Risks to Fundamental Rights stemming from Digital Tracking and other Surveillance Technologies. (2013). https://search.coe.int/cm/Pages/result_details.aspx?ObjectId=09000016805c8011

Demetzou, K. (2020). Risk to the 'rights and freedoms': A legal interpretation of the scope of risk under the GDPR. In D. Hallinan, R. Leenes, S. Gutwirth, & P. De Hert (Eds.), *Data protection and privacy: Data protection and democracy* (pp. 129–132). Hart Publishing.

Die Landesbeauftragte für Datenschutz und Informationsfreiheit. (n.d.). *Überwachung mit Videokameras: Überwachung mit Videokameras und zum Einsatz von Webcams durch nicht öffentliche Stellen* (Die Landesbeauftragte für Datenschutz und Informationsfreiheit). Retrieved May 15, 2023. https://www.datenschutz.bremen.de/ueberwachung-mit-videokameras-3744

European Commission. (2012). *Proposal for a Regulation of the European Parliament and of the Council on the protection of individuals with regard to the processing of personal data and on the free movement of such data* (General Data Protection Regulation) (COM[2012] 11 final) 1–7. https://eur-lex.europa.eu/legal-content/EN/TXT/PDF/?uri=CELEX:52012PC0011&from=EN

European Data Protection Board. (2019). *Guidelines 3/2019 on processing of personal data through video devices*, 5. https://edpb.europa.eu/sites/default/files/consultation/edpb_guidelines_201903_videosurveillance.pdf

European Data Protection Board. (2020). *Guidelines 05/2020 on consent under Regulation 2016/679: Version 1.1.* https://edpb.europa.eu/sites/default/files/files/file1/edpb_guidelines_202005_consent_en.pdf

Floridi, L. (2015). *The ethics of information*. Oxford University Press.

General Data Protection Regulation. (2012). COM(2012) 11 final, 1–7. https://eur-lex.europa.eu/legal-content/EN/TXT/PDF/?uri=CELEX:52012PC0011&from=EN

González Fuster, G. (2014). *The emergence of personal data protection as a fundamental right of the EU*. Springer.

Habermas, J. (2017). *Between facts and norms* (W. Rehg, Trans.; 15th ed.). Polity.

Hallinan, D. (2019). Data protection without data: Could data protection law apply without personal data being processed? *European Data Protection Law Review, 5*(3), 293–299. https://doi.org 10.21552/edpl/2019/3/5

Hallinan, D. (2021). *Protecting genetic privacy in biobanking through data protection law*. Oxford University Press.

Hallinan, D., & Gellert, R. (2020). The concept of 'information': An invisible problem in the GDPR. *SCRIPTed, 17*(2), 269–319. https://script-ed.org/?p=3885

Hvidsen, G., & Weitzenboeck, E. M. (2021). *Norway: Data protection laws and regulations*. ICLG. https://iclg.com/practice-areas/data-protection-laws-and-regulations/norway

Intellectual Property Rights. (n.d.). FIZ Karlsruhe – Leibniz-Institute for Information Infrastructure, Eggenstein-Leopoldshafen, Germany.

Ladeur, K. H. (2013). *Das Recht der Netzwerkgesellschft* (T. Vesting, T & I. Augsberg, Eds.). Mohr Siebeck.

Luhmann, N. (2012). *Law as a social system* (F. Kastner, R. Nobles, D. Schiff, & R. Ziegert, Eds.; K. A. Ziegert, Trans.). Oxford University Press.

Mayer-Schönberger, V. (1997). Generational development of data protection in Europe. In P. Agre & M. Rotenberg (Eds.), *Technology and privacy: The new landscape* (pp. 219–242). MIT Press.

Opdahl, R., & Gjerde Lia, P. (2021). *Norway – Data protection overview*. OneTrust DataGuidance. https://www.dataguidance.com/notes/norway-data-protection-overview

Opinion of Advocate General Cruz Villalón. (2013). Case C 293/12 Digital Rights Ireland Ltd, ECLI:EU:C:2013:845, Opinion of Advocate General Cruz Villalón, paras. 52 and 72.

Pech, L. (2021). The concept of chilling effect: *Its untapped potential to better protect democracy, the rule of law, and fundamental rights in the EU* (pp. 8–15). Open Society European Policy Institute. https://www.opensocietyfoundations.org/publications/the-concept-of-chilling-effect

Pradini, R. (2013). The future of societal constitutionalism in the age of acceleration. *Indiana Journal of Global Legal Studies*, *20*(2), 731–776.

Purtova, N. (2018). The law of everything: Broad concept of personal data and future of EU data protection law. *Law, Innovation and Technology*, *10*(1), 40–81.

Regulation (EU) 2016/679 of the European Parliament and of the Council of 27 April 2016 on the protection of natural persons with regard to the processing of personal data and on the free movement of such data, and repealing Directive 95/46/EC (General Data Protection Regulation), OJ L 119/1.

Ruhl, J. B. (2008). Law's complexity: A primer. *Georgia State University Law Review*, *24*(4), 885–911.

14. Identity, Profiles and Pseudonyms in the Digital Environment

Miranda Mourby[1] *& Elaine Mackey*

Abstract

The boundaries of personal data are determined by the concept of 'identity'. Personal data, as defined under the GDPR, is information relating to an identified or identifiable natural person. In this chapter, we argue that the informational 'identity' of an identified/identifiable person is characterised by the potential for privacy impact. Our informational identity is, in essence, the sum of all the information which can impact our rights. We use profiles and pseudonyms as an illustration of this definition. Profiles permit scrutiny of an individual – and thus 'identify' them through the intrinsic privacy impact of this evaluation. Pseudonyms alone do not allow individuals to be evaluated, which is why they are not, in and of themselves, personal data.

Keywords: identity; pseudonymisation; profiling; anonymisation; personal data

1. Introduction

What is an identification? Some information is deemed sufficiently 'us' to warrant legal protection, but this category of information shifts all the time, and the logic underpinning these shifting parameters is far from explicit. The idea of 'identity' determines the scope of data protection law in the EU, which safeguards the rights of 'identified' and 'identifiable' individuals. Without understanding when a person is – or might be – 'identified', we cannot be sure when these rights arise.

1 Miranda Mourby would like to acknowledge support from the EU-STANDS4PM consortium (www.eustands4pm.eu) that was funded by the European Union Horizon2020 framework programme of the European Commission under Grant Agreement #825843. She is also grateful to the School of Law at the University of Sheffield, whose funding supported this work in part.

Van der Sloot & van Schendel. *The Boundaries of Data.* Taylor & Francis Group, 2024
DOI: 10.5117/9789463729192_CH14

This chapter clarifies the concept of 'identity' in EU and associated national data protection law by flipping conventional wisdom on its head. It is often asserted that privacy and data protection rights arise when an individual is or can be identified. But without a clear understanding of what it means to be 'identified', this statement is not particularly meaningful. As the growth of the online infosphere increasingly detaches identity from traditional 'real-world' signifiers, the time may have come to recognise that an individual is instead 'identified' when information engages their rights to privacy and/or data protection. As profiling is thought to engage privacy and data protection rights and is proliferating within the Big Data environment (de Hert & Lammerant, 2016), it is a useful touchstone in understanding identification in digital information.

This chapter therefore attempts to delineate the contours of 'identity' in data protection law by exploring two associated concepts: profiling and pseudonymisation. We have selected these concepts because they are respectively associated with *direct* and *indirect* identification. We suggest that the parameters of 'direct' identification – information that is, in and of itself, an identification with nothing further required – help to reveal the nature of an identity in data protection law. The UK is used as a particular case study because it has, in its post-Brexit modification of the EU General Data Protection Regulation (GDPR), introduced the concepts of direct and indirect identification into a statutory definition of identifiable individuals, which adds precision to the definition that can be inferred at EU level.

The concepts of pseudonymisation and profiling under the GDPR are therefore worth unpacking because they help illustrate the circumstances in which identification takes place in the online infosphere. In the absence of a definition of 'identified' or 'identifiable' individuals in the EU Regulation itself, these subsidiary concepts provide contrasting definitions of a directly identifying 'profile' (which engages an individual's rights through evaluation of their personal characteristics) with a 'pseudonym' (which also uniquely represents people but does not permit analysis or scrutiny of them as individual subjects without further information). The 'unique' nature of the pseudonym may only be a particular variation in a hashing code; it does not signify any immediately discernible personal information. Put simply, therefore: if a profile alone is an identification, and a pseudonym alone is not, the contrast between the two helps us explain what is and is not an identity in online information.

Ultimately, we suggest that the defining feature of 'identity' in data is the capacity of information to interfere with individuals' privacy and data protection rights. As profiling data permit scrutiny of individuals in a way that pseudonymised data should not, this distinction between the two concepts provides a useful illustration of the difference this capacity of interference makes in practice.

2. Identity in Data Protection Law

As Sullivan (2011) emphasises, it is important to discern the meaning attributed to the concept of 'identity' in a particular legal context:

> Identity has traditionally been a nebulous notion and in referring to 'identity' without defining it, much of the legal literature in this area lacks precision. It gives the impression that 'identity is identity' whereas the constitution, function and nature of identity depends on context ... it is important to differentiate the 'purely legal relations' from other non-legal conceptions. (p. 6)

In order to delineate the meaning of identity in the context of data protection law, it is necessary to grapple with the GDPR's usage of the terms 'identified', 'identifiable' and 'identifier.' These occur in the definition of personal data in the GDPR:

> 'personal data' means any information relating to an identified or identifiable natural person ('data subject'); an identifiable natural person is one who can be identified, directly or indirectly, in particular by reference to an identifier such as a name, an identification number, location data, an online identifier or to one or more factors specific to the physical, physiological, genetic, mental, economic, cultural or social identity of that natural person. (GDPR, Article 4[1])

It is easy to lose one's bearings within a definition so densely packed with the terms identified, identifiable, identifier and identity. Interestingly, while the term 'identifiable' is elaborated upon as meaning someone who 'can be identified', the word 'identified' itself is not explained, leaving an ultimate ambiguity as to what 'identity' means for the purposes of the GDPR. The list of 'identifiers' is perhaps a clue, but these pieces of information appear only to refer to *means* of identification and not identification itself. As the UK Information Commissioner's Office (2020) clarifies, 'whether any potential identifier actually identifies an individual depends on the context.' For example, 'a person who enjoys the theatre' may be an aspect of cultural identity, but without further information to link this no doubt scintillating insight into one particular person, it is no more identification than it is trope, fiction or hypothesis.

We have suggested that two types of personal data can be established within the GDPR:

- information that is, in and of itself, identification (relating to an 'identified' individual);
- information that can be linked indirectly to an identified individual, including pseudonymised data, which is information on an 'identifiable' individual.

In order to answer the question of what identification is, we are principally concerned with the first type of personal data – information that is *in itself* an identification. The latter category is essentially a secondary subset of personal data, caught by the regulation if they can be linked to information that either in combination or in itself constitutes identification. The core question, therefore, is what quality or qualities of data render information an identification.

We will answer this question of 'what is identification?' by relating to direct identification, i.e. information relating to *identified* individuals. Within privacy and data protection, data that are characterised as 'personal' – and therefore as linking to individuals' 'identity' – tend to be information with sufficiently close association to an individual to justify their 'stake' in the information. As Laurie states in the context of genetic data, 'individuals have an interest in this information because it relates to them and can affect their lives' (Laurie, 2002).

2.1. Facial Images as Direct Identification

A UK case that illustrates this association with identification and the idea of a personal stake in information is the High Court judgment in *Bridges v. South Wales Police*, which was believed to be the first time any court in the world had considered the use of automated facial recognition software (AFR). The claim for, inter alia, infringement of data protection legislation was brought by Edward Bridges with the support of the campaigning organisation Liberty.

In brief, *Bridges* concerned the collection of facial images by police at rugby matches for the purposes of AFR. It was argued in submissions that the police would require further powers to match the facial images to individuals in order for them to constitute personal data (per *Breyer*). In other words, the images were not an identification in and of themselves, and 'identifiability' would only be triggered with the presence of an additional means reasonably likely to be used to identify people.

The Court rejected this argument, however, on the basis that the images were an identification in and of themselves:

> Where the data in issue is biometric facial data, we see no need for the analysis adopted by the CJEU in Breyer (in the context of information comprising dynamic IP addresses). Whether or not such information is personal data may be open to debate, as is apparent from the judgment in Vidal-Hall [2016] QB 1003. However, the biometric facial data in issue in this case is *qualitatively different* and clearly does comprise personal data because, *per se*, it permits immediate identification of a person. (R. [on the application of Bridges], 2020; emphasis added)

The phrase 'immediate identification' makes it clear that an image of a face is an identification in and of itself, having the 'quality' of being identity per se. This is reminiscent of Sullivan's description (cited above) of the 'identity is identity' mentality. Although the reasons for this are not elaborated upon, it seems overwhelmingly contextually likely that the Court bore the civil liberty implications mentioned above in mind, meaning that the location of the information within the regulatory framework of privacy and data protection was a pressing concern in this determination. The risks revealed by the evolution of AFR thus make a compelling argument for consideration of images of faces as an identification, and thus an identification in the eyes of data protection law.

2.2. IP Addresses as (In)Direct Identification

IP addresses, on the other hand, are not as straightforward a proposition. An IP address alone is not necessarily an identification because it does not create sufficient potential for consequence for, or inference about, the user of the related device, but an IP address combined with browsing history data across a number of websites *is* generally held to be an identification because it creates a profile. Evidence for this argument can be found in Recital 30 GDPR:

> Natural persons may be associated with online identifiers provided by their devices, applications, tools and protocols, such as internet protocol addresses, cookie identifiers or other identifiers such as radio frequency identification tags.
>
> This may leave traces which, in particular when combined with unique identifiers and other information received by the servers, may be used to create profiles of the natural persons and identify them. (emphasis added)

This recital seems to draw a reasonably clear distinction between potential identifiers (such as an IP address) and the combination of information that profiles an individual, adding up to enough usable information to constitute an actual identification.

Further illustration of how IP addresses can fail to meet the standard of direct identification comes from the 2016 judgment Case C-582/14 of the Court of Justice of the European Union in *Patrick Breyer v Bundesrepublik Deutschland*, which we will refer to as the *Breyer* judgment.

In the *Breyer* case, the German government collected information in case its websites came under attack and it was necessary to identify the perpetrators:

> With the aim of preventing attacks and making it possible to prosecute 'pirates', most of those websites store information on all access operations in logfiles. The information retained in the logfiles after those sites have been accessed include the name of the web page or file to which access was sought, the terms entered in the search fields, the time of access, the quantity of data transferred, an indication of whether access was successful, and the IP address of the computer from which access was sought. (CJEU, 2016, para. 14)

These retained IP addresses had no immediate privacy consequences for the associated individuals unless the German government took additional steps to build a picture of these people. It was confirmed at paragraph 38 of the judgment that the dynamic IP addresses were not personal data in and of themselves:

> In that connection, it must be noted, first of all, that it is common ground that a dynamic IP address does not constitute information relating to an 'identified natural person', since such an address does not directly reveal the identity of the natural person who owns the computer from which a website was accessed, or that of another person who might use that computer. (CJEU, 206, para. 38)

3. Pseudonyms and Profiles

The terms 'pseudonyms' and 'profiles' are used in this chapter to refer to the end products of GDPR pseudonymisation and profiling respectively. While these terms may, in other contexts, both refer to representations of individuals that fall short of an identification (e.g. a psychological 'profile' of a criminal suspect who sends letters under a 'pseudonym' but has yet to be identified), in the context of EU data protection law, they denote different levels of identifiability.

A 'pseudonym' is traditionally defined as an alternative to one's 'real' identity, for example as a 'false or fictitious name, esp. one assumed by an author; an alias' (Oxford University Press, 2007). In the context of the GDPR, personal data that have undergone pseudonymisation are associated with an 'alias' or something falling short of an actual identification. The data thus requiring additional information to be linked back to the 'real' identity of the natural person:

> 'pseudonymisation' means the processing of personal data in such a manner that the personal data can no longer be attributed to a specific data subject without the use of additional information, provided that such additional information is kept separately and is subject to technical and organisational measures to ensure that the personal data are not attributed to an identified or identifiable natural person. (Article 4[5] GDPR)

A profile, by contrast, permits the evaluation of personal characteristics under its definition in Article 4(4) GDPR:

> 'profiling' means any form of automated processing of personal data consisting of the use of personal data to evaluate certain personal aspects relating to a natural person, in particular to analyse or predict aspects concerning that natural person's performance at work, economic situation, health, personal preferences, interests, reliability, behaviour, location or movements.

This automated evaluation of personal characteristics is, we suggest, sufficient intrusion into privacy and data protection rights to constitute an identification in and of itself, even if there are no other consequences for the data subject. For example, a profile of an individual's online behaviour is likely to involve novel inferences about that person, which are of value for commercial exploitation, which then steps over the boundary of anonymous, unobserved browsing even before any attempt to 'reach' or affect the individual is made. The use of profiling in the digital environment therefore illustrates the underlying logic of identification: where there is intrusion, there is identification, even if the digital profile bears questionable resemblance to someone's 'real' identity.

Table 14.1 attempts a summary of how we distinguish the GDPR terms 'profiling' and 'pseudonymisation':

<table>
<tr><th></th><th>Pseudonymisation</th><th>Profiling</th></tr>
<tr><td>Definition under Article 4 GDPR</td><td>The processing of personal data in such a manner that the personal data can no longer be attributed to a specific data subject without the use of additional information, provided that such additional information is kept separately and is subject to technical and organisational measures to ensure that the personal data are not attributed to an identified or identifiable natural person.</td><td>Any form of automated processing of personal data consisting of the use of personal data to evaluate certain personal aspects relating to a natural person, in particular to analyse or predict aspects concerning that natural person's performance at work, economic situation, health, personal preferences, interests, reliability, behaviour, location or movements.</td></tr>
<tr><td>Information associated with the process</td><td>A pseudonym plus a string of information</td><td>A string of information that allows an evaluation of personal characteristics</td></tr>
<tr><td>Example</td><td><table><tr><td>Masked IP address</td><td>Age in bands of ten years</td><td>Gender</td><td>Employed [y/n/]</td><td>Industry of employ-ment</td><td>Number of times X website visited last 12 months</td></tr></table></td><td><table><tr><td>IP address</td><td>Website address</td><td>Date visited</td><td>Time + Duration of visit</td><td>Products viewed</td><td>Products bought</td></tr></table><table><tr><td>Masked IP address</td><td>Website address</td><td>Number of times Website visited last 12 months</td><td>Most popular product viewed last 12 months</td><td>Most popular product bought in the last 12 months</td></tr></table></td></tr>
<tr><td>How the processes differ</td><td>– A process to mask identity
– A process that reduces detail in the personal information, leaving the substance of the data untouched
– Aims to prevent direct identification</td><td>– A process to create an identity (may not match real world identity)
– A process to create new information, 'a profile', from the underlying original data
– Aims to evaluate the individual</td></tr>
<tr><td>Purpose of the process</td><td>To dissociate individuals from information. It enables the exploration of patterns within data whilst preventing direct identification.</td><td>To associate individuals with information. It enables the targeting of natural people in pursuit of a service, product or message with the potential to 'reach' the individual.</td></tr>
</table>

Table 14.1

3.1. Profiles as Direct Identification: IAB Europe

An important example of profiling is the 'Transparency and Consent', or 'TC String', generated by consent management platforms to record the consent preferences of visitors to websites regarding the use of their data.

This 'TC String' was considered in the judgment of Case DOS-2019-01377 before the Litigation Chamber of the Belgian Data Protection Authority (the APD) in a case we will refer to as the 'IAB Europe decision' (APD, 2022).

The APD handed down a decision in February 2022 as the lead supervisory authority under the 'one-stop-shop' mechanism of Article 56 GDPR. Its judgment was reviewed and approved by a number of Concerned Supervisory Authorities representing the Netherlands, Latvia, Italy, Sweden, Slovenia, Norway, Hungary, Poland, Portugal, Denmark, France, Finland, Greece, Spain, Luxemburg, Czech Republic, Austria, Croatia, Cyprus, Germany (Berlin, Rhineland-Palatinate, North Rhine, Westphalia, Saarland, Lower Saxony, Brandenburg, Mecklenburg-Western Pomerania and Bavaria) and Ireland.

This was not a judgment of the Court of Justice of the European Union, or indeed any other European court. Nonetheless, the breadth of data protection authorities represented – and the consequent scale of the litigation – makes the decision an important precedent within Europe, particularly within the world of online behavioural profiling.

Interactive Advertising Bureau Europe (IAB) is a federation of approximately 5,000 companies across Europe. IAB developed a Transparency and Consent framework as a best practice standard so that real-time bidding could be conducted in compliance with the GDPR (in theory).

Real-time bidding (RTB) was deemed sufficiently complex that it required introduction at the outset of the decision, with diagrammatic representation of the interactions. A distinction was drawn with 'traditional' advertising, in which the advert is negotiated manually between business and publisher. Instead, the machinations of RTB take place 'behind the scenes', with data subjects unaware of the identity of actors involved or even necessarily aware that their information is being automatically auctioned for the opportunity of advertising to them.

The profiling involved in RTB was deemed to be a key element of the processing that IAB had facilitated. There was no controversy that the data used for and generated by this profiling were personal data. This is interesting, as the information used for RTB was very heterogenous, potentially including:

> *URL of the visited site ▪ category or subject of the site ▪ operating system of the device ▪ browser software and version ▪ manufacturer and model of the device ▪ mobile operator ▪ screen dimensions ▪ unique user identification set by vendor and/or buyer. ▪ unique person identifier from the Ad Exchange, often derived from the Ad Exchange's cookie. ▪ the user identification of a DSP, often derived from the Ad Exchange's cookie that is synchronised with a cookie from the DSP's domain. ▪ year of birth ▪ gender ▪ interests ▪ metadata reporting on consent given ▪ geography ▪ longitude and latitude ▪ post code*

While some data included in the RTB processing are what would conventionally be deemed an identifier (gender, post code, year of birth), others are more device-orientated and not 'personal' in the conventional sense (e.g. screen dimensions, browsing software, etc.).

The element of controversy, however, lay in the TC string. The TC string is 'a character string consisting of a combination of letters, numbers and other characters' (para. 41). At paragraph 95 of the judgment, the APD (2022) found that:

> the generation of the TC String in itself constitutes, without any doubt, processing of personal data. The issue at hand is the automated creation, by a CMP registered with the TCF, of a unique and linked set of characters intended to capture a specific user's preferences regarding permitted data exchanges with advertisers. (emphasis added).

The ultimate determination by the APD that the unique set of characters capturing a user's preferences constituted personal data was transformative for the digital economy, acknowledging a whole new link in the chain of information as personal data in and of itself.

The APD's decision is congruent with the logic of this chapter. Although the relevant combination of numbers, letters and characters may not resemble the person in question in a way we would see them with human eyes, in an automated context, this string represents an actionable personal characteristic: their preferences regarding data exchange. It constitutes information that could impact upon the privacy of the person's internet browsing and is therefore, understandably, an identification.

It is important to remember that an identity for the sake of data protection law may be very different from the social, 'real-world' ways we recognise and differentiate people. Identification does not need to include a name or the capacity to physically locate the individual in the real world but could reveal enough information about them to provide an interface to affect them. McMahon and others illustrate this with the scenario of a woman who miscarries but then continues to receive ads targeted to her perceived pregnancy; a digital profile does not need to correlate accurately with a lived reality to have an impact on her (McMahon et al., 2020). Accurate or not, it would therefore make sense for this profile to be a protected digital identity in order to protect the natural living individual who will be impacted by it.

In this sense, it would not matter if the digital profile correlated poorly with the 'real-world' or 'offline' identity of the individual. Writing for the BBC, Carl Miller conducted a number of subject access requests and uncovered a strange array of inferential judgments made about him based on his browsing history, including that he was a woman trying to conceive, a 'love aspirer' and a disengaged worker with little perceived interest in reading (Miller, 2019). Even if the digital profile of an individual bears little relation to the individual's social or physiological identity, or their own subjective sense of self, it could nonetheless have consequences for them at least in terms of personalised advertisements and (as in the case of misidentification) may have all the more consequences for being wrong. When inaccurate information impacts upon individuals, there is no need to have recourse to the concept of 'fake privacy' (Burgess, 2018) if the digital identity is understood as the clusters of data that can impact a natural, living person.

The IAB Europe case illustrates the increasing penetration of the internet into our daily lives and the consequent expansion of online activity among the digitally connected majority of Europeans, meaning that many of us have an increasing proliferation of 'virtual identities' (Wachter, 2018). Any attempt to rationally delineate those virtual identities that are sufficiently connected with us to constitute a 'profile', and those sufficiently detached to be a 'pseudonym', reveals the lack of attention generally given to the question at the heart of the scope of data protection law: what is an identity in information?

If privacy and data protection are inherently connected to the 'integrity of information constituting one's identity', we cannot understand the boundary of personal data without a common agreement on what information *is* our identity. The general complacency on this issue stems from an apparent assumption that it must be obvious, that 'identity is identity' (Sullivan, 2011). The Spanish AEPD and the European Data Protection Supervisor recently collaborated to address common misunderstandings relating to anonymisation, but the ensuing guidance still falls into the 'identity is identity' trap, stating 'direct identifiers are somewhat trivial to find, indirect identifiers, on the other side, are not always obvious' (AEPD, 2021).

Our exploration of profiling versus pseudonymisation in this chapter shows that direct identifiers are *not* always trivial to define. The evolution of case law since 2016 has shown an expansion of what is considered direct identification in an online environment due to increasing recognition of the power of online profiles – even those that cannot be attributed to the 'real-world' identities of named, gendered, geographically located individuals.

3.2. Pseudonyms as 'Indirect' Identification

It is potentially confusing that a 'pseudonym' can superficially appear the same as a profile, which is also a string of letters and characters. The reason why pseudonymised data are not, however, a direct identification is that they should not permit scrutiny or other action vis-à-vis an individual (e.g. authorising the sharing of their data, in the above example). The French Data Protection Authority (the CNIL) provides the following example:

> an economics researcher has entered into a partnership with a family allowance fund (CAF) which has databases containing the names, dates of birth and addresses of applicants for housing allowance in 2019, as well as the amounts of allowances received and the number of people in the household.
>
> In order to carry out this research and meet data protection requirements, the researcher and CAF have agreed that the latter works on pseudonymised data. For this, the CAF will replace the names and dates of birth with a unique identifier (instead of deleting the columns) and will replace the complete addresses with only the municipalities.
>
> It will thus be possible for the researcher to compare identifiers between databases to find common recipients, without being able to know their identity directly. (CNIL, 2022; emphasis added)

In the above example, the researcher is crucially concerned with *trends across a dataset* rather than scrutinising or making decisions about any individual within it. As such, even if the 'unique identifier' pseudonym was similar in composition to the TC string, its presence within pseudonymised data as opposed to profiling data means that it does not immediately reveal anything about an individual that interferes with their privacy. It is only the risk of 'indirect' identification through combination with other information that makes this information personal data: it is not an identification in and of itself, as it does not directly impinge on privacy.

3.3. Direct and Indirect Identification

In the above examples, the distinction between 'direct' and 'indirect' identification is key. Direct identification requires no further information and therefore means that the data in question are a legally protected identity without the risk of further attribution. As we have seen above, the French CNIL has referred to pseudonymisation as representing a risk of 'indirect identification', and the UK Parliament has undertaken to go a step further by placing this distinction into law, in proposed updates to its Data Protection Act 2022:

> (3A) An individual is identifiable from information 'directly' if the individual can be identified without the use of additional information.
>
> (3B) An individual is identifiable from information 'indirectly' if the individual can be identified only with the use of additional information. (UK Parliament, 2022, p. 2)

The UK has even gone as far as to propose its own definition of pseudonymisation to clarify that which was set out in the GDPR, indicating that '"pseudonymisation" means the processing of personal data in such a manner that it becomes information relating to a living individual who is only indirectly identifiable' (UK Parliament, 2022, p. 3). While this is only one national interpretation of the GDPR, it does chime with the logic of the CNIL's pseudonymisation scenario, cited above. This helps to reinforce the idea that a pseudonym falls short of a direct identification because it is not immediately revelatory about an individual in a way that will interfere with their rights.

In all EU jurisdictions, the definition of identity will also establish the parameters of data protection law, which protects identified and identifiable people. The scope of this law should be understood with reference to its central purpose: the safeguarding of individual rights within a free market of digital information. Where these rights are engaged by the collection, construction or inference of information, the data should be considered an identification. The difference between pseudonymisation and profiling illustrates this acid test of intrusion in practice.

Data that have undergone GDPR pseudonymisation should not permit evaluation of personal characteristics; they should only reveal trends across individuals. Where reasonable likelihood of attribution back to particular people is removed (though control of the data environment), it may be possible for such pseudonymised personal data to be rendered anonymous. However, careful consideration should be given as to whether the same information could permit profiling in a different context; through combination with other information, or through automated scrutiny with advanced algorithms. These are among the risks of identification that must be excluded by any means reasonably likely to be used for the information to be considered anonymous, per Recital 26 GDPR.

Clarifying the digital identity as distinct from a 'pseudonym' is not just an academic exercise: our privacy and data protection rights are bound up in this concept. We therefore use profiling as a case study of intrusion and impact, which illustrates when information is of such intrinsic value that it constitutes an aspect of identity, thus warranting legal protection.

4. Profiles, Pseudonyms and Anonymity

We have previously written a paper in which we explored the introduction of the 'pseudonymisation' to data protection law within the GDPR. We argued that the data 'environment' (which includes other data, people, the presence or absence of information governance controls and infrastructure) can be managed to render such unattributed information functionally anonymous in the hands of a third party who has no access to the identifiers (Mourby et al., 2018). The controversy surrounding this question continues. Our argument drew on the concept of 'functional anonymisation' and appears to align with the UK Information Commissioner's Office draft updates to their anonymisation guidance post-GDPR (Elliot et al., 2016), but the 'bigger picture' from the European Data Protection Board (EDPB) is still outstanding, as the EU-wide board of regulators is still reviewing the 2014 European guidance on anonymisation (EDPB, 2021).

The preceding sections have shed light on the distinction between profiles and pseudonyms, which forms a central question of this chapter. We can perhaps summarise how this distinction maps onto the personal-anonymous data boundary in Text Box 14.1:

Profiles, Pseudonyms and Anonymity

Profiles: a collection of information with the potential to impact the rights to privacy and data protection of one or more natural persons through automated evaluation of personal characteristics. Profiles thus relate to an 'identified' individual and do not need any further attribution to constitute personal data.

Pseudonyms: information that has undergone GDPR pseudonymisation will still be personal if it can be attributed back to individuals through means reasonably likely to be used (rendering them identifiable per *Breyer*).

Text Box 14.1

To anonymise information, therefore, it is necessary to eliminate:

- Reasonable means of attributing information to individuals through management of the data environment (to prevent the subject becoming *identifiable*).
- The capacity of the information itself to allow individuals to be profiled and thus *identified*.

It is worth noting that longitudinal data that show an individual's behaviour over time (e.g. from a tracking cookie) will be much more difficult (if not impossible) to anonymise than a list of 'hits' on a website. Even if both types of information involve hashed or masked IP addresses, the former is far more likely to enable profiling and therefore remain personal data.

The GDPR could be described as a missed opportunity to provide a clear definition of anonymity versus pseudonymity, and indeed to address the underlying definition of what constitutes 'identification'. As it stands, however, the reader must parse an implicit definition from Recital 26:

> The principles of data protection should apply to any information concerning an identified or identifiable natural person. Personal data which have undergone pseudonymisation, which could be attributed to a natural person by the use of additional information should be considered to be information on an identifiable natural person.
>
> To determine whether a natural person is identifiable, account should be taken of all the means reasonably likely to be used, such as singling out, either by the controller or by another person to identify the natural person

> directly or indirectly. To ascertain whether means are reasonably likely to be used to identify the natural person, account should be taken of all objective factors, such as the costs of and the amount of time required for identification, taking into consideration the available technology at the time of the processing and technological developments.
>
> The principles of data protection should therefore not apply to anonymous information, namely information which does not relate to an identified or identifiable natural person or to personal data rendered anonymous in such a manner that the data subject is not or no longer identifiable. This Regulation does not therefore concern the processing of such anonymous information, including for statistical or research purposes.

Elsewhere we have outlined at length how definitions of anonymisation and pseudonymisation can be gleaned from this recital (Mourby et al., 2018). In essence, data that can be attributed to a natural person by means reasonably likely to be used are *indirectly* identifying and are thus pseudonymous personal data. Anonymous data are data for which identification by any means reasonably likely to be used is considered remote. The length of Recital 26 alone illustrates the complexity of demarcating personal and anonymous data in a way that is both logically consistent and consistent with the terminology of the GDPR. This was not unavoidable, however. When reviewing a draft of the GDPR, the Committee on Civil Liberties, Justice and Home Affairs of the European Parliament recommended clarification of these concepts back in October 2012:

> In order to reach the best level of data protection and enable new business models, we need to encourage the pseudonymous and anonymous use of services. Clearly defining 'anonymity' should also help data controllers understand when they are outside the scope of the Regulation. For the use of pseudonymous data, in sense of the data controller is able to single out individual persons by a pseudonym, there could be alleviations with regard to obligations for the data controller. (LIBE, 2012)

To reconcile this paragraph with our working definitions of profiles and pseudonyms, the mere 'singling out' of a person by reference to a pseudonym could be seen as falling a step short of evaluating their personal characteristics in a privacy-intrusive way. As such, it remains logical to see pseudonyms as indirectly identifying personal data, even when they permit singling out. This appears to have been borne out by the trends we have identified in regarding pseudonymised data as indirect identification.

In short, as pseudonymised data are only personal because of the risk of further attribution, they can be anonymised by eliminating reasonable risk of connection with additional information. Profiling data, however, are directly identifying and cannot be anonymised unless they are modified to the point that they no longer permit the immediate evaluation of personal characteristics.

5. Conclusion

This chapter has suggested that 'identity' in data protection law should be understood not in the psychological sense of how we perceive ourselves but in the 'digital' sense of information with sufficient potential impact on us individually that it should be recognised as a legally protected aspect of self. Although we have focused on profiling as an intrusion into privacy that thus constitutes an identification, the engagement of other fundamental rights could also justify treating the data as personal. For example, where the automated evaluation is of personal characteristics protected under equality laws, identification due to the engagement of the right to non-discrimination should also be considered.

The question of whether information constitutes an identification can thus be considered in two stages:

- Does the information, in and of itself, provide enough detail about the individual that they can be profiled, scrutinised, judged or otherwise experience (even without their knowledge) consequences from this information? If so, they have been 'identified' by the information.
- Can it be combined with other information – either already in the hands of the controller, or which they can obtain through means reasonably likely to be used – in such a way to achieve identification? If so, the individual is 'identifiable'.

Although the GDPR does not explicitly link the definition of profiling with that of personal data, the decisions we have reviewed have placed interference with individual rights at the heart of the concept of identification. As such, profiling provides an important illustration as to when information is sufficiently intrusive into fundamental rights in and of itself that can justifiably be called an identification. This has been contrasted with pseudonymisation, in which case the question of identification is less certain.

We have therefore considered the theoretical underpinning of the concept of identity in data protection law but also provided some practical guidance. In particular, our analysis highlights that longitudinal data that show individual behaviour over time (e.g. from a cookie) will be much more difficult to anonymise than a logfile of website visitors that only provides a single snapshot in time. Ultimately, however, our central contribution has been to show that it may now be helpful to determine the scope of identity in data protection law with reference to fundamental rights, and not (as is often suggested) the other way around. For all that the category of 'identity' shifts as technology evolves, the underlying benchmarks of privacy and non-discrimination rights are sufficiently stable to provide a reliable sense of who we are as we navigate the digital environment.

References

Agencia Española Protección Data & European Data Protection Supervisor (AEPD). (2021). *10 misunderstandings related to anonymisation.* https://edps.europa.eu/system/files/2021-04/21-04-27_aepd-edps_anonymisation_en_5.pdf

Authorité de protection de données (APD). (2022). Litigation Chamber, Case DOS-2019-01377, Concerning: Complaint relating to Transparency & Consent Framework, Decision on the merits 21/2022 of 2 February 2022

Burgess, M. (2018). *The law is nowhere near ready for the rise of AI-generated fake porn.* Wired. https://www.wired.co.uk/article/deepfake-app-ai-porn-fake-reddit

CNIL. (2022). *Scientific research (excluding health): Challenges and advantages of anonymization and pseudonymization.* https://www.cnil.fr/fr/recherche-scientifique-hors-sante/enjeux-avantages-anonymisation-pseudonymisation

Committee on Civil Liberties, Justice and Home Affairs of the European Parliament (LIBE). (2012). Working Document 2 on the protection of individuals with regard to the processing of personal data and on the free movement of such data (General Data Protection Regulation). https://www.europarl.europa.eu/doceo/document/LIBE-DT-497802_EN.pdf?redirect.

de Hert, P., & Lammerant, H. (2016). Predictive profiling and its legal limits: Effectiveness gone forever? In B. van der Sloot, D. Broeders, & E. Schrijvers (Eds.), *Exploring the boundaries of Big Data* (pp. 145–167). Amsterdam University Press.

Elliot, M., Mackey, E., & O'Hara, K. (2016). *The Anonymisation Decision-Making Framework*, 2nd ed. UKAN Publications. https://ukanon.net/framework/

European Data Protection Board (EDPB). (2021). *EDPB letter to the European institutions on the privacy and data protection aspects of a possible digital euro.* https://edpb.europa.eu/system/files/2021-07/edpb_letter_out_2021_0112-digitaleuro-toep_en.pdf

Information Commissioner's Office. (2020). *What is personal data?* https://ico.org.uk/for-organisations/guide-to-data-protection/guide-to-the-general-data-protection-regulation-gdpr/key-definitions/what-is-personal-data/

Information Commissioner's Office. (2022). *Draft anonymisation, pseudonymisation and privacy enhancing technologies guidance.* https://ico.org.uk/media/about-the-ico/consultations/4019579/chapter-3-anonymisation-guidance.pdf

Laurie, G. (2002). *Genetic privacy: A challenge to medico-legal norms.* Cambridge University Press.

McMahon, A., Buyx, A., & Prainsack, B. (2020). Big data governance needs more collective responsibility: The role of harm mitigation in the governance of data use in medicine and beyond. *Medical Law Review, 28*(1), 155–182.

Miller, C. (2019). *Would you recognise yourself from your data?* BBC. https://www.bbc.co.uk/news/technology-48434175

Mourby, M., et al. (2018). Are 'pseudonymised' data always personal data? Implications of the GDPR for administrative data research in the UK. *Computer Law and Security Review, 34*(2), 222–233.

Oxford University Press. (2007). *OED.* https://www.oed.com/

R. (on the application of Bridges) v Chief Constable of South Wales. (2020). EWCA Civ 1058.

Regulation 2016/679 of the European Parliament and of the Council of 27 April 2016 on the protection of natural persons with regard to the processing of personal data and on the free movement of such data, and repealing Directive 95/46/ (General Data Protection Regulation). (2016). OJ L119/1.

Sullivan, C. (2011). Digital identity: An emergent legal concept. University of Adelaide Press.

UK Parliament. (2022). Data Protection and Digital Information Bill. https://publications.parliament.uk/pa/bills/cbill/58-03/0143/220143.pdf

Wachter, S. (2018). Normative challenges of identification in the Internet of Things: Privacy, profiling, discrimination, and the GDPR. *Computer Law and Security Review, 34*(3), 436–449.

15. Biometric Data, Within and Beyond Data Protection

Catherine Jasserand

Abstract

The new EU data protection framework has introduced the notion of biometric data into the EU data protection landscape. Biometric data are defined as personal data resulting from the technical processing of biometric characteristics for biometric recognition purposes. When these data are processed to 'uniquely identify' an individual, they fall into the category of sensitive data and are subject to stricter rules. The legal definition of biometric data creates uncertainty as to which technical stages fall in the legal category of biometric data, what 'unique identification' means and whether biometric data, as technically defined, always relate to identifiable individuals. This chapter will answer these questions, taking the example of a facial recognition system and analysing the data generated during the recognition process.

Keywords: biometric data; facial recognition; GDPR; ISO/IEC 2382-37; unique identification

1. Introduction

Human biometric characteristics – such as the fingerprints, face, voice, iris, retina, signature and gait – are distinctive enough to recognise an individual (Jain et al., 2011). Once captured and transformed into biometric data, these characteristics can be measured. The measurement is performed by comparison between sets of biometric data. It results in a statistical score of similarity between different sets of biometric data that are compared to establish the likelihood that they belong to the same individual. This recognition process is divided into several technical stages during which biometric data are generated. As described in the ISO/IEC standard used

Van der Sloot & van Schendel. *The Boundaries of Data*. Taylor & Francis Group, 2024
DOI: 10.5117/9789463729192_CH15

as a reference by the biometric community, ISO/IEC 2382-37, on the harmonisation of biometric vocabulary, 'biometric data' is a generic term that describes the different formats resulting from the transformation of the biometric characteristics to measure them. The term covers the sample (untransformed) and the features extracted from the sample or template (reduction of the biometric characteristics into a mathematical pattern). During these technical stages, the question that arises is whether these data qualify as personal and/or biometric (personal) data.

As explained in this chapter, the EU data protection framework (composed of the General Data Protection Regulation and the Law Enforcement Directive) has introduced a new legal definition of biometric data and a legal status based on the purpose of their processing. Under the condition that biometric data are processed to uniquely identify an individual, they fall into the category of sensitive data. Not only does the notion of 'unique identification' lack clarity in the context of biometric data processing, but the definition also does not allow the determination of which parts of the technical processes fall under the regime of biometric data, sensitive data or simply personal data and which parts might not even generate personal data. To understand the limits of the legal classification resulting from the legal notion of biometric data, this chapter first explains the different technical stages of a biometric recognition system, taking the example of a facial recognition system. It then explains the legal notion of biometric data resulting from the EU data protection framework. Finally, it shows the technical stages where this legal construction seems problematic.

2. Technical Processes Through the Analysis of a Facial Recognition System

In their 2011 book, Jain et al. observe that:

> [t]he ability to identify individuals uniquely and to associate personal attributes (e.g. name, nationality, etc.) with an individual has been crucial to the fabric of human society. Humans typically use body characteristics such as face, voice, and gait along with other contextual information (e.g. location and clothing) to recognize one another. The set of attributes associated with a person constitutes their personal *identity*. ... The fundamental task in identity management is to establish the association between an individual and his personal identity. (pp. 1–2)

Thus, the purpose of biometric recognition is not to establish an individual's identity but to compare sets of data generated by a biometric system to determine whether they match. This comparison determines the likelihood in percentage that the data originate from the same person. Additional information – such as demographic or biographic information – is necessary to know who a person is or to confirm their identity.

Measurable biometric characteristics present in faces are captured and transformed to be compared for different purposes, such as identity management or categorisation. A facial recognition system will capture an image and then detect a face. Once a face is detected in the frame of an image (either still or moving), the facial features used for recognition purposes are extracted from the image. Before the feature extraction, the image is enhanced and any background noise removed. The data resulting from the feature extraction compose the biometric template, which is a reduced representation of the facial traits. As noted by Jain et al. (2011), 'The template is expected to contain only the salient discriminatory information that is essential for recognizing the person' (p. 7).

2.1. Image Acquisition

The first step is the acquisition of images that will be then transformed into different formats. It could be performed through surveillance cameras equipped with facial recognition systems or a sensor scanning a picture of an individual. Concerning live cameras, images are captured before human faces are detected. The acquisition and detection are not simultaneous but sequential processes.

2.2. Face Detection and Face Alignment

After an image is acquired, an algorithm determines whether a human face is present in the frame of a photo or in a video. As observed by Jain et al. (2011), face detection is the first stage of many applications processing facial characteristics, whether it is for facial recognition purposes, the analysis of facial expressions or classification purposes. Face detection relies on several elements, such as 'skin colour (for faces in colour images or videos), motion (for faces in videos), facial/head shape, facial appearance, or a combination of these parameters' (Li, 2011, p. 13). Many technical challenges (light, pose, environment, orientation of faces) can affect the process of face detection (Guo & Zhang, 2019). From a technical perspective, face detection is limited to finding human characteristics in a frame. The purpose of face detection is not to individualise, recognise or identify an individual or associate their identity with their face. The objective is to find whether a human face is present in an image or video frame. The result of the face detection is a classification of the object as being either a face or a non-face (Li, 2011). The facial image obtained is aligned to detect the facial landmarks (e.g. the corners of the eyes, the corners of the mouth, the tip of the nose). Face alignment identifies the geometric structure of a face. It prepares the image for the next phase. From a technical perspective, face detection and face alignment are 'pre-processing' stages before the features can be extracted (Li & Jain, 2009, 'Face Alignment').

2.3. Feature Extraction

Before extracting the features, the image is enhanced (pose, light) to facilitate the extraction of the features. As observed by Tian et al. (2011), 'Two types of features can be extracted: geometric features and appearance features' (p. 261). Geometric features relate to the shape and geometric structure of the face (such as the shape of the mouth), while appearance features relate to the texture of the skin, wrinkles and scars (Tian et al., 2011). Only the distinctive features used for recognition purposes will be extracted and compressed into a biometric template (Li & Jain, 2009, 'Biometric Template'). The template is often a numerical or mathematical representation of the geometric structure of a face.

2.4. Comparison

The final step compares the template generated from the extracted features (biometric template) with existing templates (stored on a device or in databases). A template is only compared to another in a verification application to determine if the person is who they claim to be (verification of the claimed identity). It is a one-to-one comparison. In an identification process, a biometric template is run against every template contained in one or several databases to determine if the person is known (to establish who a person is). This is a one-to-many comparison. It should be mentioned that this comparison will establish if the person is known in a database, but this process does not provide any information about the individual's identity. The verification and identification modalities are technical comparisons, which imply the existence of previously stored biometric data (either in templates form or facial images).

After this brief and simplified presentation of the technical stages of a biometric recognition system, this chapter describes how the notion of biometric data has developed and is approached from a data protection perspective.

3. Legal Definition and Classification of Biometric Data

The new EU data protection framework has introduced a legal concept of biometric data in the EU data protection landscape. Biometric data are a type of personal data generated during the technical processing of biometric characteristics for biometric recognition purposes. If they are processed to uniquely identify an individual, biometric data fall into the category of sensitive data. This section explains the notion and status of biometric data resulting from the EU data protection rules and highlights the uncertainties created by the notion of 'unique identification' and the undefined 'technical processing'.

3.1. Legal Definition

Until the adoption of the new EU data protection framework, there was no concept of biometric data in the former EU data protection regimes. When the previous Data Protection Directive (1995) was adopted, the legal nature of biometric data and the application of data protection rules to biometric technologies were not widely discussed. But as early as 2003, European bodies started to tackle the topic in policy papers. For instance, the Article 29 Working Party advising the European Commission under the previous data protection regime published a *Working document on biometrics* in 2003 (A29WP 2003) and an Opinion in 2012, where it considered that some types of biometric data could be sensitive if they revealed sensitive information, such as health or ethnicity (A29WP, 2012b, linked to A29WP, 2012a). The European Data Protection Supervisor viewed biometric data as *highly sensitive* or *very sensitive* by nature early on (EDPS 2005a; EDPS 2005b). However, the attempts to define biometric data from a data protection perspective were approximative and inconsistent (Jasserand, 2016a).

3.2. Biometric Data as a New Category of Personal Data

The notion of biometric data is defined in Article 4(14) GDPR and mirrored in Article 3(13) LED. Biometric data are:

> personal data resulting from specific technical processing relating to the physical, physiological or behavioural characteristics of a natural person, which allow or confirm the unique identification of that natural person, such as facial images or dactyloscopic data.

Article 4(14) GDPR is completed by Recital 51 GDPR concerning the classification of photographs:

> The processing of photographs should not systematically be considered to be processing of special categories of personal data as they are covered by the definition of biometric data only when processed through a specific technical means allowing the unique identification or authentication of a natural person.

Following Article 9(1) GDPR (and Article 10 LED), biometric data processed to uniquely identify an individual are sensitive data. The notion of biometric data and consequences of the criterion of 'unique identification' are analysed below.

3.3. Four Criteria: Personal Data, Technical Processing, Biometric Characteristics and Unique Identification

First, the data at stake cannot be biometric data if they do not meet the criteria applicable to personal data. According to Article 4(1) GDPR and 3(1) LED, 'any information relating to an identified or identifiable individual is personal data'. Identifying an individual from a data protection perspective means singling out or distinguishing them from a group (A29WP, 2007). The threshold of identifiability is low (see Jasserand, 2016b, for a comprehensive analysis of the definition).

Second, data are generated during the technical processing of biometric characteristics. Prima facie, the definition seems to refer to the technical stages through which biometric data are generated, i.e. from the capture of a biometric sample to its transformation into a numerical representation for comparison purposes. However, following Recital 51 GDPR, photographs (which are also considered samples from a technical perspective) are not regarded as biometric data if they are not processed to uniquely identify an individual. As analysed by Kindt, the GDPR has introduced an 'artificial distinction' between photographs (not yet processed for biometric recognition) and processed facial images. Biometric samples, which are not yet transformed, therefore seem to be excluded from the definition of biometric data (Kindt, 2018).

Third, the processing operations generate data from individuals' biometric characteristics. The description of these characteristics – be they physical, physiological or behavioural – acknowledges the diversity of human biometric characteristics that can be used for recognition purposes.

Fourth, the final criterion relates to the processing purpose, also referred to as the 'context of processing' in the Explanatory Memorandum of Convention 108+. This criterion is a critical element in the legal qualification of biometric data, but it is far from clear. In the GDPR and the LED, the processing purpose is described as *allowing or confirming the unique identification*. However, Recital 51 GDPR that specifies when photographs are considered biometric data describes the purposes as *allowing the unique identification or the authentication* of an individual. In Recital 51, it is clear that unique identification is used as a synonym for identification modality, whereas authentication refers to verification modality. Authentication is often used as meaning verification, although the biometric community does not support that usage (ISO/IEC 2382-37). The consequence of that reading is the exclusion of biometric data processed for verification purposes from the scope of sensitive data. This interpretation is consistent with the Explanatory Memorandum of Convention 108+ on biometric data (paras. 58 and 59) and the request made by stakeholders from the biometric industry to exclude biometric data processed for verification purposes from the scope of sensitive data (Consultative Committee of Convention 108, 2012). Yet Recital 51 GDPR was added during the trialogue on the proposal for the GDPR to align the text with the future modernised version of Convention 108+ (Jasserand, 2016b; Kindt, 2020). Despite the wording of Recital 51, one cannot assert that 'unique identification' refers only to the identification modality in the definition of biometric data. Both Article 4(14) GDPR and 3(13) LED describe the processing purposes as allowing or confirming unique identification. It can be argued that 'unique identification' refers to a threshold of identification where an individual is identified (i.e. singled out) thanks to their unique biometric characteristics, whether the processing is performed for identification or verification purposes. The uniqueness is not attached to a specific biometric recognition modality but to the inherent quality of biometric characteristics (Jasserand, 2019).

Not knowing what 'unique identification' means is problematic, as the criterion is also used to classify biometric data as sensitive data. Does it refer to the identification modality of biometric recognition, as it seems to be the case in Convention 108+ and Recital 51 GDPR? Or does it refer to the use of biometric characteristics that can 'uniquely link' the data to an individual, regardless of whether the data are processed for identification or verification purposes? Kindt and Jasserand have shown the limits of this definition and the use of the processing purpose as a discriminant criterion (Kindt, 2018; Jasserand, 2016b). From a technical perspective, 'unique identification' cannot refer to the identification modality. As explained by technical experts, the identification or verification process is performed through the comparison of biometric data (Jain et al., 2011; ISO/IEC 2382-37). The result of the comparison is a statistical score of similarity. From a technical perspective, it is not accurate to describe the identification process as being unique. It is not the comparison that is unique to each individual but the biometric characteristics used to recognise them. These are deemed unique or, rather, 'distinctive enough'. Forensic experts challenge the uniqueness of biometric attributes, as it has never been established. They prefer referring to their 'distinctiveness' instead (e.g. Page et al., 2011). Their approach seems to be backed up by recent studies on facial recognition showing the high similarity between faces of individuals who are not blood-related (Joshi et al., 2022).

3.4. Classification

The legal definition of biometric data and their subsequent qualification as sensitive data have created a legal maze. Biometric data generated during the technical processing of biometric characteristics fall into different categories. If processed for purposes other than identification or verification, they are personal data under the condition that they relate to an identified or identifiable individual. Such biometric data are those processed, for instance, for categorisation purposes (i.e. age, gender and ethnicity). These data could also be classified as sensitive if they reveal sensitive information.

Biometric data processed for either identification or verification purposes fall within the legal definition of biometric data. However, as explained in the previous section, the definition does not specify the technical stages of biometric recognition covered by the notion of biometric data. If biometric data are processed to uniquely identify an individual, they fall into the category of sensitive data. Based on the analysis made in this section on the meaning of the purpose of processing, it is difficult to determine when biometric data fall into that category. It could, however, be argued that biometric data processed in the context of an identification application (one-to-many comparison) are sensitive data. However, this is less clear for biometric data processed for verification purposes. Besides, the criterion does not determine which technical stage of identification (or verification modality) is considered sensitive data. The next section explores this issue based on the example of a facial recognition system.

The EU data protection framework defines biometric data and classifies them as sensitive data based on their purpose of processing rather than their nature (like other types of sensitive data). Consequently, not all biometric data are regarded as biometric data from an EU data protection perspective. The next section describes the various parts of the technical processes. Based on the legal definition, it discusses which part of the processes might fall under the regime of biometric and sensitive data, which part is only personal data and which part could be excluded from the scope of personal data.

4. Technical Processes and Personal Data

Analysing the different technical stages of the processing of biometric data in the context of a deployed facial recognition system, this section will show the limits of the definition.

4.1. Image Acquisition, Face Detection and Face Alignment

The image of an area (e.g. of a public space) will be taken by a system, not knowing whether a human face is present in the image frame. Once an image is captured, an algorithm will detect whether a human face is present. The algorithm used for face detection will only classify the objects present in the frame as face or non-face. At this stage, the question is whether face detection can be considered processing personal data, even before classifying them as biometric data from a data protection perspective. According to Article 4(1) GDPR, personal data means any information relating to an individual who can be singled out.

Face detection aims at determining whether a human face is present in frame and not whether a specific face can be distinguished from other faces. It is possible that the further processing of the image would not be of sufficient quality to perform biometric recognition. So, it could be argued that the data generated during the face detection phase might not reach the threshold of identifiability to individualise someone (i.e. single them out). From a technical perspective, face detection is limited to labelling the objects displayed in a frame, face or non-face. Thus, it could be argued that a face detection system does not process personal data. As reported by Purtova, two data protection authorities – one in Bavaria and one in Ireland – considered that face detection systems did not process personal data. However, their reasoning does not seem to be based on the threshold of identifiability but rather on the 'transient nature of the processing, where raw data of an individual processed by the detection "sensors" is discarded immediately' (Purtova, 2022, p. 164). In the Irish case, the face detection system was used for personalised advertisement purposes. As Purtova (2018) argues, the system processed personal information (age, gender or emotions) to generate 'real time personalised ads' and could single out individuals (p. 75). One could wonder whether the system at stake was just a face detection system or whether it was not analysing the expressions and emotions, and thus targeting individuals as well as detecting faces.

Based on these examples, one could argue that a face detection system that is limited to detecting the presence of a human face might not process sufficient information to individualise that face. However, as soon as such a system is used for targeting or categorisation purposes, it might generate information considered personal data. The data processed at this stage might or might not qualify as personal data, but as they are not processed for biometric recognition purposes (yet), they cannot fall into the legal category of biometric data.

Once a face has been detected, the image is enhanced, and the face is aligned to allow feature extraction and further transform the data into biometric data. An image that is ready to be processed will result from face alignment and enhancement.

4.2. Feature Extraction

During that phase, the discriminant and identifying information that a face contains is extracted to be transformed into machine-readable biometric data. It is precisely that information that will allow the individualisation and identification of individuals. There is no doubt that the format generated during that phase qualifies as personal data. From a technical perspective, it will also be considered biometric data because feature extraction is one of the technical stages of biometric recognition. What about the legal classification? As explained, biometric data fall into the legal category of biometric data dependant on their purpose of processing (referred to as biometric recognition purposes). However, the legal definition does not specify when the data fall into that category: is it when the comparison is performed (whether the result is a match or non-match) or during the process of biometric recognition? One could argue that the definition reflects the process, not just the comparison stage. According to Article 4(14) GDPR and Article 3(13) GDPR, biometric data are those that result from the technical processing, implying the different technical stages prior to the comparison itself.

Photographs also deserve a special mention here. According to Recital 51 GDPR, mere photographs, which are not processed for biometric recognition purposes, do not fall in the legal category of sensitive data. However, as soon as they are technically processed to extract facial features in view of biometric recognition, these images are classified as biometric data. As a result of Recital 51 GDPR, 'untransformed' photographs are not biometric data and do not fall into the sensitive data category accordingly. By contrast, other formats – such as biometric images and facial templates – are considered biometric and sensitive data. Yet, from a technical perspective, it seems illogical to treat facial templates, which are a reduced numerical representation of identifying characteristics, as more sensitive than 'untransformed' photographs. These images potentially provide more information about an individual than the reduced biometric template. As argued by Kindt, this distinction between photographs (which are a pre-requisite for any facial recognition system) and other biometric formats is artificial (Kindt, 2018). Besides, the GDPR does not specify when (i.e. at which stage) photographs become biometric data. Is it only after the feature extraction, i.e. when the samples are processed for biometric recognition purposes? Or should it be understood, instead, the way it is defined in border control instruments, such as in Regulation 2018/1861 on the Schengen Information System? According to Article 3(15) of Regulation 2018/1861, facial images are 'digital images with sufficient image resolution and quality to be used in automated biometric matching'. The Regulation does not require the images to be technically transformed to be considered biometric data, but only to be of sufficient quality to perform facial recognition.

4.3. Comparison

Before comparing biometric data to determine whether it is highly likely they originate from the same individual, the data are stored. The question is whether the storage of these data is considered part of the processing that allows or confirms the unique identification of an individual or whether it is not. For instance, based on Recital 51 GDPR, it could be deduced that the storage of photographs not transformed for biometric recognition purposes is excluded. It could also be argued that facial images that have been through technical processing are biometric data, even when stored. However, are these data processed to uniquely identify someone? In the application of Article 9(1) GDPR, processing *biometric data for the purpose of uniquely identifying* an individual is considered sensitive processing. It is difficult to argue that the storage of biometric data is a processing operation that uniquely identifies someone (see also Kindt, 2018). It is when the comparison is performed that the processing may result in 'uniquely identifying' someone. Still, one could question whether there is an obligation of result – that is to say, whether the comparison has to result in a match to consider the biometric data processed as sensitive. Some data protection authorities have already taken a position and hold that biometric data 'processed for the purpose of uniquely identifying a natural person ... constitute special category data regardless of whether there is a match' (e.g. ICO, 2021).

5. Conclusion

From a technical perspective, biometric data are formats resulting from the processing and transformation of biometric characteristics used for biometric recognition purposes (one individual) or categorisation purposes (shared characteristics of a group of individuals). These formats vary from the sample captured by a biometric system to the biometric template resulting from a reduction into a numerical representation of biometric attributes used for recognition or classification purposes. A step-by-step assessment is necessary to determine whether personal data and biometric (personal) data are processed at each technical stage. Depending on the purpose or context of processing, biometric data will be personal, biometric and/or sensitive data. Conversely, it could be the case that data generated during the image acquisition and face detection stages do not reach the threshold of identifiability and remain excluded from the field of personal data. Thus, it cannot be claimed that biometric data generated during the technical processing are necessarily personal data.

As explained in this chapter, the legal concept of biometric data is far from the technical notion and unsatisfactory in several aspects. It excludes some formats from the scope of biometric data, such as untransformed samples and thus photographs. It also relies on the discriminant factor of 'uniquely identifying' to classify the processed data in the category of biometric personal data. This factor is neither clear nor logical. From a technical perspective, unique identification through the processing of biometric data can never be reached. The comparison between biometric data always results in a statistical score of similarity. Therefore, it cannot be claimed that someone can be uniquely identified through their biometric data. The reference to 'unique identification' in the definition of biometric data is unfortunate. To better reflect what biometric data are, it could be suggested to revise the legal definition to get rid of this controversial criterion. This would also allow classifying biometric data processed for categorisation purposes (such as age, gender and ethnicity) in the legal category of biometric data. One suggestion would be to align the definition of biometric data with that of border control instruments. This would allow images with the technical qualities to perform automated biometric recognition to be considered biometric data. This is all the more relevant to rethink the legal approach to biometric data when, in the context of the future Artificial Intelligence Act, EU institutions are trying to circumvent that legal definition by creating new sub-categories of biometric data. Instead of adding complexity to the legal concept of biometric data, the EU legislator should simplify the current GDPR definition.

References

Article 29 Working Party. (2003). *Working document on biometrics*, Brussels, 1 August.

Article 29 Working Party. (2007). *Opinion 4/2007 on the concept of personal data*, Brussels, 20 June.

Article 29 Working Party. (2012a). *Opinion 02/2012 on Facial recognition in online and mobile services*, Brussels, 22 March.

Article 29 Working Party. (2012b). *Opinion 3/2012 on developments in biometric technologies*, Brussels, 27 April.

Bygrave, L., & Tosoni, L. (2018). Article 4(14). Biometric data. In C. Kuner et al. (Eds.), *The EU General Data Protection Regulation (GDPR): A commentary* (pp. 207–216). Oxford University Press.

Consultative Committee of Convention 108. (2012). *Modernisation of Convention 108: Compilation of comments received*, Strasbourg, 2 April.

Convention for the Protection of Individuals with Regard to Automatic Processing of Personal Data (Convention 108) adopted in 1981, Council of Europe, Strasbourg.

Convention for the Protection of Individuals with Regard to Automatic Processing of Personal Data (Convention 108+) adopted in 2018, Council of Europe, Strasbourg.

Directive (EU) 2016/680 of the European Parliament and of the Council of 27 April 2016 on the protection of natural persons with regard to the processing of personal data by competent authorities for the purposes of the prevention, investigation, detection or prosecution of criminal offences or the execution of criminal penalties, and on the free movement of such data, and repealing Council Framework Decision 2008/977/JHA.

European Data Protection Supervisor. (2005a). *Opinion of the European Data Protection Supervisor on the Proposal for a Regulation of the European Parliament and of the Council concerning the Visa Information System (VIS) and the exchange of data between Member States on short stay-visas (COM [2004] 835 final)*, Brussels, 23 March.

European Data Protection Supervisor. (2005b). *Opinion of the European Data Protection Supervisor on the Proposal for a Council Decision framework on the protection of personal data processed in the framework of police and judicial cooperation in criminal matters (COM [2005] 475 final)*, Brussels, 19 December.

European Data Protection Supervisor. (2011). *Opinion on a notification for prior checking received from the Data Protection of the European Commission.*

European Data Protection Supervisor. (2018). *Opinion 4/2018 on the Proposals for two Regulations establishing a framework for interoperability between EU large-scale information systems*, Brussels, 16 April.

European Data Protection Supervisor. (2020). *Guidelines 3/2019 on the processing of personal data through video devices*, v.2.0, Brussels, 30 January.

de Hert, P., & Christianen, K. (2013). Progress report on the application of the principles of Convention 108 to the Collection and Processing of Biometric Data. [Study commissioned by the Council of Europe]. TILT. https://rm.coe.int/progress-report-on-the-application-of-the-principles-of-convention-108/1680744d81

Guo, G., & Zhang, Na. (2019). A survey on deep learning based on face recognition. *Computer Vision and Image Understanding, 189*, 102805.

Information Commissioner's Office (ICO). (2021). *Information commissioner's opinion: The use of live facial recognition technology in public places*, 18 June. https://ico.org.uk/about-the-ico/media-centre/information-commissioner-s-opinion-addresses-privacy-concerns-on-the-use-of-live-facial-recognition-technology-in-public-places/

Il Garante. (2014). *Guidelines on biometric recognition and graphometric signature, Annex A to the Garante's Order of 12 November 2014*. https://www.garanteprivacy.it/home/docweb/-/docweb-display/docweb/3590114

ISO/IEC JTC 1 SC/37. (2022). *ISO/IEC 2382:37:2022 (EN) Information Technology – Vocabulary- Part 37: Biometrics*, 29 March.

Jain, A., et al. (2011). *Introduction to biometrics*. Springer.

Jasserand, C. (2016a). Avoiding terminological confusion between the notions of 'biometrics' and 'biometric data'. *International Data Privacy Law, 6*(1), 63–76.

Jasserand C. (2016b). Legal nature of biometric data: From 'generic' personal data to sensitive data. *European Data Protection Law Review, 2*(3), 297–311.

Jasserand, C. (2020). *Reprocessing of biometric data for law enforcement purposes: Individuals' safeguards caught at the interface between the GDPR and the 'police' directive* [Doctoral dissertation, University of Groningen].

Joshi, R. S., et al. (2022). Look-alike humans identified by facial recognition algorithms show genetic similarities. *Cell Reports, 40*, 11257.

Kindt, E. (2013). *Privacy and data protection issues of biometric applications*. Springer.

Kindt, E. (2018). Having yes, using no? About the new legal regime for biometric data. *Computer Law & Security Review, 34*(3), 523–538.

Kindt, E. (2020). A first attempt at regulating biometric data in the European Union. In A. Kak (Ed.), *Regulating biometrics: Global approaches and urgent questions* (pp. 62–69). AI NOW Institute.

Li, S. (2011). Face detection. In S. Li & A. Jain (Eds.), *Handbook of face recognition* (pp. 13–38), 2nd ed. Springer.

Li, S., & Jain, A. (2009). *Encyclopedia of biometrics*. Springer.

Li, S., & Jain, A. (2011). *Handbook of face recognition*, 2nd ed. Springer.

Page, M., et al. (2011). Uniqueness in the forensic identification sciences – Fact or fiction? *Forensic Science International, 206*(1–3), 12–18.

Purtova, N. (2018). The law of everything. Broad concept of personal data and future EU data protection law. *Law, Innovation and Technology, 10*(1), 40–81.

Purtova, N. (2022). From knowing by name to targeting: The meaning of identification under the GDPR. *International Data Privacy Law, 12*(3), 163–183.

Regulation (EU) 2016/679 of the European Parliament and of the Council of 27 April 2016 on the protection of natural persons with regard to the processing of personal data and on the free movement of such data, and repealing Directive 95/46/EC (General Data Protection Regulation).

Regulation (EU) 2018/1861 of the European Parliament and of the Council of 28 November 2018 on the establishment, operation and use of the Schengen Information System (SIS) in the field of border checks, and amending the Convention implementing the Schengen Agreement, and amending and repealing Regulation (EC) No. 1987/2006.

Tian, Y.-L., Kanade, T., & Cohn, J. F. Facial expression analysis. In S. Li & A. Jain (Eds.), *Handbook of face recognition* (pp. 247–276), 2nd ed. Springer.

Yang, M-H., Kriegman, D., & Ahuja, N. (2002). Detecting faces in images: A survey. *IEEE Transactions on Pattern Analysis and Machine Intelligence, 24*(1), 34–58.

16. Conclusions

Bart van der Sloot & Sascha van Schendel

Abstract
This chapter provides an overview of the main findings of this book, draws the general conclusions and maps the potential paths forward as well as the questions they raise.

Keywords: legal certainty; principle-based regulation; rule-based regulation; access-use debate; contextuality

1. Introduction

In this book, a varied and rich discussion was presented on the regulation of data in a broad sense. The current regulatory approach was discussed and problematised, in particular on the question of whether data should be the focus point of regulation and, if so, whether it should focus primarily on data containing information about an individual. As was discussed in the introduction, while this determination was relatively easy to make when first introduced in the 1970s, it has become increasingly difficult to maintain in light of technological developments. Two different prongs of the regulatory response were contrasted. One side of the EU regulation is concerned with maintaining a strict separation between personal and non-personal data, as well as other categories of data. The other side has focused on the extension of the scope of the concept of 'personal data' in the various data protection instruments adopted over the decades.

This book explored the extent to which either of these two strategies are feasible, the extent to which they can co-exist and the extent to which alternative approaches can be developed. To arrive at innovative and comprehensive conclusions, three perspectives were combined: technology, practice and regulation. Each of the chapters focused on a niche aspect, presenting the state of the art for that relevant topic. This concluding chapter first sets out the findings for each of these three perspectives. Subsequently, using the

Van der Sloot & van Schendel. *The Boundaries of Data.* Taylor & Francis Group, 2024
DOI: 10.5117/9789463729192_CH16

insights of each of the three perspectives, the research problem is discussed and a path forward is suggested. Finally, as should be the end of any academic book, future research questions and open-ended discussions will be highted.

2. Findings

2.1. Technology

Chapter 2, 'Object Re-identification: Problems, Algorithms and Responsible Research Practice', by Zhedong Zheng and Liang Zheng, explored techniques of object re-identification. The chapter by Zheng and Zheng demonstrated that a technique such as object re-identification is driven by and dependent on large-scale data and the AI tools to process such data – deep learning. There are arguments to be made in favour of the use of such large-scale data, in functionality and accuracy. At the same time, also in a technique such as object re-identification, privacy and data protection challenges come to the fore. Unsupervised learning, which can be necessary for such large volumes of data, comes with more problems in labelling (as there are fewer labels) and data privacy issues. In this sense, identifiability of individuals in data can be seen as a constraint, as it comes with data protection and privacy hurdles. To mitigate challenges, Zheng and Zheng propose exploring developing algorithms with synthetic data, using data anonymisation techniques and designing economical learning schemes, which are less data reliant. At the same time, they do point out that many questions around the use of synthetic data and anonymisation techniques are yet unresolved.

Chapter 3, 'The Quantum Threat to Cybersecurity and Privacy', by Nina Bindel, Michele Mosca and Bill Munson, explored the impact of quantum techniques for cybersecurity and privacy. Through this chapter, it becomes clear what the role is of quantum technologies in identifiability, in the sense of how easy it can be to break through security measures and obtain personal data. The authors foresee the release of private information combined with a loss of agency and control over personal actions as being major issues and propose strategies in transitioning to cryptography that is deemed to be quantum-safe, for which they describe various cryptography techniques. As a consequence, one can say that, unless technological protection keeps up in development with quantum technologies intended to break through information and retrieve information, the problems associated with the widespread availability of data relating to individuals will only increase. Not only will individuals be more likely to be identified in data if security measures can be undone; it also creates a sense of loss of agency over information that was thought to be confidential, since it no longer is so. One could argue that quantum computing thus not only increases the identifiability of individuals and their information in the future but can also create debates on how much data are out there and accessible, creating more and more privacy concerns.

Chapter 4, 'Realistic Face Anonymisation', by Håkon Hukkelås and Frank Lindseth, described data protection and privacy challenges of collecting and storing images, especially in terms of anonymising data. While traditional image anonymisation degrades the original data, making the images unusable for many applications, developments in deep generative models have enabled a new type of anonymisation: realistic anonymisation. Realistic anonymisation replaces privacy-sensitive information with artificially synthesised realistic content. In this way, realistic anonymisation techniques contribute to anonymous processing by attempting to mitigate data protection and privacy challenges. This chapter thus offers an interesting example of feasible anonymisation techniques, although in a specific domain of application.

Overall, the technological chapters demonstrate two points: on the one hand, there will continue to be challenges surrounding anonymisation and privacy protection given the large volumes of data out there. These challenges will likely only increase in the future with further development, such as in deep learning and quantum computing. On the other hand, the chapters demonstrate that there is a virtually unlimited range of possibilities for data processing and mitigating risks; the legal regime, however, will guide the choices that are made. If the legal regime remains focused on the identifiability of an individual, there will be a demand for (research on) certain techniques for labelling of machine data, quantum security and anonymisation. Yet from a technological perspective, this unique focus on the identifiability of a natural person may not be the most logical nor the most desirable. There are many harms that are not tackled by this approach, as it hinders processing of personal information and data techniques that, from a technological point of view, should be deemed legitimate and desirable.

2.2. Practice

The second part offered perspectives on the use of data in practice to assess what types of data are distinguished in various societal sectors and how data are viewed.

Chapter 5, 'Use of Bulk Data by Intelligence and Security Services: Caught Between a Rock and a Hard Place?', by Willemijn Aerdts and Ludo Block, described the use of data by intelligence and security services. Aerdts and Block described why and how intelligence services gather their data. From their contribution, it becomes clear that there are developments towards gathering more or placing more emphasis on bulk data, as well as a continually increasing importance of data labelled as metadata. One could conclude that such developments put strain on the GDPR and GDPR-like regimes for data, where the focus is on individual data: from jurisprudence dealing with the practises of intelligence and security services, it is nonetheless apparent that bulk data and metadata also have privacy consequences, whether or not they always classify as personal data. In addition, Aerdts and Block also discuss two data types that are not as such data types under the GDPR: data protected by provisions for persons with professional privileges and raw data. The GDPR does not see data protected by professional privilege as sensitive data as such, nor does the GDPR distinguish between raw, pre-processed and processed data. While data collection by intelligence and security services will not be regulated under the GDPR, as these actors fall outside the scope of this instrument, it nonetheless does illustrate the dilemmas between competing interests: one the one hand, there are interests such as national security and efficiency, which could be in favour of large-scale and bulk data collection, while on the other hand, there are various fundamental rights interests such as privacy, data protection and freedom of expression that might be better served with minimal data processing.

Chapter 6, 'Farm Data Sharing: Current Practices and Principles', by Sjaak Wolfert, Else Giesbers, Houkje Adema and Marc-Jeroen Bogaardt, described how the agricultural sector is one of the most data-driven sectors in our society. One crucial aspect to data that comes to the fore in their chapter is that of sharing of data. The authors describe limitations to data sharing, of which two are technological issues and regulatory limitations in instruments such as the GDPR. Digitalisation is accelerating the sharing of data, but the current abundance of data and involvement of all kinds of new smart devices and new players also raises many issues that can become obstacles for sharing data, ranging from technological and financial obstacles to the core aspect of trust. While some data fall within the scope of the GDPR or at least require a compliance check to see if they fall under the GDPR, posing hurdles for sharing, the opposite scenario can also occur: Chapter 6 brings a new argument to the fore of the GDPR debate and that is of data *unregulated* by the GDPR, as data about the farm are business data that farmers might want to protect but are not considered personal data.

Chapter 7, 'Microdata Access at Statistics Netherlands', written by Statistics Netherlands (CBS), describes microdata access at their agency. The chapter showed that microdata access is an important service and set out different ways of providing access to microdata. One specific technique to prevent identification of individuals in data is through statistical disclosure control (SDC), where the main goal of SDC is to control the risk of disclosing information on identifiable units. For public use files, this is achieved through aggregation methods for identifiers; for scientific use files, protection is awarded through a limitation in the persons who have access to the data, namely only a select group of researchers. For statistical data, not only the GDPR plays a role; the Dutch Statistical Act forces CBS to maintain the highest possible standards in the protection of the privacy of the respondents. For personal data specifically, this is enforced by the GDPR as well. To reach these high standards, CBS has adopted the 'five safes' framework. This framework aims to create different aspects of protection: safe people, safe settings, safe projects, safe data and safe output. This approach showcases protection on a multitude of levels, technical, organisational, etc. Chapter 7 in that way offers an interesting example of ways in which data can be protected beyond the GDPR, because some statistical data will not qualify as personal data and the Dutch Statistical Act also has its own specific strict rules for the protection of data.

Chapter 8, 'Atmospheric Profiling and Surveillance in the Stratumseind Living Lab: Pushing the Limits of Identifiability', by Maša Galič, discussed whether data being processed in a typical living lab could be considered personal data. The chapter focuses on the concept of identifiability, considered through the broader socio-technical lens of profiling. The particular type of profiling taking place in living labs leads to a twofold issue. On the one hand, it adds to and further complicates the discussions around the question of whether profiling constitutes a form of personal data processing simply because of its capacity to affect individuals. This issue, which has its proponents and opponents, has not yet been settled. On the other hand, it also implies a novel type of profiling – atmospheric profiling – which tries to indirectly affect persons by affecting the general atmosphere on the street rather than singling out individuals. As such, this type of profiling does not seem to constitute a type of personal data processing. The current reach of data protection law is thus very limited when it comes to living labs and smart city projects functioning according to the surveillant logic of security, based on increasing amounts of environmental data and atmospheric profiling. Broadly speaking, this chapter demonstrates that for profiling, or at least this specific type of profiling, the GDPR is more limited in scope than one might think.

Chapter 9, 'Data Used in Governmental Automated Decision-Making and Profiling: Towards More Practical Protection', by Sascha van Schendel, explored data used in profiling and automated decision-making tools used by governmental actors. The chapter put emphasis on the contextual nature of data, in that data are often gathered in a different context than that for which they will be used during profiling and automated decision-making, which causes some issues. Especially in automated decision-making and profiling applications, the context in which data were collected tends to get lost or be let go of. This is a problem not specifically addressed in data protection regulation. Other tensions with the GDPR are the bias in data bound to specific contexts, the group-oriented nature of profiles and automated decision-making and the use of aggregated data and statistical data in the creation of profiles. The author proposed that the current regulatory framework needs to be able to be contextual enough to take all these factors into account; more specifically, it must pay attention to the importance of groups in data and the importance of non-personal data. In that sense, the GDPR would be too limited.

Overall, one key point that comes to the fore is that in practice the GDPR can also be *too limited* in its scope and aim. The GDPR does not take into account or fully protect data types such as raw or bulk data, business data (such as of farmers), statistical data, living lab profiles and other profiles in general. For some of these limitations, other legal frameworks come into play, for example the right to privacy when it comes to bulk interception, as well as laws on statistical data when it comes to the protection of statistical and aggregated data. Sometimes issues seem unregulated, such as aspects of profiling data and of agricultural business data.

2.3. Regulation

The third part and final part offered a legal perspective on different aspects and ways of regulating data or categories of data.

Chapter 10, 'Data: A Very Short Introduction to the EU Galaxy and to Five Potential Paths Forward', by Bart van der Sloot, gave a broad overview of the approach in the EU to data regulation. Van der Sloot points out how the EU has invested little in the consistency between legal instruments that regulate data. To that end, alternative approaches to regulation are proposed and analysed. The alternative approaches that van der Sloot sketches are the following: one regime for all data, a fully contextual approach, changing the definitions in the GDPR, a sectoral and/or technology specific approach or regulating the different stages of data processing. Of course, not all these alternative approaches could be applied at the same time. One could thus argue that this chapter highlights the underlying rationale or choices that must be made in regulating data: what the aim is of regulating the data will determine how the data should be regulated and which data.

Chapter 11, 'The Regulation of Access to Personal and Non-Personal Data in the EU: From Bits and Pieces to a System?', by Thomas Tombal and Inge Graef, introduces the legal implications surrounding access to data, both personal and non-personal, in the EU. The chapter problematises the heterogeneity of regulatory scopes in the construction of a coherent legal system. From that perspective, the chapter forms a valuable contribution in going beyond one piece of legislation: an instrument such as the GDPR cannot be seen in isolation, but rather all the different instruments that regulate data together determine whether the regulatory strategy is maintainable. Tombal and Graef propose that whether the bits and pieces of the regulation of data will be capable of acting as a coherent system of law does not only depend on the substance of the rules but also on how market players implement and regulators enforce the various regimes. The future relationship between the GDPR's right to data portability and the Data Act's data access provisions can serve as an example or test case in this respect.

Chapter 12, 'Regulating "Non-Personal Data": Developments in India', by Rishab Bailey and Renuka Sane, discusses the regulation of non-personal data in India. This chapter presents a nice comparative example of a regulatory regime different to the EU data regulation package. Bailey and Sane demonstrate that India's regulation is driven primarily by competition concerns, as well as issues of 'fairness' and equity in distribution of the benefits of the data economy, which derive from a view that links regulation of data to India's sovereignty. The NPD Committee, established by the Government of India, adopted a design that includes designating certain datasets as HVDs, setting up the institution of a 'data trustee' to manage the datasets, creating a framework through which the HVDs could be accessed and establishing a regulator, the NPD Authority, to oversee the process.

The recognition of a community's right to benefit from the data economy and the mention of group privacy rights are notable additions to the data governance discourse in India. Bailey and Sane propose that while the proposed regulatory framework is aspirational in its goal of opening access to NPD and brings novelty by recognising the community as a distinct stakeholder in the data governance debate, the framework seeks to regulate a vast field covering a multiplicity of sectors, businesses and relationships in a fast-changing ecosystem, which may prove to be impractical. From that perspective, Chapter 12 demonstrates interesting alternatives to the regulation of data, especially a field as vast as non-personal data, but at the same time also illustrates the (practical) pitfalls of such a broad approach.

Chapter 13, 'Data Protection Without Data: Informationless Chilling Effects and Data Protection Law', by Dara Hallinan, discusses the concept of 'informationless chilling effects' and their relevance to information processing. In this chapter, Hallinan proposes that the purposes of EU data protection law should only be formulated in a broad, flexible and open-ended way. The following formulation might be taken forward: the purpose of EU data protection law is to provide protection in relation to (i) harms to fundamental rights (ii) which eventuate in relation to systems and contexts of information processing concerning individuals, (iii) while not, in advance, exhaustively defining either the forms of harms to rights encompassed nor the forms of systems and contexts relating to information processing concerning individuals, which are encompassed under this purpose. Further, the elaboration of the logic of considering the purpose of EU data protection law in a broad, flexible and open-ended manner has consequences for the conceptualisation of the boundaries of scoping concepts in EU data protection law. Building on the above, the article highlighted that informationless chilling effects might be seen as harms to rights which relate to information processing concerning individuals – albeit as a form of emergent risk parasitic to the general prevalence of information processing technologies. Accordingly, the article made the observations that: (i) informationless chilling effects constitute a form of harm to rights, which falls within the purview of the purposes of EU data protection law and (ii) scoping concepts in data protection law offer the potential to encompass systems and contexts engendering informationless chilling effects. In this sense, the chapter offers interesting argumentation on the purposes and scope of data protection law.

Chapter 14, 'Identity, Profiles and Pseudonyms in the Digital Environment', by Miranda Mourby and Elaine Mackey, showed that although the GDPR does not explicitly link the definition of profiling with that of personal data, profiling is nonetheless very relevant to the concept of identification. The chapter contained several points that are relevant to the research statement of this book. First, the chapter dealt with the argument of what is identification, to which the authors argue that profiling can be sufficiently intrusive into fundamental rights in and of itself that it can justifiably be called an identification. Second, the chapter discusses different data types in explaining which are more or less identifying than others. The chapter highlights that longitudinal data that show individual behaviour over time will be much more difficult to anonymise than information that only provides a single snapshot in time. Ultimately, the authors conclude that it may be helpful to determine the scope of identity in data protection law with reference to fundamental rights and not – as is often suggested – the other way around. For all that, the category of 'identity' continues to shift as technology evolves: the underlying benchmarks of privacy and non-discrimination rights are sufficiently stable to provide a reliable sense of who we are as we navigate the digital environment. In this sense, the chapter offers an interesting perspective on the relation between technology and legal concepts.

Chapter 15, 'Biometric Data, Within and Beyond Data Protection', by Catherine Jasserand, argued that, from a technical perspective, biometric data are formats resulting from the processing and transformation of biometric characteristics used for biometric recognition purposes (one individual) or categorisation purposes (shared characteristics of a group of individuals). A step-by-step assessment is necessary to determine whether personal data and biometric (personal) data are processed at each technical stage. Depending on the purpose or context of processing, biometric data will be personal, biometric and/or sensitive data. Conversely, it could be the case that data generated during the image acquisition and face detection stages do not reach the threshold of identifiability and remain excluded from the field of personal data. Thus, the author concludes, it cannot be claimed that biometric data generated during the technical processing are necessarily personal data. Another point the author makes is that the legal concept of biometric data is far from the technical notion and unsatisfactory in several aspects. It excludes some formats from the scope of biometric data, such as untransformed samples and thus photographs. It also relies on the discriminant factor of 'uniquely identifying' to classify the processed data in the category of biometric personal data. This factor is, according to the author, neither clear nor logical. From a technical perspective, unique identification through the processing of biometric data can never be reached. Here the author notes a gap between the technical and legal reality. To better reflect what biometric data are, it could be suggested to revise the legal definition to get rid of this controversial criterion. One suggestion would be to align the definition of biometric data with that of border control instruments. Instead of adding complexity to the legal concept of biometric data, the EU legislator should simplify the current GDPR definition.

Several points are clear from these contributions. First, most chapters are concerned with the regulation of non-personal data or are at least discussing regulation of data that traditionally goes beyond personal data. There is significant unclarity as to what exactly constitutes personal data and the scope of data protection legislation. Different competing arguments on this can be derived from the chapters. Second, arguments are brought to the table that critically reflect on the idea of an all-encompassing data regime: from Chapter 10 by van der Sloot, pros and cons to such strategies can be derived; Chapter 11 by Tombal and Graef suggests that having different legal instruments can create a patchwork with legal uncertainty and conflicts; and Chapter 12 by Bailey and Sane demonstrates the risks of far-reaching regulation and policies or tools that might be impractical or difficult to enforce. Third, some gaps between the technical and regulatory perspective come to the fore, especially in Chapter 15 by Jasserand. Finally, especially from chapters 13–15, it becomes clear that what perhaps matters most is the interpretation that is given to concepts such as identification, information and personal data and the importance of having clear definitions with, for example, explanatory memoranda.

3. Conclusions and Answers

As to the first sub-question (see Chapter 1), it can be concluded that there are various ways in which anonymous data can be linked to individuals. Examples are database reconstruction attacks (through which an aggregated database is re-identified), composition (through which two or more anonymised datasets merged together can result in [sensitive] personal data) and several de-anonymisation technologies. Information may be inferred from anonymised datasets about people who were not in the dataset in the first place, and those aggregated data, in particular, may be used for decision-making processes which may have a significant effect on citizens in general and specific groups in particular. If the latter is the case, those data may qualify as personal data. Open data means that although it may be possible to de-individualise a dataset taken in isolation, because it is possible to combine it with other data freely available online, it can never be excluded and, to the contrary, will be increasingly likely that an anonymised dataset will in time be de-anonymised by one party or another. Aggregated data, when they are made available, may be used for decision-making that affects specific identified or non-identified citizens. How data will be used cannot be controlled or estimated with certainty beforehand. However, the chance that, when data are made available online, they will be used by a party in ways that affect concrete individuals, groups or society at large is increasingly likely.

With respect to the second, third and fourth sub-questions, it is clear that it will be increasingly difficult to ensure (legal) anonymity. The democratisation of data technologies means, especially when data are made available online, that it is increasingly likely that there will be some parties around the globe that will use advanced technologies to decrypt, re-identify or de-anonymise data and invest the necessary time, energy and effort into doing so. A potentially revolutionary technological development can come in the form of quantum computing. Quantum computing is believed to be able to break most, if not all, forms of current encryption. Yet technological developments can also have a positive impact on privacy and data protection. Post-quantum encryption, for example, is believed to be much safer than current forms of encryption, and deep privacy tools (privacy tools based in deep learning models) are currently being developed.

As to the fifth, sixth, seventh and eighth sub-questions, it is clear that although the distinction between non-personal and personal is binary and absolute in its legal effect, the criteria to determine whether data are anonymous are highly contextual. From a technical perspective, the contextual approach is most apparent. Most technical experts do not believe in absolute or full anonymity but rather point to a scale of how difficult it is to de-anonymise or re-identify a database. The general availability of open data and the democratisation of data technologies will have a threefold impact on the possibilities of achieving anonymisation and pseudonymisation. First, the nature of the data in Big Data processes is not stable, but volatile. Second, as a consequence of the previous, it is increasingly difficult to determine the status of data precisely. To determine the current status of a datum or dataset, the expected future status of the data must be taken into account. Third, modern data processing operations are increasingly based on aggregate data, which can also have very large individual and social consequences. The question is whether the focus on the identifiability of an individual (natural person) and, subsequently, the notions of anonymisation and pseudonymisation built thereon are viable in the 21st century.

With an eye to the ninth and tenth sub-questions, it should be underlined that an answer depends on what is deemed to be the regulatory objective of the data protection regime: is the data protection framework to be considered from a protective angle or from the perspective of facilitating data processing within a set framework, or as a combination between both? Is the protective rationale to be understood as primarily providing protection to individual interests or to group and societal interests? Should the data protection regime be understood as laying down limitations for data processing or as providing a framework for using and sharing data? Is the protective rationale best served by limitations, or can more data processing sometimes be required to serve the best interests of individuals and/or society? Is the rationale of facilitating data use best served by an open and contextual framework or by setting strict and clear rules within which data processing is deemed legitimate? Depending on these answers, different regulatory gaps and dangers for over- and/or under-regulation will be found.

Finally, as to the eleventh sub-question and main research question, creative and innovative ideas are proposed throughout the chapters of this book to develop and improve technologies when it comes to issues such as anonymising data and protecting privacy. The combination of data, information inference and identifiability will only increase in the future, especially with the continued democratisation of technology and increased tools to break encryption and undo anonymisation (as occurs with quantum computing). This book also demonstrates various societal challenges with data-driven innovations in different societal sectors, the extent to which such challenges are considered in regulatory frameworks or not, the fluidity of data in practice and the decreased relevance of legal demarcation between different categories of data in practice. Lastly, various (new) legal approaches and concepts have been explored, either as part of the GDPR or beyond it. What also becomes clear when putting the three perspectives together is that no matter which regulatory approach would be chosen, there are conflicts in resolving different issues: some issues would require a broader application of the GDPR, some would require that there is no distinction between different regulatory modes for personal and non-personal data, some issues require a stricter regime than the GDPR and so forth.

4. Discussions and Questions

Against the background of the regulatory choices described in this book, as well as the challenges upholding these choices due to the various societal and technological developments discussed in the first and second parts, five general strategies emerge in the third part of this book that address these regulatory challenges. These can be summarised as follows:

Leaving the data protection framework as is: the data protection framework is regarded as forming a perfect equilibrium between its protective rationale and promoting data processing operations, between opting for a categorical and a contextual regulatory approach and between leaving the regulatory prerogative with the legislator and allowing judicial and executive authorities to refine concepts and rules in practice, with an eye to specific contexts and situations. Although technological practice may be said to diverge from the regulatory regime and may very well do more so over the years, this does not mean that the rules should change. Rather, more should be invested in ensuring that practice conforms with the rules. This investment should extend to the extent that processing non-personal data has an important impact, such as is already covered by the GDPR when decisions are taken in which a person is singled out or significantly affected, or by Article 8 ECHR, when policies affect the very broad notion of private life. The ECHR has been willing to develop a regime for metadata collection when necessary, and it has accepted claims in which no personal harm was endured by the claimant, instead focusing on the societal effects of large-scale data processing.

Keeping the data protection framework and investing in more precise definitions: the main outlines and contours of the current regulatory regime are deemed fit for the 21st century. However, the main regulatory challenge is the need for further clarity on the definitions of the different data categories, the boundaries between different categories and the regulation of those data. In this scenario, various regulatory alternatives are possible, such as more guidelines being issued and the introduction of a burden of proof on the data controller for showing that data are anonymous and/or encrypted. To provide more clarity on the distinction between non-personal and personal data, the contextual elements in the definition of personal data and in the description of anonymisation could be removed. This would decontextualise the question of whether personal data are processed and whether the data protection framework applies. Also, the category of pseudonymous data could be omitted. This category is critiqued both for its vagueness and because it privileges one privacy-preserving technique over others, for which no clear explanation exists. Finally, it may be considered to extend the list of sensitive personal data. Potential additional categories that were identified in this study include financial and socio-economic data, data about children, locational data and metadata.

Keeping the data protection framework and investing in more contextuality: the main regulatory challenge is regarded as the lack of contextuality and adaptability of the current regulatory regime. Again, several regulatory alternatives have emerged during this study, such as the addition of the principle of contextuality to the list of Article 5 GDPR, requiring the data controller to consider each principle, obligation and requirement under the data protection framework in light of the context in which the data processing takes place. Alternatively, reformulating the list of sensitive data in the way it was originally formulated, namely as examples rather than an exhaustive list, or including a residual category, similar to Article 14 ECHR, could be considered. Pseudonymous data could be granted a more prominent position as an intermediate category between non-personal and personal data.

Revising the data protection framework using clearly defined data categories: this scenario is similar to investing in more precise definitions. However, this scenario requires a fundamental overhaul of the current regulatory framework. In this scenario, it is believed that it is still possible to work with categories of data, even the current ones, but in light of technological developments, the regulatory regime applied to them needs reconsideration. A number of regulatory alternatives could be considered, such as adopting a 'GDPR-light' regime for non-personal data. This could imply, for example, that all data processing must accord with the principles contained in Article 5 GDPR. Also, in light of a protective regime on non-personal data, structuring the data processing regime around stages of data processing could be considered: gathering and storing data, analysing data and using data or the outcomes of data analysis. The current regulatory regime almost exclusively focuses on the moment that data are gathered and stored. There are virtually no rules on the analysis of data and no rules on the use of data, perhaps with the exception of one provision on the prohibition of automated decision-making. This is deemed problematic because the core of most present-day processing operations is in analysing data. For the analysis of data, inspiration could be sought from the rules applied to statistical agencies.

Revising the data protection framework, removing clearly defined data categories: this strategy is similar to investing in more contextuality. However, this scenario requires a fundamental overhaul of the current regulatory framework. Under this scenario, it is impossible to work with different definitions of data and to attach different levels of regulatory protection to each of those definitions. Instead, a fully contextual approach should be taken, fully dependent on a case-by-case analysis of the potential harm that could result from particular processing operations. This harm could be linked to individual and/or societal interests. Most current obligations and requirements could be left intact; however, they would be made dependent on the level of risk and harm. The GDPR could essentially be boiled down to a simple set of rules, that is to say, a list of principles and obligations for data controllers who are currently affected by the regulations. These rules could be specified so that they apply to the data controllers, taking into account the state of the field, the costs of implementation and the nature, scope, context and purposes of the processing, the nature of the data and the varying likelihood and severity of individuals and/or societal interests being affected.

The goal of this book is not to advocate for one of these five potential strategies over the others. Rather, this book demonstrated that there are alternative approaches to the current approach being taken by EU legislation and under the GDPR, each of which need to be explored further. An answer would require fundamentally rethinking the nature of regulation in the 21st century. These questions include, but are not limited to:

1. Should a data protection regime focus on the question of identifiability, or should non-personal data be treated as essentially equivalent to personal data?
2. Should a data protection regime work with binary distinctions between different types of data or rather with gradual and fluid concepts?
3. Should a data protection regime focus on the protection of natural persons, or should groups and legal persons also be covered?
4. Should a data protection regime focus on the protection of individual interests and/or on societal interests?
5. Should a data protection regime aim at limiting data flows in order to protect individual or societal interests or on facilitating data processing and transfers within boundaries?
6. How are the rationales of protection and facilitation best served?
7. Should a data protection regime allow for open data regimes, or should it prohibit those, as data may be used for different purposes, and if anonymised, should they be de-anonymised?
8. Should a data protection regime focus on gathering personal data, or should it rather or in addition focus on analysing and/or using data?

9. Should future regulation focus on data and their status, or would a focus on technologies be more effective?
10. Should there be a data protection regime at all, or is it better to work with the general principles as provided by the European Convention on Human Rights?

Author biographies

Bart van der Sloot is associate professor specialising in tech and privacy at Tilburg University. He was a co-author of the WRR Big Data Study and the WODC research into Big Data and procedural law for the 21st century. Van der Sloot has won three prestigious prices and grants: the NWO Top Talent Grant, the NWO Veni Grant and the KNAW Early Career Award.

Sascha van Schendel is a postdoctoral researcher in the field of AI and the rights to data protection and non-discrimination at Tilburg University. She was a co-author to the WRR Big Data Study and the WODC research into Big Data and procedural law for the 21st century and has many other data protection publications to her name.

Liang Zheng is a senior lecturer at the Australian National University. He is best known for his contributions in object re-identification, where he and his collaborators designed widely used datasets and algorithms such as Market-1501 (ICCV 2015), part-based convolutional baseline (ECCV 2018), random erasing (AAAI 2020) and joint detection and embedding (ECCV 2020). He received both his BS degree (2010) and PhD degree (2015) from Tsinghua University, China.

Zhedong Zheng is a research fellow at the National University of Singapore. He received his PhD from the University of Technology Sydney, Australia, in 2021 and BS degree from Fudan University, China, in 2016. He was awarded the IEEE Circuits and Systems Society Outstanding Young Author Award of 2021.

Nina Bindel is a researcher at SandboxAQ, researching the construction and cryptanalysis of post-quantum cryptography. She received her PhD from the Technische Universität Darmstadt on post-quantum digital signatures in 2018, followed by a postdoctoral fellowship at the Institute for Quantum Computing at the University of Waterloo.

Michele Mosca is a co-founder of the Institute for Quantum Computing at the University of Waterloo, a professor in the Faculty of Mathematics and a founding member of Waterloo's Perimeter Institute for Theoretical Physics. He is co-founder and CEO of evolutionQ and chair of the board of Quantum Industry Canada.

Bill Munson is a research associate at the Institute for Quantum Computing at the University of Waterloo and the managing director of Quantum-Safe Canada, a not-for-profit established to raise awareness of the quantum threat to cryptography, cybersecurity and privacy and to advocate for timely and effective responses by government and industry.

Håkon Hukkelås received his Msc in computer science from the Norwegian University of Science and Technology and is currently pursuing his PhD at the same university. His research field focuses on leveraging generative models for realistic image anonymisation to ensure privacy of individuals without compromising visual fidelity. Hukkelås is the creator of the widely used open-source framework DeepPrivacy.

Frank Lindseth is a professor in the computer science department at NTNU. His research field is visual computing with a special focus on computer vision (CV) and visual intelligence. Lindseth is a core member of the Norwegian Open AI Lab and is leading the NAP-lab (autonomous driving) with associated projects, both at NTNU. Furthermore, Lindseth also has over 20 years of experience from SINTEF/StOlav within the medical image analysis/ image-guided intervention domain.

Willemijn Aerdts is lecturer and researcher with the Leiden University Institute for Security and Global Affairs. She used to be a member of the committee on Peace & Security of the Advisory Council on International Affairs of the Dutch government. She is a member of the advisory board of WIIS-Netherland. Her research focusses mainly on intelligence oversight.

Ludo Block is a lecturer with the Leiden University Institute for Security and Global Affairs. He is a former Dutch police officer and now an independent advisor in the field of research and analysis. He obtained a PhD in 2011 on policymaking and the practice of police cooperation in the European Union. His research focuses mainly on OSINT and intelligence analysis.

Sjaak Wolfert is Senior Scientist and Theme Ambassador for 'Digital Innovation for Sustainable Food Systems' at Wageningen Economic Research. Wolfert received his MSc/PhD in crop science and information technology at Wageningen University. Current research topics are food data economy and data spaces focusing on socio-economic issues and innovation ecosystems. He is scientific coordinator of (inter)national projects, author of numerous scientific papers and a regular speaker at international conferences.

Houkje Adema, MSc, is a consumer researcher at Wageningen Economic Research. Houkje works on different projects focusing on understanding, explaining and changing consumer behaviour towards more healthy and sustainable diets. She has a background in consumer science, with master's degrees from both Wageningen University and the Technical University of Munich.

Marc-Jeroen Bogaardt is senior researcher at Wageningen Economic Research. Marc-Jeroen has a degree in engineering as well as in political science. He is mostly involved in projects commissioned by the Dutch Ministry of Agriculture, the innovative Topsector Agri and Food and the European Commission. In these projects, he focuses on the governance and institutional aspects of intra- and interorganisational and cross-border data sharing infrastructures.

Else Giesbers is researcher citizen participation at Wageningen Economic Research. Giesbers works on projects related to citizen and stakeholder engagement in food system transitions. She is mostly involved in Horizon Europe projects related to these topics focusing on understanding what drives food system transitions and how citizens play a role in this. Giesbers has a background in cultural anthropology and social geography.

Peter-Paul de Wolf graduated cum laude and earned his PhD in mathematical statistics at Delft University of Technology. Since May 1996, he has been working at Statistics Netherlands, where he now is a senior methodologist. He is an internationally respected expert in the field of statistical disclosure control.

Ivo Gorissen graduated in economics from Tilburg University. He has been working at Statistics Netherlands since December 1989. For more than a decade, he has been senior advisor in Microdata Services, dealing with the wonderful and rewarding challenge of combining secure access to data with optimal opportunities for researchers to perform their analyses.

Michel Zaaijer is legal policy advisor at CBS, Central Bureau of Statistics, The Hague, Netherlands.

Daniël von Berg is a senior advisor European and international affairs working at CBS, Central Bureau of Statistics, The Hague, Netherlands.

Maša Galič is an assistant professor in privacy and criminal procedure law at the criminal law and criminology department of the Vrije Universiteit (VU) in Amsterdam. Her current research revolves around issues connected to criminal procedure law and technology, in particular the regulation of digital investigation powers of the police. Prior to this, Galič was a doctoral and postdoctoral researcher at the Tilburg Institute for Law, Technology and Society (Tilburg University, the Netherlands), where she conducted research on privacy, surveillance, smart cities and cybercrime. At the VU and other European universities, Galič lectures on cybercrime, Artificial Intelligence, privacy (law) and smart cities.

Inge Graef is associate professor of competition law at Tilburg University. She is affiliated to the Tilburg Institute for Law, Technology, and Society (TILT) and the Tilburg Law and Economics Center (TILEC). Graef holds expertise in the areas of competition law, platform regulation and the governance of data-driven innovation.

Thomas Tombal is a postdoctoral researcher at Tilburg University. He is affiliated to the Tilburg Institute for Law, Technology, and Society (TILT) and the Tilburg Law and Economics Center (TILEC). He is part of the Sector Plan 'Digital Legal Studies', where he contributes to the research program 'From Regulating Human Behavior to Regulating Data'.

Rishab Bailey is a lawyer and technology policy researcher, currently a visiting fellow at the XKDR Forum, Mumbai. He has previously worked with the National Institute of Public Finance and Policy, New Delhi, at ThoughtWorks Inc. and various civil society organisations in India. His work focuses on telecommunications regulation, data governance, protection of digital rights, platform regulation and regulatory governance in the technology space.

Renuka Sane is research director at TrustBridge Rule of Law Foundation, India. Her research interests lie in credit and bankruptcy, pensions, insurance, financial markets regulation and the regulatory state.

Dara Hallinan is a legal academic working at FIZ Karlsruhe. He is programme director for the annual Computers, Privacy and Data Protection conference, editor of the bi-weekly Data Protection Insider newsletter and author of the recent OUP book *Protecting Genetic Privacy in Biobanking Through Data Protection Law.*

Miranda Mourby is a researcher in law at the Centre for Health, Law and Emerging Technologies at the University of Oxford. She is also a research associate within Professor Fruzsina Molnár-Gábor's chair in International Health, Medical and Data Protection Law. She is completing her PhD at the University of Sheffield.

Elaine Mackey works in information governance at the Centre for Epidemiology (University of Manchester). She is a member of the leadership team for the UK Anonymisation Network and a SPRITE+ Expert Fellow from Professional Practice. She has published on the broader aspects of data confidentiality where statistical, legal and social policy meet.

Catherine Jasserand is a postdoctoral researcher at CiTiP, within the Faculty of Law, at KU Leuven. She is a recipient of a Marie Curie fellowship (MSCA-IF) at KU Leuven, where she investigates the use of facial recognition technologies in public spaces and their impact on the rights to privacy and data protection. Jasserand is an expert in biometrics and privacy and a regular speaker at technical conferences. The research completed for the chapter is funded by the European Union's Horizon 2020 research and innovation programme under the Marie Skłodowska-Curie grant agreement No. 895978 (DATAFACE).

For Product Safety Concerns and Information please contact our
EU representative GPSR@taylorandfrancis.com Taylor & Francis
Verlag GmbH, Kaufingerstraße 24, 80331 München, Germany